International Comparative Perspectives on the Treatment of "Urban Diseases"

With an integration of theories, comparative and empirical studies, this book aims to find a treatment for Beijing's "urban diseases" and coordinate a low-carbon development plan for the Beijing-Tianjin-Hebei region in China.

Unprecedented industrialization and unconventional urbanization caused a series of "urban diseases" for developing cities across the globe. By summarizing and exploring the evolution and phased characteristics of "urban diseases", the author implements theories across classical sociology, human ecology, community school, and low-carbon city as the base for policy recommendations. This book also provides in-depth examinations and comparative studies of other metropolises' experiences in controlling "urban diseases". Cities such as New York, London, and Tokyo were modeled to propose the most appropriate low-carbon development plan for the Beijing-Tianjin-Hebei region.

With a focus on developing cities in Northern China, this book will be a great read to all scholars and students of environmental studies, development studies, urban studies, and contemporary China studies. It will also be a great addition for those who are interested in social conflicts and economic development.

Lu Xiaocheng, researcher at the Beijing Academy of Social Sciences. His main research interests include regional low-carbon innovation system, public policy, industrial economy and government bonds.

China Perspectives

The *China Perspectives* series focuses on translating and publishing works by leading Chinese scholars, writing about both global topics and China-related themes. It covers Humanities & Social Sciences, Education, Media and Psychology, as well as many interdisciplinary themes.

This is the first time any of these books have been published in English for international readers. The series aims to put forward a Chinese perspective, give insights into cutting-edge academic thinking in China, and inspire researchers globally.

To submit proposals, please contact the Taylor & Francis Publisher for China Publishing Programme, Lian Sun (Lian.Sun@informa.com)

Titles in sociology currently include:

Aging in the Context of Urbanization
Social Determinants for the Depression of the Chinese Older Population
Fan Yang

Organizational Transformation and Order Reconstruction in "Village-Turned-Communities"
WU Ying

The Many Roads to Becoming Modern
A History of Collectivism in Rural Jiangsu Province
CHEN Jiajian

International Comparative Perspectives on the Treatment of "Urban Diseases"
Reflections on the Low-Carbon Development of the Beijing-Tianjin-Hebei Region
Lu Xiaocheng

For more information, please visit www.routledge.com/China-Perspectives/book-series/CPH

International Comparative Perspectives on the Treatment of "Urban Diseases"
Reflections on the Low-Carbon Development of the Beijing-Tianjin-Hebei Region

Lu Xiaocheng

First published 2022
by Routledge
4 Park Square, Milton Park, Abingdon, Oxon OX14 4RN

and by Routledge
605 Third Avenue, New York, NY 10158

Routledge is an imprint of the Taylor & Francis Group, an informa business

© 2022 Lu Xiaocheng

Translated by Zhang Zhen

The right of Lu Xiaocheng to be identified as author of this work has been asserted by him in accordance with sections 77 and 78 of the Copyright, Designs and Patents Act 1988.

All rights reserved. No part of this book may be reprinted or reproduced or utilised in any form or by any electronic, mechanical, or other means, now known or hereafter invented, including photocopying and recording, or in any information storage or retrieval system, without permission in writing from the publishers.

Trademark notice: Product or corporate names may be trademarks or registered trademarks, and are used only for identification and explanation without intent to infringe.

English version by permission of China Social Sciences Press

British Library Cataloguing-in-Publication Data
A catalogue record for this book is available from the British Library

Library of Congress Cataloging-in-Publication Data
Names: Lu, Xiaocheng, author.
Title: International comparative perspectives on the treatment of "urban diseases" : reflections on the low-carbon development of the Beijing-Tianjin-Hebei region / Lu Xiaocheng.
Other titles: "Cheng shi bing" zhi li de guo ji bi jiao yan jiu. English
Description: Abingdon, Oxon ; New York, NY : Routledge, 2022. | Series: China perspectives |
Includes bibliographical references and index. |
Identifiers: LCCN 2021052995 (print) | LCCN 2021052996 (ebook) |
Subjects: LCSH: Urban ecology (Sociology) | Urban ecology (Sociology)–China. | Urban health. | Urban health–China. | Carbon dioxide mitigation. | Carbon dioxide mitigation–China. | City planning–Environmental aspects. | City planning–Environmental aspects–China.
Classification: LCC HT241 .L8213 2022 (print) | LCC HT241 (ebook) | DDC 304.20951–dc23/eng/20211109
LC record available at https://lccn.loc.gov/2021052995
LC ebook record available at https://lccn.loc.gov/2021052996

ISBN: 978-1-032-22531-9 (hbk)
ISBN: 978-1-032-22542-5 (pbk)
ISBN: 978-1-003-27299-1 (ebk)

DOI: 10.4324/9781003272991

Typeset in Times New Roman
by Newgen Publishing UK

Contents

List of figures vii
List of tables viii
Preface ix
Acknowledgments xvi

1 Introduction 1

2 Theoretical review of the control of "urban diseases" 46

3 Law of the evolution of "urban diseases" and its phased characteristics 67

4 New York experience in the control of "urban diseases": perspective of cross-regional coordination 107

5 London experience in the control of "urban diseases": perspective of smog control 119

6 Tokyo experience in the control of "urban diseases": perspective of subcenter construction 133

7 Ruhr experience in the control of "urban diseases": the perspective of industrial upgrading 161

8 Phenomena and causes of the problems of "urban diseases" in Beijing 178

9 Control of "urban diseases" in Beijing and
countermeasures for the coordinated low-carbon
development of the Beijing-Tianjin-Hebei region 226

10 Summary and outlook 303

References 308
Index 320

Figures

3.1 Inverted U-shaped curve for the evolution of "urban diseases" 95
3.2 Relationship of phases of urban development, urban functions and "urban diseases" 100
8.1 Resident population and floating resident population of Beijing 181

Tables

1.1	Key perspectives on the causes of "urban diseases"	5
2.1	Connotations of a livable city	57
3.1	Embodiments and treatment of "urban diseases" in typical international cities	70
3.2	Most congested cities and evening peak congested cities in 2015	78
4.1	Evolutionary phases and characteristics of New York's urbanization	110
5.1	Main measures for smog control in London	121
6.1	Japanese laws and regulations on smog control	145
6.2	Experience of main cities in levying congestion charges	155
7.1	The history of development by cultural transformation and industrial upgrading in the Ruhr area	163
7.2	Geographical advantages and the influences of industrial development in the Ruhr area	164
7.3	The process of de-industrialization in Germany and the Ruhr area	165
7.4	Models of industrial upgrading in the Ruhr area	167
7.5	Low-carbon implications for cultural transformation and industrial upgrading in the Ruhr area	172
8.1	Criteria for the classification of city size	179
8.2	Resident population of Beijing from 1978 to 2014	180
8.3	Resident population and floating resident population of Beijing in 2013 and 2014	182
8.4	Beijing's water resources from 2003 to 2014	189
8.5	Beijing's total energy consumption from 2003 to 2014	190
8.6	Beijing's environmental protection from 2012 to 2013	191
9.1	Comparison of traditional and modern urban planning from the perspective of low carbon	241
9.2	Basic characteristics of the grid management model of a city	298

Preface

As a worldwide problem, "urban diseases" have aroused great international concern. "Urban diseases" can be said to be a common problem in the development of cities throughout the world. Most cities have experienced different degrees of "urban diseases", some of them are suffering from serious urban problems, and some others have had their "urban diseases" alleviated or effectively controlled through years of governance. The so-called "urban diseases" mainly refer to a series of problems, such as population expansion, traffic congestion, environmental deterioration, social conflicts, etc., caused by the excessive and rapid agglomeration of population to urban space, resulting in the decline in the carrying capacity for population, resources, and environment of the city. Due to a lack of foresight and self-control in city planning and construction, expansion to surrounding areas occurs in a way similar to the "urban sprawl", a large amount of fertile and cultivated land is occupied and the human–landowner conflict is prominent. However, the proportion of unemployed people in cities is always high. The widened gap between the rich and the poor, housing shortage and employment difficulties restrict the harmonious development of cities and cause physical and mental diseases in the residents of those cities. The general experience of the formation and control of "urban diseases" in Western developed countries is valuable for other countries to draw lessons from; in particular, the experience in the control of "urban diseases" accumulated for a long time in international cities such as London, New York, and Tokyo is of typical significance. In the long-term and rapid development of Beijing, "urban diseases" such as population expansion, traffic congestion, frequent smog and environmental pollution, etc., have accumulated and formed, which has attracted great attention from the CPC Central Committee and the State Council. How to learn from international experience, deeply investigate the main expressions and causes of "urban diseases" in Beijing, and then put forward effective countermeasures and suggestions, is an important topic worthy of systematic study.

First of all, we systematically comb the theories related to studies of "urban diseases" to provide a theoretical basis for the treatment of the "urban diseases" in Beijing. There are commonalities in the studies of "urban diseases", but differences also exist for different countries at different points of their development. Moreover, the academic community has achieved relevant research results and theoretical systems on "urban diseases" and their treatment. We review the theories of classical sociology, human ecology, community schools, garden cities, and low-carbon cities, and propose the important theoretical underpinnings to guide the treatment of Beijing's "urban diseases" and the low-carbon development of the Beijing-Tianjin-Hebei region.

The theory of classical sociology focuses on early "urban diseases" and their treatment, and provides fundamental theoretical support for the study and treatment of "urban diseases". The theory of human ecology is an important theoretical basis for the treatment of "urban diseases", because it is a science that studies the ecological relationship and interaction between mankind and nature, the ecological environment in which mankind live, and the harmonious development of mankind and nature, as well as the spatial and temporal connections formed by mankind under the influence of their selective, distributive, and regulative effects on the environment. The community theory is a generic term for the theories, doctrines, and perspectives developed during the studies on various aspects of the community-wide issues.

This school of thought pays attention mainly to the microscopic perspectives of cities, regards cities as larger communities, and condenses the problems of "urban diseases" into a holistic investigation of the problems of "community diseases". The theories and methods for the studies of the urban community mainly include two types: neighborhoods and social networks of urban communities, and powers of urban communities. In contrast to the traditional de-ruralization model of cities, the theory of garden cities depicts a beautiful picture of the integration of urban production and life with nature. It provides an important theoretical support for solving the problems of the "urban diseases" in Beijing as a metropolis. The theory of a livable city differs from the theory of a garden city in that it places more emphasis on people-oriented urban planning and emphasizes that urban construction and development should serve people. The theory of low-carbon city offers some new theoretical tools for the treatment of urban diseases and sustainable urban economic and social development. This theory, led by the low-carbon economy and guided by the concept of low-carbon development, attaches importance to energy saving and emission reduction in the two major areas, namely production and consumption; it builds a resource-intensive and environment-friendly society, achieves good and fast economic development, ensures that the urban economy should not grow at the expense of the carrying capacity of resources, energy and environment of cities, and constructs a favorable and sustainable urban ecological system.

Second, we summarize and explore the general law of evolution and phased characteristics of "urban diseases". By defining the scope of "urban diseases" and studying their main manifestations, we analyze the phased characteristics of the evolution of "urban diseases". In the context of China's actual situation, the key point should be the characteristics at different phases during the evolution of "urban diseases" in China and Beijing since the reform and opening-up. The relationship between "urban diseases" and the functional orientation as a central city is examined, and the imbalance between different urban forms generated at different phases and the elements of cities resulting from different functional demands is studied. The American scholar Joel Kotkin called traffic congestion, environmental pollution, deteriorating health conditions, and a series of related problems caused by the Industrial Revolution the "gear brutality". There is not a uniform definition of "urban disease", which has been interpreted by scholars in different disciplines from their own research perspectives. In this book, the so-called "urban diseases" refer to the problems of population expansion, traffic congestion, serious pollution, ecological deterioration and social conflicts caused by the over-concentration of urban resources, industries and functions during long-term urban development.

Various manifestations of urban diseases include expansion and aging of population, traffic congestion, environmental pollution, resource shortage, social conflicts, etc. Generally speaking, the evolution of cities is subject to the typical phases of rapid growth of urban centers, suburbanization, and metropolitanization, each of which has different characteristics and faces different "urban diseases". The evolution of "urban diseases" is closely related to the industrial development of cities, because they are formed and developed with the rise, development, prosperity, and decline of the industry in cities. The formation of many "urban diseases" is related to continuous industrial concentration in cities, to the expansion of the size of cities and population expansion, which further lead to a shortage of resources and energy and to the stagnation of industrial development. The industrial expansion in cities is constrained by the bottlenecks in resources and energy, and the upgrading of economic structure has set new requirements for the mode of city operations, thus leading to the evolution of "urban diseases".

Third, we examine New York's experience in treating "urban diseases" from the perspective of cross-regional coordination. New York, the largest city in the United States of America and one of the most famous metropolises in the world, has always been plagued by "urban diseases" such as population expansion, traffic congestion, and environmental pollution due to the excessive concentration of heavy polluting enterprises and industries in the core areas of the city. But through effective treatment, New York is becoming the most energy-efficient and environmentally friendly low-carbon city in the United States of America. Industrialization and urbanization have many drawbacks. In the process of urbanization, a series of "urban diseases" emerged, such as population expansion, traffic congestion and housing constraints due to rapid population growth, and environmental pollution leading to the illnesses of citizens.

New York witnessed an evolution from urbanization to suburbanization. Because of the problems of "urban diseases" brought about by accelerated industrialization and urbanization, New York's government at all levels chose new development strategies, strengthened urban planning, and shifted to the direction of suburbanization based on the original urbanization. The evolution of New York from urbanization to suburbanization has effectively alleviated the problems of "urban diseases"; it roughly goes through the phases from suburbanization of the residential function, suburbanization of the commercial and industrial functions, suburbanization of the integrated functions through satellite towns, to cross-regional coordination of urban functions. Based on the transition from urbanization to suburbanization, New York further realized cross-regional coordinated development, established the coordinated pattern of the Greater New York Metropolitan Area, effectively alleviated New York's problems of "urban diseases" and promoted the coordinated development of different regions. Main experience of New York in treatment of "urban diseases" reflected the characteristics of cross-regional coordination and equal allocation, for example, building a mechanism of cross-regional coordination and enhancing the planning, organization, and implementation; strengthening the construction of public housing and emphasizing the equal allocation of public services; improving the system of public transportation and solving the problem of traffic congestion; attaching importance to the recycling of waste and to energy conservation, and strengthening low-carbon development to build a green New York. This experience is worthy of reference for Beijing.

Fourth, we explore London's experience in treating "urban diseases" from the perspective of smog control. Britain was the earliest country to witness the Industrial Revolution, and also one of the earliest countries to encounter the problems of "urban diseases" in the process of industrialization and urbanization. The well-known British labor historians, Mr. and Mrs. Hammond, called the "urban diseases" in the 19th century of Britain the "Curse of Midas", and criticized Britain for only pursuing industrial production and causing a variety of problems such as chambers of commerce, livelihood, and environmental pollution. London conducted the systematic treatment of "urban diseases" and took effective measures to turn the foggy city into a green city, which is worthy of reference for Beijing.

By combating the smog, London transformed itself from a foggy city into a green city. London's smog problem originated from the smog incident in 1952, which resulted in the British people's reflections on the bitter consequences of air pollution. From heavy fog to a blue sky and white clouds, the iron-fisted measures of pollution control of Britain became very effective. Many years of continuous control of pollution has contributed to improved air quality of London today, and it has never again been called the "capital of fog". The main experience of London in treating smog was the combined use of various means. After more than half a century of iron-fisted pollution control, London finally got rid of the shadow of smog and became an ecological and livable green capital of the world with clean air. First, with governance by law, it enacted some stringent laws such as the Clean Air Act; second, with governance by policy, it levied congestion charges and developed its public transportation; third, with governance by technology, a new type of glue was used to be "sticky" to pollutants; fourth, with green governance, it constructed green spaces and used green energy; and fifth, with social governance, it encouraged public discussion and media exposure. London's experience in smog control and its inspirations for Beijing are mainly embodied as follows: to formulate regulations regarding clean air and strengthen the institutional construction of smog control; to set up the points of pollution detection and strictly control exhaust emissions; to enhance technological research on smog control and promote control by innovation in technologies; to develop green public transportation, use clean and low-carbon energy and reduce carbon emissions, and to attach importance to public participation in controlling smog in the capital city.

Fifth, we perform a comparative study on Los Angeles' experience in treating "urban diseases" from the perspective of air pollution control. Los Angeles, a typical industrial city in the United States of America, experienced the incidents of smog and photochemical pollution. After decades of treatment, the quality of Los Angeles's air was significantly improved. The treatment of air pollution in Los Angeles went through three phases: a period of governance by organizations and regulations, a period of governance by market and technologies, and a period of transformative and collaborative governance. The phased characteristics of air pollution control and the specific policy measures taken by Los Angeles can provide an important reference for the treatment of Beijing's "urban diseases", mainly reflected as follows: building institutions for air pollution control across administrative regions and establishing a mechanism of joint prevention and control; formulating air quality plan and standards and constructing a mechanism of strict enforcement; encouraging citizens to participate in the control of air pollution, building a mechanism of joint construction and sharing, strengthening the adjustment of industrial and energy structures and establishing a mechanism for innovation of low-carbon technology; and actively building green traffic and buildings and establishing a mechanism of low-carbon development.

Sixth, we investigate Tokyo's experience in treating "urban diseases" from the perspective of subcenter construction. Tokyo, a well-known international city, also suffered from serious problems of "urban diseases" before. It took effective measures to deal with those problems and treat their multiple aspects, including planning and guidance, decentralization of functions, construction of subcenters, industrial adjustment, decentralization of population, and allocation of resources. This experience is worthy of reference for Beijing. Tokyo's "urban diseases" mainly included: a growth of population that was too fast, over-concentration of industrial enterprises in the center of the city, rapid development of steel, shipbuilding, machinery, chemical and electronic industries, concentration of large amounts of manufacturing enterprises in Tokyo, and attraction of a large portion of the population from other places, thus resulting in housing difficulties, high pressure on traffic, as well as an increase in carbon emissions and serious environmental pollution in the city caused by overcrowding of enterprises.

The main experience of Tokyo in treating "urban diseases" includes: first, strengthening the planning and decentralization of urban functions, and building subcenters; second, adjusting the industrial structure and guiding the diversion of the population; third, building the metropolitan rail system and improving the facilities of public transportation; and fourth, promoting the equalization of public services and avoiding the excessive concentration of public resources in the city. Through a comparative study of Tokyo's treatment of "urban diseases", the favorable experience can be summarized and extracted as reference for Beijing in building a world-class harmonious and livable city and advocating the low-carbon development of the Beijing-Tianjin-Hebei region. First, strengthening the planning for the construction of the subcenters and enhancing its implementation; second, strengthening the equalized allocation of public resources and effectively decentralizing the urban functions; third, guiding the transformation, transfer, and upgrading of industries and reducing the over-expansion of the population in the city center; and fourth, accelerating the construction of the capital's network of rail transit and solving the problem of urban traffic congestion.

Seventh, examine Ruhr's experience in treating "urban diseases" from the perspective of cultural transformation and industrial upgrading. Ruhr, Germany relied on coal resources to develop traditional industries, and de-industrialization led to the dilemma of urban transformation. The Ruhr area carried out the transformation and upgrading of the cultural connotation of the traditional industrial zone, and summed up the experience models of regional renovation, museums, public recreation space, comprehensive development, low-carbon development, and so on. According to Ruhr's experience, the cities in China should place emphasis on cultural transformation, formulate plans for regional rehabilitation, and never copycat other cities; in addition, they should focus on the construction of cultural infrastructures, strengthen the ecological restoration and environmental governance of the city, enhance industrial optimization and upgrading, and promote low-carbon development.

Eighth, in terms of interaction and correlation effects of population, resources and environment, through empirical study and problems exploration, we analyze the main manifestations and internal causes of the problems of the "urban diseases" in Beijing, and identify the key elements for treating them and their influencing relationships. Beijing's "urban diseases" are mainly manifested as follows: the population growth is slowing down, but the total population continues to rise, and the sustainable development of Beijing is plagued by the "urban diseases" of a metropolis; the total traffic capacity continues to grow, and the problem of "capital jam" persists; the industrial structure is not reasonable, with difficulty in decentralizing low-end industries; and the total energy consumption is on the rise, smog is becoming serious and the carrying capacity of the environment is declining. There are many influencing factors on the formation of Beijing's "urban diseases" that have complex relationships. In essence, "urban diseases" result from the accumulation of conflicts between the carrying capacity of urban resources and the environment and the speed of urbanization-oriented development.

Ninth, we conduct a research on the measures for the treatment of Beijing's "urban diseases" and the low-carbon development of the Beijing-Tianjin-Hebei region. Beijing's treatment of "urban diseases" could consult the general international experience and practice, choose scientific countermeasures for development concerning its own characteristics, adhere to the guiding concept of implementing the strategic positioning of the capital city, and regard the construction of a world-class harmonious and livable city as the basic goal, so as to accelerate the treatment of Beijing's "urban diseases" and the coordinated low-carbon development of the Beijing-Tianjin-Hebei region.

From the perspectives mentioned above, based on the integration of theory and practice, this book examines the intrinsic connections of the theories of classical sociology, human ecology, a garden city, and a low-carbon city, analyzes the law of evolution and phased characteristics of "urban diseases", compares the basic experiences of typical international cities in treating "urban diseases", such as New York, London, and Tokyo; what's more, it also makes an analysis of the "urban diseases" of Beijing and their causes, and proposes some policy recommendations for the treatment of Beijing's "urban diseases" and the coordinated low-carbon development of the Beijing-Tianjin-Hebei region, thus providing a reference for Beijing's decision-making that aims at building a world-class harmonious and livable city.

Acknowledgments

This book is a further deepening and expansion based on the final results of the key research project "International Comparative Perspectives on the Treatment of 'Urban Diseases': Reflections on the Low-Carbon Development of the Beijing-Tianjin-Hebei Region", which was supported by the Beijing Academy of Social Sciences and completed in 2014. After this project was officially concluded in June 2015, the author conducted new research and survey, systematic revision, collation and quality improvement. The manuscript of this book, which is approximately more than 300,000 words, was revised and completed in a total of nearly three years from preparation, project initiation, mid-term inspection, project conclusion, and subsequent revisions.

I would like to thank the leaders of the Beijing Academy of Social Sciences for their help and guidance in the research project of this book, and Director Wang Yanmei, Deputy Director Zhu Xiahui, Mr. Zhu Qinghua and Ms. Yu Yin at the Research Organization Department of the Beijing Academy of Social Sciences for their guidance and enthusiastic help.

Thanks to Mr. Tang Xin, Director of the Center for Municipal Survey and Research and Secretary General of the Beijing Research Base of Cities in the World, for his strong support, guidance, and concern for the research of this book. Thanks to Dr. Li Mao, Dr. Liu Xiaomin, Dr. Tian Lei, Dr. Jia Peng, Dr. Li Xiaozhuang, Dr. Zhao Yaping, Associate Professor He Renwei, Dr. Ren Chao, Researcher and Director Shi Changkui of the Institute of Management, Deputy Director Liu Bo of the Institute of Foreign Studies, Researcher and Deputy Director Gang Shuge of the Institute of Sociology, and Associate Researcher Zhao Jimin of the Institute of Urban Studies, for their help in outline design, research, discussion, and report writing during the research process of this project.

Thanks also go to the anonymous reviewers for their valuable comments and suggestions during the review process of the publication grant of the Social Science Library of the Beijing Academy of Social Sciences. This book is partially a result of the research project of the Beijing Association for Science and Technology, the decision-making and consulting project of the Beijing Federation of Social Science Circles, and the projects of the Beijing

Academy of Social Sciences. I am grateful for their financial support of my preliminary research work, and for the valuable comments and suggestions made by the review experts during the opening, mid-term and closing reviews of the related projects.

For all the quotations and references of experts and scholars in this book, I want to say thanks here. Some quotations or references may not be annotated in a timely manner, and if there is any omission, experts are welcomed to criticize and correct them. Due to the limited capability and competence, inappropriateness is inevitable, and there may be some points that deserve further discussion and demonstration. The criticism or suggestion of experts or readers will be valued.

Lu Xiaocheng

1 Introduction

1.1 Research background and the problems

As industrialization, urbanization, and informatization are accelerating, the world has been witnessing an unprecedented scale of city expansion and concentration of urban population, ever since the 1950s. "Urban diseases" as a worldwide concern are attracting great attention in the international community. Analysis of the causes and the control of "urban diseases" has never ceased in the process of urbanization. "Urban diseases" suppress the sustainable development of the urban economy and society because they are a series of contradictions and conflicts caused by the rapid concentration and expansion of the population during industrialization and urbanization, such as traffic congestion, resource and energy depletion, ecological and environmental deterioration, social problems, and insufficient supply of infrastructures in cities. The so-called "urban diseases" mainly refer to the accumulation of resource factors, the expansion of industries and employment opportunities, the continuous enhancement of city functions and the gradual widening gap between urban and rural areas, which attract more and more rural and external population to cities, but overpopulation in large cities leads to a series of economic and social problems caused by the insufficient carrying capacity of the existing traffic, infrastructure, environment, and housing. A string of problems aggravates the burden on cities and constrains urban development, including the overly expanding population, long-term traffic congestion, continuous environmental deterioration, high housing prices and housing tensions, employment difficulties, and difficulties in accessing medical care and schooling. The "pie-spreading" expansion of urban planning and construction towards the surrounding areas and the encroachment onto good farmland on the part of spreading cities result in serious conflicts between people and the land. The land for construction exceeds the ecological land, thus reducing the carrying capacity of the urban environment, restricting the harmonious development of cities, and affecting urban stability, security, and physical and mental health of citizens. In particular, the aspect of "pie-spreading" cities leads to longer time on the road, and the separation of the space between work and residence increases the

DOI: 10.4324/9781003272991-1

traffic pressure, as well as the intensity of labor and work and the pressure on the life of workers. They cause more serious traffic congestion and management problems, and the cities may lose a lot of wealth. These problems include the invisible waste of energy and resources that are not conducive to the sustainable development of an urban economy and society.

From the perspective of the international background, the general rule for the formation and control of "urban diseases" in Western developed countries is worthy of reference for other countries, especially the experience in the long-term accumulated control of "urban diseases" in world-class cities such as London, New York, and Tokyo, which is of typical significance. Faced with prominent global urban problems such as climate change, energy and resource security, ecological crisis, and the spread of "urban diseases", accelerating the transformation of urban development modes, boosting the revolution of the green low-carbon technology and developing a green low-carbon economy have become key strategies for cities around the world to adjust their economic structure, achieve rapid recovery, and seize developmental opportunities. A wave of "green revolution" is sweeping the globe. Urban transformation is a major structural change in the phase of development of the urban areas and a developmental model based on the changes in the dominant factors driving the world's urban development, as well as a comprehensive transformation involving multiple fields, multiple levels, and multiple perspectives in the urban economy, society and culture. At present, faced with the unprecedented challenge of global climate change and severe urban resource depletion and an environmental crisis, people have to re-examine the relationship between humans and nature and explore the ideal paradigm of urban development. Confronted with the serious problems of ecological degradation and environmental pollution caused by the traditional models for the development of industrialization, urbanization, and modernization, which single-mindedly pursue economic growth on a large scale, blind self-expansion, and excessive resource consumption, countries around the world have begun to concentrate on "urban diseases" and explore new developmental models from the perspectives of source control and ecological restoration.

From the perspective of the domestic background, China's rapid urbanization and its resource bottlenecks pose formidable obstacles to urban development. The traditional urban mode of development, which takes the path of extensive economic growth characterized by high degrees of consumption, emissions, pollution, and expansion, is obviously unsustainable. China is now at the peak of urbanization, and within the next 10 years, 870 million Chinese will be living in cities, accounting for more than half of the total population. Unprecedented industrialization, unconventional urbanization and extensive industrial development have caused a series of "urban diseases" such as ecological damage, environmental pollution, traffic congestion, and an imbalance in urban spaces. How to accelerate the control of China's "urban diseases" and promote the construction of an urban ecological civilization and green low-carbon development has become a key and difficult issue in the current work of the government. According to a study by Wu Guancen, Liu Youzhao, and Fu Guanghui,[1] with the accelerated integration of the world's economy and the maturity of China's market economy, the resource-based cities that grew up in the era of planned economy are facing difficulties in adapting to the trend of social and economic development.[2] In January 2013, severe smog-infested weather conditions occurred in northeastern China for several days, and serious air pollution spread from the Northeast and the North to central China and even to the Yellow River-Huai River regions and to South China. The pollution index successively exceeded the "upper limit", and the pollution was particularly severe in some big cities. The extreme weather once again gave us a warning that there is an urgent need to protect the ecological environment, build an ecological civilization, and create a beautiful China.[3] Some reports pointed out that 2015 was the "strongest El Niño year" since historical statistics have been available, with a wide range of extremely adverse weather conditions in North China, such as "high humidity", "low wind speed", and "strong temperature inversion", which contributed to the continuous accumulation of pollution.

The emergence of weather conditions of extreme smog is a phased and regionally important issue in the process of industrialization and urbanization in China. Currently, China, which is a "manufacturing power" in the world and a "global processing plant", has a relatively poor level and quality of economic development. It is in the middle and late stages of industrialization and the important stage of accelerated urbanization and transformation of resource-based cities. According to international experience, this is an important stage in which environmental problems occur frequently. Cities consume 85% of the energy and resources and emit the same proportion of exhaust gases and waste, and more than 80% of the rivers flowing through cities are seriously polluted. These facts remind us that both China and the world must change their models of urban development.[4]

The report of the 18th CPC National Congress clearly pointed out that unbalanced, uncoordinated, and unsustainable development remains a big problem; the capacity for scientific and technological innovation is weak; the industrial structure is unreasonable; agricultural infrastructure remains weak; and resource and environmental constraints have become more serious; furthermore, it indicated that many systemic barriers stand in the way of promoting development in a scientific way, and the tasks of deepening reform and opening-up and changing the growth model remain arduous. How to solve the problem of unbalanced, uncoordinated, and unsustainable development, strengthen the control of "urban diseases", and enhance the construction of an ecological civilization and low-carbon development has been elevated to an important strategy for national development. The report of the 18th CPC National Congress further emphasized the need to vigorously promote the construction of an ecological civilization, elevated it to the strategic height of "five in one", and pointed out that we should remain committed to the basic state policy of conserving resources and protecting the environment as well as the principle of giving high priority to conserving resources, protecting the environment and promoting its natural restoration, as well as striving for green, circular, and low-carbon development. The Third Plenary Session of the 18th Central Committee of the CPC clearly pointed out the need to comprehensively deepen the reform and build a system for an ecological civilization. The Fourth and Fifth Plenary Sessions of the 18th Central Committee of the CPC emphasized the need to comprehensively follow the rule of law and promote the modernization of the national governance capacity and of the governance system. These strategic deployments have become important guiding principles for the control of "urban diseases" and low-carbon development. Accelerating the control of "urban diseases" and low-carbon development is of great significance. It has already become a trend for the new round of urban development to deeply reflect on the old model of urban development and achieve urban development that is green, low-carbon, and livable. According to Li Yanjun, urban development is not linear, but cyclical fluctuations of prosperity and recession will bring shocks to urban development. How to prevent recession and maintain prosperity is one of the main issues facing urban development.[5]

On February 26, 2014, Xi Jinping emphasized the need to realize coordinated development of the Beijing-Tianjin-Hebei region, promote the construction of an ecological civilization, and boost the low-carbon development of cities in response to the problems of "urban diseases" such as smog in Beijing. Strengthening the international comparative study on the control of "urban diseases" is of great practical significance and urgency to the control of "urban diseases" in Beijing and the coordinated development of the Beijing-Tianjin-Hebei region. This research subject was selected at a proper time. Urbanization is an inevitable result of global industrialization and economic development. It is favorable for development of a global economy, but also leads to the "urban diseases" of population expansion, traffic congestion, environmental pollution, etc. Western developed countries were once plagued by "urban diseases", but through control, the urban environment has been significantly improved and urban quality has been effectively enhanced. The successful experiences of central cities in the United States, Britain, and Japan in the control of "urban diseases" can provide some important references for China that are worthy of in-depth study. A comparative study of the general experiences of these cities has an important reference value, and is even more valuable for Beijing in building an international top-class harmonious and livable city.

1.2 Literature review

1.2.1 Connotations and causes of "urban diseases"

Academically, there is not a uniform definition of "urban disease". Various negative effects and problems arising in the process of urban development can be called "urban diseases", which cover a wide range of aspects. In view of theoretical development, the term "urban disease" first originated in Britain in the late stage of the Industrial Revolution, which was known as the "dirty child" of Europe. The American scholar Joel Kotkin called the deterioration of the urban environment and a series of related problems caused by the Industrial Revolution the "gear brutality". In his Encyclopedia of Urban Problems, Eiichi Isomura pointed out that "urban diseases" are dysfunctions of individuals, societies, and groups. According to Zhou Jialai,[6] the term "urban disease" refers to the negative social and economic effects caused by the defects that affect the overall movement of the urban system due to the accelerated social and economic development and the process of urbanization at a stage when urbanization has not yet been fully realized in China. Zhang Dunfu[7] proposed that due to the complexity of urban life, many social problems inevitably arise in cities, including those related to environmental location, allocation of resources, deviant behavior, and social institutions. Cao Zhongxiong and Wu Liangcheng[8] stated that "urban diseases" are imbalance and disorder in the process of urbanization that are incompatible with urban development because of the rapidly expanding urban environment, resources, and infrastructure that cannot adapt to the rapid development of industrialization and urbanization. Zhang Hanfei[9] also considered that the essence of "urban diseases" is the imbalance between the carrying capacity of urban resources and environment and the scale of urbanization. Researchers have made a comprehensive overview of the causes of "urban diseases", as shown in Table 1.1.[10]

Table 1.1 Key perspectives on the causes of "urban diseases"

Cause	Key perspective
Theory of the size of city population	"Urban diseases" are mainly regarded as a demographic issue. It is believed that demographic disease is a key manifestation of "urban diseases", and that excessive inflow of population leads to an overpopulation that is unbearable for cities.[a] Some scholars have argued that market-oriented employment since the reform and opening-up has promoted the free movement of labors, and a large number of rural population move to developed cities, cause the overpopulation of these cities and exacerbate the problems of "urban diseases".[b]
Theory of the underdevelopment of city construction	Some scholars have proposed that the level of urban planning and management cannot keep up with the speed of urban construction, which causes a disorder in the urban system and the emergence of a series of "urban diseases". According to Zhou Jialai,[c] there are regularities of latency, outbreak and recovery behind the emergence of "urban diseases", which may be alleviated with the improvement of urban systems. Dong

(*continued*)

Table 1.1 Cont.

Cause	Key perspective
	Guoliang[d] held the opinion that the mixed construction mode of humans and vehicles in urban development does not focus on humans, so it leads to many inconveniences such as traffic and environmental problems. Wei Houkai et al.[e] indicated that China's urbanization is faster and larger than that of Western countries, but with unreasonable early planning and later underdeveloped ecological construction, the city functions cannot be improved simultaneously with the mechanical expansion of the size of the city, resulting in a series of problems.
Theory of urban–rural imbalance	The imbalance of urban–rural relationship is regarded as a root cause of "urban diseases"—over-concentration of resources in cities leads to the decline of rural areas and the outflow of the rural population to cities.[f] The imbalance and wide gap between urban and rural areas is itself a manifestation of "urban diseases". The imbalance between urban and rural areas leads to unbalanced development, and the concentration of excellent talents, technology, and capital in cities. Cities cannot play a radiating and driving role in the development of rural areas, but instead their siphoning effects on underdeveloped regions and rural areas lead to further despondency and to a decline in rural areas.
Theory of industrial transformation	Yan Yanming[g] interpreted the connotation of "urban diseases" and their internal relationship from the perspective of industrial transformation, and concluded that there is a certain logical relationship between emergence and evolution of "urban diseases" and industrial transformation, especially in the process of urban industrial transformation, which is usually a period of a concentrated outbreak of "urban diseases". This analysis implies that there are phased characteristics of "urban diseases", and each phase has its own intrinsic features and differences, and shows certain regularities with industrial transformation and upgrading. When the spatial layout and operational mode of cities can adapt to the new industrial structure as soon as possible, "urban diseases" will be mitigated; before that, it will be a period of a concentrated outbreak of "urban diseases".

a Xie Liang, 2014; Li Songtao, 2010; et al.
b Che Sirui, 2014.
c 2004.
d 2011.
e 2011.
f Liu Yongliang and Wang Mengxin, 2010; Wang Haicheng and Deng Jin, 2013.
g 2012.

In Table 1.1, researchers give insightful interpretations to the causes of "urban diseases" from different perspectives, which can provide a reference for systematic research on the causes of "urban diseases" and their characteristics.

First of all, overpopulation. The root cause of "urban diseases" is still the population issue.[11] The expansion of population is an important manifestation of "urban diseases", but they do not explain why there are too many people, or why the cities attract an inappropriately large population, and thus the mechanism for the formation of "urban diseases" is not thoroughly explained. From the perspective of the phenomenon, various demands increase due to the inflow of population and the increasing population, such as demands on employment, traffic, housing, education, medical care, culture, environment, etc., which further lead to traffic congestion, ecological deterioration, a shortage of resources and housing tension in cities. For example, Beijing's long-standing policies of household registration and restriction over housing purchases have neither prevented the inflow of population, nor effectively suppressed the skyrocketing housing prices in this capital city. The expansion of the population is not a problem relevant to the city itself only, but it is also linked to other sectors and surrounding areas, because the big gap between urban and rural areas and the lack of a link among the various sectors are also important causes. The government alone is not able to deal with the "urban diseases", which require the participation of all citizens, including the floating population.

Second, urban construction is lagging behind. "Urban diseases" are also related to the underdeveloped construction and management of the city, a lack of foresight in urban planning and unreasonable planning. Although it is difficult to accurately judge the boundaries of the future development of the city, especially the inflow of the population, urban planning must reserve the land or predict a strategic space. Urban planning failing to keep pace with the changes, unreasonable planning and the low level of management are the causes of the problems of "urban diseases". A related study points out that the fundamental cause of the traffic congestion lies in the unreasonable urban planning of Beijing. The planning is not scientific enough, and the shortsighted urban construction and development basically relies on the originally central areas forming a model of circular development, which would lead to the over-concentration of functions in the downtown area, particularly the concentration of industries in the downtown, with the residential function in the outskirts. As a result, it gives a "pie-spreading" pattern to the expansion of cities. The main drawback of this pattern of urban spaces is that the traffic network of cities is a ring-type plus radial pattern of the fast road network, which is a pattern of a concentric circle type of dispersion and easily leads to a vicious circle between the expansion of capacity and road and the traffic congestion in cities.[12] Despite the continuously strengthened urban construction, it is difficult to keep pace with the growth of population. The cycle of urban construction is longer than that of population growth, so it is not easy to adjust the planning and construction promptly according to the flow of population. In some regions, this may result in excessively farsighted urban planning and over-developed urban construction, but the growth of population is slow or the population decreases, leading to the problems of wasteful urban construction and idle infrastructures, etc. Therefore, the lag in urban construction cannot fully explain the mechanism of "urban diseases".

Third, the imbalance between urban and rural areas. According to Liu Yongliang and Wang Mengxin,[13] the "urban diseases" are caused by the imbalance between urban and rural areas.[14] Lu Lixin[15] argued that although China has obtained a series of achievements in the process of modernization, it still faces unique problems when compared with the historical process of modernization around the world and in East Asia, and the urban-rural imbalance is one of those problems. He analyzed this imbalance at the economic, political, cultural, and social levels and proposed some countermeasures.[16] The big gap between urban and rural areas, over-concentration of advantageous resources in cities and low income of farmers living in rural areas are reasons why many rural people flow to cities and further cause the overpopulation of cities. It is worthy of an in-depth analysis of this view whereby the population converges to big cities due to the enlarging gap between urban and rural areas and among different regions. Researchers believe that treatment of "urban diseases" cannot just identify the problems of cities themselves, but in fact, urban and rural areas are closely linked together. For example, the attraction of Beijing for the population from the surrounding districts and counties in Hebei, including the rural population, has led to a siphoning effect on talents and resources in those surrounding areas, which is one of the important reasons for the "urban diseases" of Beijing. The inflow of talented people of all categories at all levels from Hebei to Beijing, including those who go to school, seek medical care, and find employment, constitutes an important part of the population flowing to Beijing.

On January 25, 2015, Wang Anshun, the Mayor of Beijing, pointed out at a symposium on Beijing's "Two Sessions" that the overpopulation of Beijing is due to the fact that industries attract too many people, with those from Hebei accounting for one-fourth of the population of eight million flowing to Beijing, Beijing has gathered many resources and job opportunities, and it should work on decentralizing the core functions of the capital.[17] The rural floating population is seeking the opportunities of employment and development in cities, thus leading to many problems, such as the rapid expansion of the urban population and traffic congestion. The big gap and imbalance between urban and rural areas aggravates the problems of "urban diseases". The process of urbanization is a process of transferring rural population to cities. The habits and ways of life of the floating population, their mobility, poverty, and possible crimes can result in social instability in cities, and trigger the problem of "urban diseases", including economic, social, cultural, and ecological problems. Once the dynamic balance between urban and rural areas is broken, the growth of cities is out of order but the rural areas are at a loss, and this will lead to a lot of economic and social problems in both urban and rural areas. The over-concentration of resources in cities and the big gap between urban and rural areas makes it difficult to treat the "urban diseases" from a single urban perspective.

Fourth, the industrial transformation of cities. It is believed that the mechanism of the formation of "urban diseases" is associated with industrial development. A city may be flourishing due to industrial development and declining due to industrial decline. Types, structure, and development of industries in a city can affect its level of development, and industrial decline of a city will directly expel its population, and too many unemployed people will cause social instability in this city. Therefore, development of industries, acceleration of industrial transformation, and structural optimization and upgrading are important measures for treating "urban diseases".[18]

These points mentioned above explain the mechanism of the formation of "urban diseases" from different perspectives, and provide important insights to be considered in in-depth study of the causes of "urban diseases" and their internal regularities. However, it is noteworthy that the formation and operation of "urban diseases" are closely related to several key words, such as city, population, industry, resources, rural area, and construction. Cities emerge and develop because of population, industry, resources, and construction, while rural areas provide population and resources for cities and influence cities, and cities also influence rural areas. Hence, the analysis of the mechanism of the formation of "urban diseases" should fully consider the influence of these factors.

1.2.2 Studies on the current situation of "urban diseases"

"Urban diseases" show similar or different characteristics for different cities. The studies of these characteristics are of great significance for revealing their internal causes and regularities. A lot of researchers have conducted in-depth studies from different perspectives and according to different characteristics of the cities studied. Hu Xin and Jiang Xiaoqun[19] classified "urban diseases" into 24 categories: massive demolition and construction, disorderly development, housing issues, unfinished building projects, villages within cities, conversion of floating population on the outskirts of cities, water crisis, garbage siege, environmental pollution, road killers, engineering mistakes, greening mistakes, empty cities, heat island effect, abnormal building, damage to labor resource, over-exploitation of cultural resources, underdeveloped system of public health, urban geological disasters, traffic congestion, unreasonable layout of infrastructures, ineffective urban management, planning problems, and security problems.

Zeng Changqiu et al.[20] held the view that in addition to the generally recognized typical "urban diseases" such as population expansion, traffic congestion, shortage of energy and pollution of environment, there were also atypical "urban diseases" such as depression, youth problems, and beggar problems in the humanistic social system. Zhu Yinghui[21] put forward six symptoms of Chinese cities: disorderly convergence of population, constraints of energy resources, degradation of ecological environment, serious traffic congestion, high housing prices, and a severe situation of security.[22] According to Jiang Aihua and Zhang Chi,[23] with rapid progress in urbanization, "urban diseases" have become increasingly prominent in some of China's big cities, mainly manifested as disorderly concentration of population, congestion of road traffic, tensions of energy resources, high housing prices, and difficulties in employment.[24] Liu Jiping and Liu Chenxiao[25] indicated that as China continuously boosts its process of urbanization, "urban diseases" such as population expansion, traffic congestion, and environmental pollution have emerged, thus seriously affecting the daily work order and quality of life of urban residents.[26]

Jiao Xiaoyun[27] argued that "urban diseases" have existed to varying degrees in all countries undergoing urbanization, with the essence that the speed of the development of and the scale of the expansion of cities have exceeded the maximum load that the resources and environment of the cities can bear. The main types of "urban diseases" include: urban economic diseases, urban social diseases, urban ecological diseases, and "atypical urban diseases". The "urban diseases" had institutional root causes, and their prevention and treatment needed continuous institutional innovation and supply.[28]

Li Xuemin and Wu Zhenguo[29] pointed out that as the problems of "urban diseases" became increasingly serious, their prevention and treatment became the key link to promoting new urbanization in the new era. By the study of the prevention of "urban diseases" in big cities of Inner Mongolia pursuant to the procedure of "symptom—diagnosis—treatment", they thought that typical symptoms of "urban diseases" in the big cities of Inner Mongolia were mainly embodied in traffic congestion, environmental pollution, and housing difficulties. Through the diagnosis and analysis of the symptoms, they found that the "urban diseases" had a multi-cause multi-effect relationship with those symptoms.[30]

1.2.3 International comparative studies on the problems of "urban diseases"

The issue of "urban diseases" has been investigated by many researchers adopting the international comparative methods and perspectives. Through cross-border comparisons, the causes and general laws for the formation of "urban diseases" have been analyzed to provide a reference for the treatment of "urban diseases" in China. For example, Li Gangyuan[31] conducted a comparative study of "urban diseases" in Great Britain, and concluded that Britain, as the founder of industrial civilization, had created modern urban civilization, and driven by the commercialization and industrialization, the population of Britain rapidly moved from agricultural areas to industrial areas. The population expanded dramatically, and led to the "urban diseases" of housing, employment, public health, environment, etc. Britain's path of urbanization has experienced ups and downs. However, problem-guided and characterized by the gradual and multi-pronged reforms, it finally got out of the dilemma and explored a very characteristic model for treating its "urban diseases".[32] According to Yuan Dongzhen,[33] the rapid development of urbanization has often led to a vicious circle of a deteriorating living environment, decreasing economic activities, dividing the rich and the poor in urban areas, and increasing management costs. Such problems have been particularly evident in developing countries, represented by the "Mumbai disease" and the "Mexico disease", where there were a large number of slums and the problems of health and social security arose. Therefore, it is worthwhile for us to learn from the practices of some developed countries in dealing with "urban diseases".

Zhang Shuhua[34] studied "urban diseases" and their treatment in the United States of America during the period of social transformation, and pointed out that the rapid social transformation in the United States of America led to the emergence of various "urban diseases". Xu Zhiqiang[35] indicated that the "urban diseases" in Britain during the industrialization period were mainly embodied as the shortage of housing for workers, serious environmental pollution, and chaotic social security. The British government took a series of measures to expand the housing supply, improve the urban environment and strengthen the social security, thus achieving success to a certain degree. Wang Dawei, Wen Hui, and Lin Jiabin[36] summarized the experiences of Tokyo, London, and New York in treating "urban diseases". Wang Kaiyong and Yan Bingqiu et al.[37] studied the planning and the ideas and measures as a response in order to prevent and control "urban diseases" in foreign countries, and concluded that main manifestations of "urban diseases" in developed countries included: population expansion, overburdened cities; poverty, unemployment, and poor living conditions of urban population; traffic congestion, and deterioration of the quality of life; environmental pollution and a shortage of resources; social conflicts, criminal activities, and political corruption; the sprawling of cities and their out-of-control development, and so on. Foreign countries made a lot of attempts and accumulated much valuable experience in their urban planning and management. By learning from the planning and response ideas of the United States of America, Britain, Japan, and other developed countries in treating their "urban diseases", they will be inspirational for the urban planning and management of China. We should update the concept of urban development, strengthen the science and authority of urban planning, attach importance to the guiding role of traffic planning in urban development, actively promote the coordination and docking of various plans, shorten the cycle for the approval of the plans, and strictly guarantee the smooth implementation of those plans.[38]

1.2.4 Studies of the causes of "urban diseases"

Researchers from home and abroad have studies the causes of "urban diseases". As early as the 1960s, scholars were concerned about the social structure and economic problems caused by the urbanization of the population, and put forward their own analytical models, such as "The Impact of Migration on the Socioeconomic Structure of Cities and Suburbs",[39] and "Urbanization – The Problem of High-Density Living".[40] They analyzed the impact of population migration on the economic and social development of cities and further discussed the causes of "urban diseases". After the 1990s, Brockerhoff examined the problem of poverty in cities of developing countries and its causes. In China, researchers explained the causes of "urban diseases" mainly from three perspectives: the market, the government, and combined causes.[41]

Result of market failure. Xu Chuanchen and Qin Hailin[42] held the view that although the market mechanism could promote the optimal allocation of resources, the supply with strong externalities could not be compensated itself, and market failure led to the insufficient supply of public services, resulting in the "tragedy of the commons" in cities, namely the problems of "urban diseases". Cao Zhongxiong and Wu Liangcheng[43] pointed out that under a market economy, the problem of over-consumption arose and exceeded the carrying capacity of the city itself, while the carrying capacity of resources and the environment of the city had the property of public goods, so the market mechanism itself was not sufficient to support the development of the city, and led to the formation of "urban diseases". Wang Guixin[44] also argued that the pursuit of profit maximization under the system of a market economy resulted in continuous expansion of the size of cities, further causing "urban diseases" such as overpopulation and traffic congestion, and that the negative role or the failure of the market could cause or aggravate the "urban diseases in big cities".[45]

Result of government failure. The government should play a leading role in urban development and strengthen the governance and adjustment of "urban diseases" with the mechanism of a "visible hand". However, excessive intervention by the government or inadequate planning, design and public policy, or inadequate supply of public services can also lead to the formation of "urban diseases". In this regard, plenty of researchers have examined the causes of "urban diseases" or the failure of urban governance from the perspective of government failure. For example, Zhou Jialai[46] indicated that different phases of urban development required the provision of appropriate services or policy guidance by governance, but inadequate provision inevitably caused "urban diseases". The administrators of cities put in efforts and set goals for economic construction, while they ignored the ecological benefits and environmental pollution. The goals of the whole society focused on the economic benefits, but ignored the ecological and social benefits, and they even sought economic benefits at the expense of ecological and social benefits. Wang Guixin pointed out that the government should strengthen urban planning, and if the structural planning of urban space was not scientific and reasonable enough, it would become a direct cause of "urban diseases of big cities". According to Pan Baocai, the decision-making by multiple departments resulted in multi-centered policy decisions, the comprehensive support for cities was unreasonable, and these factors contributed to the formation of "urban diseases".[47]

Fang Yaming[48] argued that "urban diseases", the division between the rich and the poor, and "symptoms of development" such as regional disparities during the modernization of China were closely related to the imbalance in the distribution of resources, benefits, and costs due to excessive centralization of powers, and the power-dominated mechanism of resource allocation, a pattern of social development based on power hierarchy, imbalance between power and rights, inequality of rights and inherent limitations of the market economy exacerbated the imbalance in China's social development. Zeng Guangyu and Wang Shengquan[49] indicated that the impulse to pursue the GDP-based performance indicators resulted in an overemphasis on economy by the government of some cities, which disregarded the responsibility that the city government should provide public services, and also neglected the responsibilities for the improvement of livelihood, social construction, and environmental protection in the cities.

Lin Jiabin[50] studied the institutional causes of "urban diseases" and the mechanism of action in China, and suggested that the institutional causes, including cadre selection and system of performance evaluation, the fiscal and taxation system, the land system, the planning system, and the central–local relationship, became the special driving mechanism of China's urban development by influencing the behavior of the governments of cities, and also the unique institutional causes of the "urban diseases" of China. Jiang Aihua and Zhang Chi[51] argued that "urban diseases" were mainly caused by the rapid development of cities and the relative backwardness of urban planning and management in recent years, and it has become an urgent and important task for administrators of cities to accelerate the treatment of "urban diseases" from a strategic perspective.[52]

According to Ni Pengfei,[53] while urbanization was accelerating, China's infrastructure and public services could not keep pace with the growth of urbanization, and there was a lack of scientific, reasonable, and forward-looking planning and policy guidance for the spatial activities of population and industry, so urbanization in China has been facing increasingly severe challenges, and some Chinese cities have suffered from very serious "urban diseases".[54]

Result of a combination of causes. The formation of "urban diseases" is not the result of a single mechanism of market or government, but to a large extent the result of the failure of both to play their roles properly. Shi Yishao[55] argued that China's "urban diseases" were not caused by the large size of cities, but the institutional conflicts, structural disorders, policy mistakes, technical failures, out-of-control management and moral failures. Chi Zihua suggested that "urban diseases" were caused by the imbalance of resource allocation and the excessive transfer of rural labor. Liu Chunbin[56] stated that "people find the seriousness of the urban diseases of big cities and advocate the development of small towns, but actually the diseases of small towns are much more serious than those of big cities". Huang Rongqing[57] pointed out that the over-concentration of population in cities in the process of urbanization led to "urban diseases", and the rapid growth of the urban population resulted in the stagnation of or decline in the employment rate of workers, and thus the so-called "over-urbanization". According to Zhao Hong,[58] one of the important reasons why the central government positioned the coordinated development of the Beijing-Tianjin-Hebei region as a national strategy was to solve the "big-city urban diseases" in Beijing. There were many causes of the "urban diseases" in Beijing, which could be attributed to three main types: the economic development and its resulting rapid growth of population were the core causes; the unscientific and unreasonable urban planning and failure to break through the monocentric pattern were other important causes; and the institutional constraints were the most fundamental causes.[59] Liu Jiping and Liu Chenxiao[60] indicated that with the continuous advancement of urbanization in China, "urban diseases" such as population expansion, traffic congestion, and environmental pollution emerged one after another and seriously affected the daily work order and the quality of life of urban residents. The main reasons for the emergence of "urban diseases" in China included deviation in the concept of urban development, institutional defects and an underdevelopment of the building of infrastructures, etc.[61]

Wang Ning[62] argued that the existing connotations of "urban diseases" often aimed at a single city, without considering the relationship between internal and external spatial structure of the city, and hence needed to be extended in the denotations. The "urban diseases" of extra-large cities were often caused by defects in the spatial structure, that is to say, the structural layout of internal space of extra-large cities was not reasonable, and the spatial structure of inter-city system was uncoordinated, thus leading to the excessive convergence of elements and causing various symptoms of "urban diseases".[63] Li Yunzhao and Yue Wu[64] indicated that China's urbanization rate rose rapidly from 20% in 1978 to 54.77% in 2014, and with the advancement of the process of urbanization, "urban diseases" occurred, such as traffic congestion, population expansion, environmental pollution, tension in the supply of resources, increased security risks, and a lack of cultural characteristics of cities. The causes were mainly dissonance of various relationships between human beings and nature, humans and humans, and spirit and matter.[65]

According to Zhang Mingdou,[66] the new urbanization faced potential crises. For instance, the space was constrained by the dual structure of urban-rural areas, the emphasis on urban rather than rural areas led to the new "three rural" problems of migrant workers, old-fashioned agriculture and unoccupied villages, and the weak economic foundation and ability to sustain the development in small and medium towns and the serious imbalance between supply and demand of public goods and public services in large and medium cities exacerbated the consumption of resources and environmental pollution.[67]

1.2.5 The choice of countermeasures for treating "urban diseases"

In view of the above manifestations and causes of "urban diseases", the adoption of effective treating and preventive measures has become an important issue of common concern for the government, academia and all social strata. Chinese researchers, such as Gu Shengzu, proposed to implement a balanced strategy of development for large, medium and small cities, to promote the reform of the household registration system, and to realize equalization of basic public services, for the purpose of treating "urban diseases". Yang Shisong et al. suggested that the treatment of "urban diseases" should pay attention to the "local urbanization" of rural areas. According to Sun Jiuwen,[68] the prevention and treatment of "urban diseases" requires improving the level of urban governance and administrative wisdom, and "urban diseases" could be solved and prevented by relying on the enhancement of the capability of urban governance. Liu Yongliang and Wang Mengxin[69] pointed out that in order to alleviate the population pressure of big cities, a strict urban registration system was implemented and the strategy of small towns was actively developed, but these institutional and strategic measures were not effective in alleviating the problems of "urban diseases in big cities". The history and reality of the evolution of cities throughout the world showed that controlling the size of large cities and encouraging the development of small towns could not effectively solve the problems of "urban diseases". To eradicate "urban diseases", new ways must be found. Gradually eliminating the dual urban–rural structure, narrowing the gap between urban and rural areas, and achieving balanced urban–rural development are the fundamental ways for solving "urban diseases". With a view to overcoming the dual urban–rural structure, efforts should be made to solve the problem of imbalanced education between urban and rural areas, elevate the construction of rural infrastructures to strategic heights and preserve the "life-saving land" of migrant workers.

According to Lang Lang and Ning Yuyu,[70] China's industrial prosperity provides jobs for peasants in factories, but once these factories move to other areas where labor is cheaper, a large number of people will lose both land and jobs and become poor people in cities. Urban and rural problems are closely linked, and without the construction of rural areas, it will be difficult to find answers to urban problems. Si Yanming[71] proposed that the prevention and treatment of "urban diseases" requires the introduction of advanced urban management concepts, forward-looking planning, systematic construction, and refined management. Jiang Aihua and Zhang Chi[72] suggested that the treatment of "urban diseases" could be achieved through scientific building of a system of cities and towns, enhancement, and improvement of the construction of urban public infrastructures, the establishment of a scientific urban plan, and improvement in the level of urban construction and management.[73] Yang Ka[74] analyzed the nature and root causes of urban diseases and their path of treatment based on the theory of self-organizing systems.

Xiang Chunling[75] argued that the treatment of "urban diseases" must adhere to the scientific concept of being people-oriented, reduce "urban diseases" with the development of a new kind of urbanization and scientific urban planning, overcome "urban diseases" by means of institutional reform and the coordinated development of urban systems, and cure "urban diseases" by the effective protection measures for the ecological environment.[76] Zhao Hong[77] indicated that a multi-pronged approach must be taken to treat "urban diseases". Moreover, the design of new models for cities, the solution of "urban diseases" on a large regional scale, urbanization of rural life, and improvement of the quality of urbanization are some important ideas proposed by scholars. Liu Jiping and Liu Chenxiao[78] suggested that the treatment of "urban diseases" should stick to the people-oriented concept, strengthen the coordinated and sustainable economic and social development of cities, eliminate institutional shackles and various obstacles, build a new system of cities and towns, lay stress on the construction of infrastructures and improve the level of city administration.[79] According to Zhao Hong,[80] the treatment of Beijing's "big-city urban diseases" must decentralize on-core functions, regulate the industries, optimize the city space, accelerate the construction of the rail transit system, and promote the coordinated development of the Beijing-Tianjin-Hebei region.[81]

Li Xuemin and Wu Zhenguo[82] pointed out that when the problems of "urban diseases" became increasingly serious, the prevention and treatment of "urban diseases" were the key issues for advancing the urbanization in the new era, and they studied the prevention of "urban diseases" in the big cities of Inner Mongolia according to the procedure of "symptoms—diagnosis—treatment". The typical symptoms of "urban diseases" in the big cities of Inner Mongolia were embodied as traffic congestion, environmental pollution, and housing difficulties. Through diagnosis and analysis, it was found that there was a multi-cause multi-effect relationship between causes and symptoms of "urban diseases". After further analysis, they proposed the targeted countermeasures, with the expectation for effectively alleviating the adverse effects of "urban diseases" on the life of urban residents.[83]

Wang Ning[84] suggested that the spatial defects could be quantified by commuting index and utility index of extra-large cities and accordingly, he proposed that the treatment of "urban diseases" of extra-large cities should be achieved by optimizing the spatial structure, decentralizing the urban functions, and building complex cities.[85]

According to Li Yunzhao and Yue Wu,[86] the main measures for and means to treating "urban diseases" included: establishing the concept of people-oriented urban governance, cultivating citizens' awareness of environmental protection; scientific and unified planning, and improving the overall functions of the urban system; coordinating the urban and rural development, and improving the construction of infrastructures; as well as improving the mechanism of city administration, and exploring the laws of urban development.[87]

Zhang Mingdou[88] pointed out that the path of new urbanization needed to achieve the transformation from top-down man-made towns to bottom-up industry-driven towns, from the emphasis on cities while ignoring rural areas to the integration of urban and rural areas, from the areal expansion of urban construction to the improvement of people's livelihood, and from single-line promotion with a preference for quantity to a double-line balance of quality and quantity. The integration of urban and rural areas is the key to solving the contradiction of the dual urban and rural structure; solving the rural diseases depends on the inclusive development of urbanization; solving the town diseases requires necessarily the reform of land ownership system and construction of infrastructures; and solving "urban diseases" requires the intelligence of city, management, and traffic.[89]

Jiao Xiaoyun[90] argued that local urbanization of rural areas, as an important form of new urbanization, could play a pivotal role in preventing and treating "urban diseases" and solving the rural problems caused by the urbanization in other regions and the "semi-urbanization" of the transferred agricultural population. How to boost the local urbanization and solve the problems of "urban diseases" should have scientific planning as the primary task, the institutional reform as the key issue, the beautiful countryside as the goal of development, the emancipation of the mind as the driving force, and the training of skills as the guarantee of talents.[91]

Liang Li[92] proposed a technological path for treating "urban diseases" based on the background of big data era, and held the view that technology was constantly changing and shaping the new urban life, and that the interaction between urban physical space and information technology was providing the impetus for the sustainable development of cities. In the process of urbanization, "urban diseases" and other urban problems broke out and posed serious challenges to urban governance. The construction of smart cities by relying on new-generation information technology with big data at the core could bring a new technological path and effective means to the treatment of "urban diseases". Promoting the construction of smart cities was conducive to the perfection of the system of urban governance, improvement of the capability of urban governance and the quality of development, enhancement of the happiness index of cities and a solution to difficulties in the development of cities.[93] Xiao Jincheng and Ma Yankun[94] studied the treatment of "urban diseases" of the capital city from the perspective of the coordinated development of the Beijing-Tianjin-Hebei region, and put forward a specific strategy to deal with it.[95]

1.2.6 Studies on green low-carbon development and the coordinated development of cities

1.2.6.1 Interpretation of the connotations of the construction of an ecological civilization and green low-carbon development

The report of the 18th CPC National Congress proposed to vigorously promote the construction of an ecological civilization and incorporated it into the overall strategic layout of the "Five-in-One" (economic, political, social, cultural, and ecological progress). The Party and the State attached great importance to the construction of an ecological civilization, which reflected the new thinking, new concept, and new strategy of the ruling under the new economic normal, and was a positive contribution of the Party and the State to the sustainable economic and social development of cities, the improvement of the urban civilization and the maintenance of the ecological security of cities throughout the world. According to Yu Keping,[96] the ecological civilization refers to all the efforts made and results achieved by mankind in the process of transforming nature for their own benefit for the purpose of achieving harmony between mankind and nature, characterizing the progressive state of the mutual relationship between mankind and nature.[97] Lu Jun[98] defined ecological civilization as the summation of the material and spiritual achievements made by mankind following the law of harmonious development between mankind and nature and continuously promoting social, economic, and cultural development, and it is a cultural and ethical form with the tenets of harmonious coexistence, comprehensive development and sustainable prosperity between mankind and nature and among human beings.[99] Because cities are the main sites for the construction of an ecological civilization, strengthening the green development of cities means taking the construction of ecological civilization as an important direction and starting point, realizing the modernized, ecological, and sustainable development of cities through green economic growth, attaching importance to the coordinated development of many aspects, such as urban economy, society, culture, and environmental protection, and placing emphasis on the intensification of resources, environmental friendliness, and ecological protection. The green development of cities should base economic transformation on the improvement of the economic quality and ecological benefits, take the green, low-carbon and ecological development as the sustainable and core advantages of urban economic growth, social construction, and environmental optimization, and regard the green development of cities as the long-term driving force of the construction of an ecological civilization from the strategic layout and directional positioning.

Boosted by a series of global issues and challenges such as coping with climate change, scarcity of strategic resources, and a financial crisis, the green low-carbon growth and development model are increasingly receiving widespread attention from the international community. Ecological civilization is the result of the profound reflection of mankind on the traditional forms of civilization, especially an industrial civilization, and it is also a major form of progress in the concept, path, and model of the forms of human civilization and the development of civilization as well as an important direction for the process of evolution of urbanization. The construction of an ecological civilization is closely related to the long-term interests and social welfare of urban population. For the treatment of "urban diseases" and choice of a scientific development model, industrial optimization, and upgrading should be sped up by means of energy conservation, emission reduction, and green low-carbon development, the upgrading of industrial technology and industrial transformation should be strengthened, and urban transformation should be enhanced regarding multiple aspects such as social construction and ecological protection. Energy conservation and emission reduction and green development are relied upon to realize the ecological construction of cities, to build a comprehensive model of green transformation with a win–win situation of economic growth and ecological environment, to achieve the pattern of urban development by means of ecological, economic, social, and cultural integration, and to promote the construction of an ecological civilization in an all-round way. In 1985, scholars like Friberg and Hettne put forward the term "green development" and attached importance to ecological protection and green economic development. Green development is an innovation of a model based on the traditional development, and a new model of development that regards environmental protection as an important pillar to achieving sustainable development under the constraints of the capacity of ecological environment and the carrying capacity of resources. It can accelerate the treatment of "urban diseases", and change the traditional model of development that neglects ecological and environmental protection in cities. Reducing the consumption of resources and energy and the emissions of greenhouse gases is not only a common challenge for all countries, but also a driving force for transforming the mode of economic development and encouraging and developing the emerging green industries such as energy conservation and environmental protection. It is bound to become a point of breakthrough for a new round of technological revolution and an important choice for the sustainable economic and social development in cities. Many famous cities in the world lay stress on the treatment of "urban diseases", accelerate the green development of their cities, regard environmental resources as an intrinsic element of social and economic development, take the sustainable economic, social, and environmental development as the goal of green development, and then achieve the "green" and "ecological" economic activities and outcomes in cities. Of course, such theoretical and practical exploration has never stopped, and it is increasingly occupying the dominant direction of urban development and is becoming a development craze.

The construction of an ecological civilization needs to expedite the green low-carbon development of cities. In order to change the traditional modes of economic growth, resource consumption and environmental pollution that go against the requirements of an ecological civilization, the acceleration of green development must aim at construction of an ecological civilization as the goal and important direction, at the expense of the least possible input of resources and energy, as well as carbon emission and environmental pollution, so as to achieve green, circular, and low-carbon development. Accordingly, the green development of cities is an inevitable requirement and an important support for the construction of an ecological civilization. The green development of cities advocates an ecological revolution, a profound revolution involving technological, economic, social, and cultural fields of cities, and it is a transition from an industrial civilization to an ecological one, from an industrial economy to an ecological economy, from an industrial society to an ecological society, and from the industrialized model of development to a green, low-carbon, ecological, and livable model of urban development. Xiao Hong[100] argued that the green development of cities was a dialectical negation of the traditional evolutionary path of industrialization and urbanization, and that it abandoned the economy-only model of industrialized development that focuses only on the economic benefits without regard to human welfare and ecological consequences, but shifted to social, economic, resource, and environmental development that puts emphasis on overall social-economic-natural composite ecological benefits.[101]

In order to advance the construction of an ecological civilization, in the process of urban transformation, attention must be paid to the improvement of technology and efficiency regarding the utilization of resources, the cultivation and development of new economic growth points, the promotion of adjustment and optimization of the industrial structure, the enhancement of environmental protection and governance, the reduction of environmental pollution and carbon emissions, the realization of environmental friendliness and ecological balance, and the advancement of the comprehensive, coordinated, and sustainable development of the economy, society and ecological environment. The green transformation of cities means following the principles of green, ecological, and low-carbon sustainable development, achieving the modernized, ecological, and low-carbon development of cities with long-term sustainable and ecologically circular economic growth, satisfying the needs of survival and development of the current generation without damaging the interests and space for the development of the next generation, and realizing the sustainable and long-term development of long-term interests and short-term interests, local interests and global utilization. According to Li Yanjun, the development of cities is not linear, the cyclical fluctuations of prosperity and recession will bring shocks to the urban development, and how to prevent recession and maintain prosperity is one of the main issues facing urban development. At present, developed countries have entered the fifth long cycle, while China is in the third long cycle, namely in the middle stages of industrialization. In order to successfully complete industrialization and overtake the cities of developed countries, Chinese cities must experience transformation with a combination of industrial and social transformation at the core.[102]

Theories and practices regarding green low-carbon development are still in the experimental stage. Green low-carbon development is a choice of the model of transformation and a strategic decision guided by the construction of an ecological civilization, based on the theories of a circular economy, a green economy and sustainable development, with green management, green technological innovation, green transformation, and green construction as the key and driving force, and the shift of the model of development to one of sustainable development, for the purpose of achieving resource saving, environmental friendliness, and ecological balance, as well as the harmonious development of human beings, nature, and society. According to Zhuang Guiyang,[103] a low-carbon economy was a social vision, low-carbon development was a necessary process for the transition to a low-carbon economy, and the practice of energy conservation and emission reduction in China showed that China must accumulate policy experience through "learning by doing".[104] Zhang Chen and Liu Chunbin[105] argued that green transformation and development were based on the current economic and social development and the carrying capacity of resources and environment, and by changing the operational method of enterprises, the composition of industries, and the means of government supervision, the green operation of enterprises, green reconstruction of industries, and green supervision of government could be realized, so as to transform the traditional black economy into a green economy and form a scientific model of development of economic development, social harmony, resource conservation, and environmental friendliness.[106] The green development of cities has changed the past model of development of a one-sided pursuit of economic growth and expansion of material scale. Hu Angang pointed out that the so-called path of green development emphasized the unity and coordination of economic development and environmental protection, that is to say, a more active and people-oriented path of sustainable development. John Knott thought that green development was "a return to a way of development that combines new technologies and has a good impact on the climate, geography, and culture". He Jiankun[107] held the view that the construction of an ecological civilization and the realization of low-carbon development must innovate the concept of development and ideas of consumption, as well as the theories and methodologies.[108] The green low-carbon development of cities requires not only improving the way of using energy resources, but also protecting and restoring the natural ecosystems and ecological processes, thus achieving the harmonious coexistence and co-evolution of mankind and nature, and a green economy and low-carbon economic development of cities. Within the bounds of ecological limits, it lays stress on the change of the model of development, intensiveness of resources, environmental friendliness, and the innovation and application of the green low-carbon technology, improves the efficiency of energy utilization, raises the economic output per unit of input of the natural capital, increases the welfare contribution per unit of economic output, and ultimately enhances the performance of green development.

1.2.6.2 The current situation and problems of the construction of an ecological civilization and the green development of cities

International researchers have studied the current problems of cities and their inherent causes according to the realities of resource depletion and industrial decline in cities, and found that the construction of an urban ecological civilization was lagging behind, so they put forward an important proposition that the acceleration of the treatment of "urban diseases" must attach great importance to the construction of an ecological civilization and the green low-carbon development of cities. After the 1960s, with the frequent outbreaks of global economic crises and the rising prices of energy resources and labor force, many central cities in the West, such as Houston, Pittsburgh, Glasgow, and Birmingham, have shown signs of large-scale urban decline, and the problems of "urban diseases" became prominent and seriously restricted the sustainable economic and social development of cities. In this regard, some researchers have conducted an in-depth study on how the industrial structure of these cities could be adjusted and revived and how the "urban diseases" could be treated. Roberts and Sykes[109] indicated that the narrow specialized industrial groups were the root cause of economic vulnerabilities in cities, and the diversification of the industrial structure was an important path towards urban revitalization and development. Roger Perman[110] pointed out that Houston was faced with the problems of depletion of resources, deterioration of environment, decline of industries and serious unemployment, so it needed to speed up its economic transformation by vigorously extending the industrial chain, expediting the development of oil research, and driving the development of related service sectors. Landry[111] suggested that contemporary urban development needed a creative approach to transformation. Frost-Kumpf[112] argued that art played an important role in beautifying and revitalizing cities, providing employment, and attracting residents and tourists, etc. Booth and Boyle [113] explored the treatment of "urban diseases" and the transformation and renewal of cities under the guidance of cultural policies.

Many international researchers have conducted an in-depth research on the treatment of "urban diseases" and urban transformation and on development from the perspectives of green economy and low-carbon economy. Glaeser and Kahn[114] investigated the relationships of carbon emissions, size of city, and density of land development by an empirical study, and found that there was a positive relationship between the size of a city and the carbon emissions because the larger a city is the more carbon emissions it may have. Jenny Crawford and Will French[115] examined the relationship between the planning of urban spaces and the goals of green low-carbon development in Britain. W. K. Fong et al.[116] empirically studied the relationships of energy consumption, carbon emission reduction, and urban green development and urban planning in Malaysia.

Chinese researchers have studied the issue of the construction of an ecological civilization in cities. According to Weng Zhiyong,[117] China has made certain achievements in the protection of the ecological environment and natural resources, but the construction of an ecological civilization is still faced with a very serious situation and very huge challenges, which are mainly manifested in the lack of correct ecological values and ecological morality, the constraints of the phases of economic development and the model of economic growth on the development of ecological civilization, the "index" phenomenon in the construction of an ecological civilization, a not-completely-formed relevant supporting system, and the efforts and transparency of monitoring and enforcement in need of being strengthened.[118] Du Yong[119] conducted an in-depth analysis of the current situation and problems of the construction of an ecological civilization in resource-oriented cities of China, and revealed that current dilemmas faced during the construction of an ecological civilization in these cities mainly included the increasingly tightening energy and resource constraints, serious environmental pollution and obvious trend of deterioration of the ecological system, imbalance in the industrial structure, and prominent problems of livelihood.

Researchers have also conducted in-depth studies on the issue of green low-carbon development of cities. Hou Weili[120] indicated that on the road to green development, China has faced the challenges of sustained population growth, a rise in the pattern of high consumption, expansion of economic scale, shift of industrial structure to heavy industry, and rapid increase in the speed of urbanization. However, the establishment of a market mechanism, the expansion of opening-up to the outside world, the enhancement of environmental awareness, and the rise of a knowledge-based economy have also provided opportunities for China to achieve green development. Lu Jun[121] pointed out that the growth rate of the GDP had long been an unwritten criterion for evaluating the performance of officials in local governments, so that some local governments went against the laws of economics only for the pursuit of high-speed economic development. As a result, the ecological environment was seriously damaged and the sustainable development was greatly affected. The analysis of the causes of the problems in the process of building an ecological civilization in China unveiled that: first, in terms of economic factors, the deterioration of the environment was caused by economic development, and there was a conflict between economic interests and environmental protection; second, regarding human and social factors, with a large population, high pressure of resources on the environment, a generally poor public awareness of environmental protection, and intertwining of ecological problems with other social problems such as poverty, there was a tendency towards creating a vicious circle.[122] Chen Jing, Chen Ning, and Zhu Dajian et al.[123] argued that many of the problems of China's urban development stemmed from the conflict between economic and social development and the consumption of natural capital in cities, so the key to China's urban development was green transformation. However, there was a lack of effective theories and methods for evaluating and analyzing the green transformation of cities. Tian Zhiyu and Yang Hongwei[124] analyzed the current status, existing problems and challenges facing the green low-carbon development of cities in China, with a case study of the Beijing-Tianjin-Hebei region.[125]

1.2.6.3 Comparative studies of the domestic and international construction of an ecological civilization and green development of cities

Some researchers have carried out comparative studies on the domestic and foreign experiences in the construction of an ecological civilization and green development in cities. For example, Sun Yajing[126] compared the international models of the transformation of mining cities. Yuan Zhibin and Song Yajie[127] compared the models of transformation resource-based cities in China and the United States of America. Cheng Jianwen[128] proposed learning from Singapore's experience in three-dimensional greening in order to recreate green spaces in Shanghai. Lu Xiaocheng[129] studied the inspiration of New York's green transformation for Beijing. Shi Minjun and Liu Yanyan[130] conducted an international comparison of the green development of cities and indicated that the gap between green development of domestic cities and those in developed countries was mainly reflected in two aspects: environmental health and low-carbon development, and the gap in resource conservation and livability was not significant between domestic and foreign cities. The gap in environmental health was mainly reflected in two aspects: the quality of air and environmental management. The quality of air of cities in developed countries was significantly better than that of domestic cities. Domestic cities obviously fell behind those in developed countries in the field of low-carbon development. One cause of this gap was that China was in the middle stages of industrialization and urbanization, with a strong demand for energy resources; on the other hand, it was closely related to the fact that China's energy structure favored coal, while the efficiency of energy technology was low. Through a comparative study, Tian Zhiyu and Fu Guanyun[131] argued that the developed countries generally completed the process of urbanization after nearly a century of development, so their experience in this process can provide a reference for our country, and they reviewed and summarized the experience of green low-carbon development in the cities of major developed countries.

A large quantity of researchers has conducted some comparative studies on typical cases and main models of the construction of an ecological civilization and green development in domestic cities. With a case study of Zaozhuang, Liu Chang[132] analyzed the problems related to the transformation of resource-exhausted cities and put forward the specific measures to realize urban transformation.[133] Yang Bo and Zhao Liming[134] explored the model of transformation of Zhaoyuan, a resource-based city known as the "gold capital of China", studied how to overcome the "curse" of resources, the elimination of the locking effect, and the construction of a space for transformation. Lei Lei[135] proposed the "Baiyin" model for the transformation of resource-exhausted cities. Hou Jingxin and Yue Tian[136] studied the model of transformation of resource-exhausted cities from the perspective of ecological problems. Chen Jiliang[137] studied the model of transformation of Hegang from the perspective of choice of leading industries. According to

Cai Meng and Wang Yuming,[138] the creation of low-carbon tourism was an advanced stage of livable and ecological development of cities and a strategic choice of the model of transformation of tourism cities in China. Its development must be regulated, interactive, and demonstrative to accelerate the formation of a new pattern of development of low-carbon tourism cities with Chinese characteristics.[139]

1.2.6.4 Studies on the evaluation and route towards the construction of an ecological civilization and the green low-carbon development of cities

Many researchers have established evaluation index systems for the construction of an ecological civilization, and have further scientifically measured and evaluated the status of development of urban or regional ecological civilizations, so as to provide a basis for proposing effective countermeasures. Chen Jing, Chen Ning, Zhu Dajian et al.[140] divided the evaluation index systems for urban green transformation into two categories, namely, urban support systems and urban coordination systems, introduced the entropy theory to establish a model of gray entropy evaluation, and utilized relevant data of Shanghai from 2001 to 2007 to conduct an empirical study. The results of this study showed that the urban development of Shanghai was fast during the period of study, but the main problem was how to reduce per capita material consumption from the right side of the ecological threshold in order to achieve absolute disconnection. Based on the empirical analysis of four cities, namely Beijing, Shanghai, Guangzhou and Shenzhen, Lan Qingxin, Peng Yiran, and Feng Ke[141] conducted a study on the evaluation index systems for the construction of an urban ecological civilization and some evaluation methods. According to the principle of the process of analytic hierarchy, they built an evaluation index system with four layers of criteria including ecological economy, ecological environment, ecological culture, and ecological system and 30 specific index layers. By applying this index system, a comprehensive evaluation method was utilized for a horizontal comparison of the levels of construction of an ecological civilization in Beijing, Shanghai, Guangzhou, and Shenzhen in 2011.[142] Du Yong[143] argued that, as a guarantee for protecting the security of energy resources and a main battlefield for promoting new industrialization and urbanization, the construction of an ecological civilization in resource-based cities in China was in a critical period and that it was urgent to establish a scientific evaluation index system for the construction of an ecological civilization, for guiding its construction in resource-based cities in China. Geng Tianzhao, Zhu Yu, and Wang Huan[144] proposed the concept of the competitive power of urban green development and explored the relationship between the quality of environment and the level of economic and social development. From the viewpoint of a "hard environment" such as the quality of urban air environment, the quality of surface water environment, the quality of sound environment, the quality of water in the centralized drinking water sources, and the quality of ecological environment, an evaluation index system was built by combining with the industrial GDP index for measuring the degree of economic development of cities, with the environmental cost per unit of industrial GDP to characterize the competitive power of urban green development, and a case study of cities in Anhui Province.

A great number of researchers have studied the route towards the construction of an ecological civilization and the green low-carbon development of cities. According to Liu Jianping, Chen Songling, and Yi Longsheng,[145] the selection of leading industries is the key and core issue for the successful transformation of resource-based cities. By the qualitative and quantitative methods, an index system for the selection of leading industries for the transformation of resource-based cities was proposed, and the method for how to select the leading industries was discussed. Moreover, the corresponding suggestions and measures were put forward for the cultivation of leading industries for the transformation of resource-based cities.[146] Wang Yunjia[147] stated the current situation of the mineral development and environmental damage in China, analyzed the necessity for improving the mechanism of ecological compensation and accelerating the ecological restoration of mining areas, and on this basis, proposed to establish and improve the supporting policies and regulations conducive to the ecological compensation and restoration of mining areas, and to study the standard system of ecological compensation, etc.[148] Tian Zhiyu and Yang Hongwei[149] suggested that the development of urbanization should optimize the regional and urban layout, build a systematically optimized green and low-carbon system of energy supply, significantly improve the efficiency of energy utilization, innovate the system and mechanism of regional and urban management, and impel the transformation of urban development in the direction of green and low-carbon aspects as soon as possible.[150]

1.2.6.5 The current situation of studies on the coordinated development of cities

Coordinated development is an inevitable choice for cities in achieving cross-regional development. It refers to the coordination of two or more different resources or entities to collaborate with each other, to accomplish a certain goal and achieve a win–win effect of common development. The coordination covers many facets, such as technological coordination, institutional coordination, policy coordination, and management coordination, and it also includes the coordination of innovations, regional coordination and urban coordination, etc. The theory of coordinated development has become an important theoretical basis for many countries and regions in the world today, especially for metropolitan areas and city clusters in achieving sustainable economic and social development. The metropolitan areas achieve leapfrog development both economically and socially by linking cities with each other and cities with the surrounding areas.

The coordinated development of cities should be an important strategy for urban development under the new normal.

According to Shen Yufang, Liu Shuhua, and Zhang Jing et al.,[151] with the clustering of various economic resources in space and the continuous advancement of competition and cooperation in geography, coordinated development has become a popular topic in the studies of regional economics. Based on related theoretical and empirical studies on coordinated development, the development situations of industrial clusters, city clusters, and port clusters in the Yangtze River Delta region and their status of coordination were empirically analyzed. This study suggested that the Yangtze River Delta region had great room for promoting the coordination of the three major groups, and put forward some countermeasures for promoting the coordinated development of industrial clusters, city clusters, and port clusters in the Yangtze River Delta region in the light of the trend of economic integration in this region.[152]

Wang Weidong[153] utilized radar chart analysis to compare and analyze the innovation capabilities of 16 cities in the Yangtze River Delta regarding four aspects: economic basis, input capability, environment level, and output capability of innovation, thus providing a decision-making and quantitative basis for the mechanism of the coordinated innovation of city clusters in the Yangtze River Delta region. He held the view that the problems and resistance to the coordinated innovation of city clusters in the Yangtze River Delta region mainly included the imperfect dynamic mechanism of coordinated innovation, impeded the flow of innovation factors and the lack of a long-term mechanism for the sharing of science and technology resources, so it was necessary to start building a mechanism for the development of coordinated innovation of city clusters in the Yangtze River Delta region from several aspects, such as infrastructure, key areas, key carriers, guarantee mechanism, and countermeasures.[154]

Li Yingbo and Zhu Huiyong[155] explored the international experience in coordinated development of urban growth and industrial innovation from the perspective of the theory of New Urbanism, and then analyzed the effectiveness of the industrial innovation of cities in China in terms of urban industrial competitiveness, transformation and upgrading of industrial structure, the overall quality of life and the governance of urban environment. Further, they revealed the constraints, including "path dependence" in the urban industrial innovation of China, "fragmentation" of industrial policies, lack of coordination between industry and the cultural and social environment, and strong industrial homogeneity among cities. Finally, they put forward the countermeasures to be taken in order to accelerate urban industrial innovation in China in terms of the mechanism for effective intervention by the government, policy tools to optimize the industrial policies of cities, the establishment of the inter-city mechanism of industrial coordinated innovation and the construction of "beautiful cities".[156]

Zeng Lijun, Sui Yinghui, and Shen Yusan[157] argued that the resource-based cities had long provided the main means of production and made great contributions to China's economic and social development. However, the original model of extensive development caused severe difficulties to the development of resource-based cities. Resource-based cities must change the original model of development and choose a model of sustainable development supported by tech industries. The system of sustainable and coordinated development of tech industries and resource-based cities was made up of four subsystems: economic subsystem, social subsystem, environmental subsystem, and resource subsystem. By analyzing the cause–effect relationship among the factors of the four subsystems, they constructed the cause–effect model of the whole system, further built a flow chart model for the system, and integrated various methods to establish the inter-variable equations, thus initially establishing a model of system dynamics for the sustainable and coordinated development of tech industries and resource-based cities.[158]

Xing Tianhe[159] pointed out that the coordinated development of the Beijing-Tianjin-Hebei region had been elevated to a national strategy, and in order to accomplish the major tasks assigned by the State and build Beijing as a world-class city, the Beijing-Tianjin-Hebei region should highlight its comparative advantages and realize a reasonable regional division of labor; reconfigure the regional functions and construct a new spatial pattern; improve the traffic network and build a supporting traffic system; and innovate the institutional mechanisms and promote coordinated regional development.[160]

Chen Keshi, Wang Long, and Deng Tingting[161] aimed at the prominent urban problems of Beijing and the unbalanced development of the Beijing-Tianjin-Hebei region, and they analyzed the process, dynamics, and measures of Paris, a city with similar conditions of development with those of Beijing, to build itself as a world-class city by traveling along the cultural path, which provides a cultural path for reference to Beijing to build itself as a world-class city during the coordinated development of the Beijing-Tianjin-Hebei region, that is to say, with the cultural industry as the core power, by taking measures such as adjusting the industrial, demographic and spatial structures of Beijing and the Beijing-Tianjin-Hebei region, Beijing could construct a polycentric networked region of a world-class city with cultural characteristics.[162]

By a case study of the interaction and coordination between the University of London and the City of London, Shen Chen and Qie Haixia[163] studied the coordinated development of the City of London, and argued that the advancement of the industrial revolution contributed to the City's status as the political and economic center of the United Kingdom and the founding of the University of London. The development of the University of London could not have been achieved without the policy support of the City of London. In response to the needs of London's economic and social development, the University of London and local enterprises gradually moved towards mutual benefit and a win–win situation. The University of London achieved deep integration with the community while fulfilling its social responsibility.[164]

Lu Dadao[165] reviewed the economic ties, interests and contradictions of the components within the large city cluster of the Beijing-Tianjin-Hebei region, and elaborated on the characteristics of economic development and the advantages that have been gained by Beijing City, Tianjin City, and Hebei Province since the reform and opening-up. According to their respective characteristics, advantages, and the principle of serving the national strategic interests, he proposed the functional orientation of Beijing City, Tianjin City, and Hebei Province in the large city cluster.[166]

Wang Bin and Chen Yao[167] selected five indicators: per capita GDP, per capita balance of residents' savings deposit, per capita investment in fixed assets, per capita retail sales of consumer goods, and per capita imports and exports, and utilized the method of Wilson coefficients to estimate the regional differences between city clusters in the Beijing-Tianjin-Hebei region and the Yangtze River Delta region as well as the trends of changes from 1999 to 2013. The results indicated that compared with the balanced development of the Yangtze River Delta region, there were significant differences within the city cluster of Beijing, Tianjin and Hebei, with gaps in income level, potential for economic growth, and economic openness measured by the five indicators, and an unobvious trend of convergence of these gaps. The reasons for the obstacles to the coordinated development of the city cluster of Beijing, Tianjin, and Hebei were the problems such as lack of coordination in industrial support, conflicting distribution of interests within the city cluster, institutional barriers of the administrative system, and slow process in market integration, etc. By integrating with the theories and practices of the coordinated development of city clusters, they proposed the policies and suggestions to boost the coordinated development of the city cluster of Beijing, Tianjin, and Hebei.[168]

According to Zhou Jun and Ma Xiaoli[169], the growing urbanization of the Beijing-Tianjin-Hebei region was facing the problem of scarcity of resources and energy. The low-carbon planning and development was an important engine and choice of path for the coordinated and integrated development of the Beijing-Tianjin-Hebei region. They elaborated the path of responses such as the scientific planning of the structure of urban spaces, the optimization of the layout of green traffic, the adjustment of the structure of industrial zoning, the promotion of industrial transformation, the advancement of energy conservation and emission reduction, the creation of a low-carbon living environment and the enhancement of the capacity of green carbon sink, so as to promote the sustainable development of low-carbon cities in the Beijing-Tianjin-Hebei region.[170]

1.2.7 Deficiencies and review of the studies

Accelerating the treatment of "urban diseases" and green low-carbon development is an important element and a breakthrough in the advancement of the construction of an ecological civilization, in solving the "urban diseases", improving the quality of cities, building the brands of a green city and achieving the scientific development of cities at a higher level. At present, the studies on the treatment of "urban diseases" and of green low-carbon development are increasing, but the basis is still weak and there are still many shortcomings, which should be analyzed to further put forward effective policy recommendations.

Since urban diseases involve many factors and some existing studies have not taken into account the connections among various factors, there is a danger of "treating the head when the head aches and treating the foot when the foot hurts" and there are still a lot to do to achieve further improvement and a deepening of the theory.

"Urban diseases" are an effect of the rapid development of the national economy and of society. The advancement of industrialization and urbanization leads to a rapid influx of population into cities in search of more employment opportunities and developmental space, but the insufficient carrying capacity of cities themselves results in a series of problems in traffic, housing, and environment. These problems should be investigated and analyzed from comprehensive, all-embracing, and systematic perspectives. However, in reality, there are inevitably some wrong practices.[171] First, the adverse effects of "urban diseases" are overly exaggerated, and all the problems arising during the economic and social development of cities are attributed to "urban diseases". It has been suggested that the cities should not be developed, and the size and quantity of cities should be controlled to avoid the problems of "urban diseases". This idea goes against the law and the trend of urbanization, and seriously hinders the process of urbanization and sustainable development. Second, the negative effects of "urban diseases" are overlooked or underestimated. Because some cities have overly pursued economic interests and have neglected the improvement of people's livelihood, social construction, and environmental protection, especially the protection of the interests of vulnerable groups. For example, the process of urbanization is advanced by forced demolition, thus accumulating a large number of social contradictions and problems and becoming the causes of social instability. The overdevelopment of small towns and the overexpansion of cities lead to the complications of "urban diseases". This not only results in the waste of resources, but also affects sustainable development and endangers social stability. Therefore, in order to treat "urban diseases", attention should be paid to the in-depth investigation of the causes, the accurate understanding of pathology, causes, and symptoms of urban problems and their internal laws, and scientific measures and countermeasures.

International experience can be used as reference, but there still is a need to study the basic preconditions and analyze the specific situation and causes for "urban diseases".

It can be said that different countries have different symptoms and different root causes of "urban diseases", and it is difficult to adopt one solution or model of treatment. The inadequate studies on the international experience in treating "urban diseases" and blind copycatting cause a disconnection of theories and practices. There has been no systematic research on which kind of international experience can be used as reference for Beijing, and how to propose effective countermeasures in light of Beijing's actual situation.

To conduct an in-depth study of embodiments, characteristics, and internal causes of "urban diseases", the study should analyze what problems and obstacles to the low-carbon urban development exist, make a systematical analysis of the root causes of problems, select the scientific model of development and establish a system for the evaluation of the performance of the government in terms of the construction of an urban ecological civilization.

The report of the 18th CPC National Congress and the Third Plenary Session of the 18th Central Committee of the CPC clearly stated the need to vigorously promote the construction of an ecological civilization and advance green development, circular development and low-carbon development. The construction of an ecological civilization is a major plan for the well-being of the people and the future of the nation, and an important element for realizing the Chinese dream of the great rejuvenation of the Chinese nation. General Secretary Xi Jinping pointed out: "We want to have not only mountains of gold, but also mountains of green. If we must choose between the two, we would rather have the green than the gold. And in any case, green mountains are themselves gold mountains." This is a vivid interpretation of the clear attitude and strong determination of the Party and the State to vigorously promote the construction of an ecological civilization and achieve green development. The answers to these questions have not been studied in depth and systematically, namely for implementing the spirit of the central government, how to achieve green development, what problems still exist in green development in practice, what are the dynamics of green development and which model of green development will be chosen, and there is no integrated research from the facets of theoretical innovation and practice. Particularly, actually, it is difficult for local governments to choose between economic development and environmental protection, and the contradictions and paradoxes between them have not been adequately resolved. Against the background of the fact that the traditional GDP-only philosophy for the system of evaluation of the performance of the government has not changed and there is a lack of evaluation of performance regarding the construction of an ecological civilization, the Third Plenary Session of the 18th Central Committee of the CPC emphasized the need to strengthen the institutional construction of an ecological civilization, incorporate the consumption of resources, damage to the environment and ecological benefits into the evaluation system of economic and social development, and establish the system of targets, methods of evaluation, and a mechanism of rewards and punishments that reflect the requirements of an ecological civilization. However, there is a lack of in-depth studies on how to establish an effective system of evaluation of the performance of the government regarding the ecological civilization in urban green development, so it is necessary to introduce programmatic documents and guiding standards for the system of the evaluation of the performance of the government concerning the construction of an ecological civilization in cities.

To further study the inherent relationship between the construction of an ecological civilization and urban green development, the authors try to explore the significance of urban low-carbon development for the treatment of "urban diseases", and comprehensively explain the connotation and characteristics of urban green low-carbon development.

Currently, the issues without adequate studies and in need of further research are stated as follows. First, an in-depth study must be carried out on the differences between and connections among the concepts of ecological civilization, green development, low-carbon development, and circular development, so as to grasp the essential connotation of each concept, and further study how cities can achieve scientific development. At the theoretical level, the concepts of an ecological economy, a green economy, and a low-carbon economy are similar and contain each other, but simultaneously each has a different focal point. For example, the ecological economy emphasizes the simulated ecological relationship among various elements without artificial fragmentation that can lead to the alienation or distortion of development. The circular economy lays stress on the establishment of a model of resource and energy recycling, and the reduction of waste emissions, and advocates the recycle ability of waste and the reduction, reuse, and recycling of resources. The low-carbon economy attaches importance to the reduction of carbon dioxide emissions and the realization of a model of low-carbon and zero-carbon development. The green economy focuses on green development and clean production from the perspectives of production and consumption, the construction of green enterprises, green industries and green products, and the building of green cities. Second, the intrinsic connections between construction of an ecological civilization and the green development of cities should be studied in depth, and green development is the key to promoting an urban ecological civilization. Third, the connotation of green development at the level of cities must be studied deeply. Urban green development is not economic development in the traditional sense, but emphasizes a green type of economic growth, social harmony, environmental friendliness, construction of a green ecological culture, and green environmental protection at the level of political administration. By the five-in-one green revolution and development of economy, society, culture, environment, and politics, urban green transformation and construction of an ecological civilization can be advanced. Drawing on the experience of the development of cities throughout the world, the problems of "urban diseases" in Beijing can be solved by thinking from the perspective of integrated development, coordinated development, and low-carbon development of the Beijing-Tianjin-Hebei city circle. These problems have not been studied profoundly, namely how to facilitate the treatment of "urban diseases" in Beijing from the perspective of the low-carbon development of the Beijing-Tianjin-Hebei region on a large regional scale, and what policy measures should be taken. This book aims at exploring these issues.

The research tries to propose an operable and effective path for the construction of an ecological civilization and green development aiming at the functional positioning of cities.

Existing studies focus on the general issues of the development of cities, but lack explorations on the characteristics and resource endowments of cities, so it is difficult to put forward a targeted path of development for the construction of an ecological civilization and green development in cities. The functions of cities are the essential characteristics of their existence, the role and order of the urban system to the external environment, and the organic whole formed by the interconnection and interaction of various functions, rather than the simple addition of these functions. Based on the proposal of the innovation-driven strategy, transformation of the development mode, the construction of an ecological civilization, low-carbon development, and other strategies, the construction of an ecological civilization and the green development of cities should further study and strengthen the comprehensive and in-depth study of urban problems, so that urban development can better adapt to the regional economic, political, social, cultural, ecological environmental, and other functions, coordinate with the carrying capacity of the urban population, resources, and environment, and take the new path towards urban development driven by culture, innovation, and the rise of greenness. Therefore, aiming at the realities of urban overpopulation, the depletion of resources and energy, the deterioration of environmental pollution, and other issues, urban development should have a scientific functional positioning, especially in combination with the implementation of the innovation-driven strategy, to enhance cultural soft power and achieve the rise of greenness, and the effective path for urban green development should be further proposed to promote the construction of an urban ecological civilization.

1.3 Significance and purpose of the research

First of all, in terms of academic value, a systematic investigation has been conducted on the mechanism of formation, intrinsic causes, comparison of international experience, and study on the measures of treatment, so as to explore effective measures from the theoretical point of view, and construct a systematic theoretical framework for the treatment of "urban diseases". The formation, causes, and treatment of "urban diseases" have their internal laws, so it is important to dig out, summarize, and explore these laws at the theoretical level, and shape a relatively complete theoretical system, which can provide an important theoretical reference for further guiding the treatment of "urban diseases" and also have important academic value for theoretical research. This book attempts to analyze and compare in depth the common theoretical laws for the formation and treatment of "urban diseases" across different countries from the height of theoretical and academic values, make a summary, shape a relatively complete theoretical system, and promote the theoretical development for the treatment of "urban diseases".

Second, according to international comparison, this topic compares "urban diseases" that occurred in foreign countries, especially in international cities, and refines and summarizes their experience in treatment, so as to provide some references for the prevention and treatment of "urban diseases" in Beijing. There is plenty of literature on the international comparison for the treatment of "urban diseases", but very few of them have drawn a comprehensive comparison of multiple countries or cities from multiple perspectives. This book focuses on the systematic nature of international comparison, so as to not only figure out the common laws, but also highlight the differences of each city in the treatment of "urban diseases", thus giving a summary of the inherent characteristics of international experience and offering inspiration and experience for the treatment of "urban diseases" in Beijing.

Third, with regard to the practical application, effective countermeasures, and suggestions are proposed for the treatment of "urban diseases" on a large regional scale and from the perspective of the coordinated low-carbon development of the Beijing-Tianjin-Hebei region, in order to provide advisory services for the decision-making of the government of Beijing at all levels and relevant authorities in the Beijing-Tianjin-Hebei region, boost the construction of green Beijing, a harmonious and livable capital and an international city, and promote the integrated, balanced, coordinated, and low-carbon development of the Beijing-Tianjin-Hebei city circle. Beijing is currently suffering from serious problems of "urban diseases", including not only the problems of population and traffic, but also problems like frequent smog, ecological degradation, and water pollution. These problems must be taken seriously and resolved, otherwise the people of the capital city will feel unsatisfied, and we will not have a better image and power to say in the international community. These problems of "urban diseases", especially the smog, have also become an important excuse that the capitalist countries found to attack our country. Therefore, through international comparison, this book finds that "urban diseases" are common throughout the world, instead of the problems which cannot be surmounted. There are solutions, and we are full of hope. The key is to focus on the realistic problems, learn from the experience of other countries, and contribute wisdom to the solution of practical problems. This is the core theme and significance of the research for this book.

1.4 Ideas and contents of the research

The main ideas of research: based on the integration of theories and practices, we study the intrinsic connections of the theories of classical sociology, human ecology, garden city, and low-carbon city and provide the theoretical support for the treatment of "urban diseases"; analyze the evolutionary laws and phased characteristics of "urban diseases", compare the basic experience of treatment in some typical international cities such as New York, London, and Tokyo, make an analysis of the problems and causes of "urban diseases" in Beijing and put forward some policy suggestions for the treatment of the "urban diseases" in Beijing and the coordinated low-carbon development of the Beijing-Tianjin-Hebei region.

The first part is a theoretical review of the treatment of "urban diseases". It reviews the theories of classical sociology, human ecology, community school, garden city, and low-carbon city and provides some important theoretical support to guide the treatment of the "urban diseases" in Beijing and the low-carbon development of the Beijing-Tianjin-Hebei region.

In the second part, we study the evolutionary laws and phased characteristics of "urban diseases". First, the scope of "urban diseases" and their main manifestations are defined. Second, the phased characteristics for the evolution of "urban diseases" come into focus. In order to treat "urban diseases", we must accurately judge the stage of development of the city and its characteristics and give corresponding responses. Given the actual situation of China, importance is attached to the phased characteristics of the evolution of "urban diseases" in China and Beijing since the reform and opening-up. Third, the relationship between "urban diseases" and the functional positioning of central cities is examined. The core functions of a city include control functions, basic functions, and migration functions, etc. Emphasis is put on the imbalance among urban elements caused by different urban forms and different functional demands at different phases.

For the third part, the experience of New York in the treatment of "urban diseases" is explored from the perspective of cross-regional coordination. It investigates New York's urban evolution from urbanization to suburbanization and its main experience, and reflects the characteristics of cross-regional coordination and equal allocation.

The fourth part discusses the experience of London in the treatment of "urban diseases": an examination based on the Curse of Midas. The well-known British labor historians, Mr. and Mrs. Hammond, called the "urban diseases" in the 19th century in Britain the "Curse of Midas", which criticized Britain for only pursuing industrial production and causing a variety of social and living problems. Since the beginning of industrialization, the rapidly-expanding population of London led to shortage of housing, widespread slums, traffic congestion, and serious environmental pollution, thus triggering the "Smog of London". The measures taken by London to combat "urban diseases" include: to formulate the regulations on the clean air of the capital city and strengthen the institutional construction of smog control; to set up the points of pollution detection and strictly control exhaust emissions; to enhance the technological research of smog control and promote control by the innovation in technologies; to develop green public transportation, use clean and low-carbon energy and reduce carbon emissions, and to attach importance to the public's participation in the smog control of the capital city. Attention is paid to key countermeasures for the treatment of "urban diseases" in London and the experience in the systematic decentralization of urban functions.

36 Introduction

The fifth part focuses on the experience of Los Angeles in the treatment of "urban diseases": the experience based on the control of air pollution. Los Angeles, a typical industrial city in the United States of America, experienced the incidents of smog and photochemical pollution. After decades of treatment, the quality of air in Los Angeles has significantly improved. The treatment of air pollution of Los Angeles went through three phases: the period of governance by organizations and regulations, the period of governance by market and technologies, and the period of transformative and collaborative governance. The phased characteristics of air pollution control and the specific policy measures taken by Los Angeles can provide an important reference for the treatment of the "urban diseases" in Beijing.

In the sixth part, stress is laid on the experience of Tokyo in its treatment of "urban diseases": the inspiration based on the construction of city subcenters. The changes in the "urban diseases" in Tokyo were closely linked to industrial development and the resulting demographic changes. In the 1960s and 1970s, Tokyo suffered from the most serious "urban diseases". The concentration of population and labor force led to rising prices of land, environmental deterioration and increased living costs, etc. Tokyo took effective measures to deal with its "urban diseases" and treat them in their multiple aspects, including planning and guidance, decentralization of functions, construction of city subcenters, industrial adjustment, decentralization of population, and allocation of resources. This part focuses on how Tokyo's construction of public transportation, low-carbon traffic, and city subcenters can achieve the decentralization of functions, the diversion of population and low-carbon development through a comparative study.

For the seventh part, attention is given to Ruhr's experience in treating its "urban diseases": a perspective based on industrial upgrading. The experimental model of Ruhr for the cultural transformation and industrial upgrading is summarized with important implications for China.

In the eighth part, we analyze the manifestations and causes of Beijing's "urban diseases". It mainly carried out the empirical research and problem analysis of the interaction and correlation effects of these factors, such as population, resources and environment. An analysis is made of the manifestations and causes of Beijing's "urban diseases" to find out the key factors and their relationships of conduction for the treatment of "urban diseases".

The ninth part studies the countermeasures for the treatment of the "urban diseases" in Beijing and the low-carbon development of the Beijing-Tianjin-Hebei region. This part focuses on the comparative study of international experience and proposes policy recommendations. The treatment of the "urban diseases" in Beijing should consider both the general international experience and practice and the selection of the countermeasures for scientific development based on its own characteristics, adhere to the guiding concept of implementing the strategic positioning of the capital city, and regard the construction of a world-class harmonious and livable city as the basic goal, so as to accelerate the treatment of the "urban diseases" in Beijing and the coordinated low-carbon development of the Beijing-Tianjin-Hebei region. In this regard, the effective policies should be proposed, such as implementing the functional positioning of the capital city, strengthening top-level design and coordination, enhancing the balanced deployment of advantageous resources, guiding the orderly diversion of the population, accelerating the construction of rail transit, controlling the growth of motor vehicles in an orderly manner, deepening the reform of the system of the ecological civilization of the capital city, establishing the long-acting mechanism of environmental governance, building a mechanism of social participation, boosting the coordinated low-carbon development of the Beijing-Tianjin-Hebei region, accelerating the decentralization of non-capital functions, innovating the mode of urban management, advocating the intelligence of the city, and constructing a smart capital.

1.5 Key points, difficulties, and methods of the research

1.5.1 Key points and difficulties of the research

First, we systematically explore and summarize the international experience in the treatment of "urban diseases", analyze the manifestations, characteristics and causes of "urban diseases" that occurred in international cities, and examine and sum up the common laws for the treatment of "urban diseases". This is the basic research method of this book, and also an important point of innovation. From the perspective of cross-regional coordination, we investigate the experience of New York in the treatment of "urban diseases". Through the transition from urbanization to suburbanization, New York further realized cross-regional coordinated development. Beijing should pay attention to cross-regional coordination and equal allocation, and build a mechanism of cross-regional coordination. From the perspective of the control of smog, the experience of London in the treatment of "urban diseases" is summarized as follows: to formulate regulations on the clean air of the capital city and strengthen the institutional construction of smog control; to enhance the technological research on smog control and promote its control by innovation in technologies; and to develop green public transportation, use clean and low-carbon energy and reduce carbon emissions. From the perspective of the construction of city subcenters, the experience of Tokyo in the treatment of "urban diseases" is examined, such as: to strengthen planning, decentralize urban functions, and construct city subcenters. From the perspective of cultural transformation, the experience of Ruhr in dealing with "urban diseases" is explored, with a focus on cultural transformation, planning for regional improvements, and building a model of low-carbon development according to the resource endowments and industrial characteristics of the city.

Second, "urban diseases" are examined on a large regional scale. The problems of "urban diseases" mainly exist in a certain area where core functions, industries and population are over-concentrated, but over-concentration does not necessarily generate the scale effect.

Third, the "urban diseases" in Beijing should be treated comprehensively and systematically from the height of the low-carbon development of the Beijing-Tianjin-Hebei region. Overpopulation, over-concentration of industries, especially development of heavy chemical and high-energy industries, fuel-fired high-carbon traffic, and high-carbon buildings violate the principles and requirements of low-carbon development. Treatment of the "urban diseases" in Beijing requires a comprehensive, holistic and systematic consideration from multiple aspects, such as low-carbon concepts, low-carbon planning, low-carbon traffic, low-carbon industries, low-carbon buildings, and low-carbon life. These are important measures for the treatment of "urban diseases" and also important points of view and innovation proposed in this book.

Fourth, for the treatment of the "urban diseases" in Beijing, the coordinated development of the Beijing-Tianjin-Hebei region should be accelerated with the guidance of low-carbon development. Coordinated development, a path of development different from the traditional one, must be harmonious, balanced, low-carbon, ecological, and coordinated. It is the development with the treatment of the "urban diseases" in Beijing as the basic content, and should be able to effectively deal with the "urban diseases" from multiple aspects, such as long-term pollution of environment, high consumption of energy in Beijing, and even in the Beijing-Tianjin-Hebei region. However, how to achieve this coordination, boost the control of "urban diseases" by coordinated development, promote a path of development for the Beijing-Tianjin-Hebei region that is different from the traditional path of extensive development by high-carbon emissions, and choose a path of resource intensive and environmentally friendly low-carbon development are key points and difficulties for the research of this book.

1.5.2 Methods of the research

First of all, analysis of the literature. This book mainly analyzes the literature related to the theories of classical sociology, human ecology, community school, garden city, and low-carbon city, examines the progress of existing studies and their shortcomings, and further proposes the analytical framework of this book. At present, there is a vast amount of literature on the control of "urban diseases", but little of it systematically analyzes the manifestations and causes of "urban diseases" or puts forward suggestions according to the current situation of the "urban diseases" in Beijing. Hence, based on the review of much of the literature on "urban diseases" and their control, this book makes a summary and extraction and brings forward the core ideas of this book from the study of the literature.

Second, comparative analysis. This book compares the manifestations and characteristics of "urban diseases" of typical international cities and their experiences in controlling them, such as New York, London, and Tokyo, in order to summarize the common laws, and compare and refine the treatment measures and policy inspirations that can be learned from them. Through the comparison across countries, this book attaches importance to the comparison of the successful experiences of developed countries and cities, and only by learning from cities which perform better can we have the motivation and room for a breakthrough and development. Therefore, this book selects the major international cities, such as London, Tokyo, and New York, for comparison. Compared with Beijing, these cities share the same status and similarities, so they are comparable. By comparison, they can provide a reference for Beijing to deal with its "urban diseases".

Third, interdisciplinary research and system analysis. The treatment of "urban diseases" is studied by the comprehensive utilization of the professional knowledge of regional economics, urban management, institutional economics, ecological economy, and urbanology. System analysis means regarding the treatment of "urban diseases" as a complete system and analyzing the relationships among all elements. On the one hand, the formation of "urban diseases" is the result of an integrated manifestation of many disciplines, including the characteristics of urbanology, management, sociology, and economics, or the rules of geography, architecture, culture, and history. The systematic study of the treatment of "urban diseases" must put forward a scientific point of view from cross-disciplinary research. On the other hand, it is also necessary to examine the formation of "urban diseases" and the various elements to treat those "diseases" and their internal relations from the perspective of the systems theory, thus further making a profound, all-around and specific study of the problems of "urban diseases" and their solution, and proposing specific targeted, timely, and time-tested countermeasures. Therefore, this book must carry out the research from an interdisciplinary and systematic perspective.

Notes

1 2007.
2 Wu Guancen, Liu Youzhao, and Fu Guanghui, Evaluation System for the Ability of Resource-based City Transition under the Idea of Sustainable Development, *Resource Development & Market*, 2007(1).
3 Mao Xiaogang, Construction of a Beautiful China Requires the Joint Efforts of People from All Walks of Life, *Beijing Daily*, January 18, 2013.
4 Qiu Baoxing, The Transformation Trends of the Urban Development Model in China, *Urban Studies*, 2009(8).
5 Liu Chunbin and Zhang Chen, Theoretical Discussion on the Connotation of the Green Transformation of Resource-based Cities, *China Population Resources and Environment*, 2009(5).
6 2004.
7 2005.
8 2010.

9 2010.
10 Wang Ning, Defects in Spatial Structure and Treatment of the "Urban Diseases" of Extra-large Cities, *Regional Economic Review*, 2015(1).
11 Xie Jing, "The Root Cause of Urban Diseases Is the Population Issue" – Discussions about Social Governance on the Seminar of the Chinese People's Political Consultative Conference of Beijing, *CPPCC Daily*, January 22, 2014.
12 Qin Hongling, How to Alleviate the "Metropolitan Diseases" – Critical Reflections on the Urban Planning and Construction of Beijing, *Urban Geology*, 2013(1).
13 2010.
14 Liu Yongliang and Wang Mengxin, "Urban Diseases" Caught from the Imbalance between Urban and Rural Areas, *City*, 2010(5).
15 2011.
16 Lu Lixin, On the Imbalance between Urban and Rural Areas in the Process of the Urbanization of China, *Manager's Journal*, 2011(4).
17 People from Hebei Account for One Fourth of the Floating Population in Beijing.
18 Yan Yanming, Research on the Evolutionary Mechanism and Prevention of Urban Diseases in the Process of Industrial Transformation, *Modern Economic Research*, 2012(11).
19 2005.
20 2007.
21 2011.
22 Zhu Yinghui, Six Diseases of Cities: New Challenges in the Urban Development of China, *China Territory Today*, 2011(2).
23 2012.
24 Jiang Aihua and Zhang Chi, Exploration on Urban Diseases in the Process of Urbanization and Their Path of Treatment, *Academic Journal of Zhongzhou*, 2012(6).
25 2014.
26 Liu Jiping and Liu Chenxiao, An Analysis of the Embodiments, Causes and Countermeasures of Urban Diseases in China, *Journal of Jiaozuo Teachers College*, 2014(2).
27 2015.
28 Jiao Xiaoyun, Urban Problems in the Process of Urbanization: the Connotation, Types and Mechanism of Governance, *On Economic Problems*, 2015(7).
29 2015.
30 Li Xuemin and Wu Zhenguo, An Analysis to Urban Diseases of Big Cities in Inner Mongolia and the Study on Countermeasures, *Journal of Inner Mongolia University of Finance and Economics*, 2015(3).
31 2003.
32 Li Gangyuan, An Analysis of the Urban Diseases of the UK and Their Treatment – An Inquiry into the Pattern of British Urbanization, *Journal of Hangzhou Teachers College*, 2003(6).
33 2005.
34 2007.
35 2011.
36 2012.
37 2014.

38 Wang Kaiyong, Yan Bingqiu, Wang Fang, and Gao Xiaolu, Countermeasures of Urban Planning to Manage "Urban Diseases": The Experiences from Foreign Countries, *World Regional Studies*, 2014(1).
39 Goldstein et al., 1965.
40 Hauser, 1968.
41 Qin Jian, Research of Urban Disease in China: Origin, Present and Future, *Modern Urban Research*, 2012(5).
42 2007.
43 2010.
44 2010.
45 Wang Guixin, The Solution to "Urban Diseases in Big Cities", *People's Opinion*, 2010(32).
46 2004.
47 Chen Zhe and Liu Xuemin, Research Progress and Comment on "Urban Problems", *Journal of Capital University of Economics and Business*, 2012(1).
48 2011.
49 2005.
50 2012.
51 2012.
52 Jiang Aihua and Zhang Chi, Exploration on the Urban Diseases in the Process of Urbanization and Their Path of Treatment, *Academic Journal of Zhongzhou*, 2012(6).
53 2013.
54 Ni Pengfei, Some Cities of China Suffered from Serious "Urban Diseases", *China Economic Weekly*, 2013(8).
55 1998.
56 1990.
57 1988.
58 2014.
59 Zhao Hong, Beijing's Urban Diseases Treatment and Coordinated Development of Beijing-Tianjin-Hebei, *Economy and Management*, 2014(3).
60 2014.
61 Liu Jiping and Liu Chenxiao, An Analysis of the Embodiments, Causes and Countermeasures of Urban Diseases in China, *Journal of Jiaozuo Teachers College*, 2014(2).
62 2015.
63 Wang Ning, Defects in Spatial Structure and Treatment of "Urban Diseases" of Extra-large Cities, *Regional Economic Review*, 2015(1).
64 2015.
65 Li Yunzhao and Yue Wu, A Study on Urban Diseases in China from the Perspective of the Scientific Outlook on Development, *The Border Economy and Culture*, 2015(12).
66 2015.
67 Zhang Mingdou, Potential Crisis Faced by New Urbanization and Its Direction of Governance – With Rural Diseases, Town Diseases and Urban Diseases as the Chain for the Study, *Journal of Zhengzhou University (Philosophy and Social Sciences Edition)*, 2015(2).
68 2011.

69 2010.
70 2010.
71 2012.
72 2012.
73 Jiang Aihua and Zhang Chi, Exploration of Urban Diseases in the Process of Urbanization and Their Path of Treatment, *Academic Journal of Zhongzhou*, 2012(6).
74 2013.
75 2014.
76 Xiang Chunling, "Urban Diseases" in China's Process of Urbanization and Their Treatment, *Journal of Xinjiang Normal University (Edition of Philosophy and Social Sciences)*, 2014(2).
77 2014.
78 2014.
79 Liu Jiping and Liu Chenxiao, An Analysis of the Embodiments, Causes and Countermeasures of Urban Diseases in China, *Journal of Jiaozuo Teachers College*, 2014(2).
80 2014.
81 Zhao Hong, Beijing's Urban Diseases Treatment and Coordinated Development of Beijing-Tianjin-Hebei, *Economy and Management*, 2014(3).
82 2015.
83 Li Xuemin and Wu Zhenguo, An Analysis of the Urban Diseases of Big Cities in Inner Mongolia and Study of Countermeasures, *Journal of Inner Mongolia University of Finance and Economics*, 2015(3).
84 2015.
85 Wang Ning, Defects in Spatial Structure and the Treatment of the "Urban Diseases" of Extra-large Cities, *Regional Economic Review*, 2015(1).
86 2015.
87 Li Yunzhao and Yue Wu, A Study on Urban Diseases in China from the Perspective of the Scientific Outlook on Development, *The Border Economy and Culture*, 2015(12).
88 2015.
89 Zhang Mingdou, Potential Crisis Faced by New Urbanization and Its Direction of Governance – With Rural Diseases, Town Diseases and Urban Diseases as the Chain of Study, *Journal of Zhengzhou University (Philosophy and Social Sciences Edition)*, 2015(2).
90 2015.
91 Jiao Xiaoyun, The Plights, Emphasis and Countermeasures in Local Urbanization of the New Process of Urbanization: Another Idea for Controlling the "Urban Problems", *Urban Studies*, 2015(1).
92 2016.
93 Liang Li, Technological Path for Treating "Urban Diseases" in the Era of Big Data, *E-Government*, 2016(1).
94 2016.
95 Xiao Jincheng and Ma Yankun, Coordination of Beijing, Tianjin and Hebei and Treatment of the Urban Diseases in Big Cities, *China Finance*, 2016(2).
96 2005.
97 Yu Keping, Scientific Outlook on Development and Ecological Civilization, *Marxism & Reality*, 2005(4).

98 2010.
99 Lu Jun, Existing Problems in the Construction of Ecological Civilization of China and Thoughts on Countermeasures, *Journal of Socialist Theory Guide*, 2010(9).
100 2004.
101 Xiao Hong, Urban Ecological Construction and Urban Ecological Civilization, *Ecological Economy*, 2004(7).
102 Li Yanjun, Industrial Wavelength, Urban Life Cycle and the Transition of Cities, *Development Research*, 2009(11).
103 2008.
104 Zhuang Guiyang, Energy Saving and Emission Reductions: Their Significance to China's Transition to a Low-Carbon Economy, *Advances in Climate Change Research*, 2008(5).
105 2009.
106 Zhang Chen and Liu Chunbin, The Cost Analysis and Timing Choice of Green Transformation of Resource-Based Cities, *Ecological Economy*, 2009(6).
107 2015.
108 He Jiankun, The Strategic Choice of Chinese Energy Revolution and Low Carbon Development, *Wuhan University Journal (Philosophy & Social Sciences)*, 2015(1).
109 2000.
110 2003.
111 2003.
112 1998.
113 1998.
114 2008.
115 2008.
116 2007.
117 2011.
118 Weng Zhiyong, Construction of an Ecological Civilization: Study on Problems and Countermeasures, *Studies on Mao Zedong and Deng Xiaoping Theories*, 2011(11).
119 2014.
120 2004.
121 2010.
122 Lu Jun, Thoughts on Existing Problems in the Construction of an Ecological Civilization in China and Countermeasures, *Journal of Socialist Theory Guide*, 2010(9).
123 2012.
124 2014.
125 Tian Zhiyu and Yang Hongwei, Problems and Challenges of Green Low-Carbon City Development in China – Taking the Beijing-Tianjin-Hebei Region as an Example, *Energy of China*, 2014(11).
126 2004.
127 2008.
128 2008.
129 2013.
130 2013.
131 2014.
132 2012.

44 *Introduction*

133 Liu Chang, Thoughts on the Transformation of Resource-Exhausted Cities–A Case Study of the Urban Transformation of Zaozhuang, *Theoretical Research on Urban Construction*, 2012(4).
134 2013.
135 2011.
136 2013.
137 2009.
138 2010.
139 Cai Meng and Wang Yuming, A Study on the Transition of Tourism Cities Based on a Low-Carbon Perspective, *Human Geography*, 2010(5).
140 2012.
141 2013.
142 Lan Qingxin, Peng Yiran and Feng Ke, Research on the Evaluation Index System and Evaluation Methods of the Construction of an Urban Ecological Civilization – An Empirical Analysis Based on the Four Cities of Beijing, Shanghai, Guangzhou and Shenzhen, *Research on Financial and Economic Issues*, 2013(9).
143 2014.
144 2014.
145 2007.
146 Liu Jianping, Chen Songling, and Yi Longsheng, Choice and Cultivation of the Leading Industries of Resource-Based Cities' Transformation, *Journal of China University of Mining & Technology (Social Science)*, 2007(1).
147 2012.
148 Wang Yunjia, The Suggestions on Boosting the Transformation of Resource-Exhausted Cities, *China Development*, 2012(6).
149 2014.
150 Tian Zhiyu and Yang Hongwei, Problems and Challenges of Green Low-Carbon City Development in China – Taking the Beijing-Tianjin-Hebei Region as an Example, *Energy of China*, 2014(11).
151 2010.
152 Shen Yufang, Liu Shuhua and Zhang Jing et al., The Correspondence among Industrial Cluster, City Group and Port Group on the Yangtze Delta Area, *Economic Geography*, 2010(5).
153 2011.
154 Wang Weidong, A Study on the Mechanism of Coordinated Innovative Development of City Clusters in the Yangtze River Delta, *Enterprise Economy*, 2011(12).
155 2013.
156 Li Yingbo and Zhu Huiyong, Study on the Coordination between Urban Growth and Industrial Innovation under New Urbanism Perspective, *Urban Development Studies*, 2013(7).
157 2014.
158 Zeng Lijun, Sui Yinghui and Shen Yusan, Study on the Sustainable Coordinated Development of Science & Technology Industry and Resource-Based City Based on System Dynamics, *China Population Resources and Environment*, 2014(10).
159 2014.
160 Xing Tianhe, Thoughts on the Coordinated Development of Beijing-Tianjin-Hebei, *Economy and Management*, 2014(5).

161 2014.
162 Chen Keshi, Wang Long, and Deng Tingting, The Cultural Path of Building Beijing as a World-Class City from the Perspective of the Coordinated Development of Beijing-Tianjin-Hebei – Inspiration of the Paris Experience, *Commercial Times*, 2014(28).
163 2015.
164 Shen Chen and Qie Haixia, The Synergetic Development between the University and the City – A Study of Interactive Mode of the University of London and the City of London, *China Higher Education Research*, 2015(8).
165 2015.
166 Lu Dadao, Functional Orientation and Coordinated Development of the Urban Agglomeration of Beijing-Tianjin-Hebei, *Progress in Geography*, 2015(3).
167 2015.
168 Wang Bin and Chen Yao, Measurement of the Development Gap of Beijing, Tianjin and Hebei City Group and Study on Their Coordination Development, *Shanghai Economic Review*, 2015(8).
169 2015.
170 Zhou Jun and Ma Xiaoli, The Planning and Path of Low-Carbon Urban Development from the Perspective of the Coordinated Development of Beijing-Tianjin-Hebei, *People's Tribune*, 2015(32).
171 Zhou Jialai, Definition, Laws and Prevention of "Urban Diseases", *China Urban Economy*, 2004(2).

2 Theoretical review of the control of "urban diseases"

Western countries started and led the trend of industrial revolution with rapid industrialization and a high level of urbanization, but at the same time, they also encountered increasingly serious problems of "urban diseases", which attract the attention in the academic circle, especially among sociologists, urbanists, and planners. "Urban diseases" are various urban drawbacks and a series of social problems caused by the concentration of population in large cities, the blind "pie-spreading" expansion of urban planning and construction towards the outskirts, the encroachment onto arable land, the continuous expansion of the size of cities, the increasingly prominent contradiction between people and land, as well as the rapid consumption of resources and energy due to population expansion, environmental pressure, and the excessive concentration of industries. The problems of "urban diseases" know no national boundaries, and both developed and developing countries have experienced or are facing various "urban diseases". Of course, after many years of treatment and control, these problems in developed countries and regions have been alleviated or treated. However, due to the short history of developing countries and the unfinished process of industrialization and urbanization, "urban diseases" are accumulating and getting worse. There are not only common laws for the studies of "urban diseases", but also differences for different countries during the development. The academic community has developed relevant research results and theoretical systems regarding "urban diseases" and their treatment. This chapter aims to review the theories of classical sociology, human ecology, community school, garden city, and low-carbon city, and proposes some important theoretical underpinnings to guide the treatment of the "urban diseases" in Beijing and the low-carbon development of the Beijing-Tianjin-Hebei region.

2.1 Theory of classical sociology

The theory of classical sociology paid attention to early "urban diseases" and their treatment and provided a theoretical basis for the study and control of "urban diseases".[1] At that time, sociologists investigated and reflected on urban social phenomena beginning with urban problems. Tönnies, a famous

German sociologist, was very worried and pessimistic about urban problems and believed that big cities, as the "mechanical combinations" were places where people "went bad". Due to a large population in cities, people had loose and weak connections, urban society was fragmented, and selfish individualistic tendency led to a hostile state of urban life.

Durkheim, a French sociologist, on the other hand, thought optimistically and constructively about urban phenomena and their positive functions, and argued that although there were subjective differences among people in urban society, if such differences could be reasonably divided and people from different industries could be effectively organized, there would be a team effort and this would promote the development of the urban society. Of course, because of the differences in interests and diversified pursuits, urban society would lead to conflicts and fierce competition among people, resulting in a series of "urban diseases" such as personality alienation, estrangement of emotions, competition for interests, and social conflicts and confrontations.

Max Weber, a German sociologist, from the historical perspective, analyzed the inner connections and objective laws for the evolution of the urban society, and suggested that one of the important causes of urban decline was the over-dependence of human beings on capitalism, over-pursuit of material interests, and neglect of the social and ecological environment, which led to indifference and apathy of people, deterioration of urban ecology and environmental pollution, and restricted the improvement of people's connections and living environment.

2.2 Theory of human ecology

The theory of human ecology is an important theoretical basis for the treatment of "urban diseases". Human ecology is a science that studies the ecological relationship and interaction between mankind and nature, the ecological environment in which mankind lives, and the harmonious development of mankind and nature, as well as the spatial and temporal connections formed by mankind under the influence of their selective, distributive, and regulative effects on the environment. The theory of human ecology involves disciplines including biology, demography, anthropology, sociology, ecology, economics, geography, and other related disciplines, theories and methods, and the research topics include the influence of mankind on the environment, the influence of the environment on human evolution and development, and the relationship between mankind and other biological species, with a focus on ecology at different levels of organization where human beings are at the center, or the ecosystems that are closely related to, influenced by, or controlled by mankind.

Professor Wirth of the University of Chicago explored urban problems in depth, summarized the traditional theory of urban sociology, analyzed the cultural impact and influence of urban life on the material and spiritual life of people, and argued that urban areas were the relatively large residential spaces with high density, distinctive individuality, and strong social heterogeneity. The heterogeneous demographic features led to differentiation in the professions and professional structures of the population, and established the profit-oriented interpersonal relationship, thus turning urban life into a mutually exploitative relationship of interests. The high density of the population resulted in increased tolerance and deep impersonality, and the scale, density, and heterogeneity of the population became the distinctive features of the "urbanity" in urban life. Professor Burgess of the Chicago School proposed the concentric zone model based on the theory of human ecology and studied the treatment of "urban diseases". Human ecologists, according to the Darwinian theory of ecology, held the view that there was a symbiotic relationship between the urban population and the environment, the economic and social operation of the city was an ecological process, limited resources led to competition and cooperation among interest entities in the cities, and a certain "ecological balance" could be achieved through competition. In the opinion of classical ecologists, limited resources caused the deterioration of the urban environment, complicated social relations and various conflicts, which became a kind of psychopathy, and urban residents became worldly, slippery, and indifferent to their own interests. The urban living space in the high-density and high-stress state makes people more lonely, stressful, and depressed, and the relationship among people was distant and indifferent, lack of social care.[2] The emergence of urban problems, if examined from the ecological perspective, was a psychopathy that stemmed from the rural culture by changing the ecological environment and social relations of traditional rural ties, and it was difficult for the traditional rural people to adapt to the indifference, weak connections, and complicated interactions.

Given that there is a close ecological relationship between mankind and nature, urban development must attach great importance to and follow the laws of human ecology, rather than violating the laws of nature and ecological relationships; otherwise this will surely lead to the serious problems of "urban diseases". Professor Park from the Department of Sociology of the University of Chicago was an early researcher who studied the problems of "urban diseases" with the theory of human ecology. Professor Park studied the serious urban economic and social problems caused by the rapid urbanization of the United States of America, which led to the entry of immigrants from all over the world after the war and to rapid population growth. Because the urban areas were dominated by the secondary and tertiary industries such as commerce and industry, the commercial nature of cities and the excessive pursuit of market interests diluted the traditional local ties, racial consciousness, and ancestry, which had a strong impact on the psychology and values of the urban immigrant population, thus further leading to a series of urban social, psychological, and cultural problems.

2.3 Theory of urban community

The Theory of Community is a generic term for the theories, doctrines and perspectives developed through in-depth research on various aspects of the community. This school of thought mainly focused on the microscopic perspective of cities and believed that a city was a big community and the problems of "urban diseases" could be condensed into the problems of "community diseases". Because of the prominence of social organizations in the governance of community, the issue of "urban diseases" should also lay stress on the role of social organizations and emphasize their indispensable role in the urban society.[3] In the 1940s, August Hollingshead divided community studies into three phases: 1800–2915, mainly focusing on the living standards of urban residents, with special attention to the living conditions of the urban poor, and studies on the formation of urban poverty and its related social problems, which he called the phase of "conventional theory of goodness"; 1915–2929, mainly focusing on the living conditions of the urban population at different levels, and examining urban life as a whole, which he called the phase of urban life study; from 1929 onwards, community study began theory-based scientific analysis, which he called the phase of theoretical scientific analysis. The main theories and methods for the studies of urban community fall into two categories: neighborhoods and social networks of urban community, as well as powers of urban community.[4]

2.3.1 Neighborhoods and social networks of urban community

The research on the neighborhoods and social networks of urban community puts emphasis on the neighborhood relations in the living space of community residents, such as the enhancement of neighborhood rapport, neighborhood communication, the sense of cultural belonging of community, and the sense of community rules, including theoretical research on community lost, community saved, and community liberated, and many schools of thought have been formed.

2.3.1.1 Community Lost

Simmel, an important representative of this school, published an article with the title of "The Metropolis and Mental Life" in 1903, which clearly pointed out that the city, as a community environment with strong external stimuli and population concentration, was overcrowded in the living space of community. Especially in comparison with the rural areas, the crowded urban space brought strong mental pressure and a sense of urgency to community residents, triggered the overly stressful living conditions and psychological impacts, and led to the loss of the traditional rural culture, to a lack of psychological belonging, and to an increase in mental pressure. Too little communication and exchange of residents of the urban community and large cultural differences caused difficulties in communication. The urban environment changed the traditional paradigm of rural cultural life, and such changes had an even greater impact on the psychological level, especially the personalities such as snobbery, efficiency, treachery, and indifference of urban residents, which could result in their psychological discomfort or disorders. In 1938, Wirth found in his research that cities exhibited three particularities. First, a large population. The inflow of external population brought about dispersion, chaos and disorder. Second, a high density of population led to the psychology of vexation and caused anti-social behavior. In particular, the big gap between the rich and the poor urban residents would induce psychological imbalance, which was then converted into the undesirable psychological tendencies such as jealousy, hatred of the rich, and snobbery. Third, the heterogeneity it manifested itself in the differences from various aspects such as living habits, psychological state, education and race, and brought increased interpersonal conflicts. The big cultural differences easily led to misunderstanding or prejudice, lack of mutual trust, as well as the phenomenon of urban community lost.

2.3.1.2 Community saved

The researchers mentioned above adopted a pessimistic approach to the changes in urban community and developed the systematic theory of community lost, but not all community changes were bad, and there were also positive findings. Some researchers criticized the theory of community lost and proposed the theory of community saved. For example, the American sociologist Lewis published an article with the title of "Urbanization without Breakdown" in 1952, and pointed out that after the Mexican villagers moved to Mexico City, although entering the city, they did not completely give up their traditional rural habits and lifestyles, the traditional rural cultural relations among people did not completely disintegrate, human relations did not fade and become lost, communication among residents in the city was still maintained, and mutual benefit was an important psychological feature and state of mind of urban residents. Despite living in cities, urban residents still desired to communicate, care for and help each other. In particular, some community residents would consciously choose their own small circles for cultural exchanges, find a sense of cultural belonging, and maintain the traditional close cooperative relationships within the circles, such as Chinatown and Little Italy in the United States of America, and Korean Town in Beijing, etc., which became the typical examples of urban communities saved.

2.3.1.3 Community liberated

The theory of community liberated was proposed according to the phenomena of cultural conflicts and contradictions in many aspects such as loss of urban communities and lack of a psychological belonging. Only by reducing and avoiding weak ties and feelings of loneliness and alienation among community residents, interpersonal relationships, and a civilized atmosphere of community could urban communities be reconstructed, could they be liberated, and could healthy and harmonious community spaces be built. These thoughts became the focus and desired goals of many community theorists. In the 1970s, Claude S. Fischer, B. Wellman, and B. Leighton proposed the theory of "community liberated". In 1975, Fischer published "The Subcultural Theory of Urbanism", which held the view that population expansion led to social disorder and cultural loss, both of which were the root causes of "urban diseases". Urban residents as social beings could not live without interpersonal communication, care, and assistance, and they needed to establish interdependent relationships of trust. If such relationships could not be established, the residents in urban communities would be bound to being lonely, lost, and miserable. Therefore, there was a need to liberate communities, and thus human beings themselves. By reshaping the traditional close interpersonal relationships, fostering the deep socio-cultural relationships, reducing loneliness, alienation, and indifference, mutual assistance and care, communication and coordination, a good rapport could be established in communities, the interpersonal relationships could be improved, the social networks in urban communities could be built, and the disadvantages such as psychological isolation of urban residents could be eliminated.

2.3.2 Power of community

Power, as an inevitable product of social activities, is not only an important guarantee for the existence of various relationships in human society, but also an important concept in political science, international relations, and sociology. Power has the ability to integrate and allocate resources, and therefore we see "power" as a goal to be pursued by individuals or nations; "power" as a measurement of influences, that is to say, the content and quantity of resources; "power" as the results of political struggle; and "power" as an expression of the relationship between domination and dominated. Various pieces of literature and researches have interpreted power from different perspectives, such as sociology, cultural criticism, and discourse studies, which may focus on the "domination" aspect. According to Max Weber, power means any opportunity to impose one's will in certain social relations, even if faced with opposition, regardless of the basis on which such opportunity is built. Power is considered to be the basic condition for the domination of social relations and the exertion of the will. According to Parsons, power ensures the collective ability to be binding and the universal ability of the unit elements in the collective organizational system to fulfill their obligations. In urban communities, the residents come from different areas and have different cultural backgrounds, which lead to the existence of diversity and require necessary power for integration of resources. The effective implementation and orderly operation of power is an important mechanism to guarantee the harmonious development and healthy stability of urban communities.

There are mainly two types of studies on the power of community: the theory of the social elite and the theory of political pluralism. The theory of the social elite argues that the society should be managed by elites. Because social groups are of different quality, it is difficult for them to manage themselves, they need to rely on a few social celebrities for management, and elites need to play a leading role in significant political decisions. Social elites are an important force to ensure stable development of the society, and are the holders and executors of social power. Floyd Hunter, a representative of the elite theory, considers that those with power would like to befriend practitioners of business and industry, government officials, civic organizations, etc., and that most elites know each other, visit each other frequently, consult each other on community affairs, and form a close power group. Elites rule the society and play a decisive role in making decisions on all aspects of community affairs and on the handling of important events. However, the theorists of political pluralism argue that the diverse nature of the community's population, the complexity of the relations of social groups, and the plurality of values make it difficult to govern through a unified model.

R. A. Dahl, a representative of this theory, harbors the idea that the "decision-making approach" should be used to examine who is involved in making actual decisions on major urban policies. The political power of a community is not determined by a single individual or group, but is the result of the collective decisions of multiple groups and residents of the community. The political power of a community is not determined by a single individual or group, but is the result of the collective decisions of multiple groups, the residents of the community. Studies on the theories of community power provide important analytical tools for solving important problems for the development of the urban community and for examining the healthy operation of urban communities. In order to solve the problems of the urban community, an in-depth analysis in terms of the attribution and distribution of power must be made in order to find fundamental solutions.

2.4 Theory of garden city

For the purpose of avoiding the problems of "urban diseases" caused by excessive industrialization and urbanization, some researchers have proposed the idea of a garden city from the perspective of urban planning and construction. At the end of the 19th century, Howard, a famous British social activist, thought that the treatment of "urban diseases" required building a beautiful blueprint of a "garden city" which had the advantages of both urban and rural areas. By combining theory and practice, Howard actively put the idea of the garden city into practice and led the construction of two garden cities, namely Letchworth and Welwyn. It can be said that the theory of garden city aims at integrating urban and rural areas for treating "urban diseases", pursuing healthy and beautiful cities designed for living with the integration of industry and city, keeping strict control over the size of the city, and devoting oneself to the pattern of social life sufficient for meeting needs in all aspects. In 1919, the Garden Cities and Town Planning Association in the UK proposed that garden cities should be surrounded by permanent agricultural belts, the land of the city should be owned by the public and entrusted to a professional committee, and the size of a garden city should not exceed this regulation.

Garden cities should distinguish themselves from the traditional model of de-ruralization by emphasizing the close relationship between urban and rural areas. A garden city should be surrounded by vast rural areas that can provide urban residents with an abundance of fresh produce, so that agricultural products have the nearest market, but the market is not limited to the local area. Residents of a garden city can work and live in one place, and avoid the separation of jobs and housing. All the land is collectively owned by all residents, rent must be paid for the use of the land, and all the income of the city comes from the rents; and the added value from building and gathering on the land still belongs to the collective. According to Howard's vision, a garden city should reduce and avoid the combustion of coal and pollution by smoke, and the use of electricity as the main power source, and all urban waste can be reduced, recycled, and reused as resources to provide necessary materials or secondary raw materials for agricultural and rural areas. The size of cities should be strictly under control so as to avoid the "pie-spreading" development and the monotonous city made up of steel and concrete. Urban residents can be close to nature in rural areas and feel the ecological atmosphere from the natural environment. The garden city sketches a beautiful picture of the integration of urban production and life with nature.

According to Howard, the incidence of "urban diseases" and the deterioration of the urban environment are caused by continuous expansion and "magnetism" of cities. The expansion of urban boundaries, the infinite extension of cities due to land speculation, and the deterioration of the urban environment due to industrialization have led to "urban diseases" and related disasters. Based on the garden city model, Howard argued that urban boundaries should be strictly limited to prevent the unlimited expansion and the "pie-spreading" effect of cities, and that the urban land should belong to the unified body of the city. Overpopulation is the main symptom of urban diseases, and the "magnetism" of cities to attract the inflow of people is an important source of urban diseases. By taking effective measures to strictly control, consciously transplant, and moderately reduce that "magnetism", cities will no longer have the incentive to attract the excessive inflow of people, nor will they blindly over expand. In order to reduce the "magnetism" of cities, Howard envisioned a group combination model of garden cities, which consists of six single garden cities around a central city, and this shapes a cluster of garden cities between urban and rural areas. This city cluster can be a "slum-free, smoke-free city cluster", which is characterized by a planetary system in terms of spatial distribution, with beautiful rural areas between cities. A convenient system of public transportation and a well-developed information network connect cities, so the urban and rural areas can be built as a mutually permeable and complementary regional comprehensive system.

In order to reduce the "magnetism" of cities and solve the "urban diseases", Howard proposed a systemic solution to evacuate the urban population, build new cities and reform the land system. First, the urban population is evacuated to the vast rural areas, and this can solve various social problems in cities and avoid over-concentration and expansion of urban population once and for all. Second, the advantages of rural and urban areas are combined to build garden cities with a rural atmosphere and achieve their harmonious development. In other words, the urban area has the advantage of a relaxed and comfortable space in rural areas, while rural areas can also enjoy urban functions and basic public services, so that the rural and urban areas can be well integrated together. For the sake of changing the "pie-spreading" of traditional cities, emphasis should be placed on the development of clusters of towns and cities, each of which can remain relatively independent, and the residents of the towns and cities can realize most of the functions of the city locally, and become relatively independent urban communities. Third, the land system should be reformed to ensure that developers can get low added value and be attracted to developing the comprehensive functions of land. The theory of garden city provides an important theoretical underpinning for solving the problems of "urban diseases" in Beijing as a metropolis. Due to the "pie spreading" aspect of Beijing, the urban land for construction has seriously squeezed and encroached on the ecological land, leading to a series of "urban diseases" such as frequent haze, sinking water table, and environmental deterioration. In order to solve "urban diseases", we should learn from the theory of garden city and carry out urban planning and construction according to the garden city model.

2.5 Theory of livable city

The theory of livable city is different from that of the garden city because it lays more stress on people-oriented urban planning and emphasizes that urban construction and development should serve the people. Since the 1990s, Western scholars attach importance to the human-centered concept of urban planning, construction, and development, and advocate the people-oriented idea of design, to reflect the diversity, naturalness, humanity, and sense of community in the production and living atmosphere of cities, where people are no longer machines or individuals in cities. At the second Conference on Human Settlements held in 1996, the United Nations clearly proposed the establishment of habitable human settlements and that cities should pay attention to livability issues. The theory of livable city points out that urban residents should realize the organic unity of multiple elements such as residence, life, leisure, and culture within the established spatial and temporal scope, and achieve the harmonious coexistence of people and cities, and people and nature. A livable city should not only have a livable urban ecological environment, but also a livable humanistic and social environment. The natural environment is an important foundation for the construction of a livable city, while the humanistic environment is the deeper connotation of the construction of a livable city. A livable city should integrate the diversity of urban functions, sense of community, human scale, and other value standards with the real living environment to build a livable, ecological, harmonious, and balanced urban space.

The connotation of the livable city can be interpreted in the broad and narrow senses. In the narrow sense, a livable city is a city that is habitable at the natural, ecological and climatic levels, which mainly refer to a city with pleasant climatic conditions, a harmonious ecological landscape and that is suitable for people to live in. The core content for the construction of a livable city is to attach importance to making urban spaces green and beautiful, to improving the green coverage of the city, and to building a harmonious urban ecological environment between humans and nature. In the broad sense, it has a broader connotation than that in the narrow sense. A livable city is manifested as the livability at many facets, including economic, social, cultural, and natural environment, which mainly refer to a city with stable economic growth, social harmony and tranquility, cultural prosperity, and a beautiful and pleasant environment as a complex of coordinated development from all aspects, and the satisfaction and happiness of urban residents in their work, life, and residence. As pointed out by Zeng Hong,[5] a livable city is a city that achieves coordinated economic, social, cultural, and environmental development, has a good living environment, can meet the material and spiritual life needs of residents and is suitable for work, life, and residence of people. In other words, a livable city should be a city with healthy and stable economic development, continuous prosperity, social harmony and stability, whose residents live and work in peace and contentment, where there is a high degree of public safety, rich spiritual culture, a comfortable, convenient, and comfortable life, a good ecological environment, and harmony between humans and nature.[6]

With the development of the theory and practice of a livable city, its connotation is being continuously deepened and expanded and is now mainly embodied in the following aspects. First, a livable city should not only belong to the indigenous residents of the city, but also be inclusive of all groups of people who have worked and lived in the city, especially the elderly, children, women, the disabled, and other disadvantaged groups, and provide a livable living environment for all people living there; second, a livable city is sustainable, not only suitable for the present generation to live and work in, but it should also not be at the expense of the resources and environment for the next generation, and it should be suitable for future generations to live and develop sustainably in; third, a livable city should have a good "hard environment" and "soft environment" for livability, that is, a "hard environment" that meets the material needs and a "soft environment" that meets the spiritual and cultural needs of its residents.

A related study reported several basic conditions that a livable city must have. The first one is economic factors, which mean the ability to solve employment issues, many opportunities for entrepreneurship and innovation, the ability to unleash wisdom and talent, and respect for the overall development of urban talents. The second one is ecological conditions, which mean that the city must have a good environment that maintains natural ecological features, and that ensures blue sky, green land, and clean water. The third one is perfect supporting facilities, such as good conditions for traffic and travel and complete infrastructure for culture and education, healthcare, sports, and fitness to solve problems in all aspects of life. The fourth one is a good atmosphere of human relations and an environment of humanistic care, with a certain level of cultural taste and humanistic conditions for a city.[7]

A livable city should have various connotations and characteristics from the economic, political, cultural, social, and ecological perspectives, as shown in Table 2.1.[8] A livable city is not only economically prosperous or affluent, but also has a high level of social harmony, political security, ecological friendliness, and cultural enjoyment, and reflects the characteristics of livability.

First of all, a livable city is characterized by sustainable economic prosperity and high-quality growth. A city is a regional space with a high concentration of technology, knowledge, capital, and talent, and the level of economic development determines the status and competitiveness of the city. The industrial concentration in cities provides urban residents with alternative jobs and employment opportunities. The powerful economic foundation, well-developed industrial structure, and strong market demand can provide the economic support and material guarantee for the construction of livable cities, and lay an economic basis for urban social culture and ecological construction.

Second, a livable city is characterized by political harmony and stability and social security. Political stability and social security are the most basic conditions for a livable city. Political unrest and social insecurity will not attract the inflow of population. A livable city can give people a sense of security in production and life. Political stability, social harmony, social security, and good public order are the only things that allow citizens to live and work in peace and happiness.

A livable city should be a city that ensures public safety, has the abilities to effectively withstand natural disasters such as earthquakes, floods, rainstorms, and plagues, to defend and deal with man-made disasters, and respond to major emergencies and public crises, and protects the safety of life and property of urban residents. The city can achieve harmony among all classes, harmonious relationships, community affinity, and urban–rural coordination, so that people, including the migrant population, have a secure sense of belonging, enjoy modern urban functions, and view the city as a spiritual home for living and production.

Table 2.1 Connotations of a livable city

Dimension	Connotation	Main characteristics
Economic	City with sustainable economic prosperity	A city is a high-density gathering place of economic factors and a carrier of various non-agricultural industrial activities. A city should have a powerful economic foundation, a well-developed industrial structure, and a strong market potential to provide sufficient employment opportunities and high income for urban residents, and to provide an economic foundation and material guarantee for a livable city.
Political	City with political harmony and stability and social security	In a city with political stability, good public security, national unity, harmony among all classes, community affinity, and coordinated development of urban and rural areas, the residents can live and work in peace and enjoy a rich and colorful modern urban life, and regard the city as their material and spiritual home. The sense of security is a basic indicator of a livable city. A city should have the ability to resist natural disasters such as earthquakes, floods, rainstorms, and plagues, and to defend and deal with man-made disasters such as riots, terrorist attacks, and public emergencies to protect the safety of the life and property of its urban residents.
Social	City with comfortable living, convenient traffic, and good social services	Comfortable living, with housing that is well-equipped with facilities and meets health requirements; convenient traffic and a well-developed network of public transportation; good quality and adequate supply of social public products and public services such as education, medical care, health, etc.
Cultural	City with a rich culture	Being rich in historical and cultural heritages; well-equipped cultural facilities; frequent cultural activities; and a strong cultural atmosphere in the city. Only a city with cultural richness can be called a center of thought, education, science, and technology, and culture, giving full play to the function of the urban environment that nurtures people, and improving the overall quality of the city.
Ecological	City with a beautiful and pleasant landscape	A city is a complex of humanistic and natural landscapes, and it exhibits the characteristics of ecological safety, a beautiful environment, fresh air, blue sky, and clean water, and a quiet community. The humanistic and natural landscapes of a city should be coordinated with each other, and the humanistic landscape such as roads, buildings, squares, and parks should be built on a humanistic scale, and reflect ecological harmony and humanistic care.

Third, a livable city is characterized by comfortable living, convenient traffic and good social services. A livable city should have comfortable living spaces, complete living facilities, and convenient shopping to meet the living needs in all aspects, as well as convenient traffic, access to public transportation, and a well-developed network of public transportation. In large and medium-sized cities, there should also be well-developed facilities of subway and rapid transit of buses, and good social services, with access to comprehensive public services such as education and healthcare.

Fourth, a livable city is characterized by a long history, cultural heritages, and cultural prosperity. Cities cannot be built within a short period of time, but generally through a long historical period. It has accumulated rich historical and cultural heritages. International large cities such as London, New York, Tokyo, Paris, and Beijing have deep historical roots and a long history and culture. In the meantime, cities have perfect public cultural facilities like many museums and libraries, so the cultural exchanges, cultural and entertainment activities are frequent, and they have a strong cultural atmosphere with many singers, movie stars, artists, and cultural activists. With a rich cultural heritage and cultural prosperity, a city can become a regional center of thought, culture, education, science, and technology, can fully demonstrate its vigorous innovation and cultural vitality and reflect its livability and cultural attractiveness.

Fifth, a livable city is characterized by ecological friendliness and a beautiful landscape. A city is a complex of humanistic and natural landscapes, and ecological livability, beautiful scenery, and fresh air are the necessary conditions for a livable city. A livable city, which is embodied as ecological health, has the characteristics of clear water, green mountains, blue sky, quietness, and neatness, with many green spaces per capita and ecological balance. Humanistic landscapes such as roads, buildings, squares, and parks have a humanistic scale and reflect humanistic care.

The theory of the livable city provides an important basis for the research of this book. The construction of livable cities should be an important goal for the treatment of "urban diseases" and the realization of low-carbon urban development. The existence of "urban diseases" indicates that cities are not livable enough, and it is necessary to strengthen the treatment of "urban diseases" from the perspective of livability, and attach importance to the livability of cities for solving the problems such as rapid population growth, traffic congestion, high housing prices, social conflicts, and the deterioration of the urban environment, rather than only considering the achievement of the goals for economic growth. According to the theory of livable city, the prevention and treatment of "urban diseases" should consider how to achieve the livability of cities based on five dimensions: economic, political, social, cultural, and ecological. The treatment of "urban diseases" should not only require cities not to be "sick", but more importantly, to be suitable for living and with humanistic care for livability, which is also an inevitable requirement for modern urban development.

2.6 Theory of low-carbon city

Global warming has drawn special attention to the low-carbon economy, low-carbon development, and low-carbon cities. Industrial civilization enables rapid economic growth, but leads to the serious problem of high carbon emissions, which results in the greenhouse effect and climate warming, and seriously affects the safety of people's living and production space, including cities. Low-carbon originates from the process of industrialization and urbanization dominated by high carbon emissions, which triggers a deep reflection on global warming and the urban greenhouse effect. The global climate changes relate to the safety and security of people's production and life all over the world, and involve a series of issues such as ecological security, energy security, and water security. Seeking low-carbon solutions and building low-carbon cities have become important theoretical topics in the academic world. Human society has experienced several hundred years of rapid industrialization, and has relied mainly on the consumption of coal, oil, and other traditional fossil energy resources to support global economic and social prosperity and development. Simultaneously, the world is facing heavy costs and tremendous pressure from climate change, resource depletion, and environmental deterioration, etc. Both the extensive economic growth model with high carbon emissions and the urban ecological space are unsustainable, and the problems of "urban diseases" are difficult to be solved. Against this background, countries have put forward new concepts of low-carbon economy and low-carbon city.[9] Low-carbon economy is a form of economic development under the guidance of the concept of sustainable development, through technological innovation, institutional innovation, industrial transformation, development of new energy resources, and other means to minimize the consumption of high-carbon energy such as coal and oil, reducing greenhouse gas emissions, and achieving a win–win situation of economic and social development and protection of the ecological environment. The so-called low-carbon city refers to changing the traditional urban growth model of high energy consumption, high pollution, and high emissions, attaching importance to the development of a low-carbon economy, researching, innovating, and applying low-carbon technologies, developing low-carbon industries, changing the high-carbon lifestyle, and building a low-carbon society.

Cities are the important units and subjects of research for the reduction of regional carbon emissions, and the key to achieving global carbon reduction and low-carbon urbanization.[10] The international scientific community has proved that more than 90% of the current climate warming is likely to be caused by human activities, and cities – as the main sites of human activities – consume a large amount of fossil energy in their operations, emit about 75% of the total amount of global greenhouse gases, and create 80% of the global pollution. In response to the global climate changes, the development of a low-carbon economy and the construction of low-carbon cities have become the key concerns of countries and urban areas around the world, and the construction of low-carbon cities is an important way of solving the problems of urban ecological degradation, environmental pollution, and other "urban diseases". Western countries have carried out a series of explorations on the development of low-carbon cities, with remarkable achievements in controlling carbon emissions, and promoting low-carbon development.

The UK is an advocate and pioneer of the low-carbon economy and low-carbon city. The UK, where the Industrial Revolution first took place, as an island country, was faced with the difficulties such as scarcity of resources, so it was adequately aware of the bottleneck constraints of resources and energy and the threat of climate change, first proposed the concept of a low-carbon economy and attached great importance to the critical strategic significance of the low-carbon development. In 2003, in the UK's energy white paper "Our Energy Future – Creating a Low-Carbon Economy", the concept of "low-carbon economy" was first proposed and incorporated into the governmental files. In 2006, the Stern Review prepared by Nicholas Stern, the former Chief Economist of the World Bank, pointed out that globally an annual investment of 1% of the GDP could avoid a future annual loss of 5–20% of the GDP and urged the world to transform to a low-carbon economy. In April 2009, the UK became the first country in the world to announce its carbon budget to the world, which is clearly stipulated by law. In 2009, the UK Department of Energy and Climate Change delivered a report to the public with the title of "The Road to Copenhagen", which called on people around the world to act together and actively develop a low-carbon economy. In July 2009, the UK proposed the UK Low-Carbon Transition Plan, which clearly set the target of reducing the UK's carbon emissions by 34% in 2020 based on the level of 1990, and subsequently implemented a series of operational strategic plans such as the "UK Renewable Energy Strategy", the "UK Low-Carbon Industrial Strategy" and the "Low-Carbon Transport Strategy", and it took practical countermeasures to promote the development of a low-carbon economy.

The UK took the lead in the planning and practice of low-carbon cities. Local governments founded the Carbon Trusts and established low-carbon city projects together with the Energy Foundation. Bristol, Leeds, and Manchester became the first three demonstration areas for low-carbon cities, provided the experts and related technical guidance and made plans for low-carbon cities. On March 6, 2009, the Department for Business, Enterprise and Regulatory Reform launched the Strategic Vision for Low-Carbon Industries, proposed to actively develop a low-carbon new energy, vigorously develop the generation of wind power, develop nuclear energy, geothermal energy and other clean energy sources, and strengthen the technological innovation and promotion of low-carbon energy technologies. In November 2009, the UK Department of Energy and Climate Change published a draft energy plan, which clearly put forward the idea that nuclear energy, renewable energy, and clean coal are three important components of the UK's energy future. On December 1, 2009, the UK Department of Energy and Climate Change released a report with the title of "Smart Grid: Opportunities" and announced that they would vigorously promote the construction of smart grids, advance the national energy saving and emission reduction by the construction of smart grids, reduce the total amount of carbon emissions, and boost the development of low-carbon cities and of a low-carbon economy. The public are encouraged to change their traditional lifestyles and choose a low-carbon and green pattern of consumption. The British public service announcements pointed out that "unplugging a charger when not in use can save £30 a year, and replacing an energy-saving lamp can save £60 a year", which aimed to guide and encourage people to change to a low-carbon lifestyle.[11]

The implementation of the strategy for the development of a low-carbon economy and low-carbon cities in the UK achieved the obvious effects of emission reduction. In terms of the low-carbon green buildings, the UK installed cavity wall insulation in 11 million houses, which reduced the UK's heating costs by £1.3 billion in 2011. The carbon emissions in the industry decreased by 18% compared with 1990. In terms of low-carbon green traffic, due to the improvement of the energy efficiency of vehicles and the increased proportion of biofuels, the carbon emissions continuously decreased, and basically reached the level of 1990. In terms of industry, with the continuous improvement in energy efficiency in production, the industrial basis of the UK changed towards high-value, knowledge-intensive industries. The industrial production in the UK has grown at an average annual rate of 1% since 1990, while the carbon emissions have decreased by 46%.[12] It could be found that the UK has made positive progress in implementing the strategy for the development of a low-carbon economy and low-carbon cities, and has achieved a high degree of integration between theory and practice.

As an island country with relatively scarce resources and energy, Japan was well aware of the limited nature, the necessity for the intensive use of resources and energy, and the importance that must be attached to low-carbon economic development and social construction. Under the constraints of natural conditions such as geography, scarcity of mineral resources, and other resources and energy, the global climate changes had a much greater impact on Japan than on other developed countries in the world. In order to mitigate the many adverse effects of global warming on Japan's agriculture, fisheries, environment, industry, and national health, the Japanese government took the lead in building a low-carbon society.[13] It clearly proposed to build a low-carbon society and strengthen the construction of low-carbon cities at the strategic, policy, and planning levels. Japan laid stress on the government's leading role and the active participation of all citizens. First of all, starting with the government itself, it was to strengthen the planning, laws, and policies related to the construction of a low-carbon society, and call for the active participation of the general public and social organizations. In 1997, Japan established the Global Warming Countermeasures led by the Prime Minister. In 1998, the Act on Promotion of Global Warming Countermeasures was enacted. In order to mitigate the emissions of greenhouse gases, Japan's

Ministry of the Environment formulated a new environmental tax plan in November 2004, which proposed to reduce the emissions of greenhouse gases, and accomplished the tasks set forth in the Kyoto Protocol. In 2004, Japan made the plan for Japan's Scenarios of a Low-Carbon Society towards 2050. In 2007, Japan's Low-Carbon Society Model and Its Feasibility Study was released, and it put forward the study of the construction of a low-carbon society. In June 2007, Japan formulated the work called "Becoming a Leading Environmental Nation Strategy in the 21st Century".

In May 2008, the industrial sector paid much attention to the transformation and upgrading of industrial structure, emphasized energy conservation and emission reduction to achieve the low-carbon transformation and development of the industry. The low-carbon industry was the most promising market for future development, and the central government and local governments at all levels in Japan framed relevant preferential tax policies to promote the development of low-carbon industries. In May 2008, the Ministry of the Environment of Japan proposed the 12 Actions for a Low-Carbon Society, and the industry, transportation, housing, energy, and other relevant sectors were to establish the related goals for the construction of a low-carbon society. In June 2008, the Prime Minister Fukuda Yasuo put forward the new countermeasures against global warming, the "Fukuda Blueprint", which stated that Japan's long-term goal for the reduction of greenhouse gas emissions would be that: by 2050, the greenhouse gas emissions of Japan would decrease by 60--80% compared with those at present. On July 26, 2008, Japan formulated the Action Plan for a Low-Carbon Society, which aimed at achieving a harmonious coexistence between humans and nature through energy conservation and emission reduction and advocacy of a low-carbon and frugal spirit, clearly proposed to increase the efforts of photovoltaic power generation, explicitly required that by 2020 Japan's photovoltaic power generation would increase by 10 times, and that the solar-powered electric vehicles would be popularized on a large scale and the charging facilities for electric vehicles would be increased. In November 2008, the Japanese government established the Low Carbon Research Promotion Center, a strategic research institute for the creation of a low-carbon society, and released the Action Plan for the Expansion of Solar Power Generation.

In 2009, the Japanese government adopted a "carbon footprint" policy so that consumers could recognize the important role of individuals in the low-carbon society. It clearly calculated the carbon emissions of each individual, and labeled the carbon emissions of commodities such as food, beverages, and detergents, including the records in the full cycle of raw material preparation, manufacturing, distribution, use, and recycling. Therefore, consumers could be clearly aware of their emission behavior and guided towards a scientific and low-carbon type of consumption, and actively participate in the construction of a low-carbon society and low-carbon cities. In April 2009, Japan also announced the Green Economy and Social Change. In June 2009, Japan proposed new countermeasures in response to climate changes, for vigorously promoting the development of a low-carbon economy and the construction of a low-carbon society.[14] The Fukushima nuclear accident in 2011 led to a major shift in Japan's energy strategy and climate policy. The Japanese government explicitly expressed that it would reduce reliance on nuclear energy and emphasized that an energy mix consisting of nuclear energy, renewable energy and fossil fuels would be the most reliable and stable source for meeting Japan's energy needs.[15]

The characteristics of Japan's construction of a low-carbon society and low-carbon cities were mainly manifested in the government's leading role, flexibility in planning objectives, coordinated promotion by various departments, diversity in key areas and wide participation of the public. First, the government played a dominant role in the construction of low-carbon cities and a low-carbon society. From making plans, introducing policies to enacting laws, the government played an active leading role in elevating the low-carbon strategy to a national strategy, and in guiding the construction of low-carbon cities and a low-carbon society through planning, laws, and regulations. For example, levying environmental taxes is an important directional guidance for industrial sectors and social consumption. The government also actively advanced the generation of solar power and a supply of new energy, accelerated energy conservation, emission reduction, transformation and upgrading of traditional industries, and encouraged traveling by new energy vehicles, and bicycles. Second, flexibility and realism of planning objectives. Rome was not built in one day. Japan built low-carbon cities and a low-carbon society according to the actual situation. For example, for urban areas, the emphasis was put on the development of a high-density, intensive, and high-tech low-carbon society, while for rural areas, the emphasis was put on the decentralization of population and resources and the advocacy of an idyllic lifestyle that was close to nature and harmonious and leisurely. Third, the coordinated advancement of various sectors could play an active role in building a low-carbon society, ensuring the implementation of various plans, programs and policies, minimizing the carbon emissions of all sectors, and maximizing the potential for the reduction of carbon emissions in all economic sectors, which should actively participate in and coordinate the implementation of low-carbon planning. Fourth, plurality of key areas for the planning of a low-carbon society. With regard to the specific implementation, each key area of the plans had a focus. In particular, traffic, housing, and workplace, industry, consumption behavior, forestry and agriculture, land, and urban form were the key areas of low-carbon transformation. They advocated the use of clean energy and new low-carbon new energy, improved the efficiency of energy use, increased investment in technological innovation, and paid attention to the R&D and application of low-carbon technologies. Fifth, extensive public participation. The general public should recognize the importance of a low-carbon society, actively choose low-carbon means of traveling and consumption modes, respond to the actions of the government with personal actions and boost the formation of a low-carbon society and the development of low-carbon cities.[16]

According to the above basic experience of developing low-carbon cities, a low-carbon economy, and low-carbon society by the UK and Japan, it can be found that the development of low-carbon cities has already experienced a complete practical process, and the combination of theory and practice could further promote the development of the theory of a low-carbon city. The low-carbon economy is committed to forming an economic system with low-carbon industry, optimized structure, recycling, energy saving, and high efficiency, shaping a green, ecological, and low-carbon pattern of consumption, and realizing green development, recycling development, and low-carbon development of cities. Low-carbon cities are dominated by a low-carbon economy with low-carbon development as the concept. They attach importance to energy conservation and emission reduction in the two major areas, namely production and consumption; they are building a resource-intensive and environment-friendly society, and have achieved good and rapid economic development. While ensuring that the urban economy cannot grow at the expense of the resources, energy and environmental carrying capacity of the cities, they establish a benign and sustainable urban ecological system. Faced with the plights of frequent hazy weather, depletion of resources and energy, and deterioration of the ecological environment caused by high carbon emissions, it is inevitable to strengthen the prevention and treatment of "urban diseases" based on the theory of a low-carbon city, with the construction of low-carbon cities as the basic goal. It can be said that a low-carbon city is reflected in the use of clean renewable energy, increased popularization of natural gas, emphasis on urban greening and ecological construction, and focusing on waste recycling, so as to achieve comprehensive energy conservation and emission reduction in the economic, social, cultural, and environmental fields of the city, realizing the sustainable development and building a harmonious and livable city.

2.7 Summary

This chapter reviews several theories for the treatment of "urban diseases". There are both commonalities in the study of "urban diseases", and differences among countries at different phases of development. This part aims to review the theories of classical sociology, human ecology, community school, garden city, and low-carbon city, and propose the important theoretical underpinnings to guide the treatment of Beijing's "urban diseases" and the low-carbon development of the Beijing-Tianjin-Hebei region.

The theory of classical sociology paid attention to the early "urban diseases" and their treatment, which provided the fundamental theoretical underpinnings for the study and treatment of "urban diseases". The theory of human ecology is an important theoretical basis for the treatment of "urban diseases". Human ecology is a science that studies the ecological relationship and interaction between human beings and nature, the ecological environment in which human beings live, and the harmonious development of humans and nature, as well as the spatial and temporal connections formed by human beings under the influence of their selective, distributive, and regulative forces on the environment. The community theory is a generic term for theories, doctrines, and perspectives developed through studies on various aspects of community-wide issues. This school of thought mainly focused on the microscopic perspective of cities and believed that a city was a big community and the problems of "urban diseases" could be condensed into the problems of "community diseases". The main theories and methods for the studies of the urban community fall into two categories: neighborhoods and social networks of urban community, as well as powers of urban community.

Unlike the de-ruralization model of traditional cities, the theory of a garden city sketches a beautiful picture of the integration of urban production and life with nature. It provides an important theoretical underpinning for solving the problems of the "urban diseases" of Beijing as a metropolis.

The theory of livable city is different from that of a garden city because it lays more stress on the people-oriented urban planning and emphasizes that urban construction and development should serve the people.

The theory of low-carbon city provides new theoretical tools for the treatment of "urban diseases" and sustainable urban economic and social development. Low-carbon cities are dominated by the low-carbon economy with the low-carbon development as the concept. They attach importance to energy conservation and emission reduction in the two major areas, namely production and consumption, build a resource-intensive and environment-friendly society, and achieve good and rapid economic development. While ensuring that the urban economy cannot grow at the expense of resources, energy, and environmental carrying capacity of the cities, they establish a benign and sustainable urban ecological system.

Notes

1 Li Chen, Classical Theories and the Main Problems of "Urban Diseases" Abroad, *Northwest Population Journal*, 2013(3).
2 Li Chen, Classical Theories and the Main Problems of "Urban Diseases" Abroad, *Northwest Population Journal*, 2013(3).
3 Li Chen, Classical Theories and the Main Problems of "Urban Diseases" Abroad, *Northwest Population Journal*, 2013(3).
4 Xia Jianzhong, The Main Theories and Methods of Modern Western Urban Community Studies, *Journal of Yanshan University*, 2000(2).
5 2014.
6 Zeng Hong, An Exploration of Building a Livable City, *Journal of Shenyang Official*, 2014(1).
7 Huang Jiangsong and Lu Chunjiang, What Kind of Livable City Does Beijing Want to Build?, http://theory.people.com.cn/GB/41038/526534.html, January 10, 2007.

8 Livable City, http://baike.baidu.com, January 18, 2016.
9 Yuan Yi and Wang Shuangjin, Literature Review of the Theory of Low-Carbon Urban Development, *Northern Economy*, 2010(20).
10 Chen Liuqin, The Practices of the Low Carbon Cities' Development at Home and Abroad, *China Value*, 2010(9).
11 Xu Zhenghua, UK's Experience of Building a Low-Carbon Economy and Significance, *People's Tribune*, 2011(11).
12 Wu Qiaowen, UK Takes the Lead in the Low-Carbon Economy, www.ccchina.gov.cn/Detail.aspx?newsID=27742&TId=58.
13 Low-Carbon Society of Japan, www.gesep.com, June 17, 2013.
14 Zhou Xiaomeng, How Japan Integrates Low Carbon into the Whole Society, *China Energy News*, May 3, 2010.
15 Tian Chengchuan and Chai Qimin, Japan's Experience of Building a Low-Carbon Society and Significance, *Macroeconomic Management*, 2016(1).
16 Low-Carbon Society of Japan, www.gesep.com, June 17, 2013.

3 Law of the evolution of "urban diseases" and its phased characteristics

"Urban diseases" have had a long history of development. Before the Industrial Revolution, this problem was not prominent due to the small size of cities, a low concentration of industries and low convergence of population. After the Industrial Revolution, with the enhancement of industrialization and rapid urban expansion caused by mechanization in industries, the popularization of gas engines and electrical equipment improved the accessibility of traffic and further promoted the concentration of population and industries in urban spaces, and the problems of "urban diseases" accumulated. This chapter aims to analyze the phased characteristics of the evolution of "urban diseases" by defining the scope of "urban diseases" and their main manifestations. In light of China's actual situation, emphasis is put on the phased characteristics of the evolution of "urban diseases" in China and Beijing since the reform and opening-up. Finally, the relationship between "urban diseases" and the functional orientation of central cities is examined to study the imbalance between urban elements resulting from different urban forms and different functional demands at different phases.

3.1 Defining the connotation of "urban diseases"

"Urban diseases" first originated in cities in Britain, where the earliest form of urbanization occurred. In Britain, the birthplace of the Industrial Revolution, the process of industrialization gave rise to the extraordinary expansion of central cities, which led to the inadequate carrying capacity of urban resources and energy, rapid consumption of resources and energy, and the worsening of environmental pollution, and finally to the emergence of "urban diseases". The American scholar Joel Kotkin called the traffic congestion, environmental pollution, deteriorating health conditions, and a series of related problems caused by the Industrial Revolution the "gear brutality". There is not a widely recognized definition of "urban diseases", which is interpreted by different researchers in different ways according to their own research perspectives.

According to some researchers, "urban diseases" refer to the phenomena caused by the improper allocation of resources, including the inefficient overall

DOI: 10.4324/9781003272991-3

operation of cities, disorder in the urban system, dysfunction of agglomeration, and diffusion, and a decline in the residents' sense of well-being. In small and medium-sized towns, "urban diseases" are mainly reflected in the lack of employment opportunities, inefficient operation of infrastructures and basic public services due to a lack of scale demand, and insufficient effective demand for housing, with the characteristic of "over-sparseness"; in large cities, "urban diseases" are primarily embodied as excessive concentration of population, traffic congestion, oversupply of infrastructures and basic public services, and soaring housing prices, with the characteristic of "over-denseness".[1]

Other researchers argued that "urban diseases" are "negative effects" appearing in the process of urban development. In their opinion, "urban diseases" refer to the negative socio-economic effects caused by inherent defects that affect the overall movement of the urban system, because socio-economic development and the process of urbanization accelerated at a phase when urbanization had not yet been fully realized in a country, and they mainly include problems such as overpopulation, environmental pollution, spatial congestion, traffic congestion, employment difficulties, deterioration of security, low efficiency of management, shortage of resources, urban–rural conflicts, and social imbalances.[2]

Moreover, in the eyes of some researchers, the understanding of "urban diseases" should be extended beyond the scope of individual cities to urban–rural and inter-city relationships. During the process of rapid urbanization, the results of uncoordinated spatial structure in the excessive concentration of factors in certain cities, causes various social problems.[3]

"Urban diseases" indicate a phenomenon of urban alienation. Cities exist because of the concentration of people, and the development of cities is to improve people's lives, so that more people can enjoy urban functions and services, life becomes more convenient, freer, safer and more beautiful, and the traffic can become more convenient. However, a lack of self-control leads to the over-expansion of urban population, and to a decline in the carrying capacity of urban traffic, the environment, resources and energy. The more prosperous cities are the more barren and secular the spiritual homes of people seem to be. The more commodities and wealth piled up in cities, the more crime, drug addiction, prostitution, environmental pollution, and diseases. These result in the deviation of urban construction from the goal of serving people, and finally cities become alien to people to some extent. This is the so-called "urban alienation".[4]

In this book, the so-called "urban diseases" are defined as the various problems, such as population expansion, traffic congestion, serious pollution, ecological deterioration, and social conflicts caused by the over-concentration of resources, excessive clustering of industries, and over-convergence of functions during the long-term development of cities. "Urban diseases" are the dysfunctions of cities due to the over-concentration of resources, functions, population, and industrial elements in urban spaces, which leads to a decline in the carrying capacity of resources, energy, and the environment. The inherent contradictions between urban resources and social demands in a certain period of development, such as short supply or oversupply, the insufficient carrying capacity and the imbalance among the various elements of cities produce negative effects that affect the normal operation of cities.

3.2 Manifestations of "urban diseases"

Regarding the various manifestations of "urban diseases", some researchers indicate that rapid economic growth has accelerated the process of urbanization in China, and the urban population has grown dramatically. There are also a large number of "urban diseases" in large and medium-sized cities and even in small and medium-sized towns in China, which are mainly reflected in dense population, traffic congestion, environmental pollution, a shortage of resources, as well as difficulties in employment, schooling, and social management. These problems make it more difficult to treat "urban diseases".[5] This view is representative because it enumerates the important manifestations of "urban diseases". In the early period during the Industrial Revolution, the problems of "urban diseases", such as housing shortage, serious pollution, and poor hygiene, were caused by the rapid expansion of cities and their development beyond the carrying capacity of resources. Early capitalist countries took a series of measures to deal with these problems. Entering the new era, China's progress in urbanization is accelerating, the rate of urbanization has been rising, and the problems of "urban diseases" have become increasingly serious. Table 3.1 compares the embodiments of "urban diseases" in typical international cities and the measures taken to treat the problems.[6] In the table, it can be found that many cities have experienced a series of "urban diseases", such as population expansion, decline of industries, traffic congestion, housing shortage, and environmental pollution to varying degrees.

Based on the above analysis of the manifestations of "urban diseases" in foreign cities, it was found that population expansion, traffic congestion, environmental pollution, shortage of resources, and a series of social problems caused by them can be said to be the major diseases occurring in most cities. To be specific, they are manifested in the following aspects:

3.2.1 Population expansion

A city cannot be called a city without a concentration of population, and a city without popularity can only go into decline. From this perspective, many experts believe that urban population cannot be called an "urban disease". However, if the population expands and piles up too much in a small area, the carrying capacity of the city's infrastructure, traffic conditions, and housing cannot keep up with the demand of the population growth, which will cause many urban problems such as traffic congestion, housing shortage and apparent social contradictions. From this point of view, the issue of

Table 3.1 Embodiments and treatment of "urban diseases" in typical international cities

City	Main problems and embodiments	Measures taken
London	1. In the era of industrialization, large numbers of rural population rushed to cities, so infrastructure and other public service facilities were overloaded, and the housing shortage became a serious problem. 2. There were more than 20 slums in London where 10,000 people l lived, and they became the "Court for King Cholera". Workers had poor housing conditions, were lacking in public health facilities, and suffered from serious epidemic and endemic diseases. 3. Traffic congestion. Since the beginning of industrialization in London, the population has expanded too fast, and ownerships of private cars have increased, leading to limited carrying capacity and serious congestion on the streets and roads. 4. The development of the city was plagued by "smoke", which caused serious air pollution. In 1952, smog incidents occurred, and rivers were polluted by wastewater. Traffic pollution was serious. Pollutants such as nitrogen oxides, carbon monoxide, and unstable organic compounds emitted by cars formed "photochemical smog".	1. Planning and legislation were made to guide the decentralization of urban functions. New towns were built to decentralize the population in core urban areas. Education, medical care, and housing in new towns or subcenters were vigorously developed to provide good public services for new towns. The worries of employment, education, and life in new towns were solved to facilitate the effective decentralization of the urban population. 2. Under social pressures, governments at all levels began to take actions by legislating the *Municipal Corporations Act*, setting the Poor Law Commission, factory inspector office and health bureau, enacting the *Housing of the Working Class Act*, solving the problem of slums and constructing stores, parks, theaters and other facilities. 3. The plan to pay a "Congestion Charge" was proposed for controlling the quantity of cars in urban areas. The entry charge for vehicles with large displacements increased to 25 pounds per day (350 yuan per day), and a carbon dioxide tax was imposed on vehicles entering the city center. Public transportation, railway, and electric vehicles were developed, metro stations in the city center were within walking distance, city trains, light rails in port areas and bus lines diverted people from the roads, and low fares attracted the public. There were no parking areas in downtown, so that commuters were forced to use public transportation or ride bikes to work. 4. The smog incident of London resulted in the British people's reflections on the issue of pollution. They enhanced the management of industry, promulgated the *Clean Air Act*, the *Air (Prevention and Control of Pollution) Act*, and the *Environment Act*, delineated "smoke control areas", banned the burning of coal in towns and cities within these

Law of the evolution of "urban diseases" 71

areas, and set upper limits on the sulfur content of industrial fuels. All of the new vehicles sold in the UK were required to be installed with catalytic converters, and penalties were expressly prescribed to reduce pollution by nitrogen oxide. The public were encouraged to discuss the issue of urban pollution control, which was exposed on the media. Green spaces were built, greening areas were increased, and clean energy was used. London built large greening areas in the outskirts of the city, created urban green belts, and promoted the use of clean energy. By iron-fisted control of pollution, London transformed from a foggy capital to a truly green city.

1. It developed suburbs and large metropolitan areas, enhanced cross-regional institutions, strengthened construction of public housing, put emphasis on equal allocation of public services, reduced the gap between the rich and the poor, and promoted a balanced development of population.
2. A high proportion of citizens traveled by public transportation and the city created a well-developed subway system. Private cars were restricted by levying fuel taxes, bridge and road tolls, and high parking charges.
3. Importance is attached to waste recycling and energy saving to enhance the low-carbon development and to build a green New York. Waste recycling was decided as a mandatory item and legislated for protection. Traditional fuel buses were eliminated and replaced by hybrid powered buses, emissions of motor vehicles were reduced, energy-efficient lights were used, green buildings were advocated, and rainwater collection on rooftops and recycling were encouraged to conserve urban water resources.

New York
1. Population expansion and housing shortage were caused by the rapid growth of the population.
2. Social problems such as a growing gap between the rich and the poor and a high crime rate have continued to plague New York.
3. Cars became popular in families, roads could not meet the demand for travel, and traffic congestion became an increasingly serious problem.
4. Environmental pollution became serious, excessive emissions of factories led to severe air pollution, and citizens suffered from diseases such as emphysema, lung cancer.

(continued)

Table 3.1 Cont.

City	Main problems and embodiments	Measures taken
Tokyo	1. Population expansion. Tokyo is one of the world's densely populated cities, and 1/4 of the Japanese people are crowded into less than 4% of the land area of Japan. The population is growing too fast. 2. Tokyo has attracted the concentration of many people from other cities, thus resulting in a housing shortage, pressure on travel and centralization of enterprises. 3. Serious environmental pollution in cities. In 1952 and 1953, Tokyo was so polluted that it was "difficult to see the sun during the day" due to the black smoke from heating. In 1970, environmental pollution became a public hazard in Japan.	1. In order to treat the urban diseases of the metropolis, the government planned and guided by phases and steps to decentralize urban functions. City subcenters were constructed to balance the intensity of urban land use. Emphasis was put on industrial guidance and structural adjustment, and the population was diverted by decentralization of industrial guidance and adjustment, so as to effectively solve a series of problems such as expansion of urban population. 2. A traffic network dominated by rail transit was established, with few buses above ground and a low proportion of private cars driving to work. High taxes were levied, parking fees were raised, penalties for illegal parking were enhanced, and "capillaries" were opened up to divert traffic from trunk roads, thus avoiding repeated excavations and reducing traffic congestion. 3. The country proposed building a low-carbon society, enhanced the control of environmental pollution, lay stress on the development of a circular economy, and encouraged the use of low-carbon new energy. New buildings had to have green spaces and greening at the roof, in order to pursue the three-dimensional greening area. In 2003, Tokyo made the installation of filters on cars mandatory and banned diesel-engine cars from entering the city.
The Ruhr in Germany	The Ruhr area, known as the "industrial engine of Germany", has always experienced the process of urban aging and industrial decline due to the depletion of resources in the history of its development. Since 1954, it has been faced with a "coal crisis" because low-cost coal was imported in large quantities from abroad. From 1958 to 1964,	1. The government constructed new industrial parks by funding land purchases, restoring landforms, selling land and attracting investment. Investment was increased, cultural industries were developed, factories and mines were transformed into resources of tourism, and old steel mills were changed to become R&D centers for new industries and cultural exhibition centers.

27 mines were closed, and the production was reduced by 14 million tons/ year, which resulted in the unemployment of more than 5,300 workers. After the 1960s, with the continuous development of the steel industry in other countries, Germany gradually lost its cost advantage. Because the peak period of post-war reconstruction in Europe had elapsed, and there was a substitution with new materials, the Ruhr area encountered a "steel crisis". From 1980 to 1990, the city of Duisburg lost 32,000 jobs in the coal and steel industries, and the unemployment rate even exceeded 20%. As the industry declined, the structural disadvantages of the heavy chemical economy became apparent, coal and steel plants closed down, workers were laid off, economic growth slowed, unemployment increased, talents drained, pollution worsened, and a series of economic and social problems arose, such as poverty, pollution, and education for the children of laid-off workers.

2. An integrated planning agency was established to supervise the modification and transformation of mining areas. Laws were enacted, the Ruhr Regional Association was founded, and the *Regional Planning of Ruhr* was formulated to prescribe the plans for the development of the region. The relevant policies and regulations such as the *Coal Mine Adjustment Act* were enacted to enhance the integration of coal mine resources and promote the transformation of the coal industry.

3. Importance was attached to social construction and to the enhancement of re-employment and social security. Employments were subsidized, unemployment funds were promptly allocated, and the construction of infrastructure and the improvement of conditions were strengthened. Related service agencies including fund organizations, research institutions, training centers, re-employment intermediaries, etc. were established to create re-employment opportunities for laid-off workers.

4. With a focus on high and new-tech industries such as logistics, new chemical, health engineering, bio-pharmaceuticals and tourism, it developed low-carbon new energy industries like wind, solar, nuclear and biomass energy, built the largest solar cell power plant – Gelsenkirchen Power Plant, strengthened the ecological restoration and environmental control in mining areas, enhanced the public awareness of low-carbon environmental protection, encouraged citizens to plant trees and grasses, and increased forest carbon sinks.

5. Air pollution was controlled by taking measures such as limiting the emission of polluting gases, establishing an air quality monitoring system and an automatic chimney alarm system. The Ruhr industrial region has already realized an ecological green urban landscape with green mountains, clear waters, fresh and pleasant air, and residential areas and factories located in the midst of green plant communities.

(continued)

Table 3.1 Cont.

City	Main problems and embodiments	Measures taken
Mexico City	1. Urbanization was faster than industrialization, resulting in a misalignment between the level of urbanization and that of economic development. Of the 130 million people in Mexico, 50 million did not have enough income to meet the needs of housing, traffic, and education, etc. Mexico used to be one of the world's countries with the largest gap between the rich and the poor. 2. The urban population grew significantly. Mexico City, the capital of Mexico, is one of the largest and most densely populated cities on earth. Over-urbanization, an inadequate supply of urban public services, and the influx of rural surplus labor in large quantities became reasons why Mexico City was overburdened. Over-urbanization caused a significant increase in the number of poor people in Mexico City. Most of the farmers working in the city were old and lacked education and professional skills, so it was difficult for them to adapt to the demand for skilled workers in urban industries, thus leading to many slums. In addition, it was also difficult to get medical care. 3. Traffic congestion and other problems arose. Mexico City was known as the world's largest "city of traffic jams". Buying private cars became a symbol of "social status".	1. In order to control the adverse population expansion, the government of Mexico City took measures like the construction of "satellite cities" and "urban-rural parity". Since 1980, over 30 satellite cities have been built around Mexico City, with more than 15 million people living there. The city government constructed these satellite cities as livable cities with a beautiful environment, complete facilities, convenient traffic, and comfortable housing. Some prestigious universities and high schools also ran branches in satellite cities to attract people to live there. 2. In order to retain the surplus labor force in rural areas and prevent the poor from blindly flowing into cities, the Mexican government became committed to narrowing the gap between urban and rural areas and improving rural living standards. The government of Mexico City introduced a milk program to distribute free milk in rural areas to children and people aged 60 and older. The public health insurance program for the poor was available to all rural residents, and the entire family could enjoy free medical services if one person took out the insurance. The government of Mexico City also opened accounts for people aged 70 and older, and gave them a monthly subsidy of $25. In order to encourage children from poor families to attend school and reduce the dropout rate, the city government also provided scholarships to students in elementary and secondary schools of rural areas. 3. Environmental pollution was controlled by planting more trees and driving cars less frequently. In the 1990s, the government of Mexico City was determined to get rid of the title of "the world's most seriously polluted city", and so it launched the "One Tree per Household" campaign, replaced the "concrete forest" with green forests, and restored the green belt around the city. Stringent laws were enacted to protect the green vegetation, from woods in the city to flowers, trees, and grass in residents' yards, all of which were protected by laws and could not be cut down without permission.

Concentration of the population, inadequate construction of traffic facilities, and terrible planning resulted in the problems of "urban diseases" such as traffic congestion, a housing shortage, urban crimes.

4. Pollution was caused by excessive urbanization. Mexico City had seven to eight million cars driving on roads every day. In the 1990s, Mexico City, the capital of Mexico, was one of the ten most polluted cities in the world in terms of air pollution.

The government also patrolled by helicopters every day to prevent the destruction of trees in the city. The concept of green homes was deeply rooted in the minds of citizens, and it became a trend to grow flowers indoors or develop rooftops into vegetable gardens.

4. A perfect system of public transportation was built to reduce the exhaust emissions of private cars and ease traffic congestion. Since 1989, the government of Mexico City advocated the policy of "no driving today". The metro was well developed, with 11 lines and 3.88 million passengers per day. Since 2006, the city government constructed six rapid transit lines of buses, and replaced thousands of old, polluting minibuses with hundreds of large, comfortable, and low-emission buses to attract people to take them.

Los Angeles   Los Angeles, an industrial city in the United States of America, has been plagued by air pollution since early in the 20th century. The Second World War not only greatly enhanced its level of industrial development, but also brought about increased air pollution. The urban population and the quantity of motor vehicles grew rapidly. According to weather records, the visibility declined rapidly from 1939 to 1943. The "Los Angeles Smog" came in 1943. In 1952 and 1955, Los Angeles suffered two serious incidents of "photochemical smog", each of which caused hundreds of deaths of people aged over 65 due to respiratory failure. Los Angeles transformed from a "City of Angels" to a "City of Smog", and the sky of the city was mocked as a "badly developed film".

1. The city set up a specialized agency for cross-regional coordination of air quality management and aimed at providing the organizational guarantee for the environmental control of the city. In 1946, Los Angeles established the Bureau of Smoke Control, the first local air quality authority in the country, and set up the first system of gas emission standards and permits for industrial pollution in the USA.

2. Public participation and citizen campaigns advanced the legislation on the prevention and control of air pollution. In 1970, the introduction of the *Clean Air Act* was the result of a public campaign. In 1988, California promulgated the *California Clean Air Act*.

3. It introduced the market mechanism and developed advanced technologies for the control of air pollution. A trading mechanism of air pollution emissions was introduced, and emission targets were publicly listed and traded on the Chicago futures market. Technologies involving the control of air pollution were promoted, including reduction of hydrocarbon emissions and the creation of exhaust emission standards for vehicles, etc. All vehicles were required to be equipped with catalytic converters.

4. The city government strengthened industrial restructuring and regional economic development, and encouraged the development and use of clean and renewable energy. Public transportation was developed, and energy conservation at home was advocated.

population will directly or indirectly lead to "urban diseases", or it can be said that the urban population does appear to have some "diseases" that need to be treated. Of course, the key to treatment is to change the population expansion into talent productivity, and transform the negative energy into positive energy. This is the real benefit for dealing with the issue of urban population. However, in the evolution of cities around the world, the problems of "urban diseases" caused by population expansion have become increasingly prominent. The disorderly growth of and failure to control urban population have to be considered as important manifestations of "urban diseases".

Urbanization means a massive influx of people to cities, and the increase in the population leads to the expansion of cities. As China is advancing its industrialization and urbanization year by year, more rural surplus labor goes out to work at the Pearl River Delta, Yangtze River Delta, Beijing-Tianjin-Hebei, and other city circles, and so the population has further concentrated in many cities. Over the past 30 years, China's urban population has been increasing by about 20 million per year, and the rapid growth of the population has brought serious challenges to urban traffic, housing, and infrastructure, and has led to a series of "urban diseases". The Yangtze River Delta, Pearl River Delta, Beijing-Tianjin-Hebei, and a number of city clusters such as Wuhan City Circle, Changsha-Zhuzhou-Xiangtan City Cluster, and Central Plains City Cluster in central China absorb large quantities of population by employment. The influx of the working population not only boosts the rapid economic development of cities, but also puts pressure on urban management and further harmonious development. For example, Beijing, as the capital city, witnesses an inflowing population of about 400,000 each year, which results in the increasingly serious problems of "urban diseases". The disorder influx and rapid population expansion overburden the carrying capacity of existing resources, energy, the environment, traffic, and infrastructure of cities, and will inevitably lead to a series of uncoordinated, disharmonious problems in urban economic and social development, and ultimately many "urban diseases" such as traffic congestion, high housing prices, deterioration of the environment, shortage of resources, and public security.

As early as the late 19th century, Britain, which took the lead in industrialization, experienced rapid population growth due to the influx of people, which resulted in a housing shortage, the formation of many slums, inadequate public health facilities, dense distribution of heavy and chemical industries, dirty air, serious water pollution, the deterioration of the urban environment, fierce competition for jobs, many unemployed workers and difficulty in tackling crimes. In Latin American countries, many urban problems also emerged, especially in the middle of the 20th century, when industrialization and urbanization accelerated and led to the expansion of the urban population. The speed of urbanization exceeded that of industrialization, and the problem of over-urbanization emerged, with the rapid increase in the population overwhelming the carrying capacity of cities, thus causing many urban problems. In many cities of China, there is also a series of urban problems such as a growth of urban population that is too fast. China's modernization leads to the increasing concentration of industry and commerce in southeastern coastal cities. Rapid urbanization and the fast growth of the population result in the deterioration of public security in cities, with frequent crimes of kidnapping, robbery, theft, drug trafficking, drug addiction, prostitution. Traffic congestion, difficulties in employment, a housing shortage, and environmental deterioration are closely related to the rapid growth of the population and a lack of supporting facilities in cities.

When the urban population is over-expanding, especially in metropolises, the aging population also becomes a major problem that cannot be underestimated. Beijing, Shanghai, Guangzhou, and other metropolises have become truly aging cities. The aging of the population has considerable impacts on the sustainable economic and social development of cities. First, the shrinking demographic dividend, reduction in the labor force and the increase in labor cost increase the costs for the development of enterprises and affect rapid economic growth. Second, the aging population and high housing prices in cities increase the pressure on the work and life of young people. The heavy family burden and high cost of living of young people suppress the happiness of urban residents and negatively affect the improvement of the cities' capabilities for innovation. Third, aging has increased the pressure on urban retirement, and the insufficient beds for elderly care and limited services of elderly care institutions pose challenges for elderly care in cities. Fourth, the aging of the population imposes new requirements on the traditional urban planning, including industrial planning, land planning, and the planning of public facilities. Urban planning must be adapted to the realistic needs of the development of an aging society.[7]

3.2.2 Traffic congestion

An important symptom of "urban diseases" is traffic congestion, especially the congestion index during commuting hours, which directly reflects the severity of "urban diseases". Rapid population growth puts pressure on urban traffic, and the population expansion directly leads to the rapid growth of traffic needs, while the seriously underdeveloped traffic becomes a contradiction between supply and demand that is difficult to reconcile in a short period of time. Traffic congestion increases residents' time and cost of travel, affects their work efficiency, creates psychological pressure, and causes a series of problems such as urban pollution and traffic safety, thus leading to a decline in economic and social functions and becoming "stubborn diseases" that hinder development.

Beijing, as the capital city of the country, is called the "capital of traffic jam". Traffic congestion has led to a decline in citizen's satisfaction with travel in the capital city, and Beijing has become famous for its traffic congestion within the country and even throughout the world. However, according to a study, Beijing's traffic congestion is not the worst in the world, or in China. In

78 Law of the evolution of "urban diseases"

Table 3.2 Most congested cities and evening peak congested cities in 2015 Unit: %

Top 5 most congested cities		Top 5 Evening peak congested cities	
Istanbul (Turkey)	58	Istanbul (Turkey)	109
Mexico City (Mexico)	55	Moscow (Russia)	103
Rio de Janeiro (Brazil)	51	St. Petersburg (Russia)	96
Moscow (Russia)	50	Mexico City (Mexico)	89
Salvador (Brazil)	46	Chongqing (China)	84

a ranking of congested cities released by the Dutch traffic navigation service provider Tom, Istanbul, a Turkish port city topped the list of the world's most congested cities, and Beijing's congestion index was 37%, ranking 15th in the world and behind Chongqing and Tianjin among Chinese cities. But another statistic in the report showed that the congestion on the highways of Beijing (including expressways) was worse than on ordinary roads. If the congestion on highways were ranked, Beijing would rank 6th in the world. As shown in Table 3.2, in 2015, the most congested city on earth was Istanbul, Turkey, with an average congestion index of 58%, which means that during congested hours, car owners spend an average of 58% more time than normal driving, and during the evening rush hour, car owners spend 109% more time than normal driving, and the people of Istanbul waste 125 hours in traffic jams.[8]

The rapid growth of motor vehicles exceeds the existing road traffic capacity, thus leading to traffic congestion and becoming an important urban disease. According to a study, 20 years ago it took about four years to increase 100,000 cars in Beijing; and 10 years ago it took only two years. In 2002 alone, 276,000 vehicles were added. The rapid growth of motor vehicles made the already congested road traffic even worse. Unlike other big cities at home and abroad, Beijing's road construction is designed and developed with the imperial city as the center, in a chessboard pattern. The "pie-spreading" pattern from central to peripheral urban areas leads to traffic congestion in road junctions. Traffic congestion is exacerbated by the dense concentration of high-rise office buildings in downtown areas, inadequate design of parking spaces and a lack of adequate traffic facilities. In the meanwhile, most central cities in China, as administrative centers, concentrate certain administrative resources, educational and cultural resources, medical services, and other resources, which objectively increase the rigid demand for travel to work or to do business from the outskirts to downtown areas. The insufficient or underdeveloped construction of public transportation facilities, especially subways, reduces the carrying capacity of public transportation.

According to the strategic considerations of environmental protection and conservation of resources and energy, developed countries and cities in the West give priority to the development of public transportation and advocate walking systems and bicycle riding, with less frequent travel by private cars. In contrast, many urban residents in China regard private cars as a symbol of social status, and public transportation as an inferior way of life. This increases the frequency of traveling by private cars and increases the pressure on traffic to a certain extent. For example, residents in Beijing drive private cars more frequently than those in the Western developed countries. Moreover, public transportation has developed slowly without a reasonable structure of a network of public transportation and imperfect configuration of public transportation. In particular, the subway development is seriously lagging behind, there is a lack of large-capacity fast trunk lines, the accessibility of branch lines is not enough, transfer distance is too long, and the subway has deliberately increased the transfer lines and time in order to divert traffic, with the average transfer distance of more than 350 meters.[9] This causes dissatisfaction among passengers to a certain extent, and intensifies the desire to buy private cars and drive them to and from work, so it is not conducive to the alleviation of urban traffic congestion. With the improvement of people's living standards in China, the capability for the use of private cars has increased, and owning a private car has become an important symbol of successful people. People are proud of owning private cars, which have become an important means of transportation. Therefore, the rapid growth of motor vehicles in China in recent years overloads urban roads and causes traffic congestion and frequent traffic accidents. Besides, disorder and difficulty of parking are also important manifestations of traffic problems. The urban working and living environment is also affected by traffic congestion, reduced speed, time delay, and increased exhaust emissions. The main reasons for traffic congestion are the rapid growth of motor vehicle ownership, slow construction of roads, serious shortage of large-capacity and fast public transportation, and underdeveloped public transportation services, such as few lines, few seats, long waiting time, and difficulty in transfer, which all inhibit the demand for public transportation and this results in the choice of private cars by more people.

Further, the "centric development" and monocentric concentration of cities lead to the over-denseness of central resources, and the "pie-spreading" development results in an imbalance of the spatial and temporal distribution of traffic flows and excessive traffic in downtown areas. The separation of work and residence[10] and the phenomenon of a sleeping city have enhanced the rigid travel demand to and from work. The existing problems, such as unreasonable networks of roads, the "inverted pyramid" pattern with sparse networks and few branch lines and secondary roads, and old and underdeveloped traffic facilities, are the reasons for the congestion of urban traffic roads.

3.2.3 Environmental pollution

The environment is a basic condition for the sustainable development of the urban economy and society, and it is the basic responsibilities and obligations of the city government to guarantee a good quality of water quality, fresh air, healthy food, and safe spaces for urban residents. Urban environmental pollution is a key issue that urban residents complain about and that restricts the sustainable development of an urban economy and society. The phenomena of frequent smoky weather, a city besieged by garbage, water pollution, noise, and light pollution have become important obstacles to the construction of livable cities. Due to the large urban population, urban residents discharge various pollutants such as wastewater, exhaust gas, and waste into the natural environment in the process of production and living, which seriously exceeds the self-purification capacity of the natural environment, and buildings are too dense and ecological space is eroded, resulting in the mutation of nature and the function of various factors in the natural environment as well as damage to the ecological environment, which further seriously harms the physical, mental, production, and life aspects for urban residents.

At present, most cities in China are facing the dilemmas of environmental pollution, such as severe water shortage, a declining level of groundwater, serious atmospheric pollution, insufficient ecological land space, etc., in many cities, accelerated depletion of resources and energy, high intensity of carbon emissions, so the economic and social development of high-carbon cities is under severe ecological pressure. In recent years, urban environmental pollution has been intensifying, and it is manifested by the comprehensive content of pollutants, the extensive scope of pollution, the long-term nature of pollution, and the seriousness of pollution hazards. From the perspective of polluted objects, it can be divided into urban air pollution, urban water pollution, etc.; according to the causes of pollution, it can be divided into industrial pollution, traffic pollution, etc.; by the forms of pollutants, it can be divided into exhaust gas pollution, noise pollution, radiation pollution, etc.; and according to the nature of pollutants, it can be divided into chemical pollution, physical pollution, biological pollution, etc. Urban space is a place with a concentration of activities of human production and life, so urban environmental pollution can cause rather considerable harm.

First of all, atmospheric pollution. Atmospheric pollution, also known as air pollution, refers to the phenomenon that certain substances enter the atmosphere due to social activities of mankind and natural movement, and their concentration is so high that it is difficult to be purified in a short period of time, thus endangering the survival of mankind, plants, and animals, especially endangering the survival, production, physical and mental health and well-being of mankind. A substance whose presence in quantity, nature, and time is sufficient to have an adverse impact on mankind or other creatures or property can be regarded as an air pollutant. The sources of atmospheric pollution mainly include: pollutants emitted from industrial production into the atmosphere, such as soot, sulfur oxides, nitrogen oxides, organic compounds, halides, carbon compounds, etc.; harmful substances emitted from the burning of coal by stoves and heating boilers in our daily lives, such as dust, sulfur dioxide, and carbon monoxide, which can pollute the atmosphere; exhaust gases produced from burning coal or petroleum by motor vehicles such as cars, trains, aircraft, ships; smoke from forest fires, etc. Atmospheric pollutants are harmful to the human body in multiple aspects, and such harm is reflected in respiratory diseases, physiological dysfunctions, as well as diseases due to irritations to the mucous membrane tissues of eyes and noses. In China, due to the relative abundance of coal resources, the composition of total energy reserves is raw coal (87%), crude oil (2.8%), gas (0.3%) and water energy (9.5%). This composition determines the coal-dominated structure of energy consumption, and the extensive consumption of coal leads to a large amount of soot and exhaust emissions, which play a decisive role in China's air pollution.[11] The increase in motor vehicle ownership and exhaust emissions aggravate the degree of urban air pollution. Pollution from combustion, industrial waste gas, motor vehicle exhaust, dusts at construction sites and restaurant emissions are important parts of urban air pollution.

Second, water pollution. China's water pollution is very serious. With the increasing demand for water by accelerated industrialization and urbanization, the discharge of industrial wastewater is not effectively managed nor strictly controlled, the phenomenon of disorderly discharge is terrible, large amounts of industrial wastewater exceeding permitted levels is directly discharged into rivers, lakes, and seas, and some are strongly pressed into groundwater and directly cause serious pollution. The discharge of urban wastewater is also reckless, and shows an increasing trend year by year with the surge of the urban population. However, the construction of sewage treatment facilities lags behind, and domestic sewage accounts for more than 50% of the water pollution. Over-exploitation and pollution of groundwater further exacerbates the shortage of water resources. The pollution of urban water sources is becoming an important embodiment of many "urban diseases". In November 2014, The Nature Conservancy (TNC), together with the C40 Cities Climate Leadership Group and the International Water Association, jointly released the Urban Water Blueprint report, which covers the world's 100 largest cities and involves nearly 1 billion people. Due to population growth, climate change and environmental deterioration, 17 cities in China are facing the unprecedented pressure of severe water pollution, particularly Shenzhen, Xi'an, Chengdu, Qingdao, Tianjin, and Changchun. In terms of the quality of water, most urban water sources in China are heavily polluted, especially by sediment contamination.[12]

For various reasons, many people are still unable to filter and purify natural rivers or groundwater, so it is not easy for them to drink clean water. 82% of people in China drink directly from shallow wells and rivers, but these water sources are under direct threat of contamination by organic matter. There is a population of about 160 million whose drinking water sources are contaminated by organic matter. It is difficult to guarantee the safety of drinking water because tap water is affected by the contamination of water sources and there is a lack of necessary strict filtration equipment and facilities. People in suburban and rural areas do not have the sense of crisis for water safety, with a higher possibility of being threatened by pollution. Currently, international measurements of chemicals polluting nature reveal that there are more than 2,000 kinds of pollutants. The drinking standards of tap water in China are relatively low, many regions have not installed the standard filtration facilities, and some regions drink water directly after simply natural filtration or primary processing by boiling. The chlorination of tap water in cities produces many haloalkane compounds, which may cause gastrointestinal cancers in the human body.[13] The Ministry of Water Resources has often evaluated the quality of the water in more than 700 rivers, with a length of about 100,000 kilometers. 46.5% of the river length is polluted, with a Class IV or V quality of the water; 10.6% of the river length is seriously polluted, with a less than Class V quality of water, and the water has lost its value for using it; and more than 90% of the urban water is seriously polluted, with the characteristics that water pollution is developing from the east to the west, and extending from tributaries to trunk streams, from urban areas to rural areas, from surface to underground, from regions to river basins.[14] Tap water in cities is often contaminated by a variety of harmful residues such as heavy metals, pesticides, fertilizers, and detergents, and it is also a challenge to solve the problem of urban water pollution.

Third, noise pollution. Due to the concentration of the population and a relatively developed traffic system, industry, etc., the noises of traffic, industry, construction, and life overlap and cause noise pollution in cities. On the one hand, roads are densely distributed in cities, which result in not only traffic congestion, but also excessive traffic noise. Noise is also continuous at construction sites. Many places are built after demolition and demolished after building and urban construction and municipal facilities are always in a state of construction. Therefore, the construction noise and industrial noise is becoming a serious nuisance to residents. On the other hand, noise generated from life services, restaurants, vegetable markets, stores, cultural and entertainment venues make cities no longer quiet, and the noise pollution from range hoods, air conditioning units and entertainment loudspeakers transform modern cities into noisy cities.

Fourth, solid waste pollution. Solid wastes are mainly generated from industrial production and those abandoned by people in their daily lives. Due to the lack of good purification, they pollute human beings' living environment. Solid wastes by sources can be broadly divided into three types: domestic waste, general industrial solid waste, and hazardous waste. In addition, there is agricultural solid waste, construction waste, and discarded soil. Solid wastes, which are not properly collected, utilized, treated, and disposed of, seriously pollute the atmosphere, water, and soil, and endanger human health. Some solid wastes, with a long natural purification cycle, have penetrated into water sources and other ecologically fragile areas, and thus pose serious threats to the survival of plants, animals, and mankind. For example, cadmium-polluted rice is a manifestation of the direct threat to human food by heavy metal cadmium. Solid waste pollution has a big impact on the urban environment. With the accelerated rate of industrialization and urbanization, the discharge of industrial solid wastes is continuously increasing. The 2014 Annual Report on the Prevention and Control of Solid Waste Pollution in Large and Medium-sized Cities released by the Ministry of Ecology and the Environment shows that in 2013, the generation of general industrial solid wastes in 261 large and medium-sized cities nationwide was 2,383,062,300 tons, the generation of industrial hazardous waste was 29,370,500 tons, the generation of medical waste was about 547,500 tons, and the generation of domestic waste was about 161,488,100 tons.[15] Since solid wastes are not properly recycled and disposed of, they cause negative impacts on the urban environment that are difficult to repair and seriously threaten the production and living environment of urban residents.

Fifth, pollution by electromagnetic wave radiation. This kind of pollution is not easily perceived by citizens directly, but needs to be detected by certain instruments or through long-term physical impact. Hence, it rarely attracts the attention of citizens, social organizations and relevant government agencies. With the rapid development of Internet and communication technologies, the RF power of radios, TVs, microwaves and network equipment has increased exponentially, and has led to enhanced ground electromagnetic radiation. Excessive electromagnetic radiation has a serious impact on the lives of citizens, and shapes common electromagnetic pollution. High-voltage lines, substations, radio stations, television stations, radar stations, electromagnetic wave towers and electronic instruments, medical equipment, office automation equipment and household appliances in cities produce a variety of different wavelengths and frequencies of electromagnetic waves. Long-term exposure to a dose of radiation exceeding the safety criteria will endanger health. Electromagnetic wave pollution is known as the fourth largest source of environmental pollution after water pollution, air pollution, and noise pollution.

The influence of electromagnetic radiation on mankind is mainly manifested as follows. First, thermal effect of electromagnetic waves. Absorption of excessive electromagnetic waves may lead to high-temperature physiological reactions, resulting in neurasthenia, reduction in the number of white blood cells and other pathologies. Second, non-thermal effect of electromagnetic waves. When electromagnetic waves act on the human body for a long period of time, there will be physiological changes in heart rate and blood pressure and physiological reactions of insomnia and forgetfulness, and they have a very serious impact on pregnant women and fetuses. Although electromagnetic waves cannot be directly sensed by human body, the impact of excessive electromagnetic wave pollution is very serious and must urban residents must pay attention to it.

In the report "Toward an Environmentally Sustainable Future: Country Environmental Analysis of the People's Republic of China", jointly released by the Asian Development Bank (ADB) and Tsinghua University on January 14, 2013, the top 10 air pollution cities in the world were Taiyuan, Milan, Beijing, Urumqi, Mexico City, Lanzhou, Chongqing, Jinan, Shijiazhuang, and Tehran. Among them, Chinese cities included Taiyuan, Beijing, Urumqi, Lanzhou, Chongqing, Jinan, and Shijiazhuang, which accounted for 70% of the world's top 10 air pollution cities. It could be found that China's urban pollution was very serious. According to Hamid L. Sharif, the ADB Chief Representative in China, the environmental challenges facing China were arguably more complex than those of any other countries. Although China's environment had improved in many aspects, the overall situation was still in a state of deterioration due to increased environmental pressures. Before China's environmental situation can reach a turning point, there is still much to be done.[16]

3.2.4 Shortage of resources

There are many types of urban resources, such as natural mineral resources, energy, water resources, land resources, and so on. The shortage of resources is an important bottleneck for the sustainable urban economic and social development of China. Many urban spaces have emerged because of the development of resources. For example, the rise in the number of resource-based cities is based on the development of some resources. The development and exploitation of resources and energy is very important for resource-based cities. Once the resources and energy are depleted, it is likely to lead to a decline in urban industries, which will result in the closure of factories, layoffs of workers, urban decline, and serious problems of "urban diseases". Shortage of resources has become an important obstacle to the sustainable economic and social development of modern cities. The advancement of the process of urbanization is increasing the demand for energy, including electricity, coal, oil, gas, etc., which also puts strong pressure on the ecological environment.[17]

Water is the source of life, and the severe scarcity of water resources has become a worldwide problem. Water shortage is a major dilemma for the development of many cities. From the perspective of the entire hydrosphere, seawater accounts for about 97.5% of the entire hydrosphere, while the freshwater resources that can really be directly used by human beings only account for 0.00768%, in an extremely limited quantity. Water shortage is a serious shackle to the development of urbanization. It is reported by a study that nearly half of the world's river water resources are seriously polluted, climate change reduces rainfall, and freshwater resources are in an alarming shortage. Many developed cities such as Houston, Jakarta, Los Angeles, Warsaw, Cairo, Lagos, Dhaka, São Paulo, Mexico City, Singapore, Beijing, and Shanghai, are facing the dilemma of water shortage. Most cities in China are short of water, a lot of lakes are eutrophic, and plenty of rivers run dry.

China's total amount of water resources ranked sixth in the world, but its per capita amount ranked only 110th, close to the level of moderate water shortage. In 2009, China's total amount of water resources was 2.8 trillion cubic meters, including 0.83 trillion cubic meters of groundwater. According to the internationally accepted standard, per capita water resources below 3,000 cubic meters is a mild water shortage; per capita water resources below 2,000 cubic meters is a moderate water shortage; per capita water resources below 1,000 cubic meters is a severe water shortage; and per capita water resources below 500 cubic meters is an extreme water shortage. China's current per capita water resources is only 2,140 cubic meters, which is only one-fourth of the world's average, and some areas in the north and west have already experienced severe water shortage.[18] In 2014, more than 300 of the 657 cities in China belonged to the cities of "severe water shortage" and "water shortage" according to the UN-HABITAT evaluation standards. In terms of the composition of China's water resources, agricultural water use accounts for 61%, industrial water use accounts for 24%, and water use by urban residents only accounts for 13%. Cities are faced with prominent contradictions between supply and demand of water resources, a fragile water environment and great pressure on water security. Chinese cities have a great potential for water conservation. From 2000 to 2012, the per capita daily consumption of domestic water by urban residents decreased from 220 liters to 172 liters. In the past 10 years, the national urbanization rate has increased by 10% points, the population of water users has increased by 49.6%, but the total annual consumption of water in cities has only increased by 12%, basically stabilized at 50 billion cubic meters. Also, the annual wastewater recycling volume is 3.21 billion cubic meters, accounting for about 6% of the total water consumption by cities.[19]

The shortage of land resources is becoming an important manifestation of "urban diseases". Land is a basic condition for the expansion and development of urban spaces. "Land is gold" indicates the important role of land in urban construction. Land finance and the real estate industry are important pillars of urban development and have affected the production and life of every citizen in Chinese cities in recent years. The social and economic development of the country cannot be achieved without land resources, which are irreplaceable, thus being a kind of valuable and limited resource. For cities, land resources are a limited and non-renewable natural resource, and the misuse of land resources to seek short-term development is undesirable and will threaten the long-term development of a country and a city. Under the existing market economy, it becomes important for local governments at all levels to think about how to maximize the benefits of limited urban land resources, thereby expanding the economic aggregate of cities, improving their carrying capacity, enhancing their ability to absorb labor, and improving their overall competitiveness.[20] The scientific adjustment of urban land relations, protection, and development of urban land resources, the rational use of urban land, the protection of the legitimate rights and interests of land owners and users, and the promotion of sustainable social and economic development of cities are important tasks for urban development. The demand for limited land resources is constantly increasing due to the rising use of land for urban construction, overpopulation expansion and the "pie-spreading" development of cities. Land is gold in big cities, especially in downtown areas, where not only is the urban space above ground used, with numerous high-rise buildings and skyscrapers, but also the underground space is fully utilized. The problem of a shortage of land resources is still difficult to be alleviated.

3.2.5 Social problems

Social problems are typical symptoms of "urban diseases" and a key issue affecting the sustainable economic and social development and harmony and stability of cities. Urban social problems are reflected in various aspects such as urban poverty, urban employment, urban mental illnesses, juvenile delinquency, and urban beggars.

3.2.5.1 Urban poverty

Despite the well-developed economy of cities, it is difficult to alleviate the disparity between rich and poor and polarization. The problem of urban poverty is an important factor affecting the harmony and stability of cities and an important dilemma in the treatment of "urban diseases". Slums are an unavoidable social phenomenon in many cities during the process of industrialization and urbanization. The poor lack land and income sources and are concentrated in cities, especially in slums, such as Mumbai, India, and Sao Paulo, Brazil. Due to the heavy concentration of the poor, the housing, medical, educational, health, and traffic conditions are poor, and because of poverty, crimes are frequent, and young people who cannot receive normal education mostly become a factor of social instability. The urban poor are struggling at the poverty line and find it difficult to enjoy the fruits of modern urban development and the basic benefits and public services as ordinary urban residents. This huge economic difference causes emotional disconnection in urban communities, and some slums are controlled by gangs and have become dens of urban crime and an important hazard for the public security of cities.

The problem of urban poverty exists together with the problems of urban society. It is difficult to attract widespread attention and find solutions by local government and the society, thus becoming a discordant factor in urban social life. Disparities between the rich and the poor in cities, an increasing poor population and an increase in unemployment lead to the risks of social disharmony and instability. Many social problems such as fighting and brawling, spreading crime, prostitution, and begging put great pressure on social stability.[21] Various old and new conflicts are intertwined, urban residents are dissatisfied with urban construction and demolition, compensation and other issues, and unemployment, social security, distribution system, and social equity of the poor class have not been effectively solved. All of these problems intensify urban instability and disharmony.

3.2.5.2 Urban employment

Urban employment is an important facet of "urban diseases". Despite the facts that there are many enterprises, abundant information, and employment opportunities in cities, for various reasons, the high unemployment rate is a major headache for city governments. The competition for employment in cities is extremely fierce. In the period of economic downturn and recession, enterprises are closing down one after another, especially in resource-based cities where the number of layoffs is increasing dramatically due to the industrial decline. Widespread unemployment can trigger social instability and discord. Urban employment is not only an issue at the economic level, but also a big problem at the social level and family level. Cities with densely distributed resources and countless employment opportunities can attract a large inflowing population, who go to the city in order to find opportunities to get rich, and look for channels and platforms to achieve business success. Some are successful, but most of them are unemployed. The high unemployment rate is bound to turn into urban social problems. In particular, those who lack skills, educational diplomas, social connections, and other skills, such as migrant workers and laid-off workers, are facing the pressure of unemployment. The lack of social security and other assistance leads to material, mental, and psychological confusion, which further trigger begging, gangsterism, stealing, and other undesirable behaviors and even criminal acts, and this situation affects the social stability and harmony of cities. At the same time, the accumulation of "urban diseases" results in serious bottlenecks to resources and energy, environmental deterioration, industrial decline, or elimination and closure, which generates new unemployed workers and turns into new problems of urban employment.

3.2.5.3 Urban mental illnesses, juvenile delinquency, beggars, etc.

In cities, there is a large population. The pursuit of material benefits leads to a lack of humanistic care, materialistic, and profit-oriented relationships among people, increased external pressure, and reduced communication with each other, which further cause psychological disorders such as depression in urban residents. Depression can decrease the productivity of patients and impose a heavy economic burden on society. Faced with big external changes, many people cannot cope with the external environment and must adapt psychologically. Long-term discomfort causes impatience and disturbed psychological rhythm in people, and creates a sense of depression because they feel they cannot keep up with the rhythm. The problem of depression is one of the pathological problems that cannot be ignored in our country.

In addition to the problem of urban mental illnesses, juvenile delinquency is also a problem. Because of the early physiological and psychological development of adolescents, their need for sex becomes stronger. Some adolescents lack a sense of social responsibility, are indifferent to others, have poor self-discipline, lack the objective comparison and evaluation of what has happened in the outside world, and like to get into the limelight. All of these factors are important reasons for juvenile delinquency. Other important reasons include unharmonious family relations, family education short of care and that is unhealthy for young people, the formation of various deviant and incorrect values, violence, pornography, superstitious books and newspapers, audio and video products, and electronic information products on the society and the Internet.

The issue of beggars is also an important manifestation of "urban diseases". It is difficult to manage beggars due to their concealment, mobility, and uncertain identity. In history, beggars are closely related to the difficulties of some people in life. Theoretically, with the improvement of living standards, the quantity of beggars should be reduced, but in fact begging becomes a profession. People's living standards continue to improve, but the number of beggars is increasing sharply, and the structure and nature of beggar groups have undergone significant changes. Beggars use modern technology and traffic, invent new means and styles of begging, and constitute beggar groups of a complex structure, thus becoming a major problem in urban management and an important manifestation of "urban diseases". Beggars are also difficult to count and manage in terms of scale and quantity, because their composition is very complex, including the elderly, the sick, and disabled, women, children, and teenagers. The behavior of begging tends towards becoming a profession, begging means and styles are being innovated, and crimes inside and outside of beggar groups are very serious. All of these factors are important hazards to the harmony and stability of cities and cannot be eradicated. The number of vagrant beggars in cities is expanding and they are developing towards organization, diversification, and criminalization, which pose many problems to social governance. This phenomenon should be controlled by improving the relevant laws and regulations, vigorously developing the economy, establishing an effective system of social security, and strengthening the management and guidance of underage vagrant beggars.[22]

3.3 Phased characteristics of the evolution of "urban diseases"

"Urban diseases" are objective social phenomena in the process of urban development, which exist to varying degrees in cities of both developed and developing countries. The evolution of "urban diseases" has certain objective laws. "Urban diseases" are comprehensive reflections of various problems confronted in the process of urban development and transformation, behind the expansion of city size, the concentration of population, deep-seated contradictions in economic and social development. In different periods of development, the embodiments of "urban diseases" are different. Generally speaking, the law of urban evolution follows the typical phases of rapid growth of central urban areas, suburbanization, and metropolitanization, each of which has different characteristics and faces different "urban diseases".

Considering the evolutionary laws of cities, the phased characteristics of "urban diseases" can be analyzed and summarized.

3.3.1 Main phases of urban evolution

3.3.1.1 The phase of the growth of central urban areas

With the increasing number of factories in central urban areas, there is a vast influx of labor force year by year, and the demand for housing, traffic, education, health care, etc., is increasing. This leads to the growth of central urban areas, and "urban diseases" are becoming increasingly prominent. In the early period of Western countries, the rapid industrial development brought about rapid urbanization. The concentration of capital, population, traffic, and other factors in central urban areas made it difficult to balance the allocation of resources and demands for public services. The increasing number of factories increased the demands for public services such as traffic, housing, education, and medical care, while the satisfaction of these demands could not keep pace with the expansion of city size, the carrying capacity of resources and energy in cities decreased, and the urban environment began to deteriorate. Serious "urban diseases" occurred in the early industrialized and urbanized Western cities, such as the smog in London, and serious problems of environmental pollution, increasing morbidity and mortality in such cities as Tokyo and New York.

3.3.1.2 The phase of suburbanization

Central urban areas are expanding, "urban diseases" are aggravated and there is a trend for industries and population to move out to suburbs, namely this is the suburbanization phase. Suburbanization is a phase in which the population, industries, and businesses move from central urban areas to suburbs after the high concentration of population and industries, and the population in central areas declines greatly. Suburbanization is a phase in the process of urban development, which are both an extension of the urban lifestyle and an evolution of urban territorial structure.[23] With urban economic development and population expansion, it is objectively inevitable to expand to the outskirts of cities, to suburbs, and suburbanization has a huge spatial demand, developmental momentum, and market potential. Suburbanization is the result of the rapid development of industries, accelerated technological innovation and progress, improvement in urban residents' living standards, and enhancement of environmental awareness. The overcrowding of population and industries leads to a decrease in the carrying capacity of resources, energy, and the environment in central urban areas, which inevitably requires cities to expand or move out to suburbs. According to the objective laws and realities of the development of large cities abroad, the development of suburbanization goes through these processes.

A Sleeping City. This means that urban residents live in suburbs and work in central urban areas. In the late industrialization period of Western countries, the "big city diseases" emerged. Some rich people bought villas in the suburbs to enjoy the natural scenery and fresh air, while low-income citizens or inflowing population lived in suburbs to save a lot of rental costs, but they drove or took buses or subways to work in central urban areas during the day and went back to the suburbs to rest at night. This was a primary phase of suburbanization. Urban planning lacked scientific, forward-looking and strategic guidance, and did not adequately predict the "urban diseases" caused by the expansion of urbanization. Urbanization was just equivalent to the urbanization of the population, and urban expansion and outward migration were mainly the outward diffusion of the population and related production factors, thus resulting in the spatial dispersion and waste of resources. The problems of "urban diseases" could not be curbed fundamentally. Urban expansion was characterized by a disorderly "pie-spreading" pattern, separation of work and residence and the phenomenon of the sleeping city, such as Tiantongyuan and Tongzhou in Beijing and Yanjiao in Hebei, where there are no industries. Big waves of people going to work in central areas of the city increased the traffic pressure and reduced the living satisfaction of urban residents, and the long-distance travel caused physical and mental exhaustion.

Satellite City. The phenomenon of the sleeping city reflects serious problems of "urban diseases". With the urbanization of sleeping cities, suburbs could provide relatively low-cost land or housing for rent, and create conditions for the migration of some enterprises. Infrastructure in suburbs was improving, railway and buses connecting central areas and suburbs of cities were continuously improved, enterprises expanded in suburbs, and part of the suburban residents could be employed nearby, avoiding the long-standing life of getting to work at 9:00 in the morning and off work at 5:00 in the afternoon, and solving the problems of crowded subways and buses. High land prices and environmental pollution costs in central cities compelled factories and enterprises to move out and usher into the tide of industrial suburbanization. Intense business competitions in central urban areas and rising demands for business in suburbs could create market space for the migration of business enterprises. A large number of shopping malls, supermarkets, and shopping centers in central urban areas set up subcenters and branches in suburbs and provided services to suburban residents, so suburbs became relatively independent satellite cities instead of just sleeping cities.

Edge City. With further industrialization, urbanization, and informatization, suburbs are no longer villages or an urban-rural fringe in the traditional sense, but areas with new urban functions, and the service sector and offices are suburbanized, in other words, they proceed to the phase of the edge city. Since 1960, developed countries in the West and their cities have paid more and more attention to the functional radiation and development of suburbs, with service sectors such as commerce, hotels, science and technology, education, medical care, sports, culture, and fitness marching to the suburbs. The improved conditions of traffic and communication and network technologies changed the plight of isolation in traditional suburbs, high-class residential buildings, high-grade office buildings, and star-rated hotels began to run business in suburbs, suburban satellite cities started to become highly industrialized, and urban functions were spread and extended to suburbs. Suburbs became new edge cities, new centers of agglomeration after the spread of central cities and economic growth poles at the edge. This phase is the mature phase of suburbanization.

Suburbanization does not necessarily mean the expansion towards suburbs due to the development of cities, but suburbs need to enjoy the fruits of modern urban development. Suburbs greatly contribute to the urbanization of suburbs by developing industries, attracting industrial and mining enterprises and commerce, constantly improving the construction of urban infrastructures, accelerating urban–rural integration, and closely linking and integrating cities and suburbs together. It can be said that suburbanization alleviates the overconcentration of the population, housing shortage and traffic congestion in central urban areas, improves the urban production and living environment, alleviates the problems of "urban diseases" in central urban areas, promotes urban–rural coordination, and coordinated regional economic development, facilitates the coverage of urban functions and equalized supply of public services in a larger scope, improves the environmental quality of central urban areas, and helps to ease urban economic and social problems.

However, on the other hand, suburbanization is not urbanization based on maintaining the rural atmosphere of traditional suburbs. In reality, the suburbanization in many cities is actually the urbanization of suburbs, that is to say, suburbs become new urban areas and have the problems of "urban diseases" inherent in central urban areas. A study of the phenomenon of suburbanization in the United States of America argued that suburbanization had a great impact on post-war economic development and was one of the important reasons for the strong economic growth of the United States of America in the post-war period, but suburbanization was achieved at the cost of depleting resources and encroaching on the land. Suburbanization led to the occupancy of large amounts of resources and land space, compression of rural space, and an unsustainable model of urban suburbanization. According to the proportion of the population, Americans consumed far more land and mineral resources than other countries, and caused more serious damage to natural landscapes and ecological environments, which were costs that other countries could not afford.[24] The large-scale development of suburbanization in Western countries, represented by the United States of America, had a far-reaching impact on the world's process of urbanization and on global socio-economic development. The urban sprawl, spatial expansion, massive consumption of resources and ecological deterioration accompanied the process of suburbanization and resulted in new "urban diseases". It is unscientific and unsustainable to simply learn from and imitate the suburbanization process of cities in Western countries. Suburbanization is an inevitable result of the development of modern cities to a certain stage, and it also brings about a series of realistic problems of land use. Suburbanization should treat the land issue correctly. In particular, when making plans for urban development, it should adhere to the strategy of sustainable use of suburban land resources, conserve land, plan scientifically, accelerate the construction of suburban roads and other supporting infrastructure, and promote the process of suburbanization.[25] Therefore, if suburbanization is simply turned into the urbanization of suburbs and rural land is simply turned into urban land without ecological protection, the planning of natural space and the construction of related facilities, suburbanization may become an extension and expansion of "urban diseases", and this is not conducive to the long-term sustainable development of suburbs.

3.3.1.3 Metropolitanization

Metropolitanization is an advanced stage of the current urbanization development in developed Western countries.[26] A further urbanization after suburbanization is metropolitanization. It means the continuous expansion of cities turns all of the surrounding suburbs into relatively developed urban areas. A metropolitan area refers to a large city at the core extending toward many suburbs, small and medium-sized towns and urban–rural fringe in the outskirts, which are connected with the large city through subway, rapid transit and light railways, thus having strong commuting functions. With the improvement of supporting facilities, these areas are constantly integrated into central urban areas and take over some functions of central urban areas to shape a large city circle. In the 1950s, the United States of America first defined the concept of a metropolitan area, which is based on counties, with the core city having a population of 50,000 or more and a high degree of economic, social, and cultural relevance of the core city with neighboring counties.

The accelerated expansion of central urban areas turns surrounding suburbs or small and medium-sized towns into important parts or urban nodes of the city circle or metropolitan area, and hence suburbs become important parts in the metropolitan area. Suburbs become new towns around central urban areas, take over industrial and commercial enterprises from central urban areas, and rise to the new economic heights for the concentration of population and industries. There are also workers who work across administrative districts, with hundreds of thousands of commuters migrating from suburbs to central urban areas every day. Some people living in central urban areas also go to work in suburbs, such as Yanjiao in Hebei, Kunshan in Jiangsu, and Xianyang in Shaanxi. Residents of these suburbs go to work in central urban areas every day, and institutions in central urban areas have affiliated departments stationed in the suburbs. Yanjiao attracts institutions and colleges affiliated with state ministries, such as the Beijing College of Social Administration, the Transportation Management Institute of the Ministry of

Transport, and the North China Institute of Science and Technology. With the improvement of suburban housing, traffic, commercial facilities, culture and sports, science and technology, health care and other supporting facilities, the spatial structure and population distribution of suburban towns continuously form and develop towards maturity, and the pattern of a metropolitan area may take shape. For example, the subway from Shanghai to Kunshan, Jiangsu has opened and is accelerating the process of the urbanization of Kunshan, whose integration into the Shanghai metropolitan area has become a reality. Xianyang in Shaanxi plans to build a subway line to Xi'an. The Pinggu subway line of Beijing links to Yanjiao Town and Sanhe City, so it is not far away for these areas to be integrated into the Beijing metropolitan area.

It can be found that metropolitanization is an advanced stage of the development of suburbs, which basically change from agricultural areas in the traditional sense to economic heights with a high degree of integration of modern industry, commerce, agriculture, and other industries. Industries in central urban areas continue to radiate and migrate to the surrounding suburbs or nearby towns due to land cost, labor cost, and raw material cost. The production function of central urban areas is weakened and industries move away from central urban areas, while the service sector develops rapidly and the functions of social services and public administration are enhanced continuously. The development of the service sector in central urban areas can provide large quantities of jobs and opportunities. The knowledge-, labor- and technology-intensive services can attract more high-skilled, highly educated and capable talents, the development of subways, rapid buses, and small cars provides people living in suburbs, urban–rural fringe, or small and medium-sized towns around central urban areas with the possibility to work in central urban areas, and the population moves to towns and suburbs around central urban areas. The metropolitan area develops further, and suburbs also develop under the radiation of the metropolitan area, thus forming a metropolitan area or urban agglomeration of relatively closely-connected central urban areas, small and medium-sized towns and suburbs.

The metropolitanization of American cities is mainly manifested by the population growth of suburbs, which become parts of central urban areas. The central urban areas have well-developed commercial and related industries, extend or radiate to suburbs, and shape several small and medium-sized towns. Hence, suburbs gradually become parts of the city or central urban areas, and the city boundaries are extended outward to connect more small and medium-sized towns. Europe, Japan, and other developed countries and regions have experienced the process of metropolitanization. Compared with the growth phase of urban centers and the suburbanization phase, metropolitanization means a process of urbanization on a larger scale. Metropolitan areas are more of an urban clustering process across administrative regions, and their territorial scope is determined by commuting links, with the average commuting time not exceeding two hours one way. The phase of metropolitanization is mainly a state of urban spatial agglomeration driven by the self-expansion and market mechanism of cities. It is a spatial derivation under the law of unbalanced growth that has occurred in many developed countries and their cities. By decentralizing some urban functions, metropolitan areas overcome the spatial barriers to raising the level of an agglomeration economy and can achieve a higher level of an agglomeration economy on a larger spatial scale.[27]

There are also "urban diseases" in the phase of metropolitanization. It has been pointed out by a related study that metropolitanization is primarily embodied by the polycentric clusters of various types of cities that are formed in the process of metropolitanization, the distribution of resource factors are more unbalanced in metropolitan areas, and the segregation of resources and administrative divisions lead to more chaos and disorder and bring about the "Balkanization" of regional governance, which refers to the fragmentation of local authorities in many localities and the resulting fragmentation under the systems of local governments. Mumford depicted the disorderly development of metropolitan areas as "a huge, deformed mass that spreads out in all directions".[28] The diseases of a particular city can be treated through political control and effective means of the local government. However, it is difficult to form a unified administrative agency or organization to centrally manage metropolitan areas with different administrative divisions, and many problems fall within the scope of metropolitan areas, which makes management more difficult and organization weaker. Once the problems of "urban diseases" emerge, they involve a larger scope and become more difficult to solve.

The evolution of "urban diseases" is a series of economic, social, cultural, environmental, and political problems that emerge along with the expansion and economic development of cities, and the laws of urban evolution also reflect the evolutionary process of urban functions. The problems in matching the process of urbanization and urban functions result in the characteristics of "urban diseases" at different phases. To examine the manifestations and characteristics of "urban diseases" and their prevention and treatment, we need to accurately judge the phases and functions of cities, and then take effective countermeasures according to the characteristics and their intrinsic causes.

3.3.2 Analysis of the phased characteristics of the evolution of "urban diseases"

The general phases and laws of urban evolution are briefly explained above. It can be found that in the evolutionary process, as the size of cities expands, various problems accumulate and cause typical "urban diseases". It is of great significance to select the scientific countermeasures and suggestions by analyzing the phased characteristics of the evolution of "urban diseases" and consider the phase of formation and the causes of specific "urban diseases".

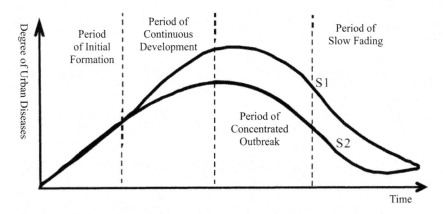

Figure 3.1 Inverted U-shaped curve for the evolution of "urban diseases".

As an inherent feature of the construction and development of modern cities, "urban diseases" are objective existences that do not depend on human will, and most cities have more or less varied types of "urban diseases". It can be said that "urban diseases" have been developing along with the evolution of cities, and are the inherent pressure and driving force of sustainable urban economic and social development. "Urban diseases" not only change with the development of the times, but are also closely related to the development level of urbanization. Different cities have different levels of development, and the embodiments and degree of their "urban diseases" are also different. If the evolutionary phases of "urban diseases" are divided, according to the general laws of urban evolution, they can fall into four phases, namely the phase of initial formation, the phase of continuous development, the phase of concentrated outbreak, and the phase of slow decline. These four phases show an asymmetric inverted U-shaped structure, as shown in Figure 3.1.[29]

3.3.2.1 Period of initial formation

The rate of urbanization in this period is relatively low, about 30% or less. Cities develop late and their size is small. Most of people are from a rural or agricultural population, and a small portion of market towns provide basic household supplies for farmers living in the surrounding areas. Economic development is backward, education, health care, science, and technology are not well developed, the scale of the city is in the primary stage, and the problems of "urban diseases" are not serious. However, because the related urban infrastructure is not well developed, urban public services are lagging behind, there is no concentration effect of industry and population, and urban functions are not complete. These can be regarded as "urban diseases" in small cities or in the period of initial formation, without "urban diseases of big cities" such as traffic congestion, population expansion, and environmental pollution.

3.3.2.2 Period of continuous development

The rate of urbanization in this period is 30–50%. The increasing urban population, the concentration of enterprises and industries, the development of cities towards suburbanization, and continuous convergence of population and industries bring pressure on the population, resources, and the environment. The structure of supply and demand of urban resources is unbalanced, such as traffic congestion in small and medium-sized towns during commuting which is the same as that in big cities. Residents suffer from the increasingly serious environmental pollution in local areas caused by the clustering of high-polluting enterprises. The underdeveloped construction of infrastructure leads to the obvious problems of a housing shortage, schooling difficulties, and difficulties in accessing medical care. Social contradictions and conflicts in urban villages, urban–rural fringe, and semi-urbanized areas become intensified, and pose the problems of a widening gap between the rich and the poor, an increase in the number of jobless people and social crimes in cities.

3.3.2.3 Period of concentrated outbreak

During this period, the rate of urbanization reaches 50–70%. The urban population dominates the entire regional population, while the rural population accounts for a relatively small proportion. Most of people work and live in cities, and large and medium-sized cities further evolve into extra-large cities and metropolises and form metropolitan areas. The problems of "urban diseases" accumulated during the period of continuous development have not been treated promptly and are further embodied in this period, including traffic congestion, population expansion, frequent smoggy weather, ecological deterioration, serious water pollution, housing shortage. These systematic problems result in the concentration of unemployed people, and many middle and lower classes live in very small rooms like ants. There are problems of an aging population before getting rich, severe public security in slums, a widening gap between the rich and the poor, and a lack of a sense of social security and happiness.

3.3.2.4 Period of slow fading

In this period, the rate of urbanization reaches over 80–90%, urbanization has reached a high level, the process of urbanization is basically completed, the urban functions are basically perfected, and the good urban space has already become harmonious and livable through the treatment of "urban diseases" and construction. At this moment, the problems of "urban diseases" have been alleviated, some of them have been basically solved, and the symptoms of "urban diseases" are fading.

As the "urban diseases" were not effectively treated in the previous period, it can have a path-dependent effect on the urban development in the later period, so that the "urban diseases" in the previous period will continue and many new "urban diseases" will be added in the later period. This makes it more difficult to treat "urban diseases". In the periods of concentrated outbreak and slow fading, there is an urgent need for the government and its social organizations to coordinate in the treatment of "urban diseases". If this is effective, the systemic risks posed by "urban diseases" can be reduced and cities can evolve towards a healthier, safer and more livable direction; otherwise, the impact will be even worse. If the government, social organizations, enterprises and citizens attach great importance to and promptly intervene on and control them, urbanization can avoid the concentrated outbreak of "urban diseases" and gradually step into a favorable state of operations, and "urban diseases" can proceed to the period of slow fading earlier, as shown by the state indicted by curve S2 in Figure 3.1. If "urban diseases" cannot be treated well, they will become more serious, and cities need to pay more costs, as shown by the state indicted by curve S1 in Figure 3.1. Of course, during the period of slow fading, the city may not necessarily be in a healthy state, and unexpected major social crisis events may bring about systemic risks to the city. It is also possible that a global economic crisis could bring about a decline in the city's leading industries, and the result may be that the city's economy could be affected and unemployment would increase. As a result, "urban diseases" may recur or evolve into new "urban diseases". Since "urban diseases" always accompany the process of urban evolution, the inverted U-shaped curve may be stretched or compressed with the extension of the time axis, and reflect the coexistence of asymmetric evolution, continuous extension, oscillation, and a local steady state.[30]

3.3.3 Urban functions and the evolution of "urban diseases"

The process of urban evolution is mainly manifested by the continuous concentration of population and industries, the increase in the size of cities, enhancing strategic position, and accumulation of various resource elements to form scale benefits and agglomeration effects, which results in cities being bound to carry a variety of urban functions. Urban functions are also changing along with urban development. Especially against the background of globalization, informatization, knowledge, and networking, the development of metropolitan areas or urban agglomerations has become an inevitable trend of global economic and social development, part of the urban functions are continuously enhanced, some functions are transferred, evacuated, or replaced with the increase in the size of the cities and also some functions are undertaken by other nodes in the region or globally. The changes in the positioning and spatial layout of urban functions, especially the core functions, become an important cause of various "urban diseases". According to some studies, the core functions in the process of urban development can be divided into the following categories:[31]

Controlling functions. They are mainly reflected in the functions of attraction and control over external resource elements. These controls are manifested in the capabilities of cities to manage, govern and compete in various aspects such as economy, society, culture, and politics in the region. The controlling functions can have the attractiveness, leadership and control necessary to accumulate external resources, integrate, and regulate various kinds of resources, and promote their own sustainable development, which mainly involves the functions of finance, trade, shipping, international politics, high-end industries, innovation, culture, high-end consumption, and other aspects. The stronger and more controlling these functions are, the more obvious the core competitiveness of cities is, the more distinctive and competitive they are, and the higher their international status and economic dominance.

Fundamental functions. They are mainly reflected as the basic services and functions that must be provided for the normal operation of cities, so as to satisfy the basic services of urban traffic, housing, health, education, medical care, infrastructure, communication, information, security, etc. The fundamental functions are different from the controlling functions because they are the basic service functions that are generally available and necessary for cities, and the fundamental conditions and basic tools that are necessary for the production and life of residents in the urban spaces. Taking the traffic function as an example, cities are generally formed because of the well-developed traffic, and they must provide and create the convenient function of a traffic hub and the basic means of transportation for residents. In terms of the medical health function, cities must establish various types of large hospitals to meet the needs of residents to see doctors, as well as the needs of surrounding areas, including suburbs and rural areas, for the treatment and diagnosis of major diseases. The functions of education, communication, security, and housing are all essential to cities.

Migratory functions. They are mainly reflected as those undertaken by cities but can be taken over by surrounding areas as the regional development and urban boundaries continue to expand. The functions of central urban areas can be replaced or extinguished without affecting their operational functions, such as non-metropolitan agriculture, high-pollution manufacturing, and low-quality housing. Migratory functions can also be called moving-out functions, which refer to the migration of the functions of agriculture and manufacturing to other areas or spaces in order to alleviate various problems in urban areas without affecting the normal operations of the area. They can even improve the effective performance of the fundamental and controlling functions of the area. In other words, migratory functions are optional. If reviewed on this condition, too many urban functions can lead to the decreasing bearing capacity of urban resources, energy, and the environment and can then cause "urban diseases". The treatment of "urban diseases" requires the decentralization and migration of these functions, which can effectively relieve the urban pressure and improve the operational efficiency of cities.

The controlling, fundamental, and migratory functions reflect the phased characteristics of urban evolution and the close relationship between these functions and cities. The change and recombination of these functions can lead to the incidence of many "urban diseases", and the evolution of "urban diseases" is related to either insufficient or excessive functions. For example, in the phase of the development of urbanization, some functions are insufficient and cause the incidence of "urban diseases"; in the initial phase of urbanization, the fundamental functions are insufficient, and the construction of infrastructure, education, health care, housing, and traffic cannot match the urbanization of the population, which inevitably leads to traffic congestion, high housing prices, environmental pollution, and many other problems. In the late phase of urbanization, especially in the phase of metropolitanization, due to the expansion of cities, central urban areas cannot carry too many functions, but plenty of migratory functions are still arranged in central urban areas, which can certainly aggravate "urban diseases". Particularly, in the phase of forming the controlling functions, a large number of resource elements, including high-quality resources, are overly concentrated in central urban areas with limited space, which increases the pressure of regional fundamental functions. The concentration of many resources such as information, technology, education, and medical health, more employment opportunities and larger space for development in central urban areas can attract greater numbers of people and industries, and intensify "urban diseases" in central urban areas. This leads to the superposition of problems and pressures at a certain phase of development. The controlling functions are reflected more in the phase of the growth of central cities, the migratory functions are reflected more in the phase of metropolitanization, and the fundamental functions are reflected more in the whole process of urban development, they have different forms and different functional demands at different phases of urban development and result in the problems of "urban diseases" in each phase,[32] as shown in Figure 3.2.

3.4 Intrinsic linkage of industrial transformation and the evolution of "urban diseases"

Industries are important pillars of urban economic and social development and can lay an important foundation for sustainable urban development. The evolution of "urban diseases", which is closely linked to the development of urban industries, is generated and developed with the rise in, development of, prosperity of, and decline in urban industries. The formation of many "urban diseases" is closely related to the continuous concentration of urban industries, to the increase in the size of cities and to population expansion.

100 Law of the evolution of "urban diseases"

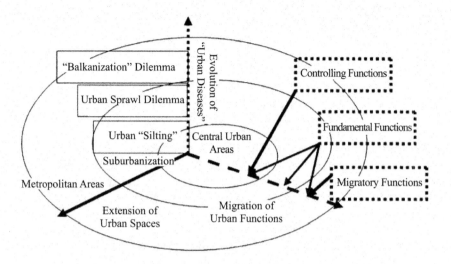

Figure 3.2 Relationship of phases of urban development, urban functions and "urban diseases".

Industrial development that is too-rapid and over-concentrated leads to a shortage of land supply, high prices of land and housing, insufficient water and land, and a serious mismatch among roads, traffic facilities, public cultural facilities, and green infrastructure and the total population. The experience of the evolution of cities abroad indicates that industrial development and transformation dominate the expansion and spatial evolution of cities, which is an important cause for the concentration and spread of the urban population and a critical reason for the incidence of "urban diseases". Especially with the continuous advancement of industrialization, informatization, and urbanization, resources are concentrated in big cities, and the mismatch between urban economic and social development and the existing carrying capacity of resources, energy, and the environment leads to the rapid outbreak of deep-seated conflicts and "urban diseases". The expansion of urban industries is constrained by the bottleneck of resources and energy, and the upgrading of economic structure creates new demands for the model of urban operations, thus resulting in the evolution of "urban diseases". The internal mechanism is manifested in the following aspects.

3.4.1 Expansion of urban industries constrained by multiple resources

The incidence of "urban diseases" is closely related to the industrial conditions. In particular, the over-expansion of the industrial scale leads to an over-concentration of the local population and enterprises, while the bearing capacity of resources, the environment, traffic, housing, and other resources of cities cannot keep up with the development, resulting in many "urban diseases". Therefore, strengthening industrial transformation is an important aspect in treating "urban diseases". Generally speaking, industrial transformation can be divided into two phases: industrialization and post-industrialization. The process of industrialization speeds up and promotes industrial development, which then attracts a large number of people and boosts the increase in the size of cities. The early and accelerated periods of industrialization are the periods of concentrated outbreaks of "urban diseases". The Industrial Revolution drives the emancipation of productive forces and actively impels machine-based mass production, the urban industries rapidly expand and the demand for resources and energy increase. However, the limited resources and energy of cities lead to the deepening of the contradiction between supply and demand and the upper limit of the carrying capacity of resources, which become important bottlenecks that restrain the expansion of the city in size. There is a lack of forward-looking planning in the early phase of industrialization, the extensive economic development aggravates the speed of consumption of resources and energy, and the environmental pollution becomes worse. For example, London in the UK, New York in the USA, and Tokyo in Japan have experienced serious urban environmental pollution due to extensive industrial development in the early phase of industrialization, because it distorted the allocation of urban resources, and the rapid growth of the urban population and inadequate infrastructure cause the problems of "urban diseases".

In the phase of late industrialization or early post-industrialization, some developed countries and cities accelerate their industrial transformation and improve their planning of urban spaces and functional configuration, but the "urban diseases" accumulated by large-scale concentration of the population cannot be alleviated in a short period of time. For example, these problems still exist, such as traffic congestion, exhaust emissions of motor vehicles, waste treatment, pollution due to urban noise, water shortage. The progress of industrialization continues to advance, cities strengthen their industrial restructuring, transformation, and upgrading, some polluting industries are eliminated, transformed or migrated, and central urban areas retain the high-quality industries with low energy consumption. The production services and life services are rapidly developed in central urban areas, and the urban functions are improved. However, population expansion has not been alleviated in central urban areas. The living standards of urban residents are rising, and their demands for social welfare and public services such as education, medical care, and culture are increasing, but the limited public services and non-equalized public facilities are not able to meet the needs of the growing population. This problem exists in many cities, and in China, it is serious in metropolises such as Beijing, Shanghai, and Guangzhou. Cities like London, New York, Tokyo, and the Ruhr area have accelerated their industrial transformation, migrated industries, increased the process of satellite towns and suburbanization, and adopted metropolitanization in order to boost urban expansion and industrial migration. The new urban patterns, systems, models and functions have impacted the traditional urban facilities, urban spaces, and urban governance models, and pose challenges to the treatment of "urban diseases". However, many cities have limited capacity for governance and appear to be at a loss and unable to cope with the complex and large scale of "urban diseases".

3.4.2 Challenges posed by urban transformation and upgrading to the traditional model of urban management

With the development of industrialization, urbanization, and informatization, the traditional cities are being transformed into modern cities, and urban transformation and upgrading pose serious challenges to the traditional model of urban management, which involves many fields such as economy, society, culture, and infrastructure. Urban economic and social development and the transformation and upgrading of industries are manifested as systematic changes, which challenge the traditional ruling and managing model of cities and require prompt responses to the diversified, multi-level and multi-domain consumer demands, and citizens have more demanding, detailed, and tedious requirements for city managers. Urban industrial transformation and economic and social upgrading are incompatible with the traditional model of urban management. These problems are "urban diseases". Urban industrial transformation, the optimization of economic structures, and the transformation of social structures require appropriate and prompt adjustments and changes in urban management. Only when the adjustments are proper or the changes are effective, can "urban diseases" be dealt with and treated well, otherwise urban development is bound to be hindered in various aspects. For example, London in the UK experienced the "urban diseases" of smog, population expansion, and traffic congestion in its process of industrialization. It strengthened the construction of new cities, and evacuated the population, industries, and traffic from central urban areas. Greater London planned to build scattered new towns in the suburbs, to establish industrial zones in the agricultural areas to attract new population and industry, to ease the pressure of population and traffic in London, and to treat the serious problem of environmental pollution. However, in the early phase of construction of new towns, there was a lack of effective management of the new towns, complete life service facilities and efficient commuting, and new towns could not satisfy the residence demands of some members of the population, and could not solve the problem of employment. This posed challenges to the traditional model of urban management, and urgently required new towns to accelerate the construction of traffic, public services, infrastructure, and other supporting facilities.

In the process of the economic and social upgrading, international cities, such as New York in the USA and Paris in France, were also faced with the challenges of various "urban diseases". These cities also experienced the typical suburbanization of residential functions in the early phase, when urban industries and populations spread to the suburbs, but the supporting functions were not perfect and posed new requirements and challenges to the model of urban operation and management. Therefore, it can be said that industrial development and urban development are processes that are mutually promoting and influencing. When the urban industries are not well developed, cities are too small and not popular, and it is difficult for cities to develop. As the urban industries continue to converge, enterprises concentrate, and the industries develop rapidly to attract a large population. Then, the urban population continues to increase, their attractiveness is enhanced, and the size of the city is forced to expand. Further development puts pressure on the carrying capacity of urban resources, energy, and the environment, and the problems of "urban diseases" are generated and worsened. When the scale of industrial expansion and sustainable development is constrained by the resource bottleneck, transformation and upgrading become necessary. The process of transformation can continuously have an impact on urban development, and industrial transformation can be regarded as the root cause of the incidence and evolution of various "urban diseases".[33]

Since the reform and opening-up, China has experienced an unprecedented process of industrialization and urbanization. The model of extensive economic growth and the path of industrial development characterized by high input, high consumption and high emissions supported the economic prosperity of cities for a short period of time, but at a high cost. They have caused the incidence of "urban diseases" in many aspects, such as deterioration of the ecological environment, the overexploitation of resources, traffic congestion, population expansion, and social conflicts. These problems are related to the phase of industrial transformation and share the common points with the evolution of "urban diseases" in other international cities. Of course, they also have their own characteristics.

3.5 Summary

This chapter analyzed the phased characteristics of the evolution of "urban diseases" by defining "urban diseases" and their main manifestations. Then, it examined the relationship between "urban diseases" and the functional orientation of central urban areas, and studied the imbalance between urban elements caused by different urban forms and different functional demands during different phases.

Defining the connotation of "urban diseases". There is not a widely recognized definition of the connotation of "urban diseases", which is interpreted by different researchers in different ways depending on their own research perspectives. In this book, so-called "urban diseases" are defined as the various problems, such as population expansion, traffic congestion, serious pollution, ecological deterioration, and social conflicts caused by the over-concentration of resources, excessive clustering of industries, and over-convergence of functions during the long-term development of cities.

Main manifestations of "urban diseases". Regarding the various manifestations of "urban diseases", some researchers indicate that rapid economic growth has accelerated the process of urbanization of China, and the urban population has grown dramatically. There are also a large number of "urban diseases" in large and medium-sized cities and even small and medium-sized towns in China. Entering the new era, China's progress of urbanization is accelerating, the rate of urbanization has been rising, and the problems of "urban diseases" are becoming increasingly serious. To be specific, they are manifested by population expansion, an aging population, traffic congestion, environmental pollution, shortage of resources, social problems, etc.

Phased characteristics of the evolution of "urban diseases". Generally speaking, the law of urban evolution follows the typical phases of rapid growth of central urban areas, suburbanization, and metropolitanization, each of which has different characteristics and faces different "urban diseases".

Internal links of industrial transformation and the evolution of "urban diseases". The evolution of "urban diseases" is closely linked to the development of urban industries, and they are generated and developed with the rise in, development of, prosperity of and decline in urban industries. The incidence of "urban diseases" is closely related to the continuous convergence of urban industries, enlarging the size of cities and population expansion. The expansion of urban industries is constrained by the bottleneck of resources and energy, and the upgrading of economic structures imposes new requirements for the model of urban operations, thus leading to the evolution of "urban diseases".

Notes

1 Song Yingchang, Explorations on the Treatment of "Urban Diseases of Big Cities", *City*, 2015(2).
2 Zhang Jingwu, Awareness, Concepts and Strategies: Discussion on "Urban Diseases" and Their Treatment, *City*, 2014(1).
3 Wang Ning, Defects in Spatial Structure and Treatment of "Urban Diseases" of Extra-large Cities, *Regional Economic Review*, 2015(1).
4 Zhang Jingwu, Awareness, Concepts and Strategies: Discussion on "Urban Diseases" and Their Treatment, *City*, 2014(1).
5 Liu Jiping and Liu Chenxiao, An Analysis of the Embodiments, Causes and Countermeasures of Urban Diseases in China, *Journal of Jiaozuo Teachers College*, 2014(2).
6 Li Gangyuan, An Analysis of the Urban Diseases in the UK and Their Treatment – An Inquiry into the Pattern of British Urbanization, *Journal of Hangzhou Teachers College (Social Sciences Edition)*, 2003(6); Wu Haiyan, Mexico City in Mexico: Poverty and Pollution Caused by Over-urbanization, Reference News, http://news.xinhuanet.com, March 1, 2013; Liu Lili, How Can Mexico City "Remove Smoke"?, *Xinhua Daily Telegraph*, September 29, 2014; Measures Taken by Los Angeles to Treat Smoke and Implications, http:/scitech.people.com.cn, March 3, 2014.

7 Tao Xidong, Inclusive Urbanization: The New Strategy of Urbanization in China, *City Planning Review*, 2013(7).
8 Zhang Yixiao, Ranking of World's Congested Cities: Chongqing and Tianjin Surpassed Beijing, *The Beijing News*, April 7, 2015.
9 Li Jiajie, What Is the Crux of Beijing's Traffic Congestion?, *Guangming Daily*, October 24, 2003.
10 The phenomenon of separation of work and residence, in a literal sense, is a problem caused by the long-distance commuting due to the separation of the place of work and the place of residence. It is also known as spatial dislocation or spatial separation of residence and job. In the 1960s, Kain, a scholar from Harvard University, first studied and proposed the problem of separation of work and residence, and his study mainly focused on the residential segregation in metropolitan areas and the relatively serious separation of work and residence of blacks in the United States of America. Due to the rapid development of industrialization and urbanization in the USA, the expansion of cities led to a concentration of the population in cities. The relatively low density of employment and population, distinct characteristics of land use by zoning, and an incomplete system of urban public transportation in most American cities resulted in the serious separation of work and residence of the low-income population in the United States of America. In China, a developing country, the lack of reasonable urban planning and design, underdeveloped public transportation, and high property prices and rents in central cities lead to an imbalanced distribution of resources and unequal public services, so there is also a relatively serious separation of work and residence in cities such as Beijing, Shanghai, Guangzhou, Shenzhen, and other megacities. Even in small and medium-sized towns, the separation of work and residence also exists to a certain extent. The separation of work and residence in China is mainly due to the spatial dislocation of residence and employment caused by the acceleration of suburbanization of residences in big cities and the slow decentralization of employment since the reform and opening-up. Qi Yunlei and Sun Shan, Sector Differences in Jobs-Housing Mismatch and Their Causes: A Case Study of Beijing Metropolitan Area, *Modern Urban Research*, 2015(1).
11 Wang Jiacheng, Clean Utilization and Structural Adjustment of Coal – An Inevitable Choice for the Sustainable Development of Coal in China, *Coal Economic Research*, 2003(4).
12 Fu Lili, 17 Cities of China Are Facing Serious Water Pollution, *Science and Technology Daily*, November 19, 2014.
13 Survey on Water Pollution of China in 2015: Current Situation of Urban Water Pollution, www.bjzq.com.cn/syjq/ShowArticle.asp?ArticleID=320251.
14 China's Water Pollution Is More Serious than Smog, www.nbd.com.cn/arti-cles/2015-03-01/899700.html.
15 Ministry of Ecology and Environment of the People's Republic of China, 2014 Annual Report on the Prevention and Control of Solid Waste Pollution in Large and Medium-sized Cities, *China Environment News*, January 5, 2015.
16 Seven of Top 10 World's Air Pollution Cities in China, http://gz.bendibao.com/news/2013115/content11472.shtml.
17 Zhang Jinggan, Resource Shortage in the Urbanization Process of China, *Urban Problems*, 2008(1).

18 Zhao Xiaohui and Fan Xi, Moderately in Short of Water in China, the Key Solving the Water Crisis Is Water Conservation, www.mwr.gov.cn/slzx/slyw/200404/t20040423_143805.html, April 23, 2004.
19 Du Yu and He Yuxin, 300 of 657 Cities Nationwide Is "Short of Water", *Beijing Daily*, May 18, 2014.
20 Yi Liqi, Current Situation of the Management of Urban Land Resources in China and Countermeasures, *Management Observer*, 2009(3).
21 Wang Dong, Urban Poverty and Social Problems in the Contemporary World, *Zhejiang Daily*, May 5, 2008.
22 Ding Xin, An Analysis of the Problem of Professional Beggars in China's Cities, *Heihe Journal*, 2008(8).
23 Xu Lin, On the Suburbanization of Chinese Feature and Countermeasures, *Journal of Fuqing Branch of Fujian Normal University*, 2009(4).
24 Wang Fengyun, Resources and Environment Cost in the Suburbanization of US Cities and Its Alarming Effects, *Shanghai Urban Management*, 2013(5).
25 Zhao Xiaohan, Study on Land Use in the Course of Suburbanization, *Journal of Huazhong Agricultural University (Social Science Edition)*, 2004(2).
26 Huangpu Yue, Zhang Jingxing, and Deng Huayuan, Metropolitanization: The New Characteristics of Urbanization in Metropolis Areas – A Case Study of Nanjing, *Modern Urban Research*, 2008(1).
27 Zhao Jian, An Appeal to Break Institutional Barriers of a Developing Metropolitan Area with a Bottom-line, *Journal of Beijing Jiaotong University*, 2015(1).
28 Yan Yanming, Research on the Evolution Mechanism and Prevention of Urban Diseases in the Process of Industrial Transformation, *Modern Economic Research*, 2012(11).
29 Yang Chuankai and Li Chen, Treatment of Urban Diseases against the Background of New Urbanization, *Reform of Economic System*, 2014(3).
30 Yang Chuankai and Li Chen, Treatment of Urban Diseases against the Background of New Urbanization, *Reform of Economic System*, 2014(3).
31 Yan Yanming, Research on the Evolutionary Mechanism and Prevention of Urban Diseases in the Process of Industrial Transformation, *Modern Economic Research*, 2012(11).
32 Yan Yanming, Research on the Evolutionary Mechanism and Prevention of Urban Diseases in the Process of Industrial Transformation, *Modern Economic Research*, 2012(11).
33 Yan Yanming, Research on the Evolutionary Mechanism and Prevention of Urban Diseases in the Process of Industrial Transformation, *Modern Economic Research*, 2012(11).

4 New York experience in the control of "urban diseases"

Perspective of cross-regional coordination

New York, the largest city in the USA and a well-known international metropolis, was once plagued by "urban diseases" such as concentration of many heavily polluting enterprises and industries in the core urban areas, overpopulation, traffic congestion, and environmental pollution. However, through effective control of "urban diseases", New York has become the most energy-efficient and environmentally friendly low-carbon city in the USA even though it still has skyscrapers, crowds, and busy streets. It has the lowest per capita carbon emissions among big cities in the United States of America, and the highest per capita public green space among big cities across the world. On the island of Manhattan where land is gold, 80% of the land area has become green spaces of the city, thus effectively avoiding problems such as serious urban pollution, insufficient carrying capacity of the environment, and squeezed ecological space. A systematic review of New York's experience in the treatment of "urban diseases" can provide an important reference for Beijing, as China's national capital and a world-class harmonious and livable city, in solving its problems of "urban diseases".

4.1 Critical problem: diseases caused by industrialization and urbanization

New York City in a narrow sense covers a total land area of 786 square kilometers and consists of five areas: Manhattan, Bronx, Brooklyn, Queens, and Staten Island. In a broad sense, it is called the Greater New York area, which comprises 26 counties and cities in New York, New Jersey, and Connecticut, with a land area of more than 32,400 square kilometers and a population of more than 16.8 million.[1] New York is the largest industrial base in the United States of America with a high level of industrialization and urbanization. The Industrial Revolution brought prosperity and rapid development to New York City, and as early as around 1920, New York had completed the process of urbanization. During its urbanization, New York encountered problems of "urban diseases".

First of all, the problems of population expansion and housing shortage caused by the rapid growth of the population. By 1921, the population

DOI: 10.4324/9781003272991-4

of New York City had reached 6.18 million, and the concentration of the population gave it a modern urban scale. By 1929, New York City had 188 skyscrapers, with a systematic urbanization. By 2003, the Greater New York Metropolitan Area had a population of 22 million. In the early period of industrialization, multifarious factories were concentrated in central urban areas and were causing a series of "urban diseases" such as population expansion. With the progress of urbanization, New York's rapid economic development attracted an influx of population, which made a series of "urban diseases" even more severe. From the 1820s to the 1920s, more than 11.3 million immigrants went to New York. The different nationalities, races, and religious beliefs of the immigrant population brought about countless conflicts with the urban culture and lifestyles and housing supply and put considerable pressure on the urban development of New York. The increase in population led to a shortage of housing supply, and the existing housing stock could not meet the housing needs of the immigrant population. At that time, a survey of the Manhattan housing market found that over half of the apartments had more than three people living in each apartment, and a small number of apartments had two people living in each apartment. In addition, social problems such as the growing gap between the rich and the poor and a high crime rate continuously plagued New York.

Second, the problem of citizens' illnesses caused by environmental pollution. In the early 20th century, air pollution in New York City was very serious because of excessive emissions from factories, and citizens suffered from emphysema, lung cancer, and many other diseases, which seriously affected their quality of life and survival. In 1910, only 5% of the people in New York City could survive to the age of 60, and 20% of young children could not live over the age of five. This could demonstrate that the ecological deterioration and environmental pollution were quite serious then, and citizens were suffering from diseases and poor health. The poor quality of air was a serious drawback of urbanization and industrialization in New York at that time.

Third, the problem of traffic congestion. In addition to the terrible ecological environment caused by the poor quality of the air and heavy and chemical industries, the traffic congestion and limited capacity of roads were also typical "urban diseases" in New York. In the 1920s, the automobile industry in New York grew rapidly and cars were quickly popularized in families, so that the roads were unable to meet the rapidly increasing demand for traffic, and traffic congestion became an increasingly serious problem.

4.2 Main phases: evolution from urbanization to suburbanization

Considering the problems of "urban diseases" caused by accelerated industrialization and urbanization, the government at all levels in New York City chose new strategies of development, accelerated urban planning, and transformed and evolved towards suburbanization based on the original urbanization. In the 1940s, New York started the process of suburbanization, and after 20 to 30 years of development, a lot of shopping malls and shopping centers were built in suburbs to meet the living and service needs of suburban residents, avoid traditional "urban diseases" such as traffic congestion caused by suburban residents going shopping in central urban areas, and achieve the goal of local consumption. With the increase in popularity and improvements of amenities, the value of the land in suburban areas appreciated upwards and many enterprises moved to suburbs and chose to invest in the development of suburbs. This led to the development and prosperity of suburban industries, and suburbs gradually realized part of urban functions. Many suburban residents shopped, lived, and worked locally, without having to repeat the daily work and life of commuting between suburbs and central urban areas. Suburbs became new towns and the destinations for work and life activities of many middle-class people. New York's evolution from urbanization to suburbanization effectively alleviated the problems of "urban diseases" through four phases, as shown in Table 4.1.

4.2.1 Suburbanization of urban residential functions

Modern cities can enjoy the convenience of the functions and amenities in life, traffic, and shopping, which attract more people to buy properties and houses in cities. However, the overcrowding of urban population and housing makes cities less convenient. Hence, the functions of housing and life services of these modern cities have migrated to suburbs, so that they can meet the living needs of suburban residents while alleviating the various pressures on central urban areas. New York solved the various problems of central urban areas by first focusing on the suburbanization of urban residential functions. In the early 20th century, most residents chose to work and live in central urban areas. As the size of cities expanded and the urban population increased, the living environment was continuously affected, and many citizens chose to live and work in suburbs. The increase in housing in suburbs and the constant improvement of living facilities enable the suburban environment to be improved continuously, so that suburbs could provide residents with a more comfortable and spacious living and working space with fresh air than central urban areas. In the 1950s, with the improvement of living standards, people aspired to living in suburbs and avoiding the overcrowded life in central urban areas. The suburbanization of New York City developed rapidly, and a large number of citizens moved to the suburbs, which became an important choice for citizens of New York then due to the development of highways, popularization of family cars, and the perfection of facilities.

4.2.2 Suburbanization of urban commercial and industrial functions

New York attached importance to the improvement in various living, production, and employment facilities in suburbs, especially the scientific planning

Table 4.1 Evolutionary phases and characteristics of New York's urbanization

Phase	Main characteristics
Suburbanization of urban residential functions	From the early 1900s to the 1950s, many citizens chose to live and work in suburbs, where housing increased, amenities continued to improve, and the suburban environment continued to be improved and enabled residents to live more comfortably than those in central urban areas. A large number of citizens moved to the suburbs. With the development of highways, popularization of cars in families and the perfection of amenities, suburbs became an important choice for citizens of New York at that time.
Suburbanization of urban commercial and industrial functions	In the 1960s, New York built large shopping malls and shopping centers in suburban towns, improved business facilities and commercial outlets, and attracted factories and industries from urban centers to suburbs. Industrial parks and commercial service outlets settled in suburbs, urban functions in suburbs could be improved and this created a large number of employment opportunities in suburbs.
Suburbanization of integrated urban functions through satellite towns	Satellite (cities or) towns are located around central urban areas like weather satellites, and were designed to relieve the pressure on central urban areas and evacuate the population, industry and traffic functions of central urban areas. New York's satellite towns included Long Island and small towns in New Jersey that are adjacent to New York. The construction of satellite towns aimed at realizing integrated functions of the city and integrating the functions of residence, shopping, education, medical care, culture and entertainment, fitness and leisure, employment, information, and law.
Cross-regional coordination of urban functions	Cross-regional coordination was achieved, a coordinated pattern for the Greater New York Metropolitan Area was built, the problems of "urban diseases" were alleviated in New York, and the coordinated development of areas was boosted. The cross-regional coordination of New York focuses on laws regarding the economic and social development among cities, the sustainability and coordination among cities, regions and urban and rural areas, and industrial restructuring, upgrading and functional complementation among regions, thus effectively avoiding the homogeneous competition among cities and the incidence of "urban diseases".

and reasonable layout of commercial and industrial functions, which could create conditions for attracting people to live and work in suburbs. New York constructed large shopping malls and shopping centers in suburban towns, completed commercial facilities and commercial outlets, attracted factories and industries from central urban areas to suburbs, and then attracted residents to work nearby. Around the 1960s, a lot of shopping malls and shopping centers were built, and industrial parks and commercial service outlets settled in suburbs, so that the urban functions of suburbs were improved and numerous jobs were created in suburbs.

4.2.3 Suburbanization of integrated urban functions through satellite towns

The concept of the "satellite city" (or satellite town), which originated in the UK, was formally introduced and used by the American scholar Taylor. Satellite (cities or) towns are located around central urban areas like weather satellites, and designed to relieve the pressure on central urban areas and evacuate the population, industry, and traffic functions of central urban areas. Satellite towns are not only the peripheral extension areas of cities that have the spatial advantage of being close to central urban areas, and can provide employment, housing, shopping, education, medical, and other supporting services for urban residents, but also relatively independent towns that are newly built or extended to decentralize the population and industries of central cities. Satellite towns are relatively independent because they maintain a certain degree of independence in many aspects such as administration, economy, culture, society, and life. With a certain spatial distance from central urban areas, they are generally separated by farmland, urban green partitions, urban forests, etc., but have certain convenient connections of traffic, such as light railways, subways, buses, and highways. Satellite towns also maintain relatively close economic ties with central urban areas.

New York's satellite towns include Long Island and small towns in New Jersey that are adjacent to New York. Based on the suburbanization of residential, commercial, and industrial functions, the urban functions in suburbs have been further developed. The construction of satellite towns aimed at realizing integrated functions of the city and integrating the functions of residence, shopping, education, medical care, culture and entertainment, fitness and leisure, employment, information, and law. Compared with central towns, the population density, building density and traffic congestion in satellite towns are smaller than those in central urban areas, thus effectively alleviating the series problems of "urban diseases" in central urban areas, such as population, traffic, housing, noise, environmental pollution, and improving the living and production space for residents.

4.2.4 Cross-regional coordination of urban functions

New York, based on the transition from urbanization to suburbanization, further realized cross-regional coordination and established a coordinated pattern of the Greater New York Metropolitan Area to alleviate New York's "urban diseases" and develop the area in a coordinated manner. The New York Metropolitan Area was formed gradually according to its own law of economic development. As the U.S. economy developed from industrialization to post-industrialization, the built-up areas of big cities became mature, and cities began to extend along the traffic axis to suburbs and gradually connected to be regional urban clusters. Through urban planning, the urban functions were decentralized and industries were transferred out of central urban areas to avoid the over-concentration of the population, traffic and industries, and give full play to the regional coordination. The cross-regional governmental agencies at all levels, social organizations, and enterprises were involved in the cross-regional developmental planning. Through cross-regional coordination, the New York Metropolitan Area was developed. The metropolitan circle of New York ranked in the order of south to north and consisted of four city clusters: Boston, New York, Philadelphia, and Washington. Moreover, some medium-sized cities such as Baltimore and their satellite towns constituted the belt-shaped metropolitan area, including 40 cities within the circle. The cross-regional coordination of New York emphasized the economic and social development laws between cites, focused on sustainability and coordination among cities, regions, and urban and rural areas, laid stress on industrial restructuring, upgrading, and functional complementarity among regions, and accentuated the industrial division of labor, cooperation, and innovation, and coordinated development between New York and its neighboring suburbs, satellite towns, and surrounding small and medium-sized cities, thus effectively avoiding homogeneous competition among cities and "urban diseases".

4.3 Key experience: cross-regional coordination and equal allocation

4.3.1 Building a mechanism of cross-regional coordination and strengthening planning, organization and implementation

Synergy is a process of integrating resources and an important tool for treating "urban diseases". New York achieved coordinated development among central urban areas and neighboring areas, urban and rural areas, and regions by developing suburbs and a large metropolitan area, strengthening the institutional construction for cross-regional coordination, enhancing the planning and coordination of city circles and organizing its implementation. The City Council of Greater New York was established as early as 1898, the Regional Plan Association of New York City was formed in 1929, and the Council of the New York Metropolitan Area was set up in 1960. These organizations fulfilled the functions of cross-regional coordination, planning, and cooperation, drove the coordinated development forward among cities and urban–rural areas, reduced regional disparities, and avoided "urban diseases". The Greater New York Metropolitan Area is one of the world's most economically powerful urban areas, which spans 10 northeastern states from Maine in the north to Virginia in the south, and consists of five large cities – Boston, New York, Philadelphia, Baltimore, and Washington – and 40 small and medium-sized cities with a population of 100,000 or more. This cross-regional multi-city metropolitan area reflects the foresight, planning, and strategic thinking of governments, social organizations, and enterprises in New York and its surrounding cities in order to control "urban diseases" and sustainable urban development.

The Greater New York Metropolitan Area built institutions and mechanisms for cross-regional coordination, strengthened industrial planning and division of labor, avoided homogeneous competition, and boosted functional and industrial complementarities among cities and regions, as well as planning and implementation. It achieved a reasonable degree of industrial division of labor that reflected the pattern of diversified development, the extension of the industrial chain and functional complementarity. New York, as an international financial center, vigorously developed financial and trade sectors and served the function of an economic leader, Philadelphia emphasized heavy and chemical industries, Boston laid stress on high-tech industries, and Baltimore developed non-ferrous metal and smelting industries. These industries had a reasonable division of labor, without homogeneous and vicious competitions. Cities had close economic ties, complemented each other in terms of industrial association, and hence boosted the coordinated development of the Greater New York Metropolitan Area.

4.3.2 Strengthening the construction of public housing and equalizing the allocation of public services

Inadequate public services are an important phenomenon and cause of "urban diseases". To solve the problems of "urban diseases", the supply of public services must be equalized. New York City emphasized the equalization of public service resources such as public housing, education, and health care, avoided regional differences in public services, drove forward the balanced development of population, and prevented the over-concentration of the population in central urban areas due to the convergence of public resources.

Housing equality is regarded as a basic right of citizens, and diversified and multi-layered housing policies are implemented to solve the housing problem of disadvantaged groups and of the employed population. New York provided public housing funding for low-income people. First, through direct government funding, there was investment in the construction of public housing and an attempt to solve part of the housing problem. For example, special support programs for public housing were developed to enhance the construction of public housing projects. Second, to provide information on the renting of housing and help renters obtain private housing. The government intervened in the increase of housing rents, reduced the cost of living, guaranteed housing for low-income families, enacted the Rent Stabilization Law and enhanced control of the housing rental market. Third, the government encouraged the purchase of housing by exempting loan interest tax and income tax and reducing property tax for low- and middle-income families who purchased homes.

114 *New York experience of "urban diseases"*

New York did not just enhance the construction of public housing, but it also equalized the allocation of public service resources in many aspects such as education, medical care, culture and science and technology, and reduced the gap in public services between central urban areas and suburbs and urban regions. The government increased investments in the construction of public service facilities, innovated the mechanism of investment and financing, and encouraged social capital to participate in the construction of public services and infrastructure. In order to strengthen the allocation of educational resources, New York spent $9,688 per suburban student in 1994, compared to $8,205 in urban areas. It enhanced the allocation of public facilities and services such as traffic, education, and medical care in suburbs and surrounding areas of the city, effectively reduced the dependence of surrounding residents on central urban areas and avoided the over-expansion of the population in central urban areas.

4.3.3 Improving the system of public transportation and solving the problem of traffic congestion

New York built a rapid transit system between regions, cities, urban areas, and suburbs, completed the system of urban public transportation, and effectively solved the problem of urban traffic congestion. It vigorously developed the system of port economy, highway, rail transportation, and shipping, which became an important basis for traffic and logistics of the metropolitan area, and favored the e-implementation of the Greater New York Metropolitan Area Plan. Ports in the Greater New York Metropolitan Area include the Port of New York, the Port of Philadelphia, the Port of Baltimore, and the Port of Boston, etc. These ports have cooperated by creating a division of work, avoiding homogeneous competition with flexible mechanisms, making up a cluster of ports on the East Coast of the United States of America and they have taken advantage of clusters and coordination. Highways and rail transit created conditions for the internal connectivity of the Greater New York Metropolitan Area. A system of traffic was formed with highways and rail transit, which strengthened the economic linkage among cities, urban areas and suburbs, realized the trend of suburbanizing the population, and effectively contributed to the treatment of "urban diseases" in New York.

In order to alleviate traffic congestion, New York laid stress on the construction of a public transportation system. A large proportion of citizens travelled by public transportation, with a per capita driving distance of 14.4 km per day, which was only one-third of the per capita driving distance per day of 41.6 km in the entire USA. This contributed greatly to the reduction of traffic congestion in New York City. New York has a well-developed subway system, which carries an average of more than 5 million passengers per day on weekdays. Bus and subway lines are operating 24 hours a day and facilitate public traveling. With a long history of construction and a century-long operation, the New York subway has not only positively contributed to the traffic problems of New York City, but it has also provided valuable experience for the development of subways in cities around the world. New York has 24 subway lines and 468 stations throughout the five areas, and it also owns more than 5,900 buses. In order to alleviate traffic congestion, New York City opened up bus lanes on roads subject to traffic congestion or high traffic flow and reflected the principle of bus priority. At the same time, because of the well-developed system of public transportation, despite the high population density, traffic congestion was alleviated. The driving of private cars was restricted by imposing fuel taxes, road and bridge tolls, and high parking fees, so the exhaust emissions of motor vehicles were under effective control. The per capita "carbon footprint" of New York was also the lowest in the United States of America.

4.3.4 Emphasizing waste recycling and energy conservation, enhancing low-carbon development and building a green New York

First, New York has encouraged and focused on waste recycling, facilitated the intensive recycling of resources, and further boosted low-carbon and green development. It attached importance to waste recycling and reuse, advanced recycling and reuse of resources and energy on the basis of reducing environmental pollution, saved resources and energy, promoted the green and low-carbon development of the city, and proposed to build a green New York. In 1989, New York determined waste recycling as a mandatory item under the protection of legislation, publicized it in all areas of the city, distributed free promotional material, launched an initiative for waste recycling, and required schools, communities, and enterprises to focus on waste recycling and reuse, save resources and energy, and reduce environmental pollution. Any violations were to be harshly punished. In the early 20th century, New York closed all landfills and shipped all wastes out of the city. It formed a waste disposal system relying on trucks, which transported nearly 84% of the domestic waste out of the city for disposal. However, the regional transfer of waste did not fundamentally solve the problem, but imputed it to other regions. The trucks for transporting wastes also increased traffic pressure, raised the exhaust emissions of motor vehicles, and polluted the urban environment. The transport of wastes added difficulty to waste disposal in the destinations. In 2006, Michael Bloomberg, the mayor of New York City, signed the 20-year Solid Waste Management Plan, which hoped to build a new environmentally friendly waste disposal system that considered ships and trains with large carrying capacities. 87% of New York City's domestic waste would be transported by ships and trains. New York City emphasized waste recycling and sorting, amended laws by the legislature, added nearly 1,000 new waste bins in densely populated areas, and recovery and recycling programs of hazardous substances for families, extended the types and coverage of waste recycling, and increased the rate of waste recovery and recycling.

Second, New York emphasized the control of air pollution and worked hard to build an ecological, livable, green and low-carbon city with fresh air. Besides strengthening legislation and implementing waste recovery and recycling to reduce urban pollution, New York also adopted effective policies and methods for control of air pollution. As early as the 1990s, New York City phased out and replaced traditional fuel-based buses with hybrid-powered buses to reduce the exhaust emissions of motor vehicles and decrease smog. From 1995 to 2006, the emissions of particulate matters from buses in New York dropped by 97% and those of nitrogen oxide fell by 58%. At present, New York City is widely using low-carbon, clean, environmentally friendly electric hybrid-powered buses, and is becoming a city with the largest number of such buses in the United States of America. New York City will further improve low-carbon environmentally friendly buses, such as increasing R&D, application and promotion of hydrogen energy vehicles, and plans to change taxis into low-carbon hybrid models.

Third, New York has advocated low-carbon energy-saving products and low-carbon green buildings and has advanced the green and low-carbon development of New York. In order to build a green city, boost green and low-carbon development, and enhance energy conservation and emission reduction, New York has also taken a series of measures such as using energy-saving lights and advocating green buildings. New York replaced traffic signal lights with energy-saving lights, which has been able to reduce energy consumption by 90%, it has replaced traditional refrigerators with energy-saving ones, and has introduced laws to encourage government agencies, social organizations, enterprises, and citizens to purchase energy-saving products, including energy-saving cars, lights, refrigerators, and air conditioners, it has encouraged the installation of energy-saving products in buildings, and has promoted wind and solar power generation. For example, the Statue of Liberty, Ellis Island, and 22 federal buildings in New York use electricity generated by wind power. New York's World Trade Center Building 7, the Hearst Tower and the Bank of America Tower were built as green buildings, which made full use of green roofs and collected rainwater on the roof for recycling and reuse and thus saving urban water resources.

Fourth, New York has built green infrastructure and advanced the city's green and low-carbon development. The concept of green infrastructure was first proposed in 1999 by the Green Infrastructure Work Group formed by the Conservation Foundation and the USDA Forest Service, which defined green infrastructure as the "Nation's Natural Life Support System", an interconnected network of waterways, greenways, wetlands, parks, forests, farms, and other protected areas to maintain the ecological environment and improve the quality of people's lives.[2] The North West Green Infrastructure Unit in the United Kingdom has defined green infrastructure as a system of natural environmental factors and green spaces with five attributes: type, functionality, surrounding environment, scale, and connectivity.[3] New York's green infrastructure, in addition to green roofs and green buildings mentioned above, has also emphasized the combined flow of rainwater and domestic wastewater.

Since New York has long been plagued by water pollution, especially during stormy periods, the discharge of rainwater and domestic wastewater has severely hindered the city's sustainable economic and social development, caused inconvenience to the life of urban residents, and has resulted in serious pollution of the urban environment due to wastewater. To solve this problem, New York made plans and invested heavily in the construction of rainwater drainage facilities. In the 20th century, New York City built 14 sewage treatment plants and nearly 12,000 kilometers of underground drainage pipes, where domestic sewage was filtered and disinfected before flowing into nearby waters. At the beginning of the 21st century, New York City began to solve the problem of diverting domestic sewage from rainwater, so that rainwater could be recycled directly, and domestic sewage could be reused after treatment. In 2010, Michael Bloomberg, the mayor of New York City, proposed a "Green City Infrastructure" project that would invest $1.5 billion over the next 20 years to reduce direct discharge of rainwater by 40% by 2030. The New York City Department of Environmental Protection decided to implement a green low-carbon rainwater drainage project and improve the city's water supply and drainage functions, considering the problem of combined rainwater and sewage caused by seawater intrusion. The "Green City Infrastructure" project included: construction of wetlands, dunes, and flood storage areas in low-lying areas, and ecological drainage ditches if conditions permit; experimentation with diverse rainwater retention projects, improvement of rooftop drainage channels by planting vegetation on roofs and using new building materials, rainwater harvesting and filtering by porous concrete; use of green vegetation, soil, and construction materials to simulate a natural water purification environment, absorb or evaporate rainwater, improve air quality, and improve groundwater and waters surrounding the city.[4]

4.4 Summary

This chapter has examined New York's experience of treating "urban diseases" from the perspective of cross-regional coordination. New York, the largest city in the USA and a well-known international metropolis, was once plagued by "urban diseases" such as concentration of many heavily polluting enterprises and industries in the core urban areas, overpopulation, traffic congestion, and environmental pollution. However, through effective control, New York is becoming the most energy-efficient and environmentally friendly low-carbon city in the USA. Industrialization and urbanization also caused many drawbacks. In the process of urbanization, it encountered the problems of "urban diseases", such as population expansion and a housing shortage due to rapid population growth, the illnesses of its citizens caused by environmental pollution, and traffic congestion.

New York has undergone a transition from urbanization to suburbanization. Considering the problems of "urban diseases" caused by accelerated industrialization and urbanization, the government at all levels of New York City chose new strategies of development, accelerated urban planning, and transformed and evolved towards suburbanization based on the original urbanization. Through the evolution from urbanization to suburbanization, New York managed to effectively alleviate "urban diseases". It approximately went through the phases of suburbanization of urban residential functions, suburbanization of urban commercial and industrial functions, suburbanization of integrated urban functions through satellite towns, and cross-regional coordination of urban functions. Based on the transition from urbanization to suburbanization, New York further realized cross-regional coordination, built a coordinated pattern of the Greater New York Metropolitan Area, alleviated the problems of "urban diseases" in New York, and boosted the coordinated development of areas.

New York's experience of treating "urban diseases" was characterized by cross-regional coordination and equalized allocation. First, it built a mechanism of cross-regional coordination, enhanced planning and organized the implementation; second, it strengthened the construction of public housing and emphasized the equalized allocation of public services; third, it perfected the system of public transportation, and solved the problem of traffic congestion; and fourth, it attached importance to waste recycling and energy conservation, strengthened low-carbon development and built a green New York.

Notes

1 Wang Dawei, Wen Hui and Lin Jiabin, International Experience and Implications to Cope with Urban Diseases, *China Development Observation*, 2012(7).
2 Pei Dan, Review of Green Infrastructure Planning Methods, *City Planning Review*, 2012(5).
3 Wu Wei and Fu Xi'e, The Concept of Green Infrastructure and Review of Its Research Development, *Urban Planning International*, 2009(5).
4 Green City Infrastructure of New York, www.gesep.com, May 17, 2013.

5 London experience in the control of "urban diseases"

Perspective of smog control

Britain was the first country to experience the Industrial Revolution, and one of the first countries to encounter the problems of "urban diseases" in the process of industrialization and urbanization. During the Industrial Revolution, the rapid growth of cities often exceeded the carrying capacity of social resources and this led to various "urban diseases", including a severe shortage of housing, serious pollution, and deteriorating sanitation. The famous British Labor historians Mr. and Mrs. Hammond called the problem of "urban disease" in Britain in the 19th century "the Curse of Midas", criticizing that Britain's pursuit of industrial production led to many problems such as various chambers of Commerce, people's livelihood, environmental pollution and so on. Since the beginning of industrialization, the rapidly expanding population of London resulted in a housing shortage, widespread slums, traffic congestion, and serious environmental pollution, thus triggering the "Smog of London". London conducted systematic treatment of "urban diseases" and took effective measures to turn their "foggy city" into a "green city", which is worthy of reference for Beijing.

5.1 Smog control in London: from "foggy city" to "green city"

5.1.1 London's smog problem originated from the smog incident in 1952

During industrialization and urbanization which lasted for more than 200 years, industrial emissions were not considered and so not effectively controlled, and air pollution became increasingly serious. As early as the Middle Ages, the problem of coal smoke pollution began to appear in London, and then UK Parliament, albeit a primitive "parliament", even promulgated a decree banning the use of coal by artisans. After the beginning of the Industrial Revolution backed by coal, many factories were built in the center of London, with chimneys everywhere, and dark clouds of smoke appeared during production. Households burnt a lot of coal for heating, and soot emissions increased dramatically. Within four days from December 5 to 8, 1952, London was plagued by foggy air pollution, and more than 4,000 people died. Two months later, another 8,000 people died. This was the

DOI: 10.4324/9781003272991-5

famous "London Smog" incident.[1] The fog was so heavy in London for several days that visibility in downtown areas was reduced to just a few feet. The fog contained sulfides and dust, and the air in London was so pungent that everyone's nostrils were filled with black dust. In that week alone, 704 people died in London from bronchitis, 281 from coronary heart disease, 244 from heart failure, and 77 from tuberculosis. In addition, there was a significant increase in the incidence of respiratory diseases such as pneumonia, lung cancer, and influenza. Due to the toxic fog, public transportation, cinemas, theaters, and stadiums were closed, a large number of flights were canceled, and even cars had to turn on their headlights when driving on the highways during the day, which proved how serious the pollution was.

5.1.2 The smog problem extended to the traffic pollution in 1980

After 1980, traffic pollution replaced industrial pollution as the primary threat to the quality of London's air. From the 1980s onwards, steadily increasing number of cars replaced coal as the main source of pollution in the atmosphere of Britain. Initially, people were mainly concerned about the impact of lead pollution from gasoline on human health, and unleaded gasoline gradually gained attention. By the late 1980s and early 1990s, other pollutants emitted from cars such as nitrogen oxides, carbon monoxide, and unstable organic compounds had also attracted wide attention. These substances underwent complex photochemical reactions under the action of ultraviolet light from sunlight, and produced a variety of secondary pollutants, mainly ozone, so it was called "photochemical smog".

5.1.3 Smog control changed the "foggy city" to a "green city"

Dense fog could hinder traffic, and high concentrations of sulfur dioxide and smog particles could endanger the health of residents. The London smog incident caused the British to reflect on the bitter consequences of air pollution. As early as 1875, Britain passed the Public Health Act in an attempt to reduce urban pollution. By the 1920s, the share of coal in industrial fuels had declined due to increased government regulation of industry, and soot pollution had been alleviated, but there was no qualitative improvement. In 1956, the British government passed the Clean Air Act for the first time. In 1968, it promulgated another clean air act. In 1974, it introduced the Air (Prevention and Control of Pollution) Act. Through effective treatment, London's foggy days were reduced from about 90 days a year at the end of the 19th century to less than 10 days, and today only a thin layer of white haze can be seen occasionally in winter or on early spring mornings. From clouds of fog to blue sky and white clouds, by the iron-fisted treatment of pollution, Britain made remarkable achievements. After years of continuous pollution control, the quality of today's air in London has greatly improved, and it is no longer called the "Foggy city".[2]

5.2 Key experience of smog control in London: a variety of measures

London learned a fatal lesson, reflected on the bitter consequences of air pollution and took a variety of controlling measures and actions. Iron-fisted pollution control for more than half a century finally changed London from a foggy city to an ecological and livable green city with clean air. London mainly adopted various means such as law, policy, technology, social participation, and green construction to achieve the comprehensive control of smog, as shown in Table 5.1.

Table 5.1 Main measures for smog control in London

Measures	Main experience
Law	Legislation could provide a legal basis for smog control, which was the fundamental experience of London. In 1954, London introduced the *City of London Act* to strictly control smog emissions. In 1956, the British government enacted the *Clean Air Act*, which designated "soot control zones" and banned the direct burning of coal in towns within these zones. After 1968, a series of air pollution control acts were promulgated, and in 1974, the *Air (Prevention and Control of Pollution) Act* was introduced, specifying the upper limit of sulfur content in industrial fuels. In 1995, Britain passed the *Environment Act*. In 2007, Britain revised its *Air Quality Strategy* and included new monitoring requirements for PM2.5 inhalable particulate matters.
Policy	The government of London was not indifferent to the problem of smog, nor did it behave irresponsibly, but it relied on laws and policies. For example, London put forward a "pay for congestion" program, namely, congestion charges. By February 2008, London's entry charges for vehicles with large displacements had risen to £25/day, equivalent to ¥350/day. Through planning, taxation, subsidies, education, and other means, the once congested traffic in the city had significantly improved. The "pay for congestion" program alone reduced traffic by 10–30% in some sections of roads in central London. The government took a series of measures to control traffic pollution, including prioritizing public transportation networks, curbing private cars, and reducing the exhaust emissions of cars and traffic congestion. It developed public transportation to reduce traffic congestion and pollution.
Technology	The government attached importance to technological innovation in smog control and decided to try a calcium-based adhesive in streets to control air pollution. This adhesive was similar to glue and could absorb dust in air. The British public could also check daily releases regarding the quality of the

(*continued*)

Table 5.1 Cont.

Measures	Main experience
	air on the Internet. In 2011, special trucks began to patrol the city and spray "calcium magnesium acetate solvents" on key roads with most heavy traffic to "stick" suspended particles of pollutants on the ground, thereby improving the quality of the air.
Green governance	In the 1980s, London built a large green ring around the outskirts of the city covering an area of 4,434 square kilometers. The government encouraged people to travel by public transportation or by bicycle and provided more green belts. London encouraged residents to buy cars with small displacements and promoted efficient, clean engine technology, and low-pollution vehicles that use natural gas, electricity, or fuel cells.
Social governance	Public discussion and media exposure were encouraged. British citizens had a tradition of self-governance and a strong social foundation for discussions, decision-making, monitoring and implementation, and environmental issues were no exception. Extensive discussion and active participation on the part of the public and prompt involvement and exposure by the media were conducive to information symmetry and to the disclosure of smog control, increasing the participation and effectiveness of social governance, advancing the progress of smog control, and alleviating the pressure of government monopoly and governance.

5.2.1 Law: the Clean Air Act

Laws regarding smog control were passed. In 1954, London promulgated the City of London Act to strictly control smog emissions, and in 1956, the British government enacted the Clean Air Act, which designated "soot control zones" and banned the direct burning of coal in towns within these zones. The law required that all power plants in the City of London be closed and rebuilt only in the Greater London area. Industrial enterprises were required to build tall chimneys for the dispersion of air pollutants. Moreover, the traditional stoves of urban residents were required to be rebuilt for reducing the amount of coal use, gradually realizing the natural gasification of residential life, and adopting centralized heating in winter. After 1968, Britain introduced a series of air pollution prevention and control acts, which imposed strict restrictions on various exhaust emissions and set clear penalties, thus effectively reducing soot and particulate matters. In 1974, the Air (Prevention and Control of Pollution) Act was introduced, specifying the upper limit of sulfur content in industrial fuels. These measures effectively reduced soot and sulfur dioxide pollution from coal burning, and produced good results. By 1975, London's fog days had decreased from dozens of days to 15 days per year, and further to five days in 1980. Since January 1993, all new cars sold in Britain have to be retrofitted with catalytic converters for reducing nitrogen oxide pollution. In 1995, Britain passed the Environment Act, which required a national strategy to combat pollution. It stipulated that each city must evaluate and review the quality of its air, and for areas that failed to meet the standards, the government was to delineate areas for controlling the quality of the air and force them to meet the standards within a specified period. In 2007, Britain revised its Air Quality Strategy and included new monitoring requirements for PM2.5 inhalable particulate matters. It stipulated that by 2020, the annual average concentration of airborne PM2.5 must be controlled below 25μg/m3, and highly polluting areas such as roads should not exceed this limit. As for areas with better air quality such as rural areas, more stringent monitoring requirements were to be imposed. The enactment of the various laws and decrees mentioned above played a crucial role in the control of air pollution and the protection of the urban environment in London.

5.2.2 Policy: congestion charges and development of public transportation

For the effective control of air pollution, the British government took strict measures on controlling emissions, which were mainly reflected in the following aspects:

First of all, the policy of congestion charges and strict penalties. London put forward a "pay for congestion" program, namely, congestion charges. Besides regulations and controls on cars and fuel, Britain tried to control the number of cars in urban areas. In 2003, it levied congestion charges to restrict private cars from entering urban areas. Laws such as the Health and Safety at Work Act required polluting enterprises to take actions for avoiding emissions of harmful gases into the atmosphere, otherwise they would face severe penalties. By February 2008, London's entry charges for vehicles with large displacements had risen to £25/day, equivalent to ¥350/day. By introducing a carbon price system and levying a carbon dioxide tax, charges were imposed on vehicles entering urban areas according to the level of carbon dioxide emissions, in order to reduce carbon emissions from ground traffic. The UK government encouraged the use of electric vehicles for reducing the exhaust emissions from fuel-powered vehicles and the level of air pollution. Through planning, taxation, subsidies, education, and other means, the once congested traffic in the city was improved significantly. The "pay for congestion" program alone reduced traffic by 10–30% in some sections of the roads in central London. It was reported that since the levying of congestion charges, London has witnessed a 25% reduction in traffic entering charged zones. The number of vehicles entering charged zones decreased by 70,000, and 50–60% of the public turned to public transportation. Congestion charges could directly reduce traffic emissions in these zones, with an 8% reduction of NOx emissions, a 7% reduction in PM10 emissions and a 16% reduction in CO2 emissions per annum.[3]

Second, the measures for smog control. The London Air Quality Strategy issued by the London City Council in 2004 emphasized that the improvement in the quality of the air in the city was not only the responsibility of environmental authorities but also required the integrated coordination and planning at all levels of the government, with the formulation of a policy on urban environmental management. From 1980 onwards, traffic pollution replaced industrial pollution as the primary threat to the quality of air in London. Currently, the content of inhalable particulate matters and nitrogen oxides in London's atmosphere is still above the maximum limits set by the national air quality objectives, and the pollutants come mainly from means of transportation. The government has taken a series of measures to control traffic pollution, including prioritizing public transportation networks, curbing private cars, and reducing the exhaust emissions of cars and traffic congestion.

Third, the development of public transportation and the reduction in traffic congestion and pollution. The subway, with a history of more than 140 years, is the first choice of most people in London. It has 11 lines and more than 270 stations throughout the city available for 3 million passengers every day. Subway stations in the center of the city are all within walking distance and the lines as dense as spider's webs cover the entire city. The London Underground has over 400 kilometers of lines, and 75% of the people who currently work in the downtown area use the subway network.

In addition to the subway, there are city trains, light rails in port areas and hundreds of bus lines that divert people on roads and solve their travel problems. Due to the well-developed public transportation and the government's high-handed approach to the use of the non-public transportation system, the public are willing to choose the subway or bus system for travel. The London City Council strongly supported public transportation and aimed to reduce traffic flow in the city center by 10–15% by 2010.

London is developing dedicated bus routes of nearly 300 kilometers, which attract the public by low fares and reduce the use of private cars. Trams and buses are free for teenagers under 18 years old. As the commercial and financial center of the Greater London area, the City of London and many downtown business districts do not have parking lots. This forces many commuters to take public transportation and to choose bicycles.

5.2.3 Technology: using new glue to "stick" pollutants

Britain has not just legislated for controlling air pollution, but it has also promoted efficient new technologies. The government attached importance to technological innovation in smog control and decided to try a calcium-based adhesive on streets to control air pollution. This adhesive was similar to glue and could absorb dust in the air. Street sweepers had already used this new product in noisy and heavily polluted urban areas. The current monitoring results claimed that particulate matters in these areas dropped by 14%. The British public could also check daily releases regarding the quality of the air on the Internet.[4] In 2011, special trucks began to patrol the city and spray "calcium magnesium acetate solvents" on key roads with the heaviest traffic to "stick" suspended particles of pollutants to the ground, thereby improving the quality of the air.[5]

Furthermore, London emphasized the improvement in and innovation of industrial technology, energy technology, and automobile technology. First, it accelerated the phasing-out of high-energy-consuming industries such as steel, textiles, and shipbuilding, improved industrial technology, advocated energy conservation and emission reduction, abandoned low-end production, gradually developed towards high-end service sectors such as design, integration, and R&D, and boosted the transformation and upgrading of traditional industries with technological advancements. Second, it advocated coal to gas technology, gradually replaced coal with oil and natural gas, reformed the coal industry, closed the backward coal production capacity, and improved the efficiency of utilization with advanced technology regarding energy from oil and natural gas. Third, it improved the residential energy technology, actively transformed residential combustion appliances, implemented centralized heating, and encouraged the use of anthracite coal. Fourth, it sped up the research and development of clean technologies, especially environmentally friendly automobile technologies, and stipulated that new vehicles must be equipped with exhaust gas purification devices to reduce nitrogen oxide emissions.[6] Fifth, a network of atmospheric monitoring was established to actively develop monitoring technologies and improve the effects of smog prevention and control. Since 1961, Britain has built a nationwide network of atmospheric monitoring, which has 1,200 monitoring points, with 450 groups participating in the monitoring. It samples soot and sulfur dioxide once an hour on average, and measures dust fall once a month. The three cities, London, Edinburgh, and Sheffield, were listed as key monitoring areas. Along with the promotion and application of environmental protection technologies, etc., they played an important role in the control of atmospheric pollution and environmental protection in London.[7]

5.2.4 Green governance: building green spaces and using green energy

London changed from a "foggy city" that was known to the world to an ecologically livable green city. The key lay in changing the traditional model of developing only heavy and chemical industries with high energy consumption, focusing on the construction of a green city and green buildings, and strengthening the green governance of the city. Green governance included building green spaces, increasing green areas, using clean energy and reducing carbon emissions. First of all, the construction of green spaces, the development of urban parks and the creation of natural ecological spaces for citizens. As early as the mid-19th century, Britain began to construct urban parks, and plan green parks on a large scale in major cities, so as to increase the greening rate of cities, add green elements for citizens and create a good living environment. This concept and the urban park campaign profoundly influenced other countries and cities. Urban parks in London also mushroomed and expanded. This effectively changed its traditional image as a city of gray or a foggy city, and formed park clusters, such as Regent's Park, St. James' Park, Hyde Park, etc., which laid a good foundation for the establishment of the urban system of green open spaces so that citizens could live surrounded by the beauty of nature.

Second, the introduction of an urban green belt and the planning of open spaces. As early as 1929, the Greater London Regional Planning Committee formulated the London open space planning, which actively introduced the green belt and designed the open space index in order to create and reserve more public space and recreational land, so that the city would be closer to nature, greener, and more ecological, and appear less crowded. The urban green belt increased green spaces in the city, and a green ring of open space was planned around London. In 1938, the Greenbelt Act was passed and large areas of land were acquired. In 1976, large urban parks, regional parks and local parks were constructed on a large scale, which were divided into different scale types for configuration according to the standards set by the Greater London Council, and the open space system was established. In the 1980s, London built a large green ring around the outskirts of the city covering an area of 4,434 square kilometers. The open space planning designed green belts, green paths or green chains to protect most of the open spaces and develop their potential for recreation. These green spaces unfolded in chains across London like a necklace of green beads and formed a perfect natural whole of the city. These "green chains" passed through densely built-up areas such as residential areas, enhanced the accessibility and environmental quality of open spaces through intensive greening and other measures, perfected the framework of London's green spaces, recreation, and nature conservation system, introduced complete slow walking systems and sports and leisure facilities, and became an important structure of London's urban development.[8]

Third, the city guided its citizens to drive less, choose green means of transportation and actively use green low-carbon energy. Thanks to the planning and construction of London's green space framework, a system of open spaces closer to nature was established to provide the basic conditions and transport environment for citizens who chose walking and bicycling. The government encouraged people to travel by public transportation or by bicycle and provided more green belts for its citizens to walk and go jogging. London encouraged residents to buy cars with small displacements and promoted efficient, clean engine technology, and low-pollution vehicles that use natural gas, electricity, or fuel cells.

5.2.5 Social governance: encouraging public discussion and media exposure

In terms of prevention, control, and treatment of air pollution in London, the government actively encouraged public participation in discussions, monitoring, and assistance of smog control. As one of the first representative systems of democracy in the world, Britain had a tradition of self-governance and a democratic foundation that encouraged citizens to participate in political discussions. Citizens can participate politically in public decision-making and major public measures, and engage in full discussion, democratic decision-making, social supervision, and implementation, etc. They have more rights to speak out on, to know and to supervise over major issues such as the control of environmental pollution and smog. The public are active practitioners of smog control, and social organizations, universities, and the public participate in the control of air pollution together. King's College London, Guy's Hospital London and St. Thomas' Hospital London jointly established the NHS Foundation to actively hold seminars on air pollution control, and study and discuss how citizens can themselves start the control of environmental pollution, and how everyone can participate in smog control, make active contributions to the social prevention and control of environmental pollution and assume their due responsibilities. King's College London developed a smartphone app for information on the quality of London's air, which sent relevant information to citizens and the society free of charge. In order to keep citizens informed of the latest environmental information, the government of London also released real-time air quality data, concentrations of various pollutants and future trend maps for the London area to citizens through the media and official networks.

Mainstream media played an active role as platforms to monitor and supervise smog control. They would not cover up for the government but boldly criticized the government's inaction.[9] In July 2012, the *Sunday Times* discussed a survey report by Clean Air in London, an environmental group, which questioned the city's efforts to beautify the air pollution index by spraying chemical solvents to clean suspended particulates near air quality monitoring points, while ignoring other areas where the quality of the air needed to be improved.

Extensive discussion and active participation of the public and timely involvement and exposure by media were conducive to information symmetry and disclosure of smog control, increasing the participation and effectiveness of social governance, advancing the progress of smog control, and alleviating the pressure of government monopoly and governance.

5.3 Policy implications of smog control in London

Beijing is the national capital where the foggy weather affects the health of citizens, has a great negative impact on economic and social development, and damages its image and international status in constructing an international city. Accelerating smog control and air pollution prevention is currently a priority for the Beijing Municipal Government. The insights from the experience of smog control in London and the countermeasures for Beijing are mainly reflected in the following aspects:

5.3.1 Enacting clean air regulations for the capital, enhancing the institutional construction of smog control

The report of the 18th CPC National Congress points out that the protection of the ecological environment must rely on the system. To control the foggy weather, the legal system for improvement of the quality of air should be strengthened. According to the 2012 Beijing Municipal Environmental Status Bulletin, compared with 2011, the annual average concentrations of sulfur dioxide, nitrogen dioxide, and inhalable particulate matters (PM10) in Beijing decreased by 1.5%, 5.5%, and 4.4% respectively in 2012, and that of carbon monoxide remained flat. The annual average concentrations of sulfur dioxide and nitrogen dioxide met the national standards, but the inhalable particulate matters (PM10) still exceeded the permitted level, with an annual average concentration of 109μg/ m3, exceeding by 9%.[10] The pollution from motor vehicle exhaust is serious, the coal-based energy structure causes serious soot-type pollution, ground dust, and sandstorms cause high concentrations of total suspended particles, and industrial pollution, especially the industrial structure of neighboring cities, leads to serious air pollution in Beijing. By drawing on London's experience, in order to build a country under the rule of law and realize the modernization of national governance capacity and governance system, there is an urgent need to perfect the laws and regulations on the prevention and control of environmental pollution, enforce the laws and regulations strictly and advance the control of smog pollution. Therefore, the Capital Clean Air Law should be introduced as soon as possible to strengthen the legal system, clearly stipulate that polluting enterprises and motor vehicle owners must take actions to avoid the emission of harmful gases into the atmosphere, and impose severe penalties on enterprises and motor vehicle owners whose sewage discharge and exhaust emissions do not meet the standards.

5.3.2 Setting pollution sampling points, strictly controlling exhaust emissions

By drawing on London's experience, first of all, Beijing must have strict regulations and controls on vehicles and fuels, and levy congestion charges during special periods in core areas (such as rush hours). The city should set pollution sampling points, strengthen the road and annual inspections of motor vehicles in order to control the quantity of vehicles in central urban areas, improve fuel standards, never add new diesel vehicles within a period, and must not allow new gasoline vehicles that do not meet the standards to be sold and licensed in urban areas; and fuel oil sold at gas stations must meet national standards. Second, it should strengthen the treatment of motor vehicle emissions, and require all motor vehicles to be retrofitted with catalytic converters for eradicating black smoke. In Beijing, pollution from motor vehicle exhaust is an important source of urban air pollution that has a worsening trend and needs to be strictly controlled. The city must strictly enforce emission standards, introduce policies that require all motor vehicles to be retrofitted with filters, and speed up the scrapping of unqualified vehicles. Motor vehicles should be mandatorily installed with exhaust emission reduction devices, strictly supervised and controlled and must not be allowed to drive on the road if they do not meet the standards. The city should also enhance the emission control of vehicles from other regions, adopt unified standards and a regulatory system, and minimize the exhaust emissions of motor vehicles.

5.3.3 Strengthening technologies on smog control, advancing control by technological innovation

Beijing should center on the continuous improvement of the quality of its air, strengthen technological regulation and technical support for motor vehicle emissions, work on solving bottlenecks that affect and restrict the regulation of motor vehicles, complete laboratory construction, the supervision of annual inspection sites and road inspections, and enhance supervision, inspection, reporting, and information disclosure on gas stations and refineries. By drawing on London's experience, Beijing should accelerate innovation in key technologies of emission reduction and achieve key breakthroughs in environmental governance. Beijing's smog control must emphasize and strengthen technological innovation and improvements, and rely on technologies to achieve environmental improvement and emission reduction. A calcium-based adhesive must be developed and used to control air pollution. In addition, it should further optimize the industrial structure, attach importance to emission reduction within the service sector, and reduce the pollution by domestic waste.

5.3.4 Developing green public transportation, using clean low-carbon energy, reducing carbon emissions

Compared with London, Beijing's public transportation is not well developed. Buses cannot meet the travel requirements of citizens, and some bus lines are seriously congested. Subway construction cannot keep up with the speed of urban development, and subway congestion is severe, with complicated interchanges and serious congestion during commuting hours. Many developed countries are accelerating the replacement of old infrastructure and the construction of new energy facilities. Although Beijing has realized the change from coal consumption to a natural gas and oil-based energy structure, it still mainly relies on traditional energy sources such as coal and oil, and the total consumption of traditional energy sources keeps increasing. Hence, it is heavily dependent on traditional and imported energy sources.

First of all, Beijing should increase its efforts in developing public transportation, in improving subway conditions, reducing congestion, and making clean energy renovation for taxis and buses within a deadline. It should successively replace urban buses with poor performance and high carbon emissions with new ones that are more comfortable and consume clean energy. The city should also vigorously advocate pollution-free means of transportation, establish a convenient and comfortable system of public transportation, extend rail transit to the urban–rural fringe, distant suburban districts and counties and surrounding urban areas as soon as possible, make plans for the construction of rail transit in Beijing's distant suburban districts and counties, the border areas and counties between Beijing and Tianjin and Hebei early, and attract the participation of social capital.

Second, Beijing should accelerate the construction of urban rail transit and public bicycles, encourage the development of electric and hybrid fuel vehicles, and increase the construction of charging stations. It should encourage the use of electric vehicles, facilitate the construction of intelligent charging and switching service networks for electric vehicles, increase charging stations, and encourage the development of electric or gas-fueled motor vehicles. It should also advance the progress of oil-to-gas conversion, strive to convert all buses and taxis to gas-fueled or electric vehicles within the next 5–10 years, and try its best to reduce motor vehicle emissions.

Third, Beijing should strengthen the construction of urban green spaces. It must suspend or delay the construction of new high-rise buildings, build more green spaces and further increase the greening rate of core urban areas. It should also accelerate the construction of new towns in the outskirts, establish a polycentric model of urban development, build green belts in core and peripheral urban areas, and strengthen environmental governance.

5.3.5 Encouraging public participation in the smog control of the capital

The prevention, control, and treatment of air pollution in London could not have been achieved without the government's emphasis on social organizations, news media, and public participation and creation of a relaxed, free, and open environment of public opinion, where everyone is responsible for environmental protection and everyone needs to participate in the control of smog. London's mainstream media do not cover up for the government but boldly attack and effectively monitor it. News media and environmental organizations can conduct open investigations, public discussions, and consultations on countermeasures. The government and the public take the same position in solving problems of environmental pollution. The government tends to encourage social supervision, participation, and real reporting, rather than be afraid of supervision, reporting, and maintaining stability.

First of all, Beijing should encourage public participation. By drawing on London's experience, the city should encourage and advocate extensive public participation in the governance of environmental pollution, build up environmental volunteer organizations and associations, and rely on social organizations of environmental protection and industry associations to strengthen the supervision, disclosure, evaluation, and reporting of various behaviors of environmental pollution. Pollution can be effectively controlled only by collective action.

Second, Beijing should advocate transparency of information and strengthen the supervision of pollution control. The city should mobilize the people of the whole society to extensively participate in environmental protection activities and supervise the behavior of the government and enterprises involving the environment. It should encourage social participation, gain the support of the masses, popularize environmental protection information, and be patient in avoiding an escalation of conflicts. It should also realize information disclosure, establish an integrated mechanism for the coordination of environmental pollution petitions, integrate various resources, strengthen organization and coordination, and form a working mechanism of upper- and-lower linkage, left-right coordination, efficient operation, and comprehensive control.

Third, Beijing should achieve four changes. For objects of governance, it is necessary to change from simply managing urban economic growth and the expansion of the scale of spaces to managing the coordinated development of complex urban economic, social, and environmental systems and pursuing the maximization of urban ecological benefits; for subjects of governance, it is necessary to change from the administrative management of the government to the comprehensive environmental governance of the government, enterprises, social organizations, and masses; for goals and performance of governance, it is necessary to change from material-oriented performance goals to people-oriented goals, and highlight the goals of improving the environment, and establishing a green and livable city, and a satisfactory urban ecological environment for the people; for scope of governance, it is necessary to change from a single center to a multi-center and joint governance of surrounding areas.

5.4 Summary

This chapter investigated London's experience in the treatment of "urban diseases" from the perspective of smog control. Britain was the first country to experience the Industrial Revolution, and one of the first countries to encounter the problems of "urban diseases" in the process of industrialization and urbanization. The famous British Labor historians Mr. and Mrs. Hammond called the problem of "urban disease" in Britain in the 19th century "the Curse of Midas", criticizing that Britain's pursuit of industrial production led to many problems such as various chambers of Commerce, people's livelihood, environmental pollution, and so on. London carried out systematic treatment of "urban diseases" and took effective measures to turn a "foggy city" into a green city, which is worthy of reference for Beijing.

London changed from a "foggy city" to a green city through smog control. London's smog problem originated from the smog incident in 1952. The smog problem extended to traffic pollution in 1980. From the 1980s onwards, the steadily increasing number of cars replaced coal as the main source of pollution in the atmosphere of Britain. The London smog incident caused the British to reflect on the bitter consequences of air pollution. From clouds of fog to blue sky and white clouds, by the iron-fisted treatment of pollution, Britain made remarkable achievements. After years of continuous pollution control, the quality of the air in London today has greatly improved, and it is no longer called the "foggy city".

The key experience of smog control in London is the variety of measures taken. First, to govern by law, it enacted the Clean Air Act and other strict laws; second, to govern by policy, it levied congestion charges and developed public transportation; third, to govern by technology, a new glue was used to "stick" pollutants to the pavement; fourth, green governance, which means the construction of green spaces and the use of green energy; and fifth, social governance, which encourages public discussion and media exposure.

The insights from the experience of smog control in London and the countermeasures for Beijing are mainly reflected as follows: enacting clean air regulations for the capital, enhancing the institutional construction of smog control; setting pollution sampling points, strictly controlling exhaust emissions; strengthening technologies regarding smog control, advancing control by technological innovation; developing green public transportation, using clean low-carbon energy, reducing carbon emissions; and encouraging public participation in controlling the smog in the capital.

Notes

1 Tang You'an, Inspirations from London's Change of "Foggy City", *Legal Daily*, January 30, 2013.
2 Wang Yahong, British Experts Say London's Experience of Smog Control Is Applicable to Beijing, www.chinadaily.com.cn, March 1, 2013.
3 In 2016, Beijing Will Try Congestion Charges, How It Will Be Levied, http://news.cngold.com.cn/20151204d1903n5870096.html.
4 Inspirations from London's Smog Control for China, www.nbd.com.cn, January 14, 2013.
5 Wang Yanhong, Never a City of Fog–History of London in Controlling Air Pollution, *Xinhua News Agency*, August 26, 2001.
6 Inspirations of Britain's Treatment of Foggy City for Our Development of the Economy, www.cfi.net.cn, January 29, 2016.
7 London's Measures of Smog Control and Implications, http://cul.sohu.com/20151201/n429116186.shtml.
8 Zhu Tianxin, The Construction of Green Open Spaces in London Started Early, *China Flower & Gardening News*, April 2, 2015.
9 Farewell to the "Foggy City": Public Participation of London under Strict Laws, http://news.xhby.net/system/2013/01/14/01593394.shtml.
10 Air Quality of Beijing Exceeded the Permitted Level by 9% in 2012, *The Beijing News*, June 1, 2013.

6 Tokyo experience in the control of "urban diseases"

Perspective of subcenter construction

The Tokyo Metropolitan Area, consisting of Tokyo and surrounding prefectures, namely Saitama, Kanagawa and Chiba, is the largest financial, industrial, commercial, political, and cultural center in Japan. Tokyo, a well-known international city, has also encountered serious "urban diseases". In the 1960s and 1970s, Tokyo's "urban diseases" were very serious, and their changes were closely linked to the city's industrial development and population migration. The overcrowding of population in the city resulted in a housing shortage, rapid rising land prices, increased traffic pressure and serious environmental pollution. Tokyo took effective measures to deal with these "urban diseases", including planning and guidance, decentralization of functions, construction of subcenter cities, industrial restructuring, diversion of population, and allocation of resources. These experiences are worthy of reference for Beijing.

6.1 Manifestations of "urban diseases" in Tokyo

Tokyo, the national capital of Japan, actually refers to the Tokyo Metropolitan Area (TMA), with a total land area of 13,400 square kilometers and a total population of nearly 37 million, including the Tokyo Metropolis and parts of the built-up areas of the three surrounding prefectures. It can be said that Tokyo is one of the largest cities in the world, where one-fourth of Japan's population is crowded on less than 4% of Japan's total land area. The Tokyo Metropolis, which covers a land area of 2,162 square kilometers, with a total population of about 13 million, is the core urban area of the TMA. The period of 1950–2970 witnessed the rapid growth of the urbanization of Tokyo, whose population quickly increased from more than 6 million to more than 11 million. The rapid growth of the population resulted in serious "urban diseases". Due to the accelerated progress of urbanization, industrial enterprises were overly concentrated in central areas of the city, and industries such as steel, shipbuilding, machinery, chemicals, and electronics developed rapidly. A large number of manufacturing enterprises concentrated in Tokyo and attracted a massive influx of population, thus further leading to difficulties in housing supply, pressure on traffic, increased emissions due to the

DOI: 10.4324/9781003272991-6

clustering of enterprises and serious pollution of the urban environment. In the 1970s, Japan suffered the most serious air pollution. The by-product of rapid economic growth was the cost to the environment. The "pollution incidents" that occurred in Japan were very serious environmental problems at that time. After the Second World War, Japan adopted limited development of heavy and chemical industries and used coal as the main energy source. With the Keihin, Chukyo, Kitakyushu, and Hanshin industrial zones at the core, it vigorously developed related industries, and the results were smokestacks everywhere and terrible exhaust emissions. Severe air pollution made it difficult to see blue sky, white clouds, and the sun in Tokyo, the visibility on roads was only 30–20 meters and there was a pungent smell of sulfides everywhere. The inhabitants of many neighboring cities suffered from severe asthma and other diseases. Japan was tortured by serious air pollution then, and the PM2.5 levels were literally off the charts. Air pollution was mainly photochemical smog, which was a phenomenon of smog pollution formed by the mixture of two pollutants after the secondary pollutants generated by the photochemical reaction when the primary pollutants emitted by cars, factories, and other sources into the atmosphere were exposed to sunlight (ultraviolet light).[1] In 1968, thick clouds of smoke were hanging over the sky above the steel works in the Tokyo Bay. Thermal power plants supplied electricity for the city while causing serious environmental pollution and smoggy weather. At that time, the number of people in Japan suffering from respiratory diseases caused by inhaling sulfide emissions reached 3% of the population in 1964. By 1970, more than 500 people had been diagnosed with asthma in Yokkaichi, and by the end of 1972, more than 6,000 people had been diagnosed with the disease nationwide, of whom more than 10 eventually died. It could be found that Japanese cities, including Tokyo, have experienced serious pollution to their urban environments.

6.2 Key experience of the control of "urban diseases" in Tokyo

6.2.1 Strengthening the planning and decentralization of urban functions, constructing subcenter cities

In order to effectively deal with the "urban diseases" of the metropolis, Tokyo planned and was guided by phases and steps for decentralizing its urban functions. In the 1950s, Japan's economy was growing at a rapid pace, and the central business district of Tokyo was no longer able to meet the needs of economic and social development, because government offices, the headquarters of large companies, national economic management agencies, and commercial service facilities were overly concentrated, with traffic congestion and a high density of buildings. For alleviating the over-concentration in the central district, Tokyo accelerated the construction of subcenter cities to reduce the pressure of industry, traffic, and population in central urban areas and to balance the intensity of urban land use. In 1958, 1982, and 1987,

Tokyo implemented the urban development strategy of "subcenters" (namely Shinjuku, Shibuya, and Ikebukuro) to enhance the urban functions of subcenters and take over and decentralize some functions of core urban areas. After years of development, the Tokyo Metropolis formed a multi-center, multi-ring, balanced, livable, and low-carbon urban agglomeration of "central areas–subcenters–surrounding new cities–neighboring county centers".

With the acceleration of urbanization, globalization, and industrialization, the size of cities is expanding, and the single-center, "pie-spreading" pattern of urban expansion cannot meet the requirements of the sustainable development of urban spaces. The construction of "subcenters" and the realization of multi-center development has become the trend and strategic choice of most metropolises. "Subcenters" are mainly distributed in the outskirts and take over partial functions of the central city. They are second only to the comprehensive new urban space in the main city center. The construction of subcenter cities can effectively alleviate the contradictions of development spaces in central urban areas and a series of problems of "urban diseases".

Tokyo followed the strategy of subcenter development three times in 1958, 1982, and 1987, respectively. In 1956, Japan enacted the National Capital Region Planning Act, which clearly specified the territorial scope of the metropolitan area with Tokyo at the center and a radius of 100 km. The capital region of Japan was not an administrative region, but a planning or policy-oriented region. Mainly through planning at the national level, national resources, and efforts were coordinated to advance the construction of the capital region, instead of being confined to self-planning of the administrative region. This could enhance the authoritativeness of planning and the effectiveness of implementation, greatly facilitate the formation of a large urban agglomeration of Tokyo, solve a series of "urban diseases" caused by over-concentration of population in a single city, and be conducive to the formation of an interrelated economic circle in a large space. Subsequently, Japan prepared and implemented the National Capital Region.

Basic Plan several times, emphasized the construction of subcenters and new cities, and strengthened the decentralization of functions out of central urban areas. The decentralization of functions aimed to facilitate balanced allocation of resources, prevent central urban areas from undertaking too many functions and concentrating excessive advantageous resources, and break the monopoly of resources and solidification of interests of the privileged class. In 1999, a new plan was prepared to build a new urban structure of "decentralized network structure" in the Tokyo area by 2015.

By now, seven subcenters have been shaped in Tokyo to undertake some functions of Tokyo as an international city. They have already become important centers of activity for local residents and inflowing population. The inflowing population does not necessarily have to work and live in central urban areas, but many of them choose to work, develop, and live in these subcenters. This can greatly relieve the pressure of population, traffic, housing, employment, and the environment in central urban areas. For example, Shinjuku, an important subcenter city of Tokyo, is located to the west of the central urban areas of Tokyo. Its pillar industries are consumption, tourism, and entertainment by becoming a subcenter. Now, this subcenter is an important urban function area second only to Ginza and Asakusa-Ueno.

After nearly 30 years of planning and construction, the Shinjuku subcenter has taken shape. In order to take over the functions of central urban areas, Shinjuku has vigorously developed service sectors such as finance and insurance, real estate, retail and wholesale trade, information, and commerce. The concentration of economic, administrative, cultural, and information sectors in the Shinjuku subcenter might attract a large number of people to work there, and some government agencies of the Tokyo Metropolis have moved to Shinjuku. These measures might reduce the pressure of population in central urban areas and promote economic prosperity and social development in Shinjuku. The working population in Shinjuku is already close to that of Tokyo's central three wards. As an important subcenter of the Tokyo Metropolis, Shinjuku has evolved into an important area for the development of the financial sector and other high-end services. Within a radius of 7,000 meters from Shinjuku Station, there are nearly 200 banks and financial institutions. Shinjuku is also home to administrative and commercial centers. It has a lot of cinemas, fitness, and entertainment facilities, dance halls, concert halls, restaurants, shopping malls, and other industries. For instance, Nishiguchi Underground Mall and Odakyu Underground Mall have become important commercial spaces in Shinjuku, which attract a large number of working population and businessmen, reduce the pressure of population in Tokyo, boost Shinjuku's economic development and have become new economic growth points.

Tokyo has vigorously developed subcenters, improved the quality of surrounding cities, taken over part of the functions of Tokyo as an international city by market-oriented means, reduced its pressure of resources, energy and the environment, and has alleviated "urban diseases" and the pressure of population on Tokyo. The model of large urban agglomeration with subcenters can create an urban economic, cultural, and social circle which is an interconnected, complementary and cooperative geographic space. It can increase the carrying capacity of the urban circle, but reduce that of resources, energy, and the environment in local areas, especially central urban areas.

6.2.2 Adjusting the industrial structure, guiding the diversion of the population

Tokyo laid stress on industrial guidance and restructuring to avoid an overexpansion of the population in central urban areas, diverted the population by decentralization and adjustment of industries and has effectively solved a series of problems such as the expansion of the urban population. In the mid-20th century, Tokyo developed heavy and chemical industries such as steel, shipbuilding, machinery, electronics, and chemicals, which attracted a massive influx of working population and resulted in increasingly serious "urban diseases". In this regard, Tokyo enacted the Industrial Control Law to accelerate urban planning in the Tokyo Metropolitan Area, decentralize labor-intensive, heavy, and chemical industries to the suburbs, to small and medium-sized towns and abroad, and reduce the pressure on the urban resources, energy, and the environment of Tokyo. The city improved the quality and efficiency of industries by adjusting the industrial structure and optimizing the industrial system. It controlled industrial projects of a certain scale and new projects of universities, etc., developed knowledge-, resource- and technology-intensive service sectors in central urban areas, enhanced the value and competitiveness of these industries, and realized the sustainable economic and social development of the city by a high degree of efficiency. Technological innovation and urban service industries were energetically developed to achieve economic revitalization and prosperity on the basis of reducing the total population.

6.2.3 Building a rail transit system of the metropolitan area, improving public transportation facilities

6.2.3.1 Establishing a traffic network dominated by rail transit, with only a few buses and a low proportion of driving to and from work, effectively reducing traffic above ground

First of all, a three-dimensional network of public transportation dominated by rail transit was established. Tokyo is a densely populated international city where the traffic problems should not be underestimated, but it paid attention to the control of traffic congestion relatively early. Tokyo mainly adopted the policy of restricting ground traffic while developing underground rail transit and it built a three-dimensional network of public transportation dominated by rail transit to facilitate the scientific control of urban traffic congestion problems. Tokyo's urban traffic was characterized by a three-dimensional rapid transit network on, under and above ground, which referred to a three-dimensional network of transportation integrated with roads, viaducts, underground subways, and suburban rapid trams.[2]

The construction of subcenters in the Tokyo Metropolitan Area could not have been achieved without a system of rail transit made up of fast, high-density, high-capacity subways, and light railways. After decades of construction, building and improvement, a well-developed network of subways and light railways was established in the Tokyo Metropolitan Area, which includes more than 280 km of subway lines and nearly 3,000 km of railroads. It was not only possible to transfer passengers of subways every 500 to 1,000 meters, so it also built duplicate urban rail lines on busy roads and major city arteries to serve the function of fast transportation. In order to increase the source of funds for the construction of rail transit, the Tokyo Metropolitan

Government attracted social capital and issued bonds for the financing of rail transit, which effectively expanded the scale and speed of the construction of rail transit in Tokyo. The high-density, multi-station, and wide-coverage system of rail transit effectively decentralized the population of Tokyo's core urban areas. An important feature of Tokyo's control of traffic congestion was that everyone could take the rail transit to any corner of Tokyo.

Taking the Tokyo JR line (Japan Railway) as an example, it links the urban areas of Tokyo and also extends to all parts of Japan.

The JR line forms a circular Yamanote Line, which is the largest rail transportation artery of Tokyo. The circular route connects almost all of the most important areas and tourist attractions in Tokyo. Trains on the Yamanote Line operate in an "outer circle" (clockwise) and an "inner circle" (counter-clockwise). Outer circle: Osaki → Shibuya → Shinjuku → Ikebukuro → Ueno → Tokyo → Shinagawa → Osaki. Inner circle: Osaki → Shinagawa → Tokyo → Ueno → Ikebukuro → Shinjuku → Shibuya → Osaki. In addition, there is a central line in the middle of the Yamanote Line (Tokyo Station to Shinjuku Station) that goes straight to both the east and west. And this central line has an express line that does not stop in the middle, so it can cross the whole city quickly.

The Tokyo Metro line connects nine subway lines in the center of the city, including Ginza Line, Chiyoda Line, Hibiya Line, Marunouchi Line, Yurakucho Line, Hanzomon Line, Tozai Line, Namboku Line, and Fukutoshin Line. These tandem subway lines achieve full coverage of the major areas of Tokyo and basically cover all of the important stations and tourist attractions, thus providing great convenience for citizens and tourists, and offering a means of transportation to reduce the driving of motor vehicles.

With such a well-developed and densely distributed urban rail network, 43% of the people travel by rail transit each day, 86% of commuters who go to work or study take rail transit, and during the morning rush hours, 91% of all commuters enter central urban areas of Tokyo by rail transit. This is worthy of reference and learning by Beijing. Only with a full-coverage, high-density subway network is it more cost-effective for citizens to travel by subway than by motor vehicles. In this way, the city can effectively guide the public to choosing the subway, and thus reduce and minimize the intensity and frequency of using motor vehicles.

The advantages of Tokyo's rail transit, including trams and subways, are elaborated as follows. First, accurate arrival, even in seconds. Tokyo's trams and subways are mainly made up of JR East, Tokyo Metro, and Toei Tram and Subway, and each route has its own schedule. The time of trains arriving at the platform is counted in seconds. In this regard, trams and subways in any other places of the world cannot be comparable to those in Tokyo. Second, the distance between stations is short. Tokyo subway stations are less than 500 meters apart. There are also many entrances and exits, most of which are connected to large commercial buildings and office buildings. For those who live in Tokyo, trams and subways are very convenient means of transportation.

Third, they are in good order. According to statistics, the average number of people taking trams and subways in Tokyo is over 11 million per day. The good manners of Japanese people prevent disorders. Even during the morning and evening rush hours, passengers still line up and no one cuts in line or talks loudly or eats inside the train. It is a deeply rooted culture of Japan "not to bother others".

In the second place, there are relatively few buses above ground, which mainly serve the function of transferring, and they solve the last-mile problem. In Tokyo, the railroad circular track around the urban center connects the subcenters organically, so that there is a relatively fast and high-capacity traffic network among the cities. Starting from each subcenter, there are many light rail lines built in a radial pattern, extending to suburbs or neighboring cities, and new small and medium-sized cities and industrial centers have developed at the end of the lines. Thus, it is unnecessary to have more coaches or buses for long-distance travel. Tokyo has relatively few buses above ground, which is different from Beijing. Beijing relies heavily on buses, especially for traveling over long distances and across districts and counties. In Beijing, the frequent buses, especially on major transportation arteries, are used to relieve traffic pressure. Buses are very important, but however, their carrying capacity lags behind that of rail transit, so adding more buses is actually an important cause of traffic congestion that cannot be ignored. Tokyo, on the other hand, avoids the above problem, as its rail transit system carries more than 20 million passengers per day and takes 86% of all passenger traffic of the city. Only 6% of the people drive cars, thus avoiding traffic congestion caused by motor vehicles.

6.2.3.2 Overpasses and subway transfers are connected by elevators to ensure convenient, punctual and smooth transfers and a seamless connection

Tokyo's overpasses are designed with elevator connection to facilitate diversion of pedestrians at road junctions, reduce traffic lights and ensure traffic safety. Relatively speaking, overpasses in Beijing have no elevators, it is inconvenient for pedestrians to use overpasses, so there are too many pedestrians on the ground, which reduces the speed of ground traffic and causes many safety hazards. Elevators are used in the Tokyo subway to ensure convenient and punctual transfers, and a large number of rail lines can ensure transfers within 3 minutes. More often than not, passengers can transfer trains directly across the platform. Beijing, by contrast, has to restrict passenger flow and artificially design more circuitous lines to increase transfer times due to the limited carrying capacity of the subway. In Tokyo, it is convenient to transfer in subways and guarantee a smooth and flawless passenger flow. Moreover, there are many subway exits, and large stations even have several dozens of exits that direct the flow of passengers to large office buildings, shopping malls, government agencies and companies. They can effectively divert the passenger flow, increase the carrying capacity of rail transit, and reduce the cost in time of transfers via public transportation. Considering the costs in time, the economy, and environmental protection, rail transit is more attractive and competitive, and hence most citizens in Tokyo choose rail transit.

6.2.3.3 Tokyo levies high taxes and fees, raises parking fees and increases penalties for parking violations, so as to moderately increase the operating costs of private cars and achieve the goal of reducing the use of private cars

First of all, the city levies high taxes and fees to encourage a reasonable use of cars. It adopts a high taxation policy for vehicles, which must pay nine items of taxes, including consumption tax, vehicle acquisition tax, vehicle weight tax, light vehicle tax, fuel tax, diesel trading tax, and oil and gas tax. Most taxes and fees must be paid by consumers themselves.

Second, the city controls the total number of parking spaces and raises parking fees. On the one hand, individuals are required to have parking contracts in order to buy cars. The monthly rent of parking space in Tokyo is between 20,000 and 40,000 Japanese yen, so the high rent of parking spaces can prevent some people from buying cars. On the other hand, parking fees are expensive. There are a few free parking spaces for government offices, companies, and other institutions in Tokyo. However, transportation subsidies are included in the salaries of commuters, and employees are encouraged to choose rail transit. Those who go to work by private cars must pay for expensive parking fees themselves. Designated parking spaces in downtown areas of Tokyo charge 300 Japanese yen an hour. Car owners are only allowed to park for one hour, and after one hour, they will receive a fine of 15,000 Japanese yen. In self-service parking spaces, parking fees are charged from 600 Japanese yen to 1,500 Japanese yen per hour.[3] The high parking fee effectively restricts the driving of private cars to and from work, and most private cars travel only about one-third of the time on holidays. This can reduce the traffic on the ground and decrease pollution from the exhaust of motor vehicles.

Third, severe penalties are imposed on parking violations. The Tokyo government has adopted severe penalties for parking violations, which has also changed from the previous 30-minute "grace period" for temporary parking to "immediate enforcement". Parking violations of general cars are subject to a heavy fine of 15,000 Japanese yen and two points deducted from the driver's license. The Japanese driver's license has 6 points a year, so the penalties are relatively severe. The enforcement of penalties was enhanced, and retired veteran police officers are hired as civilian supervisors to combat parking violations. In comparison, Beijing's penalties for parking violations are too light and poorly enforced. This condones parking violations and further worsens traffic congestion, especially on community roads and non-trunked traffic routes, where parking violations are not well controlled. In this regard, Tokyo's policy of strict control and severe penalties should be borrowed.

6.2.3.4 Tokyo opens up "capillaries" to divert traffic from trunk roads, avoid repeated excavations and reduce traffic congestion

First of all, Tokyo attaches importance to traffic diversion from trunk roads, with special attention to the construction of feeder roads. The construction of feeder roads is an important complement to trunk roads because they can play a critical role in relieving traffic congestion. By opening up "capillaries" such as "cut-off roads" and small roads in each area, traffic flow on trunk roads can be effectively diverted. When the researchers at the Tokyo Metropolitan Government's Police Department in charge of countermeasures against traffic congestion observe a road that is prone to congestion, they will promptly explore the possibility of finding a nearby place and building a feeder road. This is of great significance for Beijing, which lacks experts and institutions to think about and solve congestion on key sections of roads. There is an urgent need for a specialized administrative agency of road traffic to identify, study and develop feeder and capillary roads that can relieve congestion at frequent congestion points. In Tokyo, more than 300 renovated feeder roads are used to effectively divert traffic from trunk roads.

Second, Tokyo reduces the frequency of road excavation and reconstruction as much as possible, emphasizes one-off planning and construction, avoids repeated excavations and reduces traffic congestion. Tokyo is very cautious of road construction, which generally requires planning and strict investigation and study before a decision is made on whether or not to excavate and rebuild a road. The local government coordinates underground projects with various parties, and the road administration, together with police and utility companies, constitutes local liaison and coordination committees for the coordination and prevention of traffic and construction accidents. In order to avoid repeated construction, the government invests enough budgets for the construction of underground pipelines, collects data on road refurbishment, develops software for underground drainage systems, and reduces the frequency of road excavations and repeated constructions. Road excavation is generally conducted at night to prevent inconvenience to the public and to ensure smooth traffic flow.

6.2.3.5 Multi-center distribution can avoid the separation of work and residence and reduce the total traffic demand for commuting

Like other well-developed cities in the world, Tokyo's rapid economic development led to population expansion, over-concentration of industries, high land and housing prices in core urban areas, traffic congestion, and environmental deterioration. For this reason, Tokyo has put forward the strategic philosophy of decentralized development and multi-center distribution early on, advanced multi-center urban development, and has built seven subcenters such as Shinjuku, Shibuya, and Ikebukuro in the metropolitan area in different phases, so as to avoid over-concentration of urban functions in a certain area and form an urban pattern of multiple centers. The multi-center urban layout can enable some urban residents to work and live nearby, or realize the integration of work and residence and the integration of industry and city in a certain center, thus effectively avoiding the excessive separation of work and residence and reducing the total rigid traffic demand that must be transported long distances to and from work. Unlike Beijing, which relies primarily on public transportation, a well-developed radial network of urban rail transit has been established between multiple centers to achieve high-capacity, fast and one-stop transportation, effectively relieving the population and traffic pressure in urban centers, and easing the pressure on the urban environment.

Due to the well-developed traffic in the subcenters, especially the subway, Tokyo realizes equalization of public services such as education, medical care, and culture. Equalization can prevent citizens from being overly concentrated in one central urban area because of their preference for particular resources. In Beijing, non-equalization of resources and public services attracts people to crowd into core areas and leads to population expansion, traffic congestion and high housing prices. For example, Dongcheng District, Xicheng District and Haidian District are three areas of Beijing that are overcrowded with high-quality educational and medical resources, and school district housing becomes a core influencing factor for concentration. The high housing prices in these school districts seem to be unattainable. The excessive concentration of high-quality resources inevitably causes traffic congestion and population expansion, so that it is difficult to solve the problems of "urban diseases". Learning from Tokyo's experience, Beijing should promote coordinated development based on a multi-center and balanced distribution of resources. There is no big difference in public services between working or living in central urban areas and in subcenter cities, because the multi-center urban layout can effectively decentralize non-capital functions and relieve the pressure of population, traffic, and environment on central urban areas.

6.2.3.6 Intelligent, digital, and information-based system of transportation can improve the operating efficiency of traffic and effectively ease congestion

Despite its well-developed network of transportation and high ownership rate of vehicles, Tokyo does not alleviate traffic pressure by continuously widening and increasing traffic mileage, but by controlling traffic congestion through complete road facilities and an intelligent, digital, and information-based system, so as to effectively coordinate various means of transportation. It mainly includes the following three systems:[4]

First, the vehicle information and communication system. This system is a digital communication system that provides drivers with information regarding traffic nearby from the vehicle navigation system, which contributes to the safety and smoothness of road traffic and improves the road environment. The system center transmits edited and processed information about road traffic such as traffic jams or control to vehicle navigators promptly for offering information to drivers.

Second, the toll collection system. This system can be installed in all highway toll booths to eliminate or avoid hand-operated toll booths and effectively reduce traffic congestion.

Third, the advanced road support system. This system includes support for safe driving, optimization of traffic management, improvement of the efficiency of road management, support for public transportation, pedestrian support and support for emergency vehicle operations, etc. It is widely applied to the formulation and adjustment of traffic policies, construction and renovation of roads, improvement of safety infrastructures, the manufacturing of vehicles, and the perfection of the functions of technological systems, thus creating favorable conditions for the development, promotion and application of an intelligent transportation system and the establishment of a safe and optimized traffic environment. Moreover, several vehicle makers are involved in the development of the advanced safety vehicle system, with focus on the development of alarm devices for drowsy drivers, automatic braking devices, etc., in which information and communication technology plays a critical role. The development of intelligent, digital, and information-based systems can become an important means for and basic tool in solving traffic congestion, ensuring traffic safety, and reducing environmental pollution.

Further, the high quality of traffic, publicity valuing the awareness of traffic safety, education, and cultivation are also important means to effectively control the traffic congestion in Tokyo.

6.2.4 Promoting equalization of public services, avoiding excessive concentration of public resources in cities

Tokyo has valued the equalized supply of public services, prevented overconcentration of resources in central urban areas, achieved a balanced distribution of the population, and avoided phenomena such as school district housing. Taking education as an example, Tokyo strengthened its regional equalization of education funding according to the regulations of the Japanese government and adopted a job rotation system of teachers, so that the quality of education among schools could be balanced to advance equalization of education. Compulsory education was primarily funded by higher-level government authorities. For example, the prefectural governments in the Tokyo Metropolitan Area were responsible for more than 40% of the funding for compulsory education, while the central government was responsible for about 60% of the funding. The central government provided the main part of education funding and guaranteed the source of funding for the operation of compulsory education.

In terms of teaching staff, teachers in Japanese public elementary and secondary schools, who enjoyed the same salary levels as civil servants were under uniform management and guarantee of the government. The government adjusted the regular rotation and mobility of teachers, so that each teacher could not work in the same school for more than five years and had to be rotated at the end of the period, so as to ensure the relative balance of regional strength and levels of teaching, avoid school choice and school district housing due to difference in teaching quality in schools and prevent price rises that were too rapid and overcrowding of students who made their choice of school in local areas. By adjusting resources of public service, Tokyo tried to equalize and balance such resources, input education, medical and cultural and sports facilities to the ring-shaped residential area, avoided over-concentration of public resources and alleviated the problems of "urban diseases" such as population expansion and traffic congestion.

6.2.5 Treating "urban diseases" such as the control of environmental pollution by law

The central and local governments formulated complete laws and regulations to deal with "urban diseases". Taking the control of environmental pollution as an example, Japan passed a lot of laws to control smog, as shown in Table 6.1. In order to better control environmental pollution, Japan mobilized experts to study the sources of air pollution, and found that air pollution was mainly due to the cross-chemical reaction between factory emissions and motor vehicle exhaust, which form photochemical smog. Japan spent nearly 50 years in fighting these two kinds of sources of pollution. Among them, the first 20 years were mainly used to strengthen the treatment and rectification of factory emissions, and the last 20 years were mainly used to control the pollution of motor vehicle exhaust.

For treating the exhaust emissions from factories, according to the laws enacted in Japan, initially they were targeted at factories, such as the Factory Effluents Control Law in 1958, and the Law on Emission Control of Soot and Smoke in 1962, which focused on the treatment of toxic gases such as hydrogen sulfide emitted from factory chimneys. The government set the corresponding emission standards according to the heights of factory chimneys and air pollution in the areas where factories are located. The city adopted the progressive treatment from first controlling and then reducing, it continuously improved the emission standards of enterprises, and effectively controlled the problems of waste gas emissions from factories. The Japanese government enacted the Air Pollution Control Law in 1968, which elevated emission standards to the legal level, increased penalties and punishments for corporate emissions, and specified that local governments and residents could conclude agreements on prevention of environmental pollution, and directly enter factories for monitoring the emission of pollutants. Japan also strengthened technological innovation in emission reduction, launched special research projects that encouraged research institutions to carry out research on devices for the removal of harmful substances from factory windows, and

Table 6.1 Japanese laws and regulations on smog control

Year	Main law or regulation
1958	Japan enacted the *Factory Effluents Control Law*.
1962	Japan enacted the *Law on Emission Control of Soot and Smoke*.
1967	Japan enacted the *Basic Law for Environmental Pollution Control*.
1968	Japan enacted the *Air Pollution Control Law*.
1970	The Japanese Parliament discussed the issues of environmental pollution and it was called the "Pollution Session".
1971	Japan created the Environment Agency, which was promoted to Ministry of the Environment in 2001. Environment agencies were established in 47 administrative prefectures, 12 large cities and 85 designated cities, and basically formed a national integrated system of administrative management with the Ministry of the Environment at the core.
1978	Japan followed the example of the USA and launched the "Japanese version of the Muskie Act" for toughening vehicle emissions control.
1981	Japan took measures for restricting emissions of nitrogen oxides in major cities.
1992	Japan enacted the *Law Concerning Special Measures to Reduce the Total Amount of Nitrogen Oxides Emitted from Motor Vehicles in Specified Areas*.
2000	Japan enacted the *Environmental Regulations for Ensuring the Health and Safety of Residents*.
2001	Japan enacted the *Law Concerning Special Measures for Total Emission Reduction of Nitrogen Oxides and Particulate Matters from Motor Vehicles in Specified Areas*.
2003	Tokyo introduced a new legislation that required installation of filters in vehicles and banned diesel-engine vehicles from entering Tokyo. At that time, Nissan Motor had the most advanced exhaust filtration technology in the world.
2009	Japan sets the PM2.5 environmental standards.

encouraged enterprises to purchase and install new equipment and materials for the reduction of emissions and waste.

After having made phased achievements for control over the air pollution from factories, Japan proceeded to control the exhaust emissions of motor vehicles. The Japanese government attached importance to the research of devices installed on vehicles for desulfurization and emission reduction, and scientific research institutions worked together with vehicle manufacturers to improve engines, upgrade them to engines with good performance and low emissions, and phase out vehicles with high fuel consumption and high emissions. Japanese manufacturers developed clean energy vehicles and encouraged the promotion of electric vehicles and oil-hybrid vehicles. The use of motor vehicles was also reduced by building urban rail networks and tram systems, thus effectively reducing vehicle emissions.[5] In order to combat urban environmental pollution, the government of Tokyo and the city's public emphasized urban greening and beautification. The government of Tokyo clearly stipulated that new buildings were to have green areas and rooftop greening, which rarely meant planting grass, but planting trees to improve the effect of spatial greening.

With respect to environmental governance, the public played an important role in pollution litigation and legal recourse. The Japanese public launched a social campaign to resist environmental pollution, which swept over the country in the latter half of the 1960s and early 1970s, so that the Japanese government had to emphasize the problems of environmental pollution and enact relevant pollution laws. Victims of pollution became aware of their rights, actively asserted those rights by filing lawsuits regarding environmental pollution, put great pressure on polluters and government authorities, and impelled the control of environmental pollution by people from all walks of life. The most influential case was the Tokyo air pollution lawsuit, in which victims filed a lawsuit against the government and seven major vehicle manufacturers for damages, and demanded immediate cessation of the exhaust emissions of vehicles. It took 11 years from 1996 to 2007 to settle the case. In the end, the defendants were forced to fund and establish a medical subsidy system for patients suffering from air pollution, the government promulgated the policy of controlling vehicle emissions, and vehicle manufacturers spent 1.2 billion Japanese yen for the settlement. During the hearing of the air pollution lawsuit, a victim relief system with Japanese characteristics was also developed.[6]

6.3 Learning from these experiences and policy implications regarding the control of "urban diseases" in Tokyo

Through the above comparative study of Tokyo's treatment of "urban diseases", useful experiences can be summarized and extracted as reference for Beijing in building a world-class harmonious and livable city and promoting the low-carbon development of the Beijing-Tianjin-Hebei region. Tokyo effectively eases the pressure of central urban areas by the construction of subcenters, which effectively attract some industries and population from central urban areas, and reduce the pressure on resources and energy as well as on the environment. Through industrial restructuring, traffic construction, decentralization of functions, construction of infrastructure, and equalization of public services, it has become an important model city for controlling "urban diseases". It can provide effective reference and policy implications for Beijing in building a world-class harmonious and livable city and achieving low-carbon green development.

6.3.1 Strengthening the planning for construction of urban subcenters, enhancing the execution of planning

According to Tokyo's experience of phased and step-by-step planning and construction of urban subcenters, the planning for the construction of urban subcenters in Beijing as the national capital should be strengthened to effectively decentralize the urban functions of the capital and ease the pressure in many aspects, such as urban resources and energy, the environment, population, and traffic. At present, Beijing clearly requires building Tongzhou District as an international new town and Beijing's subcenter, but not enough effort is being put into it and the district is not playing a significant role in decentralizing urban functions. Tongzhou should be more important for taking over population, traffic, industries, and public services, instead of serving a new sleeping city. As a result, a tidal traffic flow forms on Batong Line and traffic arteries from Tongzhou to central urban areas during rush hours, and this leads to congestion. Therefore, there is still a long way to go to speed up the plans for the construction of urban subcenters. It is necessary to strengthen the construction of rail transit, industrial planning, education, medical, and other public services, and add to the atmosphere and resource advantages that can attract people. Only in this way can the urban subcenter truly become an important destination for decentralizing urban functions of the capital.

First, a coordination agency should be established. According to Tokyo's experience, Beijing should plan and build a multi-center, multi-ring, balanced, livable and low-carbon capital economic circle with the pattern of "central areas–subcenters–surrounding new cities–neighboring county centers" and enhance cross-regional planning and coordination. The construction of a multi-center and multi-ring capital economic circle can effectively decentralize non-capital urban functions and promote balanced and coordinated regional development. There is a need to establish a cross-regional coordination agency to carry out unified planning, coordination, and interaction for the development of cities in the capital economic circle, and advance cooperative and coordinated development. The cross-regional coordination agency of the capital economic circle should take the lead in strengthening the formulation, implementation and guidance of the coordinated plans for the development of the Beijing-Tianjin-Hebei region, build a large capital city circle covering Beijing, Tianjin, Hebei, and other cities in the region with joint actions, reasonable industrial division of labor and complementary functions, and narrow the gap for development of cities in the city cluster.

Second, the implementation of planning should be strengthened. While enhancing the plans for urban subcenters, Tokyo strengthens the authoritative implementation of planning, and gives authority to this by legislation. In the planning, decision-making and formulation phases, the city fully seeks public opinion, encourages public participation in the demonstration of plans, improves the scientific nature and operability of urban planning, considers the interests of stakeholders, and forms a unified opinion for the implementation of the plans. In the implementation phase, planning legislation is drafted. For example, it delineates the boundary, direction of the extension and industrial development of the metropolitan area through legislation, and promulgates regulations, such as the National Capital Region Land Development Planning Act, the Act on Restriction of Industries, etc. in the Built-up Area of the National Capital Region, the Act on the Conservation of Suburban Green Zones in the National Capital Region, and the Multi-Polar Patterns National Land Formation Promotion Act, which clarifies the legal status of urban planning and ensures its effective implementation. Beijing's urban planning is characterized by a lack of unified planning authorities, planning of land and industries by multiple government agencies, improper enforcement, inability to supervise and curb violations of planning promptly, continuous expansion of city size, serious over-utilization of land, and illegal construction that cannot be prohibited. It needs to learn from the experience of Tokyo, strengthen the implementation and planning, enhance the authoritativeness of planning, particularly unifying various plans, strictly plan and implement, avoid the occurrence of various violations and prevent violation first and then revision of rules and regulations.

6.3.2 Enhancing the equalized allocation of public resources, effectively decentralizing urban functions

According to Tokyo's experience in treating "urban diseases", either the construction of subcenters or industrial transfer and diversion of population highlight the equal distribution of public resources and public services and avoid excessive local concentration of resources. By decentralization of advantageous resources, equalization of public resources and equal supply of public services, it reduces the regional difference and creates basic conditions for decentralization of urban functions. Tokyo fully fulfils the role of government regulation and market guidance to effectively control the size of the city by equalized configuration of public resources and public services, guide the diversion of population and industries towards surrounding areas and avoid over-concentration in the core area.

First of all, it should establish a high-density and wide-coverage system of rail transit, build a fast flow channel among central urban areas and the surrounding areas, and create convenient conditions of decentralizing urban functions. Convenient traffic can provide a condition for the diversion of the population and create prerequisites for equalized allocation of public resources.

Second, it should improve the integrated service functions of new cities such as urban subcenters. New cities are not only sleeping cities, but they also have basic production and living conditions for livability and workability, so as to reduce the long-distance travel demand of the commuting population. Urban subcenters and various new cities should become important functional service areas to effectively take over the population and industries from central urban areas.

Third, the equalized configuration of education resources should be strengthened to avoid the over-concentration of high-quality education resources in central urban areas. For example, Tokyo legislates to facilitate the reasonable flow of excellent teachers among regions and achieve the equalization of the quality of education. Prestigious universities are distributed around suburban areas, and famous schools are moved to new cities or distant suburban districts and counties and towns to avoid over-concentration of high-quality education resources in central urban areas and the phenomenon that citizens pursue "school district housing".

According to the law of talent development and people's demand for education, high quality education resources should be increased moderately, such as enrollments into key universities, so that more people have the opportunity to receive high-quality education, instead of setting unfair education thresholds by indicators in the era of the planned economy, which inevitably results in unfairly different admission standards with the same score. The reasons behind such unfairness include a privileged way of thinking, and limited enrollments into key universities. The model of admission or management system of key or famous universities "with enrollments in short supply" is bound to lead to fierce competition.

In order to achieve the equalized allocation of education resources, especially the equalization of high quality education resources, first of all, the opportunity for fair competition for such resources like key and famous universities should be increased from the source, otherwise the decentralization of high-quality education resources is a false proposition, because after the decentralization of old high-quality education resources, new concentration will be formed and will result in new school district housing requests.

Beijing should accelerate the decentralization of urban functions, enhance equalized allocation and balanced distribution of public services and public resources, divert the highly concentrated quality education and medical resources in central urban areas, and accelerate the supply of public resources to surrounding new cities and other cities in the city cluster, so as to guide the transfer and diversion of the population, industry and capital to surrounding areas. The decentralization of non-capital functions of Beijing does not mean relocating all public resources in the core area to other areas, but a quantitative decentralization and qualitative improvement based on guaranteeing the supply of basic public services in the core area. After guaranteeing basic public services such as education, medical care, and culture in the core area, new education, medical, and cultural projects are compressed, with the focus on increasing the supply of public services such as education, medical care, and culture and optimizing the allocation of resources in the destinations of diversion, impelling a relatively balanced distribution and an equalized allocation of public resources in spaces, and avoiding the concentration of too many high-quality resources in the core area.

6.3.3 Guiding industrial transformation, transfer and upgrading, reducing the over-expansion of the population in central urban areas

Industry is the core of urban economic development that is necessary for supporting urban development. However, industrial development may attract an influx of population which exceeds the established size and capacity of the city, thus leading to excessive concentration of industry and an over-expansion of the population, and further causing a series of "urban diseases" such as population, transportation, resources, energy, the environment, high housing prices, and social instability. Therefore, in order to treat "urban diseases", the industry issues should be scientifically, objectively, and rationally analyzed. A city needs to develop industries, which however does not mean over-development of industries, nor does it mean the development of just any industry, or the indefinite expansion and agglomeration of industries. It should consider the carrying capacity and constraints of urban resources and energy, transportation, infrastructure, the environment, etc.

Regarding Tokyo's experience, it effectively treated "urban diseases" by diverting, restructuring and upgrading industries to facilitate the diversion of population. For example, the Industrial Control Law was enacted to transfer heavy and chemical industries to other distant suburban areas, improve the quality and efficiency of industries in central urban areas, and vigorously develop knowledge- and technology-intensive service sectors. Beijing does not have very high-quality industries. On the one hand, it should continue to phase out, transform, and relocate industries with relatively high pollution, water consumption, and energy consumption. On the other hand, the city should vigorously develop knowledge- and technology-intensive service sectors and improve the quality and efficiency of its service sectors. At present, the proportion of service sectors in Beijing reaches more than 70%, but they do not have high quality or competitive power. The scale of productive services is not large, the proportion of life services is high, and the level of energy consumption is also high.

Beijing needs to reduce the intensity of industrial energy consumption and the level of carbon emissions through industrial restructuring, transformation, upgrading and transfer, improve its industrial quality, continue to phase out and transform low-end industries in some suburban districts and counties, enhance industrial restructuring in central urban areas, take the opportunity of functional decentralization to transfer low-end industries and some labor-intensive industries to distant suburban districts and counties and neighboring areas in Hebei and Tianjin. By industrial transfer and guided diversion of pollution, the city may avoid over-expansion of the population in central urban areas. Beijing should highlight the coordinated development of core urban areas and peripheral areas, especially distant suburbs, distribute high-end service sectors and high-tech industries to these areas, and facilitate the industrial transformation and upgrading of these backward areas. In this way, not only can the quality and efficiency of industries in distant suburbs be improved and can energy consumption and environmental pollution be reduced, but also high-end employment can be increased in peripheral areas to avoid over-concentration of population or talents in core areas. If the CBD or new construction projects can be moved to distant suburbs, this may ease the traffic congestion and environmental pollution in this area, prevent people in Yanjiao, Tongzhou, Tiantongyuan, and other major "sleeping cities" from being busy for work, and reasonably and effectively divert the population.

6.3.4 Accelerating the construction of a regional rail transit network, thus solving the problem of urban traffic congestion

Compared with Tokyo, Beijing's rail transit lags far behind in terms of construction density, mileage, coverage, and related facilities. Rail transit does not play a very important role in the traffic of Beijing. Beijing should take the following measures to speed up its construction of the regional rail transit network. First, the city should innovate the model of investment and financing of rail transit construction. It must enhance the construction of the existing subway lines in Beijing, start the construction as early as possible, improve the speed and scale of rail transit construction, use PPP, BOT and other modes, fully attract social capital to participate in rail transit construction, change the traditional model of rail transit development and construction, improve the return on investment of rail transit construction in the form of subway properties and institutional mechanisms, and change the traditional model of planned economy relying solely on government investment. Subway properties can further raise the value of land along the subway, grant land development rights to the rail transit investors along the subway, carry out commercial development of land within the scope of the existing land planning and relevant regulations, obtain part of land revenue to make up for deficiency and return of capital, revitalize the various revenue capitals brought by rail transit construction, thus improving the benefits and advancing the progress of rail transit construction. Second, the institutional mechanisms must be innovated. Taking the opportunity of the coordinated development of the Beijing-Tianjin-Hebei region, with reference to the Tokyo metropolitan development model, Beijing should vigorously complete rail transit construction among central urban areas, surrounding areas and adjacent towns, expand the coverage of rail transit, create the basic conditions for transportation in order to decentralize the functions, population and industries of central urban areas, lay a foundation for promoting the coordinated development among regions and solve the problem of traffic congestion.

6.3.4.1 With reference to Tokyo's experience, Beijing, as a national capital that will be built as an international city cluster, should build a traffic network dominated by rail transit as soon as possible and increase the supply, carrying capacity and convenience of the subway

First, Beijing, also the Beijing-Tianjin-Hebei region, should accelerate the establishment of a three-dimensional traffic network dominated by rail transit, and form a three-dimensional system of rapid transit on the ground, underground, and above ground. Beijing should speed up the construction of rail transit around the city center to connect urban subcenters and satellite towns organically, so that cities are interconnected by a relatively fast and large-capacity network of rail transit. It must construct many light railway lines in a radial pattern, extending to suburbs or neighboring cities, and develop new small and medium-sized cities and industrial centers at the end of these lines, in order to further reduce the long-distance transportation by buses on the ground and ease the environmental pressure caused by traffic congestion and exhaust emissions.

Second, at core areas of the city, especially within the fourth ring or even the fifth ring, the subway should be available for transfer every 500–2,000 meters. In the meanwhile, complex railway lines should be built at busy roads and main arteries, such as Line 1, so as to achieve high density, multi-site, wide coverage of the rail transit system, and connect all the districts of Beijing and surrounding counties of Hebei and Tianjin by one or two lines of rail transit.

Third, while increasing the number of express trains, subway lines in core areas must ensure that the station-to-station distance is designed to be less than 500 meters, and more entrances and exits must be added, which should be connected to large commercial buildings and office buildings. The goal is that people taking rail transit in Beijing must be more than 80% of the total travelling population. This can effectively divert the capital's population and create transportation conditions that can decentralize the non-capital functions. Rail transit should be connected to all hotels, shopping malls and office buildings, and designed with convenient accesses.

Fourth, Beijing should do well in maintaining the traffic order of rail transit, advocate civilized manners that encourage people to queue up to get on and off the trains, not to cut in line and not to talk loudly in the train, accelerate the construction of civilized traffic order and create a good environment for traveling. The civilization of traffic order reflects the civilization of a city. To build an international first-class harmonious and livable city, Beijing should highlight the traffic education of citizens and emphasize the civilization of traffic order. Traffic wardens and volunteers can be added to actively guide the public to obey traffic rules, handle traffic violations and infractions in a prompt manner, stop uncivilized behavior, and maintain a civilized traffic order. The city should also provide the job training of traffic police, so that they can be meticulous at work, promptly remind motor vehicles of not occupying non-motorized lanes, and educate promptly and resolutely prevent electric bicycles, motorcycles, cars driven by elderly people or motor vehicles which drive on the wrong way or run the red light, or pedestrians who have uncivilized behaviors such as not using crosswalks. During law enforcement, traffic police should actively advocate polite manners, refuse rigid requirements, supervise more, smile more, and pass civilized manners to every citizen. Anyone who violates rules should be mandatorily required to be wardens or traffic volunteers for one month, so as to improve their traffic civilization and learn to consciously obey traffic regulations.

6.3.4.2 The government should play a leading role, strengthen the coordination among the various means of transportation, solve the problem of the last mile, perfect the design of bus lines, open up the "capillaries" of traffic, reduce the number of long-distance buses in core areas, and increase the frequency of buses in remote suburban areas where rail transit is not yet available, so as to facilitate travel

First, the government of Beijing should play a leading role in strengthening the coordination among the different means of transportation, especially the plans regarding the subway and buses. In Tokyo, the government at all levels has always played a leading role in controlling traffic congestion and they value the planning and design of traffic and the coordination and integration of the various means of transportation. Beijing should strengthen the interface among subways, buses, railroads, and other sectors, boost the integrated planning and interconnection of various means of transportation, avoid and reduce sectoral protectionism, and facilitate passenger traffic and transfers.

Second, efforts should be devoted to solving the last mile problem and reducing long-distance buses in core areas. Because Tokyo's rail transit is well developed, there are almost no buses on the ground. The only buses are those serving the function of connecting subway stations and the last mile. Compared with Beijing, if many bus lines are designed in busy areas, including where the subway may be constructed, this can put certain pressure on the traffic capacity. Some buses compete for passengers and driving lanes, and this also causes certain traffic hazards. With reference to the experience of Tokyo, the number of buses and private cars in core urban areas should be reduced, all buses and private cars should be changed to underground passages, the ground is mainly used for pedestrians and bicycle lanes, so as to reduce urban traffic hazards, decrease urban noise, and create the conditions for building a quiet and livable city.

Emphasis should be put on the traffic diversion of main and tributary lines, the last mile of traffic construction, opening up "cut-off roads" and "capillaries" in various areas, and the effective diversion of traffic congestion on trunk roads. The frequency of road excavation and reconstruction should be reduced to void repeated excavations and reduce traffic congestion.

Third, the number of buses in areas where rail transit may be constructed should be moderately decreased, especially long-distance buses in core urban areas with developed rail transit, so as to reduce the flow of ground traffic. However, the number of lines and the frequency of buses should be increased where there is no subway line, for facilitating the traffic in distant suburbs.

Fourth, bus hub stations should be changed as a design that focuses on subway stations out of the fifth ring, and bus hub stations such as Dongzhimen should be canceled or reduced to ease the traffic congestion in central urban areas, especially around bus hub stations.

154 *Tokyo experience of "urban diseases"*

The city should accelerate the construction of overpass elevators and subway transfer elevators, strengthen delicate management, ensure convenient, punctual, and smooth transfer and achieve flawless interfacing. For building an international first-class harmonious and livable city, Beijing should reflect the level of modernization of the city, and a people-oriented philosophy and convenient traffic conditions. Elevators should be installed for overpasses at important road sections to provide convenience for the public, reduce the occurrence of red light running between pedestrians and motor vehicles, ensure traffic safety, and enhance the modernization of transportation in the capital city. While ensuring elevator safety, elevators should be installed at subway interchange stations and stops, to improve the passenger transfer capacity of the subway, save the time of traffic, increase the subway's attractiveness, meet the traffic demand of the system of public transportation dominated by rail transit, and ensure a smooth and flawless flow of passengers.

6.3.4.3 Beijing should guide the reduction of the frequency of driving private cars in phases, introduce road congestion charges and motor vehicle pollution taxes as soon as possible on particularly congested sections of roads, during peak periods, and in severe foggy weather conditions, raise the standards of parking fees by time, enhance monitoring and penalties for parking violations, improve the skill of motor vehicle owners and traffic order, and effectively control traffic congestion

Private cars only account for 6% of the traffic in Tokyo, so this greatly reduces the pressure on urban traffic and decreases the exhaust emissions and environmental pollution caused by motor vehicles. The government of Tokyo plays a leading and enforcing role, and behaves strictly in combating traffic congestion, restricting traffic, restricting cars, and imposing congestion charges. It must ensure administration strictly according to law, impose various traffic taxes and parking charges to guide or restrict private cars, and guide citizens to choose buses and subways. Besides Tokyo, other cities also impose congestion charges, as shown in Table 6.2.[7]

In Beijing, the capital city, traffic relies heavily on private cars during rush hours, and this is an important cause of traffic congestion. Meanwhile, according to the analysis of the sources of smog in Beijing, motor vehicles contribute more than 31%. According to Tokyo's experience, as important measures of traffic congestion control and emission reduction, the use of private cars must be restricted or reduced.

First of all, the insufficient carrying capacity of rail transit and the limited carrying capacity of buses cannot keep up with the current demand of commuters in Beijing. Hence, it is unrealistic to fully restrict or control motor vehicles in a short period of time. Private cars must be guided to reduce the frequency of use in phases and steps.

Second, it should gradually change the current way of obtaining license plate numbers by lottery, learn from the experience of other cities, auction

Table 6.2 Experience of main cities in levying congestion charges

City	Experience in levying congestion charges
London	Since 2003, London has levied congestion charges on vehicles in the city center, from Monday to Friday 7:00 a.m. to 6:30 p.m. Vehicles must pay these charges when driving on streets, but taxis, police cars, fire trucks and ambulances are exceptions. Not just British dignitaries, but also foreign dignitaries, in fact, Obama's car also had to pay such charges, which are 5 pounds per a period of time and lately, this has risen to 8 pounds. They can be paid at parking lots, gas stations, kiosks, post offices, and other specially designated tax payment points, or by network or telephone. If frequent driving to downtown is needed, car owners can also make payments per week, month or year.
Lisbon	Buses also pay the charges. In the center of Lisbon, there are two old urban areas where vehicles other than those of local residents are prohibited, and the other areas of the city levy congestion charges. All "vehicles entering the city center" must pay these charges, without any restriction on private or public vehicles.
Tokyo	It adopts a high taxation policy for vehicles, which must pay nine items of taxes, including consumption tax, vehicle acquisition tax, vehicle weight tax, light vehicle tax, fuel tax, diesel trading tax, and oil and gas tax. Most taxes and fees are to be paid by consumers themselves. The city raises parking fees, and individuals are required to have parking contracts in order to buy cars. The monthly rent of parking space in Tokyo is between 20,000 and 40,000 Japanese yen. Designated parking spaces in downtown areas of Tokyo charge 300 Japanese yen an hour. Car owners are only allowed to park for one hour, and after one hour, they will receive a fine of 15,000 Japanese yen.

license plates, regulate the total number of motor vehicles by the market mechanism, and allow for trading of license plates of motor vehicles on the market and aim at lawful mobility. The total number of motor vehicles in Beijing should be limited through scientific forecasting, and no new license plate numbers should be added within this scope of limitation.

Third, an electronic toll collection or fine system (ETC) should be designed to collect congestion charges on vehicles passing along important congested roads, at different time points, such as rush hours or congestion periods. No charges will be collected at non-rush hours or non-congestion periods. In severe smoggy weather, motor vehicle pollution tax should be levied on fuel vehicles, together with congestion charges. A vehicle information and communication system like that in Tokyo may be designed to inform and guide private cars in advance through on-board radio. No pollution tax should be imposed on new-energy vehicles such as electric vehicles, and the market mechanism and social capital should be introduced to enhance the investment and construction of charging piles and guide citizens to choose new-energy vehicles. After the gradual improvement of the rail transit system, it is recommended to abolish the restriction based on the last digit of license plate numbers, adopt the policy of levying congestion charges within the fifth ring or the sixth ring on commuting to and from work by time periods and road sections, thus guiding citizens to reduce the use of private cars and make a real contribution to the control of traffic congestion and smog.

Fourth, parking charges should be raised by time periods. All parking spaces in the city should be registered with a unified numbering system, and an electronic registration system should be established for both public parking spaces and those owned by companies. Parking is paid for by credit cards, and charged on the basis of the time one parks his/her vehicle, and the charging standard may stipulate the lowest price. Parking spaces designated in urban areas should charge 50 yuan per hour, and vehicles can only be parked for one hour. After automatic deduction through the electronic system, the charges can be returned to the owners of different parking spaces in a certain percentage. A parking space monitoring system should be established throughout the city to enhance the penalties for parking violations, especially parking on roads, which are also levied by the electronic scanning and automatic deduction system. Raising parking charges may effectively restrict the use of private cars, and reduce the frequency of driving motor vehicles on roads, thus achieving the goal of controlling traffic congestion.

Fifth, the skill of motor vehicle owners and traffic order should be improved to effectively control traffic congestion, which aims at not restricting motor vehicles and citizens, but at creating an easily accessible and smooth traffic environment. Therefore, it is necessary to improve the skills of motor vehicle owners, and maintain good traffic order and traffic civilization. Traffic safety awareness education and publicity should be enhanced.

Sixth, citizens who have the need to purchase vehicles are encouraged and guided to buy new-energy vehicles, and government agencies and civil servants should take the lead in buying new-energy vehicles. The government of Tokyo at all levels buy hydrogen-fueled vehicles for official use, and the government makes it mandatory for civil servants to choose new-energy cars. Due to the relatively serious smoggy weather and environmental pollution, Beijing should accelerate the transformation and upgrading of its energy consumption structure. The government should take the lead in purchasing new-energy vehicles, and guide and encourage citizens who have the need to purchase vehicles to buy those powered by new energy. The government should strengthen the construction of supporting facilities and charging piles for new-energy vehicles.

6.3.4.4 Multi-center distribution can avoid the separation of work and residence and reduce the total traffic demand for commuting to and from work

Beijing should strengthen the construction of Tongzhou as a subcenter, form a multi-center pattern of urban spaces as soon as possible, clearly specify The strategic positioning of the capital city, decentralize non-capital functions, and divert the education, medical, cultural, and other high-quality resources from core areas of Beijing such as Dongcheng District, Xicheng District, Haidian District, and Chaoyang District to subcenters or establish branches.

First, the increment of high-quality resources in central urban areas such as those within the Fourth Ring Road should be reduced, and conditions should be created to guide the diversion of high-quality resources. On the premise of ensuring the necessary public services of education, medical care, and culture in central urban areas and that the quality of life does not deteriorate, the high-end education, medical care, culture, and other high-quality resources should be fully or partially diverted, and the docking and interconnection with neighboring areas should be strengthened.

Second, those subcenters and satellite towns should speed up docking with high-end resources of central urban areas, strive for the decentralization of state organs and state-owned enterprises and institutions to subcenters and satellite towns and for the establishment of branches, they should create more employment opportunities and development space for subcenters and satellite towns, guide the local resident population to work locally, and to avoid or reduce the distance between work and residence.

Third, it is necessary to enhance the construction of education, medical, cultural, and other public service resources in subcenters and satellite towns, accelerate the construction of rail transit in subcenters and satellite towns, and improve the attractiveness to population and industries, so that industries and population in central urban areas can be retained and develop well in subcenters and satellite towns, thus truly achieving the goal of diverting non-capital functions and reducing the total traffic demand for commuting to and from work.

6.3.4.5 Beijing should accelerate the establishment of an intelligent, digital, and information-based system of transportation in the capital city to improve the operating efficiency of traffic and effectively reduce congestion

Intelligence, digitalization and informatization are the trend and tide for future urban development inclusive of urban traffic. The use of modern information technology, network technology and traffic technology can effectively improve the current efficiency and governance of traffic, not only to enhance road accessibility, but also to effectively avoid and reduce traffic congestion. Attention should be paid to the establishment of a vehicle information and communication system, which can provide drivers with information about the surrounding traffic, enhance the safety and smoothness of road traffic, and improve the road environment. A toll collection system should be established as soon as possible. In particular, an ETC system should be installed at the toll booths accessible to Beijing as soon as possible, and hand-operated toll booths should be cancelled or reduced. This system should be opened at all highway toll booths to effectively reduce traffic congestion. A road support system should be established to serve safe driving and emergency vehicle supports, optimize traffic management, and improve the efficiency of road management.

6.3.5 Improving laws and regulations, controlling the pollution of the urban environment

First of all, the government at all levels, especially the central government, should highlight the institutionalized governance of environmental pollution by enacting the Law on Emission Control of Soot and Smoke and the Air Pollution Prevention Law, raise the emission standards of enterprises, restrict their emissions, and reduce the total amount of industrial pollution. By legal provisions, the city can eliminate all backward production capacity, raise the standards of industrial emissions, strengthen industrial transformation and upgrading, and reduce industrial and other emissions. For Beijing, in order to control urban environmental pollution, regulations should be enacted to strengthen industrial transformation and upgrading, eliminate backward industries, raise emission standards of enterprises, and enhance supervision of and punishment for enterprises exceeding the permitted levels according to regulations.

Second, Beijing should promulgate rules and regulations to restrict the exhaust emissions of vehicles, mandatorily require motor vehicles to install exhaust emission reduction devices, continuously reduce the total number of fuel vehicles, decrease the use of fuel vehicles, and encourage the purchase and use of new-energy vehicles such as electric vehicles.

Third, Beijing should encourage social organizations and the public to participate in the control of environmental pollution. Public participation can enhance the power of prevention and control of urban pollution. Social organizations and the public are also victims and producers of environmental pollution, and their active role and interaction are certainly indispensable for the prevention and control of environmental pollution. Relying on the government only, or pushing the government to the point of being opposed to by the people, is not conducive to the enhancement of the government's image, or to the prevention and control of various kinds of environmental pollution. Hence, it is necessary to fully mobilize the enthusiasm, initiative and creativity of social organizations and the public, actively participate in the control of environmental pollution, achieve and share the fruits of urban environmental protection, and jointly create a green and livable urban space.

Fourth, Beijing should focus on urban greening, expand urban ecological spaces, require green roofs for new buildings and attach importance to the construction of green buildings. It should encourage the use of energy-saving and environmentally-friendly materials, promote three-dimensional greening, realize greening on walls, roofs, and other areas exposed to the sun, reduce the loss of energy in buildings, and actively use green materials and green spaces, which can increase certain carbon sink, but also beautify the environment, and reduce carbon emissions and energy consumption.

6.4 Summary

This chapter examined Tokyo's experience of treating "urban diseases" from the perspective of subcenter construction. Tokyo, a well-known international city, has also encountered serious "urban diseases". Tokyo took effective measures to deal with these "urban diseases", including planning and guidance, decentralization of functions, construction of subcenter cities, industrial restructuring, diversion of the population, and allocation of resources. These experiences are worthy of reference for Beijing.

The manifestations of "urban diseases" in Tokyo include rapid population growth, over-concentration of industrial enterprises in central areas of the city, rapid development of industries such as steel, shipbuilding, machinery, chemicals, and electronics. A large number of manufacturing enterprises were concentrated in Tokyo and attracted a massive influx of population, thus further leading to difficulties in housing supply, pressure on traffic, increased emissions due to the clustering of enterprises and serious pollution of the urban environment. The key experience of the control of "urban diseases" in Tokyo can be spoken of as follows: first, strengthening the planning for and decentralization of urban functions, constructing subcenter cities; second, adjusting the industrial structure, guiding the diversion of the population; third, building a rail transit system in the metropolitan area, improving public transportation facilities; and fourth, promoting equalization of public services, avoiding an excessive concentration of public resources in cities. Through the comparative study of Tokyo's treatment of "urban diseases", useful experiences can be summarized and extracted as a reference for Beijing in building a world-class harmonious and livable city and promoting the low-carbon development of the Beijing-Tianjin-Hebei region. First, strengthening the plans for the construction of urban subcenters, enhancing the execution of those plans; second, enhancing the equalized allocation of public resources, effectively decentralizing urban functions; third, guiding industrial transformation, transfer and upgrading, reducing the over-expansion of the population in central urban areas; and fourth, accelerating the construction of a regional rail transit network, thus solving the problem of urban traffic congestion.

Notes

1 Lin Xi, Valuable Experience: How Japan Controlled Smog, *Life Times*, March 11, 2014.
2 Zhang Xuan, Delicacy and Traffic Demand Management: Tokyo's Control of Traffic Congestion, *Journal of Jiangxi Radio & TV University*, 2014(4).
3 Zhang Xuan, Delicacy and Traffic Demand Management: Tokyo's Control of Traffic Congestion, *Journal of Jiangxi Radio & TV University*, 2014(4).
4 Zhang Xuan, Delicacy and Traffic Demand Management: Tokyo's Control of Traffic Congestion, *Journal of Jiangxi Radio & TV University*, 2014(4).

5 Lin Xi, Valuable Experience: How Japan Controlled Smog, *Life Times*, March 11, 2014.
6 Qu Yang, The Legal Path of Air Pollution Control in Japan, *Legal Daily*, January 22, 2013.
7 Zhou Weili, Four Questions on Trial Levying of Congestion Charges in Beijing in 2016, *Guangzhou Daily*, December 14, 2015.

7 Ruhr experience in the control of "urban diseases"

The perspective of industrial upgrading

As the progress of urbanization accelerates, the consumption of resources and energy and environmental pollution increase, and seriously restrict sustainable urban economic and social development. Many resource-based cities are facing the problems of "urban diseases" such as resource depletion, ecological deterioration, and environmental pollution. To change the traditional labor-intensive urban development model of high energy consumption and high carbon, and speed up the construction of new urbanization necessarily require the promotion of an urban ecological civilization and low-carbon development. Urban industrial upgrading and low-carbon development based on cultural transformation has become an important model for and experiential choice of many Western countries in strengthening the treatment of "urban diseases". The problems, such as depletion of coal resources, declining industries, closing of resource-based enterprises and the laying off of workers in the Ruhr area, seriously constrain sustainable urban economic development. For treating "urban diseases", the Ruhr area was successfully built as a modern, ecological, low-carbon, and livable city through cultural transformation, industrial upgrading, and ecological construction, by vigorously promoting industrial culture tours, renewing, and transforming old industrial sites, turning several abandoned industrial buildings into forest parks, art galleries, and design centers, and developing cultural tourism. It is important to study the experience of cultural transformation and industrial upgrading in the Ruhr area of Germany, which can be of great practical significance for Beijing in strengthening its treatment of "urban diseases" and in realizing low-carbon development.

7.1 The history of development: important reasons for industrial upgrading in the Ruhr area

The Ruhr area was once the industrial lifeblood of western Germany, and the main base of German coal and steel production, with an industrial area of 4,593 square kilometers. However, the long-term mineral exploitation and industrialization as well as the development of heavy industries such as coal, steel and mechanical engineering led to serious environmental pollution and

DOI: 10.4324/9781003272991-7

ecological deterioration in the Ruhr area, which was once known as one of the dirtiest areas in Europe. The Ruhr area successfully realized urban transformation by cultural transformation, ecological restoration and low-carbon governance of traditional industrial towns and improving the quality and efficiency of its industries. The history of the development in the Ruhr area is reflected as a process from the prosperity of the traditional coal industry and industrial development, to de-industrialization, and then to cultural transformation and industrial upgrading for achieving urban transformation and low-carbon development, as shown in Table 7.1.

7.1.1 Phase of industrial boom: development of traditional industries in the Ruhr area relying on coal resources

The Ruhr area of Germany, emerging in the mid-19th century, was known as the heart of German industry. The development of the coal industry, the steel industry, and rail transportation enabled the Ruhr area to develop as an important industrial city belt within a few decades. The Ruhr area had extremely abundant coal resources and good geographical advantages, as shown in Table 7.2. The development of coal minerals and related resources led to the prosperity of traditional industries and the formation of an industrial system dominated by the exploitation of coal resources. Due to the concentration of large quantities of enterprises, factories, and houses for developing coal resources, and the relatively developed traffic facilities, the region between the Ruhr River and the Emsher River in the southern part of the Ruhr area shaped a well-developed industrial system and a functional urban region. The Ruhr area had geological reserves of 219 billion tons of coal, which accounted for three-quarters of the total reserves in Germany, and included economically recoverable reserves of about 22 billion tons, which accounted for 90% of those of the country. Surrounding the development of coal resources, the Ruhr area formed a series of industries such as coking, electricity, and coal chemistry, and developed the steel industry, chemical industry, machinery manufacturing industry, the nitrogen fertilizer industry, and the building materials industry. The Ruhr area produced 80% of Germany's hard coal and 90% of Germany's coking coal. In addition, it also had two-thirds of Germany's capacity for steel production, as well as that of electricity, sulfuric acid, synthetic rubber and oil refining, and the military industry played an important role in Germany and accounted for half of Germany's economic development. The Ruhr area also had a certain influence in Europe and the world because of the industrial development of its coal resources.

7.1.2 The phase of industrial decline: de-industrialization causes "urban diseases" in the Ruhr area

After the 1950s, the Ruhr area's economy gradually declined. With the decline of traditional industries such as coal and steel, the Ruhr area, like other old

Table 7.1 The history of development by cultural transformation and industrial upgrading in the Ruhr area

Main phases	Time	Key features	Leading industries
Phase of industrial boom	In the mid-19th century	Based on coal resources, it formed heavy and chemical industries, produced 80% of Germany's hard coal and 90% of Germany's coking coal, owned two-thirds of Germany's capacity for the production of steel and played a prominent role in Germany.	Coking, electricity, coal chemistry, iron and steel industry, chemical industry, machinery manufacturing, nitrogen fertilizer industry, building material industry, synthetic rubber, oil refining capacity, military industry, etc.
Phase of industrial decline	In the 1950s	De-industrialization created a dilemma of urban transformation in the Ruhr area. The declining traditional industries, resource depletion and environmental pollution led to "urban diseases".	Industries such as coal, steel declined, the number of coal mines in Germany, and coal production in the Ruhr area were decreasing year by year.
Phase of industrial transformation	In the 1960s	The Ruhr area enhanced integrated regulation, cultural transformation and industrial upgrading, conducted cultural transformation and the comprehensive use of abandoned mines, factories, and industrial relics, strengthened the construction of cultural infrastructure, and achieved urban transformation and low-carbon development.	It strengthened the development of industrial heritage tourism, developed cultural industries, built museums, and transformed machine shops and coke factories into industrial innovation bases for drama, opera, fine arts, pop music, jazz, and concerts in the Ruhr area.

industrial areas in the world, faced a structural crisis, and the depletion of resources and environmental pollution caused many "urban diseases". Due to the impact of the world energy crisis and the technological revolution, the global overcapacity of steel and the decline in the status of coal energy, the Ruhr area's steel and coal industries plunged into recession, the industrial development went into the doldrums, growth slowed down, unemployment increased, it was brain-drained, pollution worsened,[1] and a series of

Table 7.2 Geographical advantages and the influences of industrial development in the Ruhr area

Geographical advantages		Main influences
Traffic location	Located at the crossroads of land transportation in central Europe, railway and road transportation were convenient; the Rhine River, Lippe River, Ruhr River, and canals formed a network of inland rivers, which was connected to the ocean through the port of Rotterdam at the mouth of the Rhine River.	Its well-developed and convenient water transportation could provide a precondition for the importation of raw materials and exportation of products in the Ruhr area, and the status of a traffic hub promoted the rapid development of industries.
Resource endowments	Abundant coal resources were able to provide resources for the industrial development of the Ruhr area. The Ruhr coalfield had high-quality coal resources with abundant reserves and good mining conditions.	Abundant coal resources lay an important basis for the development of the coal industry, the steel industry, the power industry, and the chemical industry in the Ruhr area.
Upstream industries	Iron ores came initially from the iron ore mines of Lorraine, France close to the southwest of the Ruhr area, and later from Sweden. The Ruhr area was relatively close to these iron ore mines.	This was conducive to saving freight costs and reducing production costs. The convenient connection of upstream industries created conditions for the industrial development of the Ruhr area.
Consumer market	The well-developed industries and product demand in Germany and Western Europe provided a broad consumer market for industrial products from the Ruhr area.	It facilitated the sale of industrial products and the development of industry.

economic and social problems arose. Industrial development was constrained and the international competitiveness of local manufacturing enterprises declined continuously, leading to the de-industrialization of the Ruhr area. De-industrialization was mainly manifested as a series of industrial decline in which factories and enterprises went bankrupt, closed down, moved to other regions or switched to other industries, as shown in Table 7.3.[2] The number of coal mines in Germany, and the coal production in the Ruhr area decreased year by year. Because of the over-reliance on coal and other energy-intensive industries, the disadvantages of the economic structure dominated by

Table 7.3 The process of de-industrialization in Germany and the Ruhr area

Year	1957	1960	1965	1970	1975	1980	1985	1990	1995	2000
Number of coal mines in Germany (mines)	153	133	101	69	46	39	33	27	19	12 (Zin Ruhr)
Coal production of the Ruhr (millions of tons)	123.2	115.5	110.9	91.1	75.9	69.2	64.0	54.6	41.6	25.9

heavy and chemical industries became even more obvious, and the traditional coal and steel industries gradually declined. The reasons for the de-industrialization of the Ruhr area and its urban transformation were the decline and increasing depression of the coal industry with the rise of oil and gas, and the withdrawal of the steel industry from the historical stage due to the globalized division of labor.[3] De-industrialization had serious economic and social impacts, with a large number of unemployed workers and increasing environmental pollution. The Ruhr area was facing various problems of transformation and "urban diseases", such as how to deal with the problem of de-industrialization and how to dispose of abandoned mines, old factories, and ancillary facilities.

7.1.3 The phase of industrial transformation: the Ruhr area strengthens comprehensive improvement to achieve low-carbon development

After the 1960s, the Ruhr area implemented comprehensive improvements to strengthen cultural transformation and industrial upgrading, which features low-carbon development with low energy consumption and environmental pollution, and lay an important basis for urban economic restructuring and the enhancement of cultural soft power. In the early 1990s, the depletion of resources, industrial decline, and high unemployment rates prompted the Ruhr area to explore the importance of cultural industry and its inherent potential for the creation of jobs. Faced with the dilemma of the depletion of the coal resources and urban transformation, local governments highlighted the transformation, upgrading and renovation of traditional industries, transformed and comprehensively utilized abandoned industrial mines, factories and industrial heritage for cultural renovation, incorporated cultural connotations, strengthened the construction of cultural infrastructures, realized the intensive use of resources and energy and environmental improvement, and achieved the low-carbon development of the economy and society. It strengthened the construction of cultural infrastructures, the development of industrial heritage tourism and of the cultural industry, reduced energy

166 *Ruhr experience of "urban diseases"*

consumption and environmental pollution, and realized industrial upgrading and low-carbon development. The Ruhr area planned and built dense cultural infrastructures, and cultural facilities and activities were often funded by local governments and accounted for about 5% of the annual local budget. In the early 21st century, 5 million Ruhr citizens had five opera houses. The German Mining Museum in Bochum became a world-known thematic museum, thanks to the 260,000 miners who worked in the region half a century ago. The Ruhr Museum, which was converted from a coal-washing plant, would become a monument to the region's industrial history. These museums hosted many cultural events that contributed to the transformation and prosperity of the local economy. The Ruhr Music Festival, for example, was founded in 2002 with the aim of using the Ruhr's monumental industrial structures for large-scale performance events of music, drama, and dance. The old machine shops and coke factories became an innovative base for drama, opera, fine arts, pop music, jazz, and concerts in the Ruhr area.

7.2 Important experience: models of industrial upgrading in the Ruhr area

The Ruhr area transformed and upgraded traditional industrial areas with cultural connotations, changed old steel mills as R&D centers for new industries and cultural exhibition centers, renovated old buildings to become amusement parks, rock climbing bases and other recreational places, constructed modern natural landscape parks by redesigning and transforming coal gangue hills and developed them as important places for cultural industries, sports and fitness, entertainment, and leisure. With cultural transformation and industrial upgrading, one out of every 13 enterprises in the Ruhr area was engaged in the cultural industry in 2003. The cultural industry was gaining ground in the Ruhr area, with 7.5% of the regional business taxation being paid for by the 10,000 local businesses and individual operators engaged in the cultural industry. At present, more than 52,000 people are employed in the cultural industry in the Ruhr area. In 2010, over 2,500 cultural events were held in the Ruhr area, attracting more than 3.4 million tourists, and the Ruhr was elected as the "European Capital of Culture". The following models can be summarized from the cultural transformation of old factories and industrial heritage in the Ruhr area, as shown in Table 7.4.

7.2.1 Regional rehabilitation model of industrial heritage

The industrial heritage roadmap means to transform the industrial heritage in the Ruhr area into new cultural sites, organically linked them to form a 400km-long circular bicycle path, and showed the local industrial heritage to local residents and tourists in a system of tourist roadmaps. The former industrial anchor points were transformed as core nodes of the path, including various museums of science and technology and social history, panoramic viewpoints,

Ruhr experience of "urban diseases" 167

Table 7.4 Models of industrial upgrading in the Ruhr area

Main models	Important examples	Basic features
Regional rehabilitation model of industrial heritage	Emscher	Integrated design and improvement was carried out on the industrial heritage tourism resources in the entire Ruhr area, including the development of regional tourism routes, marketing and promotion, planning and combination of tourist attractions and other resources. It created an integrated regional blueprint for industrial heritage tourism, organically linking main tourism sites of industrial heritage in the area, and planning and renovated systematically "a road of industrial heritage tourism".
Museum model for renovation of industrial facilities	Henry Steel Works, Zollern Colliery and Zollverein Coal and Coking Plant	By the cultural transformation of many existing industrial facilities and heritage, the area enhanced the upgrading and transformation of traditional industries, and renovated factories and mines to be industrial museums of unique style and tourism resources with investment by the government.
Public recreation space model of industrial landscape integration	North Duisburg Landscape Park, Gelsenkirchen Nordstern Park	Through cultural transformation, large cultural landscape parks were built based on the industrial landscape of coal and iron and steel, the former waste gas storage tanks were transformed as training pools for diving clubs, concrete yards were changed as activity sites for young people, and walls were renovated into a rock climbers' paradise. Ecological landscape and green corridors for bicycles were designed in vast industrial parks to connect sewage rivers, which were transformed into a waterfront area for cultural tourism and recreation through treatment and ecological restoration.
Integrated development model of a shopping and entertainment center	Oberhausen Center shopping mall	It utilized the abandoned land of factories, integrated the cultural concept of Shopping Mall, organically combined shopping and recreation and industrial heritage tourism for comprehensive development, realized cultural transformation and industrial upgrading successfully, and built large new shopping and recreation centers.
Low-carbon development model of industrial transformation and upgrading	Gelsenkirchen Power Plant, Mont-Cenis Academy Solar Power Plant, Emscher Regional Park	It enhanced the transformation and planning of traditional industries such as coal, made full use of existing resources and industrial bases, reduced reliance on and consumption of traditional resources, and advanced low-carbon transformation and upgrading. It actively developed new energy industries, built the Gelsenkirchen Power Plant, the largest and most advanced solar power plant in Europe, developed clean and recyclable chemical products from coal and natural gas, and promoted the transformation of the pattern of urban energy consumption and the change of development mode.

and a series of important worker settlements. The transformation and industrial upgrading of resource-based cities were effectively achieved through the construction of an industrial heritage, provision of industrial culture tours, and a multi-objective, multi-node integrated remediation. For example, the Ruhr area carried out a multi-objective comprehensive development of Emscher, namely the International Building Exhibition (IBA) program. This program started in 1989 with the establishment of a regional management committee, the KVR, which developed and implemented a 10-year comprehensive rehabilitation and revitalization plan for the area, focused on the restructuring of traditional industries, infused cultural connotations into old industrial buildings, factories and mines, and abandoned sites, enhanced their in-depth transformation and comprehensive utilization, highlighted the improvement of the natural environment and ecological restoration, alleviated the environmental pollution and continuously solved a series of social problems such as employment and housing. The regional rehabilitation model was mainly the integrated design and renovation of industrial heritage tourism resources in the entire Ruhr area organized by the regional management committee KVR. It developed resources such as tourism roadmaps, marketing, and promotion, plans for and combinations of tourism attractions, drew a regional, integrated and combinational roadmap for industrial heritage tourism, and organically linked main tourism attractions of industrial heritage tourism in the area. The Ruhr area developed nearly 50 industrial tourism attractions based on the original industrial heritage sites by means of regional rehabilitation and cultural innovation. The Ruhr Tourism Bureau specially designed an industrial culture route to package attractions in the Ruhr area as a whole and enhance the cultural brand of the industrial tourism industry. At the same time, a bicycle path linking these attractions was created to provide relatively inexpensive and perfect public bicycle services for tourism. Various forms of tourism concessions such as annual and joint tickets were also available to tourists. These measures reflected the low-carbon, green, and harmonious urban culture concept.

7.2.2 Museum model for renovation of industrial facilities

The museum model for renovation of industrial facilities mainly transformed industrial heritage and relics into museums with industrial characteristics. Instead of simply closing down factories, splitting plants, and backfilling coal mines, the government in the Ruhr area made use of existing industrial facilities and relics for cultural transformation, enhanced the upgrading and transformation of traditional industries, and renovated factories and mines as industrial museums with unique styles and transformed them into tourism resources.[4] This model was represented by the Henry Steel Works, the Zollern Colliery, and the Zollverein Coal and Coking Plant. The Henry Steel Works was founded in 1854 and closed down in 1987. Through cultural transformation, the abandoned steel works became an open-air museum where children can play and explore. The museum uses abandoned industrial facilities to attract family tourists, and the guides of the museum are volunteers who are former workers, thus enhancing the local workers' sense of cultural belonging and participation.

The Zollern Colliery, located in Dortmund, preserved and renovated old factory and office buildings to show the classical style. Used trains were renovated as tour tools in the park so that it could have the cultural heritage with an industrial history. Zollverein, a coal and coking plant in Essen, ran coal wells beginning in 1847 and was always the largest coal well in Europe. The plant was the second largest steel company in the world, but it was shut down in December 1986. It was later transformed into a historical and cultural monument by a management company formed by the local asset acquisition agency (LEG) and the city government of Essen, and the provincial and municipal government established a dedicated development fund for the cultural renovation, planning, and industrial upgrading of the plant. The abandoned railroad and old trains inside the mine were transformed into a performance venue for the children's art school in the community, and the coke plant was renovated as a restaurant and children's swimming pool. This attracted not only many children and other tourists, but also artists and creative design companies, associations, and societies. This plant became the office space for a lot of cultural and creative design companies as well as a place for the exhibition of their works, making it an important center for modern industrial art and design industries in Germany.

7.2.3 Model of a public recreation space of industrial landscape integration

Old factories were transformed into public recreation spaces, such as the North Duisburg Landscape Park and the Gelsenkirchen Nordstern Park. The North Duisburg Landscape Park was transformed from Thyssen Steel, which was originally a large industrial base integrating several industries such as coal mining, coking, and steel. After being forced to shut down in 1985, it was renovated as a large cultural landscape park based on the industrial landscape of coal and steel through cultural transformation. The former waste gas storage tanks were transformed into training pools for diving clubs, concrete yards were changed into activity sites for young people, walls were renovated and became a rock climbers' paradise, and some warehouses and factory buildings were changed into concert halls. The original industrial plant area was converted into a green ecological landscape and green corridors for bicycles, thus becoming a paradise for bicyclists and ecology advocates. The Nordstern Park in Gelsenkirchen was also a large public recreation space transformed from a former coal plant. Tall coal well shafts were retained as an important landscape item of the park, and gardens were created on the abandoned land of the coal mine, where various large cultural events and German garden exhibitions have been held. This area also organically connected the Emscher River, once the most polluted sewage river in the

Ruhr industrial area, renovated and designed it through river treatment and ecological restoration, and transformed it into a waterfront area for cultural tourism and recreation in the Ruhr area, which added to the cultural charm and natural landscape of the public recreation space.

7.2.4 Integrated development model of a shopping and entertainment center

A typical example of this model is the Centro shopping mall in Oberhausen. Originally an important industrial city rich in zinc and metal ores, Oberhausen established the first iron foundry in the Ruhr area in 1758. With the advent of de-industrialization, factory closures, workers' unemployment, and economic decline forced Oberhausen to undergo an industrial transformation. The area successfully achieved cultural transformation and industrial upgrading by using the abandoned land of factories, integrating the cultural concept of a Shopping Mall, organically combining shopping and entertainment with industrial heritage tourism, carried out comprehensive development, built a large new shopping and entertainment center, opened up industrial museums and retained a giant gas storage tank with a height of 117 meters and a diameter of 67 meters. This shopping and entertainment center is not only an important shopping destination for local residents, but it also has the auxiliary facilities of food and entertainment, such as a café, a bar, a food and culture street, a children's playground, a tennis and sports center, a multimedia and video entertainment center, and an artificial lake transformed from an abandoned mine pit. With a well-developed traffic network, Oberhausen's Center shopping mall becomes an important shopping, entertainment, and cultural center for the Ruhr area and the largest shopping and tourism center in Europe.

7.2.5 Model of a low-carbon development of industrial transformation and upgrading

In order to mitigate the pollution and damage to the environment caused by energy-based industries, the Ruhr area carried out the low-carbon transformation and industrial upgrading of traditional industries, vigorously developed low-carbon high-tech industries, new-energy industries, and modern cultural industries, and promoted low-carbon development and green transformation of resource-based cities. First, it strengthened the transformation and planning of traditional industries such as coal, made full use of the existing resources and industrial base according to local conditions, reduced reliance on and consumption of traditional resources, and advanced the low-carbon transformation and upgrading of industries. Second, it actively developed new-energy industries, established the largest and most advanced solar cell power plant in Europe – Gelsenkirchen Power Plant, developed clean and recyclable chemical products from clean and recyclable coal and natural gas, and promoted the transformation of the urban pattern of energy consumption and a change in the mode of development. To achieve low-carbon development, the Mont-Cenis Academy in Herne was built on the site of a former coal mine and used a solar power plant to supply all energy consumption. Third, the ecological restoration and environmental governance of the mining area were enhanced, and trees and grass were planted at the site of closed-down companies. The government emphasized the publicity of the knowledge of environmental protection to enhance citizens' awareness of low-carbon environmental protection, encouraged them to plant trees and grass, increased forest carbon sinks, and jointly promoted the low-carbon development of the city by a multi-faceted approach. The Ruhr area greened former factories, mines, industrial sites and other areas on a large scale to wipe the dust off the Ruhr's "face", change the image of polluted cities, and achieve green transformation and low-carbon development. The Ruhr area strengthened the construction of urban green infrastructure, built many mining parks throughout the area, and provided green space for recreation, sports and air purification of surrounding citizens, with a total of 15,000 hectares for forest recreation areas. These green spaces were interconnected through green corridors, and formed the main east-west green structural system in the Ruhr area with the Emsher Regional Park at the core.[5] Through urban greening and upgrading, the Ruhr area chose a low-carbon development model to revitalize declining industrial cities and achieve a multi-win situation in terms of economic recovery, social construction, and ecological civilization, which is worthy of reference for other cities.

7.3 Policy suggestions: implications of low-carbon development of industrial upgrading in the Ruhr area

The report of the 18th CPC National Congress and the 3rd, 4th, and 5th Plenary Sessions of the 18th Central Committee of the CPC proposed to promote the construction of an ecological civilization, green development, circular development and low-carbon development, and to realize the modernization of national governance. Strengthening the construction of an ecological civilization and low-carbon development is the basic requirement to realize the transformation and upgrading of cities and the modernization of governance. According to the experience of low-carbon development by cultural transformation and industrial upgrading in the Ruhr area of Germany, many resource-based cities in China are facing the dilemma of transformation. In order to solve the bottleneck constraints such as depletion of resources and energy and environmental pollution, it is necessary to strengthen cultural transformation and industrial upgrading, and enhance the low-carbon development and green transformation of Chinese cities from the strategic heights of global warming, ecological civilization, and low-carbon development. To be specific, the implications of cultural transformation and industrial upgrading in the Ruhr area for the low-carbon development of Chinese cities (see Table 7.5) are mainly manifested in the following aspects.

172 *Ruhr experience of "urban diseases"*

Table 7.5 Low-carbon implications for cultural transformation and industrial upgrading in the Ruhr area

Key areas	Important implications	Policy recommendations for low-carbon development
Strategic planning	Development of rehabilitation planning	To establish the concept of low-carbon development, formulate plans for urban transformation, and set up a coordinating planning agency to guide the rehabilitation and transformation of mining areas.
Development model	Choosing the model of low-carbon development	According to local resource endowment and industrial characteristics, it should not be the same for all cities. Cities need to have a scientific design, strengthen the transformation and upgrading of traditional industries, increase the technological content of industries, focus on the development of strategic emerging industries, high-tech industries, cultural industries, and new-energy industries, and reduce carbon emissions.
Capital investment	Diversified funding sources	Cities should raise funds for cultural transformation and industrial upgrading through various channels, increase financial investment, set up seed funds for cultural and creative industries, encourage social capital to be invested and to finance cultural and creative industries, enhance the construction of cultural infrastructure, and accelerate the construction of a basic system of public cultural services.
Development environment	Enhancement of ecological restoration and environmental governance	Cities should vigorously publicize knowledge of environmental protection, enhance citizens' low-carbon awareness, strengthen urban ecological restoration and environmental governance, plant trees and grass at the former sites of closed enterprises, construct green infrastructures, and build forest cities.
Industrial upgrading	Emphasis on technological innovation and development of low-carbon industries	Cities should emphasize the integration of local cultural characteristics into transformation and industrial upgrading, become competitive on the market by technological innovation, develop a cultural and creative industry, a tourism industry, an exhibition economy and other service sectors, and boost industrial upgrading and structural optimization.

7.3.1 Emphasizing cultural transformation, developing regional rehabilitation plans, and improving the capacity for urban governance

The transformation of traditional energy-based cities must attain new strategic heights, find opportunities and make plans in economic globalization and industrial upgrading, and determine their own plans for development and effective policies. In terms of policy philosophy, according to the experience of the Ruhr area in cultural transformation, industrial upgrading and low-carbon development, cities should pay attention to ecological civilization, establish the concept of low-carbon development, formulate strategies and targets for low-carbon urban transformation, and encourage the vigorous development of green and low-carbon industries. The experience of cultural transformation in the Ruhr area indicates that traditional industrial areas and resource-based cities can achieve an urban rebirth through cultural innovation and development of cultural industries. Local governments should be innovative and guided by enlightened and strategic public sectors. They need to invest a considerable amount of public funds to advance the protection, restoration, and transformation of old factories, mining areas, and industrial heritage. They should establish the concept of low-carbon development, make plans for urban transformation, enhance cultural transformation and development of cultural industries, and create job opportunities for educated and skilled workers as well as hard-working people. The Ruhr area established an integrated planning agency to guide the rehabilitation and transformation of mining areas. The German government, considering the state of coal resources at that time, determined in advance the time frame for closure of some coal mines and targets for reduction of production and staff, and formulated plans for the step-by-step and phased implementation to avoid the pressure on the society caused by the concentrated resettlement of workers after resources were depleted. The Ruhr area introduced policies for the adjustment of industries and built and nurtured many service supporting organizations. For China's urban transformation, cities should formulate effective plans for transformation and policies of development, take into account their local characteristics and actual situation, highlight the modification and cultural transformation of original industrial heritage, improve the capacity for urban governance, and boost low-carbon urban development.

7.3.2 Choosing the low-carbon model for the development of industrial upgrading according to resource endowments and industrial characteristics

In the Ruhr area of Germany, the regional rehabilitation model of industrial heritage, the museum model for renovation of industrial facilities, the model for public recreation space for integration of industrial landscapes, a model of the integrated development of shopping and entertainment centers, and a model of the low-carbon development of industrial transformation and upgrading are all scientifically designed according to resource endowments and the industrial characteristics of each city, thus being able to successfully realize cultural transformation and industrial upgrading and solve the problems of "urban diseases", such as industrial decline. The practice of development in the Ruhr area reveals that in order to achieve a smooth economic transformation, resource-based cities must facilitate the continuous flow of capital, people and information through tourism and cultural industries, which then can drive the comprehensive development of other related industries.[6] The transformation of Chinese cities needs to consider their respective resource endowments and industrial characteristics, and choose an effective model of development. There should not be the same model for thousands of cities, who are then subject to homogeneous competition. Chinese cities should focus on the cultural characteristics and green low-carbon development, and build their own model of low-carbon development.

First of all, cities should strengthen the transformation and upgrading of traditional industries, change the traditional model of economic growth with high-energy consumption, high pollution, and high emissions, increase the technological content of industries, drive traditional industries continuously from low-end industries to high-end parts of the smile curve and enhance the competitiveness of the value chain. With regard to traditional industries, closed down enterprises, factories, and mines should not be simply closed and dismantled, but they should learn from the cultural transformation and museum model of the Ruhr area, strengthen cultural transformation, vigorously develop the industrial cultural tourism industry, and venture down the road towards an industrial culture.

Second, cities should focus on the development of strategic emerging industries, high-tech industries, and cultural industries, which are typically characterized by high technological content and a high level of innovation and possess their own core competitiveness. Since the 1980s, the policies of the Ruhr area have changed from relocating and phasing out old enterprises and building new industries in the past to actively developing characteristic strategic emerging industries in combination with the renewal and renovation of old enterprises, so that it could enhance industrial upgrading and economic vitality.[7]

Third, cities should pay attention to the development of new-energy industries and change the traditional mode of high energy consumption. They should vigorously develop new-energy industries such as wind and solar energy, improve the efficiency of energy utilization and reduce the intensity of energy consumption. China's urban transformation should highlight the development of new-energy industries, change the long-term dependence of economic development on traditional sources of energy such as coal and oil, continuously transform the structure of energy consumption and the pattern of consumption, increase the proportion of new energy in urban energy consumption, continuously reduce the intensity of carbon emissions of energy consumption, and promote low-carbon urban development.

7.3.3 Strengthening diversified financing and attaching importance to the construction of cultural infrastructures

Because urban industrial transformation and industrial development require large amounts of funds, the Ruhr area raised funds on all fronts, at multiple levels and through multiple channels. It strengthened funding by the government, formulated and introduced corresponding investment policies, and simplified approval formalities. A "coal surcharge" and a "coal subsidy tax" were levied on users. It also made full use of EU funding, loans or funding from financial organizations, established state development management companies, and issued bonds for land development to raise funds, etc. The Ruhr area strengthened the construction of infrastructures and improvements, and created an environment favorable to investments for industrial transformation in resource-depleted areas.[8] China's urban transformation should raise funds for cultural transformation and industrial upgrading through various channels. The government should increase its financial investment, set up seed funds for the development of cultural and creative industries, activate social vitality, and encourage social capital to participate in the investment and financing of cultural and creative industries. The government should also enhance the construction of cultural infrastructure and realize the dream of cultural power, which requires the accelerated construction of a basic system of public cultural services. The construction of cultural infrastructure is a prerequisite and foundation, as well as a basic guarantee for the development of a cultural industry.

7.3.4 Raising awareness of low-carbon development and strengthening urban ecological restoration and environmental governance

In order to achieve low-carbon development, the Ruhr area strengthened the ecological restoration and environmental governance in mining zones and planted trees and grass at the original sites of closed-down enterprises. For the urban green transformation of the Ruhr area, the government spent a lot of money on cleaning up abandoned mines, treated harmful substances on the ground, carried out large-scale afforestation and urban greening projects, transformed the Ruhr industrial area, which was full of garbage and sewage and suffered from ecological deterioration, into a modern "European garden". The green transformation of urban development highlighted energy saving and emission reduction, seriously controlled pollutant emissions, energetically facilitated the progress of energy technology and the conversion of the energy structure, accelerated low-carbon development, and improved the environmental quality.[9] According to the experience of the Ruhr area,

176 Ruhr experience of "urban diseases"

China's "urban diseases" should be treated by strengthening environmental control and restoration, adopting a circular economy model to enhance the transformation of abandoned factories and waste treatment, and strengthening the construction of infrastructure for environmental protection, traffic, water and other fields, so as to create conditions for urban green transformation and low-carbon development. The governments of Chinese cities should have a sense of low-carbon development, actively publicize the knowledge of environmental protection, enhance citizens' low-carbon awareness, strengthen the construction of green infrastructures, encourage tree planting, and build forest cities. They should actively take measures of environmental protection, restrict emissions of polluting gases, establish air quality monitoring systems, and promote ecological governance and low-carbon urban development.

7.3.5 Strengthening industrial optimization and upgrading, emphasizing technological innovation, and developing low-carbon industries

The Ruhr area emphasized the integration of local cultural characteristics into transformation and industrial upgrading, carried out cultural transformation based on original factory buildings, mining areas, and industrial sites, actively developed low-carbon cultural creativity and tourism industries, and boosted urban low-carbon, high-end, and green development through cultural transformation and industrial upgrading. Facing the situation of the development of a stagnant economy, the Ruhr area actively transformed traditional industries, facilitated the optimization and upgrading of its industrial structure, and vigorously developed tourism and cultural industries. According to the experience of the Ruhr area, China's urban transformation should strengthen the optimization and upgrading of the industrial structure, develop low-carbon cultural and tourism industries, take the road towards an industrial heritage with Chinese characteristics, and strongly combine a low-carbon economy with technological innovation.[10] Chinese cities should upgrade the level of technological innovation in traditional industries and the technological content of products, strengthen the technological innovation of traditional industries, introduce new technologies and equipment, increase the technological content and added value of products, improve competitiveness, and create brands. They should develop new industries, obtain market competitiveness by technological innovation, drive urban industrial design by information technology, vigorously develop the cultural creativity industry, the tourism industry, an exhibition economy, and other service sectors, promote industrial upgrading and structural optimization, realize the reduction of the proportion of high-energy-consuming industries in the industrial structure, and promote low-carbon development and the construction of an ecological civilization in Chinese cities.

7.4 Summary

This chapter examined the experience of treating "urban diseases" by the Ruhr area of Germany from the perspectives of cultural transformation and industrial upgrading. The Ruhr area relied on coal resources to promote the development of traditional industries, but the de-industrialization caused dilemmas of urban transformation. It transformed and upgraded traditional industrial zones with a cultural connotation, and concluded the experiential models of regional rehabilitation, museums, public recreation spaces, integrated development, and low-carbon development. According to the experience of the Ruhr area, China's urban development should focus on cultural transformation, make plans for regional rehabilitation, never adopt the same model for thousands of cities, emphasize the construction of cultural infrastructures, strengthen urban ecological restoration and environmental governance, enhance industrial optimization and upgrading, and boost low-carbon urban development.

Notes

1 Li Chenghui, Study of the Industrial Structural Adjustment of Mining Cities – Taking the Ruhr as the Example, *China Population Resources and Environment*, 2003(4).
2 Li Leilei, De-industrialization and Development of Industrial Heritage Tourism: The Actual Process and Development Model of the Ruhr Area in Germany, *World Regional Studies*, 2002(3).
3 Wu Hongyan, Mode and Enlightenment of the Ruhr District Industrial Heritage Tour in Germany, *Journal of Taiyuan University*, 2010(3).
4 Li Xuemin and Zhao Hui, The Experience of Industrial Transformation in the Ruhr Industrial Area of Germany, *China Economic Times*, November 24, 2005.
5 Chang Jiang and Feng Shanshan, The New Dynamism of the Ruhr Area, *Dongfang Daily*, November 1, 2012.
6 Chen Shuhua, The Development of Industrial Tourism in Northeast Resource-based Cities – Analysis from the Perspective of the Ruhr Area in Germany, *Academic Exchange*, 2010(3).
7 Wang Jun and Qiu Shaonan, Mode Shift and Structure Adjustment: Thinking about the Transformation of the Old Industrial Area of Qingdao with the Experiences of Ruhr in Germany as Reference, *China Development*, 2012(3).
8 Lu Xiaocheng, *Urban Transformation and Green Development*, Economic Press, China, 2013, pp. 94–95.
9 Shi Minjun and Liu Yanyan, Urban Green Development: An International Comparison and Perspective of Problems, *Urban Development Studies*, 2013(5).
10 Lu Xiaocheng, Exploring the Model for Low-Carbon Innovation System of Green Transformation in China's Cities, *Journal of Guangdong Institute of Public Administration*, 2013(2).

8 Phenomena and causes of the problems of "urban diseases" in Beijing

Beijing, as a metropolis, has accumulated the problems of "urban diseases" such as population expansion, traffic congestion, frequent smoggy weather and environmental pollution during its long-term rapid development, which attracts the attention of the CPC Central Committee and the State Council. Beijing is beset with acute problems in energy, traffic, medical care, schooling, employment, housing, and security, all of which are closely related to population size, structural distribution and population management. On February 26, 2014, aiming at Beijing's "urban diseases" such as smog, General Secretary Xi Jinping proposed to accelerate the coordinated development of the Beijing-Tianjin-Hebei region, so as to solve Beijing's "urban diseases". It is of important practical urgency and strategic significance to implement the strategic positioning of the capital city, strengthen the treatment of "urban diseases", and accelerate Beijing's treatment of "urban diseases". This chapter carries out an empirical study and examines the problems from the perspective of the interactive effects of population, resources, and the environment, analyzes the main manifestations and internal causes of Beijing's "urban diseases", and finds the key factors and their relationships regarding transmission in order to treat "urban diseases".

8.1 Phenomena of the problems of "urban diseases" in Beijing

The problem of "urban diseases" is a global dilemma of urban development. "Urban diseases" refer to a series of economic, social, cultural, political, and ecological problems that arise during the process of urbanization and industrialization as the population grows, industries concentrate, resources, and energy are consumed faster, and environmental pollution worsens. "Urban diseases" are manifested as traffic congestion, environmental pollution, shortage of resources, employment difficulties, social unrest, and many other contradictions of development. The existence of "urban diseases" seriously affects the quality of life and the social development of urban residents, and poses a great threat to the further improvement of urban quality. As a national capital city and a metropolis, Beijing is faced with the increasingly serious problems of "urban diseases". The problems of atmospheric pollution,

DOI: 10.4324/9781003272991-8

population expansion and traffic congestion are not effectively solved. The treatment of "urban diseases" of the capital city has become an urgent political task assigned by the central government to the government of Beijing at all levels, and also an important issue for Beijing in the period of the 13th Five-Year Plan.

On February 27, 2014, Comrade Xi Jinping, General Secretary of the CPC Central Committee and President of the People's Republic of China, pointed out during his visit to Beijing that the city had the features and advantages of high status, large size, superior strength, rapid changes, and good quality but at the same time, the growing city was also facing many alarming problems, such as overpopulation, traffic congestion and high housing prices, as well as very serious ecological and environmental problems, such as the invisibility of blue sky and night stars, rivers drying up, over-exploitation of groundwater and ground subsidence. These are typical manifestations of the "urban diseases" of the capital city.

8.1.1 Population growth is slowing down with the continuous rising of total population

According to the new criteria in the Notice on the Adjustment of Urban Scale Classification Standards issued by the State Council in 2014, cities are classified into five categories and seven levels, among which cities with a resident population of 10 million or more are considered metropolises, as shown in Table 8.1. In 2013, the resident population of Beijing was 21.148 million, including 2.212 million in the core areas of capital functions and 10.322 million in the extension areas of urban functions. Beijing is a typical metropolis that is confronted with the pressure of a growing population on resources, energy and the environment. The problems of "urban diseases" are constraining the sustainable development of the capital city Beijing.

Table 8.1 Criteria for the classification of city size

Categories	Population	
Metropolises	City population > 10 million	
Extra-large cities	5 million < city population < 10 million	
Large cities	1 million < city population < 5 million	Type I: 3 million < city population < 5 million
		Type II: 1 million < city population < 3 million
Medium-size cities	0.5 million < city population < 1 million	
Small cities	City population < 0.5 million	Type I: 0.2 million < city population < 0.5 million
		Type II: city population < 0.2 million

Table 8.2 Resident population of Beijing from 1978 to 2014

Year	Resident population (10K)	Floating resident population (10K)	Birth rate of resident population (‰)	Mortality rate of resident population (‰)	Natural growth rate of resident population (‰)
1978	871.5	21.8	12.93	6.12	6.81
1988	1061.0	59.8	14.43	5.08	9.35
1998	1245.6	154.1	6.00	5.30	0.70
2008	1771.0	541.1	7.89	4.59	3.30
2009	1860.0	614.2	7.66	4.33	3.33
2010	1961.9	704.7	7.27	4.29	2.98
2011	2018.6	742.2	8.29	4.27	4.02
2012	2069.3	773.9	9.05	4.31	4.74
2013	2114.8	802.7	8.93	4.52	4.41
2014	2151.6	818.7	9.75	4.92	4.83

Currently, the symptoms of Beijing's "urban diseases" have become very serious. Overpopulation is an important manifestation. The problem of population control is an important issue that Beijing can hardly avoid. As shown in Table 8.2 and Figure 8.1, the permanent resident population of Beijing increased from 8.715 million in 1978 to 21.148 million in 2013, with an average annual growth rate of 35.52%. The floating resident population increased from 218,000 in 1978 to 8.027 million in 2013. It can be found that the rapid growth of the floating population is an important feature and cause of the "urban diseases" of the capital city.

In recent years, Beijing has taken a lot of measures to control the excessive population growth and obtained a certain number of achievements. According to statistics, the resident population of Beijing was 21.516 million at the end of 2014, with an increase of 368,000 compared with that at the end of 2013, and the growth rate was 1.7%. The increment decreased by 87,000 people, and the growth rate decreased by 0.5% points from the previous year. Among this population, the floating resident population was 8.187 million, with an increase of 160,000 or 2% over what it was at the end of the previous year, although the increment decreased by 129,000, the growth rate dropped by 1.7% points compared with the previous year, and the population increment and growth rate gradually slowed down.[1] Extra-large cities attract a massive influx of population because of industrial development, economic activity, advanced technology and information, and the high quality of education and medical services. The rapid concentration of population further facilitates the expansion of the size of the city and economic growth. However, urban construction, supporting services and management, housing, traffic, and other constraints limited by urban planning and urban investment often lag behind economic growth and population expansion, leading to a series of contradictions, such as traffic congestion, housing shortage due to

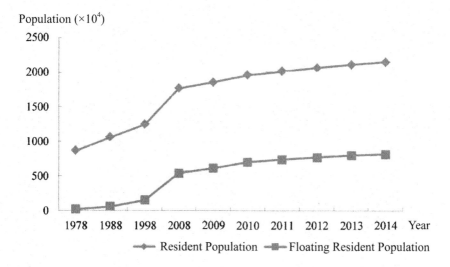

Figure 8.1 Resident population and floating resident population of Beijing.

overpopulation, employment difficulties, increased social conflicts, deterioration of public security, and other "urban diseases".

In terms of population growth, the increment in 2014 was 87,000 fewer than what it was of 2013, and the growth rate was 0.5% lower than that of the previous year, but according to total population and density, with what it was in 2013 as a benchmark, the resident population reached 21.148 million in 2013, with an increase of 455,000 compared to 2012, of which the floating resident population reached 8.027 million, with an increase of 289,000 compared to 2012. With respect to population density in 2013, core areas reached 23,942 people/square kilometers, and Xicheng District had the highest population density in Beijing that reached 25,787 people/square kilometers. As far as the population distribution of different areas is concerned, as shown in Table 8.3,[2] the resident population in the core areas of capital functions was 2.213 million, that in the extension areas of urban functions was 10.55 million, that in the new areas of urban development was 6.849 million, and that in the development areas of ecological conservation was 1.904 million.

Xicheng District and Dongcheng District are the most densely populated areas, and the analysis should focus on the internal reasons why Xicheng District, Dongcheng District, and the extension areas of urban functions attract a greater population. All of them are highly concentrated areas for central ministries and commissions and their affiliated institutions and units, as well as for headquarters of central enterprises, state-owned enterprises and banks, international organizations, various types of companies, office buildings, shopping malls, etc. They are also areas where the most famous

Table 8.3 Resident population and floating resident population of Beijing in 2013 and 2014 unit: 10K

District/county	Resident population 2014	Resident population 2013	Floating resident population 2014	Floating resident population 2013
Whole city	2151.6	2114.8	818.7	802.7
Core areas of capital functions	221.3	221.2	54.0	55.4
Dongcheng District	91.1	90.9	21.2	21.0
Xicheng District	130.2	130.3	32.8	34.4
Extension areas of urban functions	1055.0	1032.2	436.4	426.0
Chaoyang District	392.2	384.1	179.8	176.1
Fengtai District	230.0	226.1	85.1	85.0
Shijingshan District	65.0	64.4	21.2	21.4
Haidian District	367.8	357.6	150.3	143.5
New areas of urban development	684.9	671.5	296.9	289.6
Fangshan District	103.6	101.0	26.7	24.6
Tongzhou District	135.6	132.6	55.5	53.6
Shunyi District	100.4	98.3	38.9	37.3
Changping District	190.8	188.9	100.2	100.6
Daxing District	154.5	150.7	75.6	73.5
Development areas of ecological conservation	190.4	189.9	31.4	31.7
Mentougou District	30.6	30.3	4.9	5.0
Huairou District	38.1	38.2	10.4	10.6
Pinggu District	42.3	42.2	5.3	5.3
Miyun County	47.8	47.6	7.2	7.2
Yanqing County	31.6	31.6	3.6	3.6

Chinese universities and research institutions and Grade 3A hospitals are located. These institutions serve numerous functions of the capital city such as administration, economy, education, culture, and medical care, and are also the most high-end, dense, authoritative, and perfect heights of interest for all kinds of resources in China.

The increasing and expanding population is bound to put greater pressure on traffic, housing and employment and lead to a further worsening and exacerbation of Beijing's "urban diseases". From the perspective of patients seeking medical services, it is estimated that 800,000 people come to Beijing for medical treatment, and this figure may reach 1.6 to 1.7 million including escorts. There are probably several million people in Beijing for purposes of study or accompanying their children who study in Beijing. Beijing's reliance on corporate development and land sale to increase fiscal revenues, support its huge fiscal expenditures, and meet GDP targets set by the government at higher levels inevitably leads to a strong incentive to develop the economy. The mechanism of transmission is: increase in fiscal revenues – the need to develop industries – attracting more enterprises – population growth – increased building and traffic needs – increased pressure on resources, energy, and environmental carrying capacity.

8.1.2 Total traffic capacity continues to grow, and the problem of "capital jam" persists

In recent years, Beijing has accelerated the construction of roads and has improved the traffic conditions to a certain extent, but the phenomenon of "capital jam" has not been fundamentally curbed. The construction of traffic infrastructures has been increasing, the total mileage of roads and highways and the rail transit operation lines in the territory have been extended, and the passenger capacity of rail transit is close to that of electric buses. In recent years, the construction of traffic infrastructures in Beijing has increased; the total mileage of roads and highways in the territory increased from 28,585 km in 2012 to 28,808 km in 2013. In 2013, the mileage of expressways reached 923 km, the mileage of urban roads reached 6,295 km, the area of urban roads reached 96.11 million square meters, the number of overpasses on urban roads reached 414, and the number of overpasses crossing streets reached 520. According to the number of operating buses, the number and length of operating lines, and passenger capacity of buses, as well as the passenger capacity of taxis, Beijing obviously increased its investment in public transportation, and the passenger capacity further grew. This indicated that the traffic demand in Beijing has not been relieved and the pressure on public transportation continues to exist.

As the population in the capital city grows year by year and the number of motor vehicles is increasing, despite the extension of subway lines and the improvement in traffic facilities year by year, the traffic congestion in the capital city has not been significantly alleviated, and the problem of "capital jam" has not been fundamentally curbed. Due to the overcrowding of industries in central urban areas, the housing problem cannot be solved, and the high housing prices and rents also restrict the local accommodation of the working population in central urban areas, who have to choose the relatively cheap distant suburban districts and counties as the destination for buying and renting houses. However, the distant suburban districts and counties have the limited capacity of employment, thus becoming typical "sleeping cities" (such as Tiantongyuan, Tongzhou). As a result, traffic congestion is even worse during rush hours, with countless cars on trunk roads, overcrowded subways and difficulty in walking at interchange points. The problem of "capital jam" is closely linked to the growing number of cars in Beijing in recent years. The number of motor vehicles in Beijing increased from 4.983 million in 2011 to 5.437 million in 2013, and continued to increase to 5.591 million in 2014, and the number of cars increased to 3.165 million. If there is no control, at such a growth rate, the number of motor vehicles would reach 5.9 million in 2020 or even exceed 6 million. This would put tremendous pressure on Beijing's limited carrying capacity of roads. If without stringent measures to strictly control the total number of motor vehicles, it will be difficult to alleviate Beijing's problem of traffic congestion.

In order to alleviate traffic congestion, Beijing has introduced the policies of license plate lottery of motor vehicles and traffic restrictions, which have eased the already congested urban traffic, but cannot really solve the problem of traffic congestion. In recent years, Beijing has also been investigating and studying the issue of congestion charges, but this is still in the research stage and has never been tried out or implemented.

The traditional way of controlling traffic congestion is mainly to restrict vehicle ownership rather than the number of vehicles on the roads, and this approach has little effect and only causes social injustice and complaints by the masses to a certain extent. According to the experience of motor vehicle control in London, New York, and other developed cities, it is important to reduce the use of motor vehicles, change the habit of driving cars to and from work, and increase the cost of using them. How to increase the cost of using them and collecting congestion and parking fees is an important policy option. Collecting congestion charges means optimizing the allocation of road space resources in central urban areas by the limited economic means and market mechanism. With the gradual weakening of the government's administrative intervention in various fields and the further strengthening of the role of the market, it is the right time to play the decisive role of the market mechanism in resource allocation, and control traffic congestion in metropolises like Beijing mainly by economic means and market regulations.

8.1.3 Industrial structure is not reasonable, with difficulty in decentralizing low-end industries

Beijing has built a service-oriented economic structure with the tertiary industry as the mainstay. In 2014, Beijing's tertiary industry accounted for 77.9% of the regional GDP, with an increase of 0.4% points compared with what it was in 2013, the secondary industry was compressed again, accounting for 21.4% of the regional GDP, and the primary industry accounted for only 0.7%. This reveals that the proportion of Beijing's industrial structure is relatively optimum and has no big difference with that of developed cities around the world. However, among tertiary industrial sectors, the financial sector makes the biggest contribution, followed by wholesale and retail trade, but the information transmission, software and IT services, and scientific research and technology services make poorer contributions. This indicates that the structure of service sectors in Beijing is not optimized enough, and low-end industries such as wholesale and retail trade still account for a large proportion. This is inconsistent with the requirements of the central government to decentralize non-capital functions, especially low-end and extensive industries. These wholesale and retail trades are also the key targets for decentralizing non-capital functions and low-end industries in Beijing.

On April 30, 2015, the Central Political Bureau meeting considered and adopted the Planning Outline for the Coordinated Development of the Beijing-Tianjin-Hebei Region. The outline points out that promoting the coordinated development of the Beijing-Tianjin-Hebei region is an important national strategy, with the core being orderly decentralization of Beijing's non-capital functions. Beijing has fully implemented the important national strategy of the coordinated development of the Beijing-Tianjin-Hebei region, it strictly controls the increment and diverts the stock, and has achieved remarkable results in the diversion of industries. However, Beijing proposes to build a high-grade, precision, and advanced economic structure, and there are many difficulties in diverting low-end parts of the industrial chain and low-end markets.

Promoting the integrated and coordinated development of the Beijing-Tianjin-Hebei region and diverting non-core functions of the capital city are considered a systematic project that will not be achieved overnight, and industrial transfer and undertaking is one difficulty. The targeted and detailed lists and path design and the coordinated advancement and initiative of Beijing, Tianjin and Hebei are required to determine which industries to move out, which industries to introduce. Although many industries are at the low end, they are closely linked to the life of citizens. For example, agricultural wholesale in the capital city is faced with a complex and serious situation. Some low-end parts and markets can meet the basic needs of Beijing's citizens and economic and social development, and they cannot be fully decentralized in a clean sweep.

For example, the Xinfadi wholesale market of agricultural products is mainly to ensure the most basic supply of agricultural products to central leaders, state units and capital citizens, thus being the shopping basket for citizens in the capital city. This market can neither be considered a non-capital core function, nor a target for decentralization and relocation. Our research team has visited the Xinfadi wholesale market of agricultural products four times. It is located in the South Fourth Ring of Beijing, built on May 16, 1988, covers a land area of 1,820 mu, and accounts for more than 80% of the supply of agricultural products in Beijing. In 2014, its trading volume exceeded 14 million tons with a turnover of 53.5 billion yuan. It is a wind vane for agricultural wholesale markets throughout the country. The overall layout of agricultural markets in Beijing is "one large, 12 medium and 100 small": "one large" refers to Xinfadi; "12 medium" are the medium-sized wholesale markets, namely Zhongyang, Xinanjiao, Jingshen, Yuegezhuang, Jinxiudadi, Dayang Road, Wangsiying, Baliqiao, Shimen, Huilongguan, Shuitun, and Nanhua; "100 small" are more than 100 community markets in various urban areas. In terms of business pattern, the Xinfadi Market supplies more than 80% of the vegetables and fruits in Beijing; the Xinanjiao Market is known as the big freezer of Beijing because it is the core base for the supply of frozen products in Beijing; the Jingshen Seafood Market is the largest distribution center for fresh aquatic products in Beijing, with an average daily sales volume of more than 1.3 million tons; and the business of dried fruits and spices of the Jinxiudadi Wholesale Market tops all markets. In terms of land area, "one large" and "12 medium" cover a land area of more than 8,000 mu and have nearly one million practitioners. Most of these markets were formed spontaneously in the 1980s and 1990s, and they not only guarantee the supply of the capital city, but also serve the non-capital function as a place of national distribution. About 60% of the agricultural products in Beijing's large agricultural markets are distributed to Jilin, Liaoning and Heilongjiang in the northeastern part, Shanxi, Inner Mongolia, and Ningxia in the northwestern part and Hebei and Tianjin in the northern part of China.

The decentralization of Xinfadi and other agricultural wholesale markets cannot be done in a clean sweep. They should not be simply relocated, but they require in-depth research and the introduction of a detailed plan for diversion, transformation and upgrading. On February 25, 2015, General Secretary Xi Jinping proposed during his visit to Beijing to clarify the city's strategic positioning, adhere to and strengthen its core capital functions as a national political center, cultural center, international communication center, and scientific and technological innovation center, and strive to construct Beijing as an international first-class harmonious and livable city; adjust and decentralize non-capital core functions, optimize the selection of industries, especially industrial projects, highlight high-end, service, agglomeration, integration and low carbon, effectively control the size of the population, and enhance the balanced distribution of the regional population. Hence, the decentralization of non-capital core functions should not be simply closing wholesale markets of agricultural products, but it requires scientific research and a phased decentralization according to the needs for developing core capital functions and the actual needs of Beijing citizens to buy daily necessities. In this regard, Beijing has also clearly proposed the following four categories of non-capital functions: general manufacturing, regional logistics bases, and regional wholesale markets, some public service functions such as education and medical care, and some administrative and institutional service organizations. For decentralizing non-capital functions, the plans will be made by categories and decentralization will be carried out in three phases: near, medium, and long-term. Further research and key analysis are required for determining whether large agricultural wholesale markets are a core function of the capital, whether they should be diverted and how to divert in the integrated development of the Beijing-Tianjin-Hebei region.

The Xinfadi wholesale market of agricultural products, the shopping basket for citizens in the capital city, should not be simply relocated, but partially decentralized and upgraded to achieve high-end, brand, and sustainable development. Some functions of these markets do not belong to the core functions of the capital, such as storage, cold store processing, and transit of bulk agricultural products, which are non-capital functions that can be promptly diverted, while other functions may be transformed and upgraded. In August 2015, Xinfadi, which has an annual trading volume of 14 million tons of agricultural products, started to plan for upgrading and transformation. After transformation, Xinfadi retains and upgrades its distribution function in Beijing, but diverts some non-core businesses such as warehousing and primary processing to Tianjin and Hebei. The modern, three-dimensional vegetable trading center, fruit trading center, and cold chain center, have replaced the existing scattered trading market. They cover a land area of 660 mu to achieve efficient and economical use of land resources. The vacated land is fully used for greening and building a park-style market.[3] Because it involves the supply of agricultural and sideline products to the whole city of Beijing, the Xinfadi wholesale market of agricultural products will not be relocated, but it needs to be transformed and upgraded, and the transition from traditional "hand-to-hand sales" to "e-commerce and unified payment" is being considered, so as to enhance its functions.[4] At present, the Xinfadi market has established sub-markets in Gaobeidian, Hebei, and other areas, to facilitate the decentralization of some functions. Meanwhile, it has been further upgraded through transformation to decentralize some low-end small traders, strengthen electronic and information management, support large, outstanding, and strong ones, plan the transformation of photovoltaic power generation, use new energy, and reduce the waste of resources.

Our survey of the Xinfadi wholesale market of agricultural products found that traffic congestion is very serious in this area. The dense traffic flow, unreasonable road planning and design, particularly poor diversion of branch roads and construction of capillary roads, result in serious "hard obstruction" of roads. This precisely indicates that the government has not fulfilled its functions of traffic construction and management in this area, and the phenomenon of being dirty, disorderly, and bad also reveals that the local government has not seriously performed its service and supervision functions. The transformation and upgrading of the Xinfadi wholesale market of agricultural products does not just mean decentralizing some non-capital functions and low-end projects that are not suitable for Beijing, but more importantly, it means strengthening orderly rectification, transformation, and upgrading of traffic, environmental construction and housing in this area according to the requirements of modern city construction and management, making plans scientifically, reasonably diverting, and upgrading in an orderly manner. Only in this way can the development problems in this area be truly solved, so as to guarantee the construction of the vegetable basket project for citizens, scientifically solve problems of traffic, environment, resources, and energy, and the distribution of population in this area, as well as achieving sustainable development.

The Shilihe Wholesale Market is used as another example, 80% of which aims to meet the needs of Beijing citizens for life services. In Beijing, large wholesale markets for clothing, stones, and lamps are relatively concentrated. Most of them are regional wholesale markets with a low threshold for entry, so they can attract a large number of low-end industries, and most practitioners are non-Beijing locals, who often bring their family members and friends.

Low-end industries are also popular for employment of migrant workers who work in Beijing. Hence, the decentralization of non-capital functions needs to divert and relocate these low-end industries that are not suitable for Beijing's development. For example, on November 16, 2015, the largest stone market in North China–Beijing Xizhihe Stone Market was decentralized. On December 9, Tianyi Di'anmen Store officially ceased operations, and the wholesale markets such as Guanyuan and Wantong ushered in a wave of closures one after another. On December 10, 14 large integrated markets in Haidian District, such as Wanjiadenghuo, Shenghongda, and Yaoshun building material market, were relocated before the Spring Festival. Taoranting ornamental flower market was officially closed on January 1, 2016. On December 19, 2015, the task of decentralizing 200,000 square meters of wholesale market in Beijing Zoo was completed. On December 25, all trading markets in Huilongguan in the north of Changping were to be cleared out by the end of the month.[5] However, the living and production services that are basic functions of the capital cannot be decentralized. We lack effective solutions to the problems such as traffic congestion and disorderly markets caused by industrial development in these areas, as well as specific studies and differentiated measures of control.

Although high-end industries and areas can create high GDP and fiscal revenues, they are faced with the problems of being labor-intensive and over-concentrated in core urban areas. Overly dense office buildings concentrate too many jobs and working population, thus causing serious problems such as population expansion, traffic congestion, housing shortage, and environmental pollution. Beijing's "urban diseases" are largely related to overly dense office buildings, business towers, shopping malls, and inadequate traffic infrastructures in the core areas, and also to the incentive of economic growth to develop high-end industries and attract more people. We lack top-level design and action plans for the systematic research and scientific governance of these problems.

8.1.4 Total energy consumption rises, smog becomes serious and the carrying capacity of the environment is declining

Since a long time ago, Beijing has suffered from smoggy weather and a scarcity of resources and energy. These problems seriously hinder the construction of a beautiful Beijing and an international first-class harmonious and livable capital, and become obstacles to social harmony and stability. Citizens are eagerly looking forward to changing the image of environmental pollution for the capital city. In general, Beijing has enhanced its treatment of environmental pollution, but the problem of smog is serious and the task of controlling environmental pollution is becoming more and more difficult. Beijing is strengthening its control over environmental pollution, and the capacity of sewage treatment, the use of reclaimed water, and its capacity for harmless waste treatment continue to improve.

Table 8.4 Beijing's water resources from 2003 to 2014

Item	2013	2014
Total amount of water resources (million cubic meters)	24.8	20.3
Per capita water resources (cubic meters)	118.6	94.9
Total annual water supply (use)	36.4	37.5
Water consumption per 10,000 yuan of gross regional product (cubic meters)	18.37	17.58
Decline in water consumption per 10,000 yuan of gross regional product (%)	5.87	3.93
Divided by uses		
Agricultural water use (million cubic meters)	9.1	8.2
Industrial water use (million cubic meters)	5.1	5.1
Domestic water use (million cubic meters)	16.2	17.0
Environmental water use (million cubic meters)	5.9	7.2

Source: Beijing Municipal Bureau Statistics, Survey Office of the National Bureau of Statistics in Beijing: Beijing Statistical Yearbook for 2015, China Statistics Press, 2015.

There is a rigid water demand and a large gap in sewage treatment, so it is difficult to ease the problem of water shortage in metropolises. As shown in Table 8.4, the total annual water resources decreased from 2.48 billion cubic meters in 2013 to 2.03 billion cubic meters in 2014. The decreasing trend remained, and the per capita water resources decreased from 118.6 cubic meters in 2013 to 94.9 cubic meters in 2014.

The unified scheduling platform of water resources for Beijing points out that the inflowing water at Huinanzhuang in the Beijing section of the central line of the South-to-North Water Diversion Project amounted to 509 million cubic meters. Water works of the city "drank" water for an amount of 365 million cubic meters, Daning and Huairou reservoirs "stored" water for an amount of 50 million cubic meters, and 94 million cubic meters were used to refill the groundwater. However, Beijing still suffers a water shortage of nearly 100 million cubic meters.[6] Beijing's water consumption per 10,000 yuan of gross regional product fell by 0.79 cubic meters compared to that in 2013, with a decline of 3.93%.

As shown in Table 8.5, in terms of uses, agricultural water use decreased from 910 million cubic meters in 2013 to 820 million cubic meters in 2014, industrial water use remained the same as the previous year, but domestic water use increased from 1.62 billion cubic meters in 2013 to 1.70 billion cubic meters in 2014, and environmental water use increased from 590 million cubic meters in 2013 to 720 million cubic meters in 2014. It can be found that with industrial restructuring, optimization and upgrading in Beijing, agricultural water use is effectively under control and the total use of industrial water is not increasing, but with the increase in population, domestic water use has increased significantly, environmental problems are serious and environmental water use has also increased significantly. On the one hand, there is

Table 8.5 Beijing's total energy consumption from 2003 to 2014 Unit: 10k tons of standard coal

Year	Total energy consumption	Primary industry	Secondary industry	Tertiary industry	Consumer goods
2003	4648.2	99.9	2476.7	1391.0	680.6
2006	5904.1	92.3	2773.1	2129.3	909.4
2009	6570.3	99.0	2544.2	2760.3	1166.8
2012	7177.7	100.8	2426.1	3252.1	1398.7
2013	6723.9	97,3	2079.2	3109.1	1438.3
2014	6831.2	91.7	1998.4	3236.5	1504.6

a large constant demand for water use, and the increase of sewage discharge puts pressure on the supply of water resources; on the other hand, sewage treatment has a relatively large gap, and water resources are wasted seriously, which makes it difficult to alleviate the problem of urban water shortage, and water conservation needs to be strengthened.

Beijing's energy production and total consumption are rising and putting serious pressure on energy consumption and on the intensity of carbon emissions, which results in a continuous decline in the environmental carrying capacity. In 2013, Beijing's energy production continued to grow. The production of primary energy reached 5.368 million tons of standard coal, which increased by 350,000 tons of standard coal compared to that in 2012, the production of secondary energy decreased to 31.709 million tons of standard coal in 2013, and the production of gasoline, kerosene, diesel, fuel oil, and liquefied petroleum gas also decreased. However, the production of electricity increased from 28.47 billion kWh in 2012 to 32.81 billion kWh in 2013.

According to Table 8.5, the total energy consumption of Beijing in 2014 was 68.312 million tons of standard coal, which had increased slightly over 2013. In terms of the structure of energy consumption, the primary industry decreased slightly, the secondary industry diminished significantly, the tertiary industry, and domestic consumption obviously increased. Energy consumption is dominated by the tertiary industry and domestic consumption, but that of the secondary industry has decreased. This is consistent with the service-oriented economic structure of Beijing, but the increase in total energy consumption may put more pressure on energy and cause the problem of emissions.

Beijing is subject to the pressure of population expansion, the current situation of inadequate energy supply and smoggy weather cannot be changed in a short term, the construction of environmental protection facilities lags behind economic development, and there is no optimism regarding the water environment. According to Table 8.6, the total wastewater discharge continued to grow, and reached 1,445,799,300 tons in 2013, with an increase of 43,063,400 tons over 2012; in terms of air environment-related indicators, sulfur dioxide

Table 8.6 Beijing's environmental protection from 2012 to 2013

Item	2013	2012
Water environment		
Total wastewater discharge (10K tons)	144579.93	140273.59
Chemical oxygen demand emissions (tons)	178475	186501
Ammonia nitrogen emissions (tons)	19704	20483
Sulfur dioxide emissions into the atmospheric environment (tons)	87042	93849
Nitrogen oxide emissions (tons)	166329	177495
Smoke (dust) emissions (tons)	59286	66829

emissions, nitrogen oxide emissions, and smoke (dust) emissions decreased, but the smog in metropolises has not been effectively curbed.

According to the existing results of research on Beijing's air pollution, especially the components of the PM2.5 analysis, in Beijing, motor vehicles are the largest cause of pollution and account for about 31.1%, coal combustion accounts for 22.4%, industry and other sources account for 18.1%, and dust and restaurants account for 14.3% and 14.1%, respectively. PM2.5 comes from both direct emissions from pollution sources and secondary generation; both anthropogenic sources and natural sources.

First of all, it is a dilemma of pollution that the ownership of motor vehicles is not decreasing, the number of motor vehicles in stock is increasing and the exhaust emissions have become a regular source of pollution. The exhaust emissions of motor vehicles contribute to 31.1% of the local pollution. Due to the absence of necessary measures for motor vehicle ownership and use, the exhaust emissions of motor vehicles have become a rigid or constant and stable source of air pollution in Beijing. There is no overall target control or rigid constraint on new motor vehicles. Although the annual increase has slowed down, and Beijing has lowered its annual increment from 240,000 to 150,000, including 20,000 new-energy vehicles, the total number of fuel vehicles still increased by 130,000 per year. It means that the limited air capacity of Beijing is subject to the emissions of at least 130,000 new vehicles, thus resulting in the "deteriorating" total pollution of motor vehicles. New motor vehicles offset the effect of motor vehicle elimination and emission reduction. The promotion and use of new-energy vehicles is confronted with many problems, such as low awareness, low technology, difficulty in cost reduction, and insufficient facilities. The exhaust emissions not only lead to serious air pollution, but most terribly affect the physical and mental health of citizens and result in the hazards of lung cancer and cardiovascular disease. Without resolutely controlling and reducing motor vehicle emissions, the stained image of Beijing as a polluting city cannot be removed, and the construction of a world-class harmonious and livable city will become an empty phrase.

Second, coal reduction is effective, but the full implementation of natural gas and energy substitution is plagued by the poor planning of energy facilities and difficulties in laying gas pipelines, etc. The goal of coal-free urban areas in Beijing can be achieved, but there is no systematic plan for gas pipelines in many distant suburban districts and counties, and it is difficult to lay gas pipelines in rural areas, especially in mountainous areas. In some areas, there are difficulties in demolition, relocation and subsidies for laying gas pipelines. The limited subsidies for high-quality coal, the declining prices of poor-quality coal and ineffective supervision of coal burning facilities lead to the use of poor-quality coal by part-time farmers or residents. The enforcement of coal-free use is weakly supervised in distant suburban districts and counties, there is limited space to avoid coal burning and reduce coal use, and the coal reduction in Beijing makes little contribution to the smog control. Moreover, there are technical and cost challenges for new energy consumption and restructuring.

Third, the phasing-out of polluting industries is facing difficulties in eradicating dead ends on the urban-rural fringe of Beijing, transformation and upgrading of polluting industries outside Beijing, and regional transmission. Beijing is pillared by the tertiary industry, with a limited space for reduction of industrial pollution. By closing and transferring polluting industries, either the scale or total emissions of polluting enterprises in Beijing are diminishing, and there is limited space for not developing industries completely, or reducing industrial emissions to a minimum level. The pollution emissions of service sectors, including production or life services, also attract attention, but the overall space for emission reductions is not very large, and the effect on smog control is not very obvious.

The regional transmission of smog comes from the surrounding areas of Beijing to some extent, especially heavily polluting industrial cities in Hebei Province, and it is difficult to achieve strict control and effective governance on the industrial scale and pollution emissions in the surrounding areas. Thus, strengthening the control of several typical heavily-polluting cities in China such as Tangshan, Xingtai, Handan, and other areas around Beijing is a difficult point for the control of air pollution in the capital city.

Fourth, dust control needs to slow down the frequency and speed of urban demolition and reconstruction, and the process of urbanization cannot always pursue GDP growth in the cycles of demolition and reconstruction. Developed cities in Western countries highlight planning, and after a period of construction, they basically do not carry out demolition and reconstruction on a large scale. Many cities attach importance to the preservation of old buildings and do not build more new towns or new buildings. This is a common phenomenon in Europe and the United States of America, where most buildings are more than 100 years old. This can not only effectively preserve historical monuments and urban history and culture, but also avoid new energy consumption and environmental pollution during reconstruction.

Beijing must reduce or slow the frequency of building demolition and reconstruction, pay attention to the preservation of ancient buildings, and stop the planning and construction of new buildings in core urban areas or relatively mature urban areas to reduce the density of urban buildings and retain more urban ecological space. Furthermore, it should moderately enhance its control over pollution emissions within the urban life service sectors, and it should not compress rigid living demands in its control over pollution of the catering industry because there is limited room for control, nor adequately advocate green life and consumption.

Fifth, no adequate efforts are being devoted to the control of several key pollution sources and there is a regulatory and control vacuum. For example, the emissions of airports in the capital are not controlled. These airports can draw on the experience of Europe, where aircraft with excessive emissions are strictly prohibited from landing at the airport and a tax is levied on aircraft with excessive emissions. But no such regulations are promulgated by airports in our capital. The daily fuel emissions from airplanes of Capital Airport and Nanyuan Airport have a serious impact on the air pollution in Shunyi, Tongzhou, Chaoyang, Daxing, Changping, and other areas.

Sixth, it is difficult to cure the cross-infection of population, industrial and traffic diseases with environmental diseases. Atmospheric pollution is directly caused by "urban diseases", which further results from a series of problems such as industrial concentration, traffic congestion and a housing shortage due to the over-expansion and concentration of the population in urban areas. Overpopulation may cause problems such as difficulty in reducing the rigid demand for emissions, the increase in exhaust emissions owing to traffic and car purchasing on the part of the new population, and various emissions of new buildings and industries because of the housing and offices of the new population. There is a lack of top-level design and specific action plans for the comprehensive diagnosis, full examination, and systematic remediation of these diseases.

Seventh, Beijing is not sufficiently greened, and many urban greening isolation zones are encroached upon and squeezed, thus weakening the role of green space for urban dust reduction and smog control. A lot of lands originally planned as green partitions have either been converted into industrial, commercial, or residential land, or turned into land for illegal construction. The low greening rate of the city has lost its proper effect on the purification of urban air pollution.

Eighth, there are no operating agencies at points of air pollution prevention and environmental control, particularly environmental law enforcement at the levels of streets, towns, and communities. The capacities of public security, urban management, family planning, and other departments are not integrated, and work on air pollution control and environmental protection at the grassroots level lacks executors, participants, supervisors, and social supporters.

8.2 Analysis of the causes of "urban diseases" in Beijing

Beijing's "urban diseases" have not only the basic features of general metropolises, but also the special characteristics of a national capital city, especially the capital of a large developing country and a socialist country, so their causes are more complex. There are many influencing factors on the formation of Beijing's "urban diseases" that have complex relationships. In essence, "urban diseases" result from the accumulation of conflicts between the carrying capacity of urban resources and the environment and the speed of urbanization-oriented development.[7] On the one hand, Beijing, as a metropolis, has the general rules of metropolitan development, and its "urban diseases" share commonalities with other cities. A lot of "urban diseases" are not unique to Beijing, but common to other cities, such as population expansion, traffic congestion, housing shortage, environmental deterioration, and depletion of resources. On the other hand, the formation of Beijing's "urban diseases" is also closely linked to the city's historical development, cultural characteristics, regional realities, and political status, and needs to be analyzed in the context of Beijing's geographical location and current situation. General Secretary Xi Jinping proposed to implement the strategic positioning of the capital city and to decentralize non-capital functions. This provides a guiding direction for treating Beijing's "urban diseases" and analyzing the causes for the formation of "urban diseases".

8.2.1 Lack of a top-level design and overall mechanism of coordination for the treatment of "urban diseases"

8.2.1.1 Lack of top-level design and action plans to solve the problems of "urban diseases" in the capital, and unreasonable urban plans

At present, although Beijing has done a lot of work on implementing the spirit of General Secretary Xi's speech and has made some progress and achievements, there are still many problems and a lack of in-depth analysis, systematic thinking and top-level design on the causes of these problems. According to the mechanism of "urban diseases", the emergence of "urban diseases" is a manifestation of incoordination and disorder among various elements and subsystems in the operation of the urban system. As a huge open system and self-organization, the city is constantly exchanging energy within and outside the system, including information, talents, knowledge, and materials. Without these exchanges, the operation of the city will be hindered, and the whole system will malfunction and be disordered if any one part fails. Exchanges and mechanisms of system feedback are essential to maintaining the overall balance of the city. Once exchanges and input and output systems fail, or the mechanism of information feedback does not work, the urban system will become unbalanced, and in serious cases, the operation of the city will be paralyzed.[8] "Urban diseases" are often generated along with the process of urbanization and industrialization, because there is non-coordination in the material transmission and energy exchange within the urban system, which leads to a disorderly, chaotic, and uncontrolled state of urban operations. Therefore, the analysis of the causes of "urban diseases" should be considered from the perspective of the whole system, especially the top-level design of urban development and the height of systemic development. From a holistic and systematic self-organizing point of view, there is a lack of top-level design and action plans to implement the strategic positioning of the capital city and treat "urban diseases". Since there is no resolution on the implementation of the capital's strategic positioning from a macroscopic, holistic, and systematic height or specific action outline and strategic planning in the form of documents, it is difficult to form unified deployment, unified action, and unified measures at both the level of Beijing city or the level of district or county, and this eventually leads to no target and inability to achieve the expected goals and results.

There are a number of reasons for Beijing's "urban diseases", but the core problem is that the capital has too many urban functions, which affect the core functions. President Xi Jinping proposed to further clarify and implement the strategic positioning of the capital city, and fully affirm the idea that it is a national political center, cultural center, international communication center, and center of science and technology innovation. This positioning, inheriting the previous one, adds the statement of science and technology innovation center, which is the new mission and new requirement for the development of the capital city when China responds to the new trend of global competition for innovation and implements its innovation-driven national strategy. The typical manifestation of Beijing's "urban diseases" is overpopulation, which has reached the "ceiling". But the reasons why the population is flowing into Beijing include not only the natural absorption capacity of population of Beijing as a metropolis, but also too many urban functions, a concentration of too many resources and unequal public services. Beijing is the national political center, cultural center, economic center, financial center, science and technology center, education center, medical center, etc., and these large, all-embracing, high-end, and numerous central functions are bound to attract a massive influx of population. For example, people from other places concentrate mainly in Dongcheng and Xicheng districts for seeking medical treatment, and there are also a certain percentage of children from other places who attend schools in these areas. More functions mean the concentration of more advantageous resources, which implies the acquisition of some benefits and unfair distribution. As a national center of politics, culture, science, and technology, it will naturally gather high-end political resources, cultural resources, scientific and technological resources, educational resources, medical resources, etc., and may provide more high-end employment opportunities, which are the prerequisites for attracting high-end talents.

Beijing intends to deal with its "urban diseases" of a capital city, but it has failed to scientifically position the functions of the capital city and has lacked a top-level design and clear action plans for decentralizing non-capital functions and treating "urban diseases". As a result, the various measures for treating "urban diseases" can "treat the symptoms but not the root cause", thus being difficult to solve the fundamental problems of too many functions and overly intensive resources in the core urban areas. For example, the single-minded policies of population control can reduce the inflowing population in the short term, such as eviction of low-end industries and their working population, expulsion of people from housing or basements for group rental, but it cannot slow down the trend of population expansion in Beijing in the long term. As long as the incentives and conditions for attracting the influx of population remain unchanged, the problem of Beijing's population expansion will persist for a period of time. This requires an in-depth analysis of the capital's "urban diseases" and its causes, enhancement of top-level design, systematic formulation of action plans and strategic planning, and better coordination among all parties. However, there is a lack of top-level design and action plans in this regard, and the Action Outline for the Coordinated Development of the Beijing-Tianjin-Hebei Region is nothing but a document, and it will take a period of time to implement it and observe the effects it produces.

The core and non-core functions of the capital city are not analyzed deeply, nor are they defined. Which functions should be diverted and which basic functions cannot be relocated has not theoretically been recognized, without good study, design, and plans, thus leading to the difficulty in continuous, steady and effective advancement of the specific work. For example, there is a lack of clear plans of functional decentralization and urban development for the Beijing Zoo wholesale market, the Dahongmen market, the Guangyuan market and the Shilihe market. It does not have an in-depth study, a clear design and perfect plans regarding whether these markets should be relocated or not, whether they should be relocated completely or partially, where to relocate, how to relocate, and how to transform or utilize the lands or vacant lands after relocation. And there are also no detailed plans and implementation schemes on how to compensate for the interests of these market players, how to divide property rights, and how to connect the relocated markets.

The formation of "urban diseases" in the capital is closely related to the lack of reasonable urban plans. Too many urban functions, overly concentrated industries, excessively dense high-rise buildings and underdeveloped construction of infrastructures are associated with the unscientific and imperfect urban plans. Because the urban plans lack sufficient foresight, scientific prediction and sufficient planned space for the expansion of the size of the city, an increase in the urban population, urban industrial development, urban traffic facilities, and urban development is subject to restrictions. The problems of urban planning are mainly manifested in the following aspects.

First, the urban plan lacks in-depth research, strategic thought and scientific demonstration, without considering the characteristics of urban development and the trend of future urban expansion. Some urban planning has changed the will of individuals or some leaders and is short on foresight, science, and strategy. Urban planning is eager for success and profit, and focuses on vanity projects and performance projects, thus being unable to keep up with the trend of urban development.

Second, the planning is not serious and is not coordinated. The unreasonableness of the planning itself makes it difficult to implement it effectively; the planning lacks sufficient demonstration and research and does not meet the needs of the actual development; and the planning cannot fully deal with the interests of all parties, so it is difficult to coordinate the relationships of all parties and becomes something done in vain. During the execution of urban planning, relevant authorities consider their own interests only, without communication and coordination, making it difficult to implement the plan. For example, there are no scientific planning and effective mechanism of planning execution for many green belts and urban–rural fringe areas in Beijing, where private buildings and illegal construction encroaching on urban green areas cannot be monitored and controlled promptly, thus resulting in urban traffic congestion, concentration of low-end industries in urban–rural fringes, and in the rapid growth and expansion of the population.

Third, urban planning pursues GDP and economic interests only, but does not thoroughly consider the carrying capacity of resources, energy, and the environment of the city. For example, the core urban areas mainly pay attention to the growth of the GDP, blindly introducing more industries and projects, building denser and high-rise buildings, and a lack of plans and institutional constraints on resources, energy, and the environment. The overly dense building land use has seriously encroached on the ecological land use and public cultural spaces, leading to the accumulation of "urban diseases" such as overpopulation, traffic congestion, depletion of resources, and energy and environmental pollution. Fourth, urban planning is not strictly carried out, and violations are not dealt with in promptly and resolutely. As the national capital, Beijing's urban planning, once adopted, should be firmly implemented, but numerous local violations have not been stopped and dealt with properly, and it is lack of adequate mechanisms of monitoring and enforcement. For example, some green isolation zones were occupied by illegal constructions, but no effort was made to detect, supervise, and stop such acts in time, and after being found, they could not be resolutely investigated and demolished, resulting in relatively weak execution and lack of authoritativeness of the planning. Some plans have been changed by individual leaders, and hence the plans cannot be carried out according to the intended goals. In the urban–rural fringes and green isolation zones, there are especially many illegal constructions, which are relatively difficult to deal with and demolish, thus restricting the effective execution of urban planning. For decentralizing non-capital functions, these areas are also difficult and tricky places to act on.

8.2.1.2 Lack of a relevant legal basis for the decentralization of non-capital functions and operable policies and measures

The lack of clear plans and a relevant legal basis leads to the fact that the decentralization of non-core functions of the capital has no legal basis, and relies solely on leaders' speeches and governmental files, all of which are administrative actions directly interfering with the market, contrary to the basic spirit and requirements of giving play to the decisive role of the market mechanism in resource allocation as proposed in the report of the 18th CPC National Congress, and its implementation is also very ineffective. For example, for general enterprises and operators who commit no obvious violations but conform to the functional positioning of the capital, the mandatory requirement for merchants to terminate their contracts and move out by a deadline is obviously contrary to the laws and basic principles of market economy, and actually an excessive administrative intervention in the market. There is no clear compensation for the interests of these relocated enterprises or support from relevant policies, and the government lacks a sufficient basis for decentralization and a means of regulation. There is a lack of operable policies and measures to support the diversion of industries and population and land control during the decentralization of non-capital core functions. The lack of implementation rules for relevant policies and regulations has led to the common problem that there is no legal basis and it is difficult to implement such measures when the control of the population is assumed at the grassroots level. For example, no relevant policies are available to guide the process of shantytown renovation, involving the demolition of units with central and municipal property rights, as well as the big gap between the required housing for demolition and the funding. Moreover, after a number of backward industrial production projects are phased out, due to the lack of macroscopic policy guidance and detailed implementation methods for the nature of the land, planning adjustment and administrative approval, the lands of the original projects are left idle, without a clear direction of development, thus preventing other industries from moving in and making it impossible to achieve the successive development of industries. The imperfect policies directly lead to inefficiency in the regulation of the population.

Regarding the control of traffic congestion, disorderly parking, and exhaust emissions, there is also a lack of an effective legal basis, and systematic and detailed Clean Air Act and Regulations on Urban Traffic Congestion and Pollution Prevention, so it is difficult to punish and control traffic congestion and disorderly parking according to law.

8.2.1.3 Lack of an effective body for coordination, an insufficient compensation mechanism, and underdeveloped urban management

First, due to the lack of an effective coordinating body, it is difficult for an individual entity to advance governance. The implementation of the strategic positioning of the capital city and the decentralization of non-capital core functions involves the defining of land property rights, compensation for interests, relocation, and cultivation of the market, public services, traffic conditions, financial and taxation policies, etc. No coordination mechanism has been established from Beijing at the levels of city, districts, counties, towns (streets), and even market entities, and many tasks require the coordination and collaboration of multiple agencies such as a planning commission, a development and reform commission, a commission of transportation, and an administration for industry and commerce. It is difficult for a single agency or entity to effectively work on them. For example, Fengtai District has responded positively to the spirit of General Secretary Xi's speech and the relevant deployments of the municipal government, and set up a practical department which is the Dahongmen Decentralization Office, but the office is unable to effectively interface with the various functional departments at the municipal level in Beijing. A lot of work needs instructions from multiple sides. If there is no coordinating mechanism at the municipal level, it is difficult to solve various problems during decentralization, and the process of decentralization suffers from the problems of multi-sided management and mutual shirking of responsibilities. The decentralization of non-core functions also involves many interested entities such as central organs, the military, central enterprises, state-owned enterprises, etc., and concerns multiple levels of administrative units such as district and county governments, townships, and streets, and the governments of Beijing, Tianjin, and Hebei, with multiple interested entities, a complex nature of property rights and cross-jurisdictional relationships, thus making it difficult to coordinate effectively not only within Beijing, but also between Beijing and central organs, military, central enterprises, and other governments and institutions at all levels of Tianjin and Hebei.

Second, due to a lack of an effective mechanism for compensation, it is difficult to fundamentally incentivize the inherent vitality of decentralization. The implementation of the strategic positioning of the capital city, the decentralization of non-core functions, and the treatment of "urban diseases" all involve complex interests, high decentralization costs, and high social risks. Taking population diversion and control as an example, it faces the seven contradictions among continued urbanization, a gap in the development of Beijing, Tianjin, and Hebei, sufficient local developmental momentum, uneven the distribution of public resources, the pressure of maintaining social stability, rules of industrial decentralization, legality of means and Beijing's control of the population.

Due to a lack of an effective mechanism for compensation, it is difficult to solve many problems regarding the game of interests. There are multiple games, competing interests, and dilemmas in implementing the strategic positioning of the capital city, decentralizing non-urban core functions, and treating "urban diseases". There are also contradictions between government intervention and market mechanisms, between central government and municipal government, between municipal government and district and county governments, between the Beijing municipal government and central enterprises, state-owned enterprises and central organs, and among the interests of different market entities. Industrial decentralization and market relocation will create conflicts of interest between the original owners and tenants, but how to compensate them? The land where the industry is located involves different kinds of ownerships such as original state-owned enterprises, farmers' collective land, and an enterprise's own land, and there is a lack of a clear mechanism for interest compensation and risk sharing. Beijing lacks institutional arrangements for input of compensation funds, distribution of compensation funds at the urban and district levels, and compensation standards, which reduce the willingness of market entities to be decentralized.

Beijing has introduced incentives for the relocation of polluting industrial enterprises, but without incentives for those below designated size and other entities to be decentralized. If these deficits of interest cannot be compensated promptly or given expectations at the policy level, it is difficult to prompt the relocation and decentralization of these enterprises or industries. Even if it is mandatory to close enterprises and compress industrial space, the goal of diverting the population will fail; even if certain industries or markets are diverted, the population or markets are transferred to surrounding areas, but the problem of population expansion cannot be solved. The purpose of industrial decentralization is to divert the population. When the purpose of population diverting cannot be achieved, industrial decentralization will put the cart before the horse and end up in vain.

Third, there is no market condition for functional decentralization, public services in the destinations are poorly developed, and the deficits of interest cannot be balanced. Non-core functions and industries of Beijing are diverted to the surrounding areas in Hebei and Tianjin, but these areas do not have a market environment similar to Beijing's, and they lag behind Beijing in terms of market demand, upstream and downstream industries, traffic conditions, and public services. The objective differences in public services, education, medical care and traffic in the destinations make them difficult to take over diverted population and attract the entry of market factors. Mandatory industrial relocation may lead to the demise and loss of interests of certain industries and enterprises due to the non-availability of market conditions in the destinations, thus reducing the motivation and willingness of industrial relocation and leading to relocation without leaving and decentralization without solving problems. In the meanwhile, there is a lack of reasonable institutional arrangements and policy regulations in GDP accounting, transfer payments, tax sharing and rebates, etc., and Beijing and destinations for industrial transfer cannot reach a consensus on the interests of development, which hinders the relocation and transfer of enterprises.

Fourth, the coordinated development of the Beijing-Tianjin-Hebei region is not promoted by a real institution, so it cannot take the form of a long-lasting mechanism for cooperation. The Beijing-Tianjin-Hebei region includes two municipalities directly under the central government and one province, and there are central ministries and commissions and their national enterprises and institutions within the municipality of Beijing, with multiple entities, complex hierarchies, and cross interests. The lack of strong mechanisms for organizational leadership and coordinated advancement for the coordinated development of the Beijing-Tianjin-Hebei region makes it difficult to advance substantially even if each side has a desire for cooperation and development. The coordinated development of the Beijing-Tianjin-Hebei region is not only a matter of Beijing, Tianjin and Hebei, but it also involves the maintenance and balance of the central interests. On the one hand, solving the problems of "urban diseases" in Beijing is not something that can be successfully achieved by unilateral actions at the Beijing municipal level. Industrial and population decentralization should not only include the relocation of Beijing's municipal enterprises and units, but also the relocation and decentralization of some state-owned enterprises, central enterprises, and central institutions belonging to non-capital core functions, which have a stronger ability to absorb population compared to Beijing. It is impossible for the Beijing municipal government alone to control the population and decentralize industries, which is something that requires the coordination of the central government at the national level. On the other hand, Beijing should play the role of a big brother in the coordinated development of the Beijing-Tianjin-Hebei region, but it lacks the power of direct administration and control. Beijing alone is unable to realize the actual balance of interests and coordination of development. The central government must establish a real institution at the national level to advance this matter, and without adopting a practical benefit-sharing mechanism and implementation plan, it will be difficult to realize the coordinated development of the Beijing-Tianjin-Hebei region.

Fifth, the level of urban planning, construction, and management cannot keep up with the requirements of building an international first-class harmonious and livable city. As the capital of a large developing country with a large population, Beijing is objectively and inevitably overpopulated with traffic congestion, but the lack of urban planning talents, underdeveloped urban planning, construction, and management, and a lack of urban construction concepts have aggravated the "urban diseases". Constrained by the traditional object-oriented concept of urban construction, urbanization is simply equated with the construction of avenues, scenic areas, luxury city squares, skyscrapers, and shopping malls, it ignores the city's carrying capacity of resources, energy, and the environment and the livability of urban residents, it does not have sufficient urban facilities, and lags behind in urban service facilities. In terms of management, the city highlights control while ignoring services, highlights fines while ignoring rules, highlights ruling while ignoring participation, with limited management talents and capacity, its detailed and professional management seriously lag behind the level of urban development, and the social services are of bad quality. The phenomena of multi-sided management, governance by several organs, and fragmentation are prominent, the efficiencies of the construction of infrastructures, use, operations, and management are low, the quality of the construction of infrastructures is poor, and accidents occur frequently.[9] As a result, there are problems of there being few life service points, inconveniences for life, traffic congestion, and disorderly parking of private cars. Furthermore, there are various difficulties in development, such as difficulties in admission to kindergartens, schooling, medical care, and elderly care, which restrict the construction of a harmonious and livable capital and the sustainable economic and social development of the city.

8.2.2 Lack of a scientific substitute mechanism of GDP-based performance assessment, but with an arduous task of industrial restructuring

The report of the 18th CPC National Congress and the 3rd and 4th Plenary Sessions of the 18th Central Committee of the CPC proposed to deepen reform in an all-around manner, change the traditional GDP-based performance assessment system, and give play to the decisive role of the market in resource allocation, but in the actual political operations and government system, no files have been issued to change the traditional fiscal and taxation system, or the traditional GDP-based system of performance assessment. There is a lack of a scientific new system and mechanism that can replace the traditional GDP model of performance assessment. In the process of treating "urban diseases" and decentralizing non-capital functions, the cites are not immune to the institutional influence on the incentive to pursue the GDP.

China's urban development is influenced by various institutional factors, which are not only the important driving force of urban expansion and economic growth, but also the important causes that hinder sustainable urban economic and social development and form "urban diseases". According to related studies, these factors mainly include the mechanism for the selection of cadres and system of performance assessment, the financial and taxation system, the land system, the planning system, etc.[10] Such factors can be said to be the important characteristics of China's urban development, and also the important shackles that restrict further sustainable, scientific, and healthy development of cities, and the analysis of these factors can provide the theoretical basis for choosing a scientific path of governance.

The influence of the mechanism for the selection of cadres and the system of performance assessment.

China attaches great importance to the strict selection of cadres and adopts the basic model of democratic recommendation, personnel survey, discussion by the party committee and approval by the higher level. For example, in January 1986, the procedure for selecting cadres as stipulated in the Notice of the CPC Central Committee on Selecting and Appointing Cadres Strictly Pursuant to Party Principles is: first, democratic recommendation, extensive listening to opinions and proposing candidates for selection; second, survey by the personnel department, collective discussion and decision by the party committee and then reporting to the superior according to the authority of cadre management; third, further consideration by the superior organization and then submission to the party committee for discussion and approval. The files such as the Provisional Regulations on the Selection and Appointment of Leading Party and Government Cadres in 1995, the Regulations on the Selection and Appointment of Leading Party and Government Cadres in 2002 and the Decision of the CPC Central Committee on Strengthening the Party's Governance Capability in 2004 modified and improved the system for the selection of cadres, in which leadership nomination, survey by the personnel department, and discussion and decision by the party committee are the key procedures for this selection and appointment. This is actually a top-down system of cadre appointment.

The selection and performance assessment of leading cadres by the superior units are decisive factors influencing the behavior of subordinate units and their leading cadres. This mode of selecting and appointing cadres, which mainly relies on the assessment and decision of the superior, determines that the subordinate units and their behaviors are guided by the preferences and needs of the superior. Performance assessment, under the long-standing basic principle of insisting on "economic construction" at the center, focuses too much on economic growth indicators, with GDP as the dominant factor, and pays little attention to social development, improvement in people's livelihood, environmental protection, sustainable development, and other indicators, which account for only a small proportion. The economic growth indicators determine the performance assessment of subordinate units and their main leading cadres. In this model, subordinate units put excessive emphasis on GDP and economic growth, and urban development gives way to economic growth, and cities with fast economic growth are valued and praised by superior leaders, and then the cadres can get promoted.

The system of performance assessment, which focuses on economic growth indicators, has a serious influence on the sustainable economic and social development of cities, with too much emphasis on the economy, but neglect of social construction, improvement of people's livelihood, public services, and the construction of infrastructures, which become an important cause of "urban diseases". Due to the excessive focus on economic construction and GDP growth, urban functions are overly concentrated. The central urban areas have higher land prices and better conditions for industrial development, so they can build more and denser high-rise office buildings to achieve economic growth goals, while the development goals of ecological land, improvement of traffic facilities, and public cultural services are often neglected or replaced.

The government at the municipal level encourages industrial clustering and attracts large projects, thus resulting in the overburden of urban resources, the environment and infrastructure. They excessively pursue visible economic construction and vanity projects, but neglect projects regarding people's livelihood, social construction, and ecological protection. Construction of cultural plazas and other vanity projects can be easily noticed by superior leaders during their visits and included in the evaluation and assessment, so these projects are given priority in investment and construction. The projects related to people's livelihood and social construction, such as urban drainage, roads, urban ecological restoration and protection, social security, etc., are not easily noticed, their development is not valued and their construction seriously lags behind. This mechanism of performance assessment leads directly to an insufficient construction of urban infrastructures, but the excessive development of commercial real estate in central urban areas can attract more working population and traffic. Therefore, it is difficult to avoid the problems of "urban diseases" such as population expansion, traffic congestion and environmental deterioration.

8.2.2.1 The influence of the current fiscal and taxation system

At present, China's fiscal and taxation system has an important influence on the government at the municipal level. On the one hand, due to the tax sharing system, the good tax sources are collected centrally, but the excessive responsibilities of public services and other affairs are seriously mismatched with the limited local fiscal sources. Some local governments have too few corporate tax sources because industries are not well developed, and some local governments not only basically have little local fiscal tax revenue, but also lack strong support from the superior fiscal transfers, resulting in payroll finance and land finance. In 1994, China adopted the tax sharing system, which implemented tax division and tax sharing ratio more favorable to the central government, and did not delineate the affairs and fiscal expenditure responsibilities of governments at all levels. As a result, the financial powers were centralized, but the affairs were decentralized; local governments lacked financial resources, but they assumed excessive responsibilities of affairs and expenditure. Taxes from enterprises is the most important source of revenue from local fiscal taxation, but in regions with fewer enterprises or less favorable development, local governments do not have enough sources of fiscal taxation, thus leading to payroll finance and land finance. Payroll finance reflects the fact that local governments have limited revenue from fiscal taxation. They can rely on land finance only, as taxes related to real estate such as deed taxes, property taxes, land value-added taxes, and urban land use taxes are all important components of local fiscal revenues, which, together with land transfer fees, constitute "land finance". The mismatch between local governments' affairs and financial resources forces the government at the municipal level to seek sources of revenue other than taxes, and "urban operations" and land finance become prevalent. The tax structure, in which enterprise-related taxes are the main source of income, leads to the phenomenon by which local governments try all means of attracting investment in order to expand their sources of taxes. They carry out high-intensity real estate development in the renovation of dilapidated buildings, so that the population and economic activities become more intensive and the urban infrastructure more overburdened.

8.2.2.2 The influence of the land system

The land system in China has a significant influence on urban development. Due to the dual system of public land ownership in urban and rural areas, the property rights of urban land and rural land are different; urban land is owned by the State, but rural land is collectively owned by farmers. Except for land of the rural collective construction type, only state-owned land can be used for construction. Collective organizations are not allowed to purchase state-owned land, and the State may compulsorily expropriate collective land. Under the current legal framework, the property rights of rural land owned by farmers collectively are incomplete, and the owners and ownership of the rural collective land can only be changed through expropriation by the State. These regulations on the land system can lead to the monopoly of the land market by the government at the municipal level, thus creating convenient conditions for them to enclose and sell land and practice "land financing". Governments at the municipal level are owners, managers, and operators of urban land, so there are excessive non-market-oriented factors in the allocation of land resources. The government at the municipal level has the incentive to expand the scale of demolition and reconstruction, which intensifies the complication and fragmentation of the internal spatial structure of cities, and results in an insufficient supply of public services, encroachment onto ecological land and public facilities by construction land, an agglomeration of population and industries in old urban areas, an aggravation of traffic congestion, and other symptoms of "urban diseases".

8.2.2.3 The influence of the planning system

Because urban planning is not reasonable and the decision-making power of planning is highly centralized, its problems are easily caused, problems like diagonal decision-making, asymmetry of responsibilities and powers, non-scientific and unreasonable planning, and planning falling behind changes, so that the problems of "urban diseases" cannot be fundamentally solved. For example, the planning of urban traffic lags behind the growth of the urban population; the planning of construction land is not reasonable enough and exceeds the carrying capacity of urban resources, energy, and the environment. The planning lacks authoritativeness and remains without implementation, and many localities "change the plans after the appointment of a new leadership". The new leaders change the plans at will to reflect the new ideas and achievements of the current government leaders. The punishment for illegal development and construction is too weak to deter violations of the law. Moreover, the planning is not timely because its approval procedure lags behind, the planning process has no public participation, the planning cannot guarantee the scientific development of the city, and local governments pursue political achievements, economic growth, land enclosure, and sales and maximization of fiscal revenue. All these situations lead to the continuous deterioration of "urban diseases".

For the above reasons, the negative influence of the mechanism for performance assessment of pursuing GDP, taxation system, and land system still exist, the incentive of economic development to the government at the district and county levels has not been fundamentally changed, and there are not enough efforts made at carrying out industrial decentralization.

First of all, the mechanism of performance assessment of pursuing GDP has not changed, and it is difficult to balance the interests. The purpose of vacating the cage to change birds is to achieve a higher economic growth and attract more industries, enterprises, and population, while an increase in population will lead to more serious traffic congestion and other "urban diseases". For example, the outward expansion of financial streets and CBDs in core areas further aggravates the problems of "urban diseases" such as population expansion, traffic congestion, and environmental deterioration. Due to the GDP-based performance assessment, the governments at all levels of Beijing, Tianjin and Hebei have an incentive to actively develop the economy, and economic growth needs to attract the inflow of industries and population, thus leading to more serious "urban diseases" such as population, traffic, resources, energy, and the environment.

Second, the decentralization of low-end industries results in the reduction of GDP. When high-end industries are temporarily unable to enter and replace them, the incentive and motivation of local governments to decentralize industries are reduced, or the decentralization of old low-end industries leads to the entry of new low-end industries, making it difficult to crack the problems of "urban diseases" such as traffic congestion. In addition, since the intrinsic motivation based on economic development and the pursuit of GDP still exists, the industries with good efficiency, low energy consumption, low pollution, and potential to be explored but not belonging to the core functions of the capital are not diverted via a prompt decision. In the case of Beijing, including core areas, the incentive to develop the economy has never weakened despite the realistic problems of serious population expansion, traffic congestion and environmental pollution, and the phasing-out of low-end industries is not aimed at decongesting the population and traffic, but at developing GDP and acquiring more tax revenue.

Third, a green and ecological low-carbon industrial system has not been established, and the extensive model of economic development restricts the construction of an ecological civilization in the capital. There isn't enough innovation for green low-carbon technology, and the technical support system has not been built. The construction of an ecological civilization needs rid itself of the concept of "technical rationality first" by the traditional industrial civilization, and the value orientation of neglecting ecology and the environment with economic interests first. The solving of resource and environmental problems depends on the innovation and development of a series of green and low-carbon technologies. At present, the innovative supporting system of green low-carbon technology in the Beijing-Tianjin-Hebei region has not yet been established, and the financial and taxation, investment and financing policies are not yet suitable to the construction of an ecological civilization. As a heavily polluted region, in Hebei, the proportion of high-carbon industries is too high, the low-carbon ecological industrial system has not been built, and there is still a long way to go for the shutdown and transfer of polluting enterprises.

Although Beijing is a tertiary industry-pillared service economy, with the tertiary industry accounting for more than 70% of the GDP, the industrial structure of service sectors is low-end with a high proportion of life services, such as catering, traffic, logistics, wholesale and retail services, which are big sources of pollution, and with a small proportion of knowledge-intensive, technology-intensive, and low-carbon services. As a result, Beijing still has a high intensity of industrial emissions. Reducing the proportion of heavy and chemical industries around Beijing, including those within Hebei Province, decreasing pollutant emissions, and strengthening industrial transformation and development of ecological industries are the top priorities in promoting the construction of an ecological civilization in the Beijing-Tianjin-Hebei region, and the key to boosting ecological construction in the capital, reducing smog and improving the environment. How can the proportion of heavy and chemical industries in the Beijing-Tianjin-Hebei region be reduced, how can the environmental protection of enterprises be improved, and how can the emission of pollutants really be reduced? These problems require cooperation and mandatory initiatives in the three areas, namely Beijing, Tianjin, and Hebei. They cannot be solved only with awareness, or relying on the one-time central action similar to APEC, but it is necessary for both the central government and the government at all levels in Beijing, Tianjin, and Hebei to take real action to stop the mere pursuit of GDP.

Fourth, from the perspective of the Beijing-Tianjin-Hebei region, the air pollution in Beijing comes mostly from regional transmission, the most seriously polluted cities of China are mostly located in Hebei, and one-third of the smog in Beijing has its sources in the surrounding areas. If some industrial cities in Hebei do not transform their model of development, polluting industries are not eliminated, and pollution is not controlled, it will be difficult for Beijing to succeed in controlling its air pollution. However, if the incentive of these polluted cities to pursue GDP and the mechanism for performance assessment of pursuing economic growth are not changed, it will be difficult to close and transfer polluting industries in the short term. In the Beijing-Tianjin-Hebei region, Hebei and Tianjin pursue GDP and continue to develop polluting industries, and they have inadequate incentive to phase out all the high-polluting industries as soon as possible. Fundamentally, the outbreak of Beijing's "urban diseases" is closely related to China's current system of performance assessment and fiscal management system. Governments at the levels of city, district, and county and even townships and streets are under multiple pressures of economic assessment and tax increase. Due to the incentive of land finance, there is a pattern of development based on "selling land–constructing buildings–selling houses–inflow of people", which inevitably brings about disorderly industrial expansion, rapid population growth and continuous environmental pollution.

Because the financial system in the capital is not established, and the system of performance assessment of Beijing's districts and counties and cities and counties of Hebei and Tianjin has not changed, driven by the pressure of GDP, it is difficult to delink the finance from its own economic development. The decentralization and phasing-out of low-end industries do not have the effective balance and sharing of interests, and the homogenous competition of industries is becoming intensive, so the coordinated development of the Beijing-Tianjin-Hebei region is hindered. The development of various areas in this region is unequal and unbalanced, and in particular, there is a big gap in economic development.

8.2.3 Lack of the fundamental measures for population control, with difficulty in controlling population expansion without diversion of advantageous resources

According to the measures taken by Beijing since the implementation of the spirit of President Xi's speech, population control has failed to grasp the essence of what attracts the influx of people, and merely diverting the population is treating the symptoms but not the root cause. Beijing has set a target of population control at 23 million by 2020. In recent years, the districts of Beijing have included reasonable control of population size and orderly management of the floating population in their reports on the work of government. They are taking measures such as reducing the demand for low-end labor to curb the disorderly and blind concentration and improve the effectiveness of orderly management of the floating population. For example, Shunyi District, through measures such as "attracting people by industries, controlling people by business, and controlling population by housing", rectifies and regulates the "five types of small stores" such as restaurants, baths, beauty salons, and various markets such as small department stores and building material markets, integrates and clears up a number of small stores and businesses that do not have the basic conditions for business operations, reasonably plans and regulates the development of the life services industry such as recycling of resources, property management, and household services, and reduces the excessive demand for low-end jobs for the floating population. Fangshan District has adopted residence permit management for the floating population, is preventing labor-intensive, low-technology, and low-end industries from absorbing a large number of inflowing population, and it clearing out five types of small businesses, including small garment, small processing and small workshops, and six small places including small hotels, small restaurants, and small Internet cafes. It is reasonably diverting industries and workers that are not suitable for development in the district and reducing the demand for low-end labor.[11]

The above strict control over the mobility of the low-end population is effective in the short term, but in the long term, it is difficult to curb the objective demand for the influx of population to Beijing. Currently, the government is emphasizing the diversion of the floating population or the so-called low-end market and low-end working population. The measures of population diversion are not systematic enough and focus only on the surface by simply setting a numerical target and assigning the task of population control.

First, the existence of low-end industries and a low-end job market demand will certainly attract more floating population. No city can be developed with a completely high-end population alone, and a moderate proportion of the working population in low-end industries and low-end market is necessary for the development of the city. It is impossible to divert all of the floating population. Taking the cleanup of low-end industries as an example, low-end industries are mainly business service industries, which are providing services for the population. Even if these low-end service industries are diverted and high-end industries with high added value are retained, it will still be difficult to effectively control the population growth. Simply setting numerical goals and indicator tasks for population diversion in districts and counties can result in the transfer of population among districts and counties, and difficulty in the control of population in the urban–rural fringe areas.

Second, without the decentralization of advantageous resources, it is difficult to curb population expansion. Beijing takes advantage of its policies to concentrate high-quality resources nationwide, thus being able to provide more and better opportunities for jobs and development. There is no sufficient number of competitive large and medium-sized cities within a 500-kilometer radius of Beijing, and the first choice for people in the northeast China, northwest China and north of the Yellow River seeking jobs after graduation is Beijing. As the capital of China, Beijing has the advantages of high-end political resources, high-end educational opportunities, high-end medical opportunities, high-end employment opportunities, as well as fair opportunities of development and smooth information resources, which are resources non-existent in other places and are also the core factors attracting the influx of population. For example, the admission rate of Beijing's students to first-tier universities is 24.33%, but that of students in Hebei Province is only 9.03%.[12] If these advantageous resources are not decentralized and the gap of resources is not narrowed, it will be difficult to advance the decentralization of population and industry, or realize coordinated development of the Beijing-Tianjin-Hebei region.

Due to the concentration of advantageous resources, a population that is too highly densely located in core areas and there is excessive pressure on infrastructure, it is not easy to solve the problems of "urban diseases". "Urban diseases" are a collective term for a series of problems such as traffic congestion, environmental pollution, high housing prices, and coexistence of slums due to the concentration of massive numbers of the population in cities.[13] The increase in population and its continuous expansion are bound to put greater pressure on traffic, housing, and employment, leading to the further deterioration and intensification of Beijing's "urban diseases". Infrastructure, as a basic condition and service guarantee for the employment and life of the population, is subject to a lack of adequate investment and mismatch with the increment in the population, which will surely reduce the supply capacity of infrastructures, and aggravate the problems of "urban diseases". The construction and development of infrastructures in the fields of traffic, energy, resources, and environment are objectively slow to improve, and subjectively, because the population is relatively floating and the population growth cannot be easily controlled and predicted, it is difficult to match the investment in the construction of infrastructures with the population growth. Accordingly, this inevitably leads to "urban diseases" such as traffic congestion, environmental deterioration and high consumption of resources and energy, which cannot be curbed in a short period of time.

The most prominent problem of Beijing's development is the large number of people. So why are there so many people and what are the main reasons for attracting the influx of population to Beijing? An in-depth analysis reveals that there are too many functions. Beijing has the functions of a political and cultural center as the capital, as well as other functions such as an economic center, a financial center, a research center, an education center and a medical center. The core interests of these functions are induced by the excessive concentration of political resources, more high-quality educational resources (especially the resources of famous universities), a higher level of medical resources, more employment resources, etc., which form the heights of interests and potential differences in resources with surrounding areas. Without equalized decentralization and allocation of these resources, it will be still attractive to the floating population, and as a result, other population control and industrial decentralization policies cannot be truly effective.

If the vast majority of general administrative institutions that are not closely linked to the functions of the capital are difficult to decentralize, a large number of military command organs and their affiliated institutions, education, medical, and other public service institutions in the core areas are not diverted, and high-end advantageous resources are not decentralized and diverted, Beijing will not only attract more inflowing population, but it will also be unable to realize true diversion and effective relocation of industries. The lack of appropriate decentralization or diversion of these advantageous resources to the surrounding areas of Beijing will lead to a long-term siphoning effect. For example, a large portion of inflowing population in Beijing comes from Hebei, accounting for 22% of Beijing's total population, or about 1.56 million people, who exacerbate population expansion and traffic congestion in Beijing, and widen the economic gap between Hebei and Beijing.

The reason behind Beijing's outbreak of "urban diseases" is that it carries too many functions and is overly concentrated, and that its surrounding areas are poorly developed. For example, an important reason for Beijing's population expansion is the large gap between the economic and social development of the surrounding areas and Beijing. Beijing has sufficient employment opportunities and high-quality public service resources, which are very appealing to the surrounding population and attract them to converge at Beijing. Therefore, it is impossible for Beijing to solve the problems of "urban diseases" alone, and strong support must be provided in the surrounding areas to solve the problems of development on a larger scale.

Third, there are a large number of old houses owned by central and municipal authorities in the central urban areas, which are used for renting and operations and attract massive numbers of the floating population. It is not easy to have accurate data regarding the population because there is a lack of accurate and timely population statistics, uniformity in the statistics of different departments such as public security, flowing population management, traffic, and development and reform commission, or an objective platform for the information about the floating population.

Fourth, the reform of increment is not proper, and that of stock cannot be adjusted. The treatment of "urban diseases" in the capital city and the coordinated development of the Beijing-Tianjin-Hebei region are faced with the problems of improper reform of increment and difficulty in adjusting the reform of stock. In order to divert the population, on the one hand, some of the population has been decentralized by administrative means, but there are still a large number of new populations every year, resulting in the number of diverted population being offset by the number of new population. On the other hand, the population in the core areas is adjusted to the surrounding districts and counties, but there is no fundamental change in the total population, and it has no practical effect on the population of Beijing and traffic congestion. Due to the improper reform of increment, the growth speed is not under control, the districts and counties have a strong demand to develop the economy, attract industries and increase the number of enterprises. The increment in population and traffic and the total exhaust emissions have not been reduced, so that the treatment of atmospheric diseases and "urban diseases" cannot become effective.

For industrial decentralization, the stock of industries and enterprises in the core areas, such as state-owned enterprises and central enterprises belonging to non-capital core functions, is not adjusted. Administrative intervention and mandatory decentralization of low-end markets alone cannot make a real contribution to the decentralization of Beijing's population, especially the total population of the core areas. Due to the existence of self-controlled entry indicators of state-owned enterprises, central enterprises, central government agencies and institutions, it is difficult for Beijing to effectively control the increase in its population, control and slow down the new population in the core urban areas, and effectively decentralize the mass of the population, thus being unable to regulate and control the population of Beijing.

For the development of new towns, due to the adoption of a unified target control of the population, the construction of new towns in Beijing is restricted by space for the growth of the population which is too small. The development of new towns is short of the motivation and conditions to attract the population and industries from the core areas. For the coordinated development of the Beijing-Tianjin-Hebei region, there is a lack of the capacity and conditions to absorb the incremental population from Beijing. The important stock of resources established in Beijing, such as state-owned enterprises, central enterprises, and central institutions belonging to non-capital core functions, is not diverted to Hebei and Tianjin, so it cannot have an agglomeration effect on resources, and it is difficult to actually advance the cooperation and coordinated development of the Beijing-Tianjin-Hebei region.

8.2.4 Lack of total control targets of motor vehicles, with slow construction of rail transit

The mismatch between the carrying capacity of urban public service facilities and urban development or the rapid expansion of the population is one of the main causes of "urban diseases". Compared with developed countries and even developing countries, China has a low level of per capita occupancy of urban infrastructures, and the scale of the construction of infrastructures and management level cannot keep up with the speed of population growth. With the rapid advancement of urbanization, the inadequate quantity and quality of infrastructures become major contradictions and important bottlenecks to our accelerated progress of urbanization and to the promotion of the healthy and sustainable development of cities in China. The number of motor vehicles in Beijing is growing year by year, making the congested roads even worse and the contradiction between supply and demand of road resources even more acute. Traffic congestion is mainly related to the construction and management of urban traffic infrastructures, and the slow construction of rail transit leads to the failure of rail transit serving as the main means of transportation for people in metropolises.

First of all, the traffic will continue to grow due to the population growth of Beijing in the future, and the difficulty of treating "urban diseases" restricts the speed of treating "traffic diseases".

Second, a high proportion of commuters drive private cars to and from work, and this increases the pressure on traffic. The parking fees are too low as are the costs of using motor vehicles, which cannot effectively curb the increase in motor vehicles and traffic needs.

Third, subways, express railways and suburban railways are still facing a serious shortage, the dilemma of "crowded subways" and "slow buses" still exists, and the construction of rail transit is confronted with the problems of insufficient funds, institutional barriers, and inadequate participation of social capital. The problems of "urban diseases" are exacerbated by insufficient subway coverage, the slow speed of construction lagging behind the development needs of metropolises, tremendous traffic pressure on buses and continued increase in the number of motor vehicles. In recent years, Beijing has accelerated the speed of building rail transit. In 2013, the length of operating lines of rail transit was 465 kilometers, and it was 442 kilometers in 2012. The subway lines are being extended every year, and the subways transport more and more passengers, which accounted for 39.82%, with an increase of 7.5% points compared with 32.32% in 2012. This indicates that the role and status of subways in the entire system of public transportation is improving. However, compared with developed cities such as New York, London, and Tokyo where rail transit accounts for 80% of all public transit or traffic, the coverage and capacity of subways in Beijing is still far from enough.

The subways in Beijing have not fully covered all districts and counties of Beijing, such as Pinggu, Huairou, Miyun. Many areas still have only one or two subway lines available, resulting in congestion during rush hours, such as Batong Line, Changping Line, 15# Line and Fangshan Line. The waiting time is also more than five minutes, and the transfer of lines may take 15–20 minutes. In order to divert the traffic, the transfer lines are deliberately extended, and this not only wastes time, but also triggers more complaints from passengers. Although the subway lines in the core areas are relatively dense, the high concentration and density of high-rise buildings, residential areas, industries, universities, and tourist attractions such as Tiananmen Square have led to a serious convergence of tourists, students, and commuters. Neither underground nor above-ground transportation can handle such a large capacity, and hence Beijing is becoming one of the most congested cities and a city in which it is difficult to effectively guarantee public security.

Moreover, Beijing does not have a subway line access to other areas outside of Beijing. The existing bus lines are mostly congested. For example, the bus lines driving to Yanjiao, Xianghe, Gu'an, Zhuozhou, and other surrounding areas are overburdened. Due to the monopolistic supply of public transportation, there are few buses, with long waiting time, insufficient market competition, poor service quality, and short operating hours in the morning and evening, thus being unable to meet the traffic needs of passengers. These objective problems severely restrict the integration of urban and rural areas and the coordinated development of the Beijing-Tianjin-Hebei region, and it is becoming very difficult to guide and encourage low-end industries and enterprises to move out.

In terms of motor vehicle ownership, the number of civilian cars and private cars has grown to a large extent. The number of civilian cars reached 5.189 million in 2013, which increased by 232,000 over 2012. The number of private cars reached 4.265 million in 2013, with an increase of 190,000 over 2012. Both of them "worsen" and "delay" the already congested traffic in the capital city, and add "pollution" and "emissions" to the serious smoggy weather in the capital. The yearly growth in the number of motor vehicles and the increase in emissions can do nothing but worsen the congestion and environmental deterioration of Beijing. The policy experience of Singapore, London, and other developed cities in imposing congestion charges on private cars can be drawn upon, but Beijing is very slow to introduce relevant policies and adopt various means such as economic and legal means for comprehensive governance.

Fourth, the "difficulty" and "disorder" of parking cannot be curbed, with unclear parking spaces and confusing management. The problem of "cut-off roads" and "obstructed roads" has aroused social concern, the design of traffic signal lighting lacks "green wave" intelligence, and the slow urban walking system is not perfect.

Beijing's existing phenomena of parking difficulties and disorderly parking exacerbate the "capital jam", and make the congested road conditions even worse. It is common to find cars parked on arteries, branch lines, and in bicycle lanes, and some branch lines have been used as parking spaces since their construction, without any remediation. The parking problems are threatening the healthy development and effective operation of the city, or even endangering safety in some communities. According to the current policy restricting the purchase of motor vehicles, the increase of 200,000 vehicles every year will mean thousands of kilometers long in a queue, but the urban roads of Beijing are just over 6,000 kilometers. If most of the vehicles are parked at the side of roads, they will soon occupy the roads.[14]

According to international experience, parking fees are generally paid directly to the state treasury or parking fee collection system by technological means and the parking supervisors are law enforcement officers who do not collect payments in person. And some communities, roadsides and corporate yards are free for parking. A survey shows that free parking for small cars in Beijing's six urban districts accounted for 73% in 2005, which rose to 86% in 2010. A car occupies a parking space larger than the space needed by one urban resident, and the parking is free.[15] As the total number of motor vehicles continues to increase, there is neither an upper limit, nor an accelerated phase-out of existing license plates, resulting in a serious mismatch between the total number of motor vehicles and parking spaces. More vehicles and fewer parking spaces will inevitably cause difficulty in parking. The construction of three-dimensional garage and underground parking spaces lags behind, many communities are old ones that basically have no reserved and planned underground parking lots, the three-dimensional garage is faced with problems such as insufficient investment funds, and hence motor vehicles have no place to park but at the side of roads.

The management responsibilities of parking spaces and parking fees and the responsibilities of executing bodies are unclear, so disorderly parking behavior cannot be controlled, and no one is responsible for this affair. For example, disorderly parking is mainly concentrated on branch lines, small roads, hutongs, and communities, which do not fall within the scope of traffic supervision, become a vacuum for the regulation of disorderly parking, and fail to attract the attention of the higher authorities, especially the traffic authorities. Generally speaking, communities and their surrounding areas off of trunk roads should be managed by community residents' committees, but such committees or property companies do not have the power to regulate disorderly parking, and, on the contrary, persuade them or take other soft measures. Even if there are some parking spaces, because the parking spaces are bought out or on long-term rent, they are occupied or locked, and this leads to a waste of parking resources or restrictions in communities.

Furthermore, as far as developed cities internationally are concerned, a lot of urban communities, institutions, units, schools, and hospitals do not have excessive fence walls, but all cities in China, including Beijing, owing to localism and departmental interests, build walls to isolate their own departments spatially from the outside. This results in the cutoff of many spaces, and the idleness of space resources and road resources. Objectively, this increases the demand for roads and occupied areas, and to a certain extent, has exacerbated the problem of parking difficulties.

Fifthly, traffic is inconvenient. In particular, the rail transit system of the Beijing-Tianjin-Hebei region with the nature of public transportation has not been established, the work mechanism of traffic integration is not complete, and the traffic structure at the regional and municipal level fails to achieve the integration of two networks. It does not have enough internal carrying capacity or sufficient external expansion, so it is difficult to provide the necessary conditions for the outward migration of the population and industrial decentralization.

8.2.5 Lack of a long-lasting mechanism for environmental governance and effective measures for the prevention and control of smog

On February 26, 2014, President Xi Jinping delivered an important speech on air pollution control during his survey in Beijing. President Xi pointed out that the prevention and control of air pollution is one of the most prominent problems facing the development of Beijing. The prolonged and extensive smog that has occurred in recent years not only harms the health of citizens, but also stains the image of China and the capital. With the acceleration of urbanization and modernization, major environmental pollution problems occur frequently, such as excessive PM2.5 and smoggy weather, which directly affects the sustainable economic and social development of Beijing, and damages the good image and expectations of the construction of a harmonious and livable city and beautiful China. Serious air pollution is also one of the main causes of the current economic and social conflicts in the capital, and the citizens of the capital are very dissatisfied with the serious pollution of the atmosphere. Since the reform and opening-up, the rapid economic growth of Beijing and its surrounding areas has been a world-renowned achievement, but energy consumption remains high and air pollution is becoming more and more serious, with increased pollution of fine particles (PM2.5), inhalable particles (PM10), and suspended particles (TSP). Due to the use of coal and other minerals as fuel in industrial production, a large number of pollutants are emitted into the air, and together with massive exhaust emissions of vehicles, cause the suspension of countless tiny dust particles, smoke particles or salt particles in the atmosphere and these form smog. This is why atmospheric pollution continues to plague Beijing, and the quality of the city's air has seriously deteriorated. Especially for a period of time, smog has frequently attacked the Beijing-Tianjin-Hebei region, the severity and urgency of air pollution has caused the growing concern of people from all walks of life. The quality of Beijing's air is a matter of public interest, national image, and the image of the capital, and the control of air pollution and PM2.5 is a difficult problem and a primary task that cannot be avoided, bypassed or escaped by Beijing in order to achieve sustainable development and the building of a harmonious and livable city. President Xi proposed the great goal of Beijing to build a world-class harmonious and livable city. If atmospheric pollution is so serious, Beijing will not be a livable city, and environmental pollution will seriously stain the image of Beijing and restrict the construction of a livable city, a premier area, and a green Beijing.

In recent years, Beijing has enhanced its efforts in environmental protection and pollution control, and all districts and counties have attached great importance to environmental protection and obtained a series of achievements, but the environmental situation in the capital is still quite serious. From an objective point of view, the reasons for the formation of atmospheric environmental problems include:

First, overburden of resources and environment. General Secretary Xi pointed out that due to long-term development and construction, Beijing's natural ecosystem is in a degraded state and the resources and environment are clearly in an overburdened condition. The frequent smoggy weather is superficially a phenomenon of atmospheric pollution, but it is actually the pressure of Beijing's population, resources and the environment. Over a long period of time, the rapid development of industrialization and urbanization in Beijing and the surrounding areas has brought about an increase in population, industrial emissions, resource, and energy consumption and environmental pollution, and hence the pressure and contradictions of population, resources and the environment have become increasingly prominent. General Secretary Xi pointed out that the noticeable problem of Beijing's development is the population. When there are more people, the pressure on resources and environment will be higher. Overpopulation will lead to a continuous increase in the rigid demand for emissions, such as the increase caused by the traffic needs of the new population and car purchases, as well as various emissions of pollution by new construction and industries for housing and work for the new population. The direct cause of atmospheric pollution comes from "urban diseases", which is caused by a series of problems such as industrial concentration, traffic congestion, and housing shortage due to the over-expansion and concentration of the population in urban areas.

Second, little ecological space. The basis of environmental capacity is ecological space. Because serious regional environmental pollution exceeds the limited ecological space and environmental capacity, the industrial land and living land encroach upon the ecological land, the ecological space like forests, lakes, and wetlands decreases in size, and groundwater is overly exploited, the retaliation from nature is naturally increased.

Third, one-third of the PM2.5 is sourced in coal combustion. President Xi Jinping pointed out in a speech during his survey of Beijing on February 26, 2014 that one-third of the PM2.5 in the Beijing-Tianjin-Hebei region stems from coal combustion. The traditional mode of energy consumption for domestic and industrial use in the Beijing-Tianjin-Hebei region is coal combustion. The huge consumption of coal leads to high emissions of sulfur dioxide, nitrogen oxides, and atmospheric mercury. And the emissions of these pollutants are the main cause of air pollution. There is an urgent need to change the coal-based structure of energy consumption. Besides coal combustion, the exhaust emissions of motor vehicles are also an important cause of smog in Beijing. The root cause of smog in Beijing may be numerous volatile organic compounds and nitrogen oxides emitted by the urban traffic and sulfur dioxides emitted from the production, which are then converted to particles through chemical reactions. Control of these three types of gaseous pollutants is the key to controlling air pollution in Beijing.

In terms of the system of management, the current system of environmental governance appears to be incompetent in the face of the severe situation, and lacks a long-term mechanism for environmental governance and effective measures for the prevention and control of smog.

8.2.5.1 Unreasonable division of functions, unclear responsibilities of environmental governance and cross-management

The division of functions among resource, environmental, and ecological authorities is unreasonable, environmental supervision is weak, it is difficult to implement and pursue responsibility for environmental protection, and the system of environmental governance for regions and water basins urgently needs to be reformed. The lack of a legal basis for cooperation among regions and the lack of effective procedures and dispute resolution lead to numerous cross-regional environmental problems, especially with regard to the prevention and control of water pollution in river basins. The above-ground and underground sewage treatment in Beijing is characterized by intentional separation, multiple responsible parties, unclear responsibilities, and mutual shirking of responsibilities. Environmental authorities are allocated with only a small quota of staff and unequal powers and responsibilities, and the environmental protection work cannot ensure that laws are observed and strictly enforced and that anyone who violates the law is held to account. For the technical operations of environmental governance, Beijing has made great progress, such as a significant increase in the investment of environmental equipment, personnel, and funds. However, in terms of the system of environmental governance, Beijing is still in a state of multiple authorities, which means "nine dragons taming the water". The functions of environmental governance of sewage, garbage, and ecological pollution are distributed among authorities such as environment bureau, gardening and greening bureau, municipal commission of urban management and water authority, and waste disposal alone involves several authorities. The system is not flawless, the functions are overlapping, and the government is absent, and all these situations seriously reduce the administrative efficiency of environmental governance in Beijing[16] and restrict the construction of an ecological civilization in the capital.

8.2.5.2 Difficulty in gatekeeping of construction projects, investigating and punishing enterprises with illegal emissions, and collecting sewage charges

Environmental supervisory agencies lack the necessary coercive means to implement the "three simultaneous" management actions of construction projects, and are unable to fully implement construction projects, environmental impact assessment and the system of "three simultaneous" actions. Construction projects still commence without declaration and approval by environmental authorities. Some construction projects involve illegal construction, some are unlawfully constructed on the collective land by using green partitions, without approval and supervision, and it is difficult to investigate and deal with these projects and enterprises with illegal emissions. Some enterprises play the game of "hide and seek" with the environmental supervisory authority. If the supervision occurs in the daytime, they work at night. Also, there are a lot of highly polluting enterprises in the urban and rural interface and remote rural areas that cannot be supervised.

8.2.5.3 Lack of supervision of the pollution site, resulting in the improper or abnormal operation of polluting facilities, with serious "hidden" emissions of pollution

At present, many new projects at the grassroots level are commenced before approval, and some are even completed without approval; if enterprises with illegal emissions are investigated today, they will remain so tomorrow; sewage charges cannot be collected in their full amount. Enterprises above designated size are governed by the government affairs center, with fixed amount and time of collection, and within the specified time, the environmental authority has no power to collect such charges. Once an enterprise fails to make payment, it is late for the environmental authority to enforce it, and the enforcement procedure will take a period of time. The environmental authority lacks the necessary administrative power, including the constraints on the environmental violations of the local government. The existing environmental laws and regulations are more often than not "advocates without operability, or strong punishments". Environmental enforcement cannot get the active cooperation and attract the attention of the local government, especially the person in charge, so environmental protection is slow to make progress. A series of normal activities of supervision and management, such as inspection of enterprises by the environmental authority, collection of sewage charges, and handling of letters and visits, often cannot be carried out without the cooperation of other functional departments of the local government. Environmental law enforcement officers are also threatened by violent incidents of resistance to the law, resulting in much less enthusiasm for their work.

8.2.5.4 Emphasis on the surface rather than the connotation, the end rather than the source

The so-called "emphasis on the surface" means that excessive attention is paid to the cityscape and environment, such as whether the roads are clean. Less emphasis on the connotation means that not enough attention is paid to the environmental quality, especially aiming at the increasingly serious pollution of garbage and the exhaust emissions of vehicles, and without effective measures. Emphasis on the "end" rather than the source means that environmental governance in Beijing focuses more on the cityscape and environment, garbage and treatment of the exhaust emissions of vehicles, and there is not enough attention to the control of the source where these problems arise.

8.2.5.5 Emphasis on government investment rather than social participation, and insufficient use of economic means

The government is currently the absolute dominator of environmental governance in Beijing, but enterprises and the public, who are the important parts of urban operations, are seriously lacking in the awareness for their participation in environmental governance. On the one hand, the government expends a lot of financial, material and human resources, but the effect of environmental governance is not good; on the other hand, the mode of environmental governance of the government is not be widely accepted by the public. The emphasis on administrative means rather than economic means refers to the alternate number plate restrictions on motor vehicles that Beijing implemented for more than two months to ensure the air quality of Beijing during the Olympic Games, which is a typical model of environmental governance by administrative means. In order to ensure the success of the 2014 APEC conference in Beijing, the capital city took administrative measures such as vehicle restrictions, production shutdowns and work stoppages to achieve a brief period of "APEC blue" through human intervention.

Beijing's environmental authority released the Assessment of the Effectiveness of Air Quality Protection Measures during APEC. After the measures were taken, the daily average PM2.5 concentration in Beijing was reduced by more than 30% during the period of November 1–22, 2014, and the average PM2.5 concentration in the surrounding areas of Beijing, Tianjin, and Hebei decreased by about 29% year-on-year. The emissions of other indicators including sulfur dioxide, nitrogen oxides and volatile organic compounds were reduced by 50% on average. During the conference, the measures of alternate number plate restrictions on vehicles, site closures, and factory shutdowns brought about a significant reduction in pollutant emissions. However, after the APEC conference, these measures were stopped and the smoggy weather in the capital returned to normal. The tax and charge system commonly adopted in developed countries for environmental pollution is still not established in Beijing. The mechanism of cooperation and constraints between environmental and economic authorities is not effective, the sewage charges are relatively small, and the punishments for excessive emissions are too few. The administrative penalties under environmental regulations are mainly in the form of fines, and the amounts are too low.

8.2.5.6 Lack of strict environmental law enforcement and weak supervision

Some environmental regulators enforce the law in a formal way, and the enforcement behavior is not regulated. Some regions have serious local protectionism, and the government even becomes the umbrella of environmental violations of enterprises. China's system of environmental protection is a "unified kind of supervision and management by the environmental authority, by which each department is responsible for its own work". The environmental authority manages a wide range of complex areas, which require the close cooperation and support of all functional departments of the local government, and cannot be done alone. Thus, the effectiveness of law enforcement is always unknown. Unified supervision and management and joint law enforcement often cannot be realized. First, there is not a clear division of responsibilities and a relationship between the environmental authority and other authorities. Second, the environmental authority and other authorities are parallel in the government, and whether other authorities cooperate with the environmental authority in the environmental protection work depends on whether the local government attaches importance to such work. In many regions, the powers of economic authorities are greater than those of the environmental authority, and the environmental authority and non-economic authorities are marginalized. The result is a sharp decline in sewage charges, failure to promptly handle dispute cases regarding environmental pollution, and increasing complaints from the public, which seriously affects the prompt governance of pollution and the improvement of environmental quality.

8.2.5.7 Mismatch between the number of law enforcement officers and the actual needs for environmental protection work, poor quality of law enforcement teams, and a lack of operating agencies at the terminals

Under the current dual management system, the power of allocating the quotas of staff is vested in the local government, resulting in unreasonable staffing of some environmental authorities, poor working conditions and few law enforcement officers. It is also common to find that one officer does several jobs, so that many environmental enforcement tasks cannot be carried out. Since the local government has the power over the cadres of the environmental authority, some local governments do not attach importance to environmental protection, and they often transfer incompetent people to the environmental protection team. In addition, because some local governments also have the financial control of the environmental authority, they allocate insufficient fiscal expenditures to the education and training of environmental protection personnel with the excuse of limited fiscal revenue, which also affects efficient and unified environmental law enforcement. There are no operating units at the terminals for the prevention and control of air pollution and environmental remediation. In particular, there is a lack of environmental enforcement forces at the levels of streets, towns, and communities, the public security, urban management and family planning authorities are not integrated, and there are not enough enforcers, participants, supervisors, and social support forces available for the treatment of air pollution and environmental protection at the grassroots level.

8.2.5.8 Insufficient innovation in ecological and environmental protection systems, unscientific control of concentration indicators, and ineffective prevention and control of smog

The current ecological and environmental situation in the capital is serious, and the general public is eagerly awaiting effectively increased efforts at ecological and environmental protection and the construction of an ecological civilization. In recent years, the central government and many localities have taken a series of measures to accelerate the transformation of the mode of development, promote the green development and improvement of the ecological environment, and strengthen the control of environmental pollution. Generally speaking, there are many measures of administrative regulations and financial input, with long-term, overall, and exemplary management, but few institutional innovations that can give full play to the decisive role of the market in the allocation of resources. The root cause is often not the lack of attention by the local party committees and governments, but insufficient institutional innovation. It is not resolutely determined to reform the institutions and mechanisms of ecological and environmental protection, without an institutional system of extensive social participation, or a fundamental change in the ideological and operational disconnections or an improvement of the environment. Actually, all of us are involved in environmental pollution, and there is a lack of mandatory, authoritative, and fundamental institutional guarantees.

The control of smog lacks the actual control of pollution sources and their transmission processes, nor are there long-lasting mechanisms and necessary measures for environmental governance. The Clean Air Action Plan of Beijing 2013–2017 clearly specifies indicators such as the reduction of the annual average concentration of fine particles in the air and the control of micrograms in each district and county, which are obtained by regular testing of the air, but due to the randomness of changes in the meteorological conditions, such as air mobility and reduction of the concentration of fine particles, it is difficult to reflect the actual effects of smog control in each district and county. According to the existing research on the formation mechanism of smog, the sources of pollution in Beijing mainly include coal combustion, exhaust emissions of motor vehicles, and dust, but there is a lack of fundamental measures to control them. For example, there are no systematic and fundamental institutional regulations to reduce coal combustion and control the exhaust emissions of motor vehicles. Farmers in remote suburban counties and areas are prohibited from burning coal, but there is no alternative energy, nor citywide natural gas pipeline plans and construction, so the natural gas is not available in many areas. Ostensibly, local residents are strictly prohibited from burning coal, or encouraged to use high-quality coal, but actually this practice is unsustainable.

Measures to control the exhaust emissions of motor vehicles are also ineffective. On the one hand, substandard motor vehicles are banned or eliminated; on the other hand, new license plates of motor vehicles are issued. The number of new motor vehicles not only worsens the already congested traffic conditions, but it also increases exhaust emissions. From the perspective of regional transmission, Beijing is phasing out some polluting enterprises, but these enterprises move to the surrounding areas in Hebei and continue to emit pollution, the regional transmission of smog has not been fundamentally controlled, and the smog control of Beijing cannot be effective.

8.2.6 Lack of effective public participation and synergy in the treatment of "urban diseases"

The formation of "urban diseases" such as traffic congestion and environmental pollution in Beijing is a typical "tragedy of the commons". The implementation of the strategic positioning of the capital city, decentralization of non-capital functions, adjustment of the industrial structure, strengthening of the construction of urban infrastructures, improvement in urban management and prevention of air pollution are not just unilateral actions of the government, but they involve the long-term development of the capital city, the needs for the treatment of "urban diseases", and the expectations of citizens to build a beautiful capital. However, the lack of effective social organizations and extensive, active, timely, effective, and orderly participation of the public makes it difficult to raise awareness. Without joint efforts in the treatment of "urban diseases" in the capital, there will be no innovative vitality of group efforts.

First of all, the responsibilities for the formation and treatment of "urban diseases" are all placed on the government, which is considered to be omnipotent and should take full responsibility. In reality, the government is not omnipotent. Under the system of a planned economy, the government does everything and monopolizes, but causes grave consequences of destructing productivity, and under the system of a market economy, the government is even less competent. It must govern by law and adhere to public participation and coordinated governance. However, the public and citizens are not aware that they are also important sources of air pollution and traffic congestion, so they do not have a strong sense of self-discipline and willingness to assume the responsibility. The treatment of "urban diseases", especially major planning involving the overall interests of the capital, has not been actively participated in by social organizations and citizens with common action. It is difficult to raise social awareness, achieve unified action, and obtain sufficient support and wide participation, and therefore the implementation of the strategic positioning of the capital city cannot be effectively advanced.

Second, ideological mobilization is not adequate, the publicity and education are not sufficient, and there are various one-sided perceptions and suspicions of people from all walks of life, who have the strong emotions of waiting, watching, and fearing. For example, there is no unified social action, social voice, and social support for the treatment and remediation of traffic congestion, disorderly stalls, and environmental pollution.

Third, the treatment of "urban diseases" and the solving of other social problems do not value the power of social organizations, which are not well developed, the channels for social participation are not smooth, and there are no long-lasting mechanisms. The relationship between the government, the market and society has not been rationalized, the government does not decentralize its powers, the market is not effective and the society does not participate, thus leading to the dilemma of the treatment of "urban diseases" in which the government is incompetent, the market is dysfunctional and the society complains. Many cities in developed countries in the West have also experienced "urban diseases", such as London in the UK and Tokyo in Japan, but through effective treatment, they have already gotten rid of the dilemma of "urban diseases", and their experience is worthy of reference for Beijing. However, in practice, there are many difficulties in learning and transplanting. For example, London levied fuel charges and congestion charges in the central urban areas for the control of the exhaust emissions of motor vehicles and traffic congestion, with obvious effectiveness, but it has not been possible to introduce such measures in Beijing until now. On the one hand, there is great social resistance, and on the other hand, it also reflects that the public has not formed a consensus on the treatment of "urban diseases" such as traffic congestion. It neither plays the role of collective efforts, nor takes effective and innovative measures, nor does it activate public participation in the treatment of "urban diseases".

8.3 Summary

This chapter primarily carried out an empirical study and examined the problems according to the interactive and associative effects of population, resources, the environment and other factors, analyzed the main manifestations and internal causes of Beijing's "urban diseases", and pointed out the key elements and their transmission relationship for treating "urban diseases".

Beijing's "urban diseases" are mainly manifested as follows. First, the population growth is slowing down, but the total population continues to rise, and because of the pressure of resources, energy, and the environment caused by the growing population, the sustainable development of Beijing is plagued by the "urban diseases" of a metropolis; second, the total traffic capacity continues to grow, and the problem of "capital jam" persists; third, the industrial structure is not reasonable, with difficulty in decentralizing low-end industries; and fourth, the total energy consumption is on the rise, smog is becoming serious and the carrying capacity of the environment is declining.

There are many influencing factors on the formation of Beijing's "urban diseases" that have complex relationships. In essence, "urban diseases" result from the accumulation of conflicts between the carrying capacity of urban resources and the environment and the speed of urbanization-oriented development. First, there is a lack of top-level design and a mechanism of overall coordination for the treatment of "urban diseases"; second, there is a lack of a scientific substitute mechanism of GDP-based performance assessment, but with an arduous task of industrial restructuring; third, there is a lack of the fundamental measures for population control, with difficulty in controlling population expansion without diverting advantageous resources; fourth, there is a lack of total control targets of motor vehicles, with slow construction of rail transit; fifth, there is a lack of a long-lasting mechanism for environmental governance and effective measures for the prevention and control of smog; and sixth, there is a lack of effective public participation and synergy in the treatment of "urban diseases".

Notes

1 Resident Population of Beijing at the End of 2014 Reached 21.516 Million, www.cnr.cn/, January 25, 2015.
2 District/County Population and Employment Data of Beijing in 2014, www.bjstats.gov.cn, January 18, 2016.
3 Solutions Urgently Required for the Decentralization of Agricultural Wholesale in Beijing, *China Food Newspaper*, December 31, 2015.

4 "Xinfadi" Will Not Move, But Must Be Transformed and Upgraded, *International Business Daily*, March 10, 2014.
5 Solutions Urgently Required for the Decentralization of Agricultural Wholesale in Beijing, *China Food Newspaper*, December 31, 2015.
6 Zhang Fang, Water Shortage of Beijing Still Reaches 100 Million Cubic Meters, *Beijing Times*, September 8, 2015.
7 Jiang Aihua and Zhang Chi, "Urban Diseases" in the Process of Urbanization and Analysis of the Treatment Path, *Academic Journal of Zhongzhou*, 2012(6).
8 Yang Ka, Analysis of the Nature and Root Causes of "Urban Diseases" and Their Paths of Treatment Based on the Theory of a Self-organizing System, *Jinan Journal (Philosophy and Social Sciences)*, 2013(10).
9 Jiang Aihua and Zhang Chi, "Urban Diseases" in the Process of Urbanization and Analysis of the Path for Treatment, *Academic Journal of Zhongzhou*, 2012(6).
10 Lin Jiabin, An Institutional Analysis of China's "Urban Diseases", *Urban Planning Forum*, 2012(3).
11 Population Control of Shunyi, Beijing: Attracting People by Industries, Controlling People by Business and Managing People by Housing, *Beijing Youth Daily*, January 7, 2011.
12 Admission Ratios and Number of Admitted Students by First-tier Universities in 2013, http://gaokao.gaofen.com/article/42224.htm.
13 Zhao Hong, A Good Remedy to Beijing's "Urban Diseases", http://finance.sina.com.cn, May 4, 2014.
14 Beijing Municipal Commission of Transportation: Solving "Disorder" First and Then "Difficulty" of Parking, *Beijing Morning Post*, January 22, 2014.
15 Beijing Municipal Commission of Transportation: Solving "Disorder" First and Then "Difficulty" of Parking, *Beijing Morning Post*, January 22, 2014.
16 Qi Benchao and Zhou Da, Environmental Management of Tokyo and Enlightenment to Beijing, *Social Sciences in Ningxia*, 2010(5).

9 Control of "urban diseases" in Beijing and countermeasures for the coordinated low-carbon development of the Beijing-Tianjin-Hebei region

According to the experience of urbanization around the world, China's urbanization is still in a period of rapid development, which may also be a period of concentrated outbreak of various urban problems. The prevention and treatment of "urban diseases" during the rapid progress of urbanization has become a major practical problem that needs urgent attention and must be taken seriously.[1] Beijing, as the capital of a large developing country, has entered the phase of post-industrialization with the industrialization and urbanization of the country, and urbanization is an inevitable trend of the economic and social development of the capital city, and also coincides with the general law of urbanization in Western developed countries. For example, London has also experienced these "urban diseases", such as environmental pollution, population expansion and traffic congestion, and after long-term treatment, it has built a green and low-carbon international city. The treatment of "urban diseases" of Beijing should not only consider the general experience and laws of international treatment of "urban diseases", but also the choice of scientific countermeasures of development according to Beijing's own characteristics. Beijing should accelerate its treatment of "urban diseases" and a coordinated low-carbon development of the Beijing-Tianjin-Hebei region under the guiding principle of the implementation of the strategic positioning of the capital, aiming at the basic goal of building an international first-class harmonious and livable city. To be specific, the following countermeasures should be taken.

9.1 Realizing the functional positioning of the capital, and enhancing top-level design and unified coordination

9.1.1 Implementing the functional positioning of the capital, and clarifying the direction of urban development

In February 2014, President Xi Jinping, aiming at the "urban diseases" of environmental pollution, traffic congestion, population expansion in the city, clearly defined the functional positioning of Beijing as a national political center, cultural center, international communication center and scientific and

DOI: 10.4324/9781003272991-9

technological innovation center, and the overall goal of building an international first-class harmonious and livable city. The strategic positioning and developmental goals of the capital city make the direction clear for the treatment of "urban diseases" in the capital, and reflect the ardent expectations of the State for Beijing as the national capital and the voices and expectations of the general public. In order to treat the "urban diseases" of the capital, we should first clarify and implement the strategic positioning of the capital city, strengthen the top-level design for the treatment of "urban diseases", and establish a long-term mechanism for coordination.

In recent years, Beijing's rapid economic growth at the rate of more than 10% guarantees the rapid development of the capital, but at the same time, rapid economic growth also causes the alarming "urban diseases" of air pollution and traffic congestion. The treatment of "urban diseases" in the capital is related to Beijing's sustainable economic and social development, to the progress of building a harmonious and livable capital in Beijing, and to the expectations and interests of citizens in the capital for an ecological environment in Beijing. Thus, in order to treat Beijing's "urban diseases", we should be guided by the implementation of the capital city's strategic positioning, and take this opportunity to determine the highlights and direction of development in various fields such as economy, society, culture, politics, and the environment, as well as matching urban spatial capacity with the carrying capacity of resources, energy and the environment according to the capital city's strategic positioning, and it is necessary to strengthen top-level design and coordination.

We will fully understand the functional positioning of the capital and adhere to and strengthen its core functions. The positioning of the capital functions as four centers defines the status, direction, and highlights of Beijing as the national capital in the overall landscape of national economic and social development. The expansion of the capital city, sustainable economic and social development, formulation of urban development strategies, and the choice of urban development models should not conflict with the capital's functional positioning, and they must be compatible, coordinated, and mutually promoted. We should not introduce industries that are not suitable for the capital's functional positioning and exceed the capital's carrying capacity of resources, energy, and environment by considering the economic growth factor only, but we need to solve the deep-seated problems such as there being too many functions and too much concentration behind the population expansion.

9.1.1.1 Implementing the functional positioning of the capital and building a national political center

As a national political center, Beijing has to fulfill its political responsibility of serving the central government, provide the basic conditions and service guarantees for the functioning of the CPC Central Committee, the State Council, national ministries and commissions and international organizations, leave space, especially ecological space, for their development, and create an environment in the capital that can demonstrate the national political functions better. Therefore, from a strategic point of view of building a national political center, a top-level design should be created to ensure the security and stability of the political center, guarantee the normal organization of various political activities and major political meetings, and improve the political influence. This requires the State to plan and build "Central Administrative Districts"[2] in Beijing. The Dongcheng District and Xicheng District should not be economic but should weaken the industrial function and strengthen the functions of political and cultural services. Given that the Central Committee of the CPC, the State Council, and national ministries and commissions are mainly concentrated in the Dongcheng District and in the Xicheng District, it is important to speed up the establishment of "Central Administrative Districts" and build a financial system in the capital to serve such districts under the strategic opportunity of implementing the functional positioning of the capital and decentralizing non-capital functions. On the one hand, the central urban areas (Dongcheng and Xicheng) should accelerate the relocation and decentralization of institutions and departments that do not serve the central government; on the other hand, the financial system of the capital should be adopted to support the basic financial expenditures of Dongcheng District and Xicheng District as the "Central Administrative Districts" in the form of central transfer payments, which cannot rely on self-supporting and self-industrial expansion to generate revenue. The problems of "urban diseases" such as overly dense buildings, over-concentration of industries, and overpopulation in the Dongcheng District and Xicheng District are all related to the multiple pressures of developing the economy while serving the central government, thus leading to the most prominent "urban diseases" there. In order to implement the strategic positioning of the capital and build a national political center, we should strengthen the top-level design of the central administrative districts, and relocate and decentralize institutions, organizations, and enterprises that do not serve the central government, or serve the whole of Beijing, to subcenters such as Tongzhou or surrounding areas as soon as possible.

9.1.1.2 Implementing the functional positioning of the capital and accelerating the construction of a national cultural center

Beijing has a very limited geographical space, especially in terms of the ownership of resources and energy, so it cannot develop the resource and energy-based industries in the long term, and trade-offs need to be made. It should exploit and preserve its own cultural resources with a long history, and the economic construction and industrial development should not encroach on land for historical and cultural monuments. Beijing is the cultural center of the country, with the most concentrated top-level scientific research units, educational institutions, literary and sports groups, and news media in the country. The city holds numerous international and domestic cultural, artistic and sports exchange activities every year, which have an influence in Asia and even in the world. For constructing a national cultural center, we should pay attention to and protect the existing cultural resources, instead of overemphasizing economic development while neglecting the cultural preservation and cultural construction. In order to implement the basic functional positioning of the capital that aims at building a national cultural center, we must determine the scope, fields, leading industries and public services, strengthen the strategic plans, and clarify the goals, priorities, directions, and fields for the construction of the national cultural center. How can it be combined with the decentralization of non-capital functions, and how can the strategic planning and supporting construction of the national cultural center be carried out on this basis? First, the construction of the national cultural center should highlight the protection, construction, and branding of local cultural resources. It should not be culture alone, but must be combined with its own cultural resources, cultural characteristics, and cultural elements for construction and development that preserve. It should not carry out the so-called archaized and rebuilding during construction and development at the expense of destroying local cultural resources and cultural heritage. Second, we should emphasize the balanced development of the system of public cultural services, and realize the balanced distribution and reasonable development of cultural advantageous resources. From the perspective of decentralizing non-capital functions and treating "urban diseases", we should highlight the construction of the system of basic public cultural services in each area, avoid excessive concentration of advantageous cultural resources in local or core areas, and achieve the balanced and equalized construction and support of public cultural facilities. If the central urban areas have excessive cultural resources and abundant cultural facilities, while the distant suburban districts and counties or surrounding areas are extremely lacking in cultural resources and seriously uneven in cultural facilities, the result will certainly be overly abundant advantageous cultural resources in the central urban areas, which can attract more population and employment, and cause new "urban diseases". Hence, we must focus on the construction of the system of basic public cultural services, balanced public cultural resources and equalized allocation and distribution of public cultural services. Third, the development of the cultural industry should focus on characteristics, differentiation, and branding. The construction of a national cultural center should give play to the Beijing's role as a cultural leader, reflect the cultural characteristics, cultural brand, and taste of the capital, and go into differentiated competition to continuously improve quality and efficiency, enhance the competitiveness of Beijing's cultural industry and further improve the capital's cultural soft power and build a national cultural center.

9.1.1.3 Implementing the functional positioning of the capital and accelerating the construction of a national scientific and technological innovation center

With the advent of economic globalization, scientific and technological innovation becomes the eternal driving force of economic growth. It is the core competitive power of a country or region that determines the economic status and scientific and technological strength of that country or region in the international arena as well as the future fate of social development. Beijing, the national capital with incomparable scientific and technological resources and strengths in the country, is leading the country in terms of scientific research equipment, laboratory construction, scientific and technological talents, scientific and technological information and knowledge. In order to build a national scientific and technological innovation center, it must make full use of these resources, strengthen the integration of resources and the activation of inner innovation, and drive the sustainable economic and social development of Beijing by means of scientific and technological innovation. First, the city must highlight the driving and leading role of scientific and technological innovation, give value to the strategic position of science and technology as the primary productive force, increase investments in scientific and technological innovation and industry-university-research cooperation, advance the transformation of technologies, improve the rate of technological transformation, strengthen the use and protection of intellectual property rights, reform the system, and activate the momentum of scientific and technological innovation, play the dominant role of enterprises in scientific and technological innovation, encourage experts and highly-skilled talents from research institutions to cooperate and bring innovations to enterprises, and emphasize technological transformation and industrial incubation. Second, it must give play to the prominent role of scientific and technological innovation in transforming modes, adjusting structure and promoting growth, improve the economic quality and growth efficiency through scientific and technological innovation, enhance economic strength with technology, build a "high-grade, precision and advanced" economic structure, vigorously develop high-tech industries and drive the transformation and upgrading of the traditional industries with scientific and technological innovation. Third, it should build industrial brands for the capital with scientific and technological innovation, create fine products, brands and taste, highlight the high end, services, concentration, integration, and low carbon, and form a high-end, innovation-driven, green and low-carbon model of industrial development. Fourth, it should give play to the strategic position and leading role of Zhongguancun National Independent Innovation Demonstration Zone, take the construction of science and technology parks and innovation parks by Zhongguancun and various districts and counties as a platform, expand the field, scope, and level of scientific and technological innovation, boost the in-depth cooperation between Zhongguancun and various districts and counties including those in Hebei and Tianjin, promote the deep integration of scientific and technological innovation and regional economy, advance the profound cooperation of scientific and technological innovation in Zhongguancun and different industries and sectors, improve the capital's capabilities of scientific and technological innovation and international competition, continuously promote the model of independent innovation in Zhongguancun and enhance the status of and global influence of the national scientific and technological innovation center.

9.1.1.4 Implementing the functional positioning of the capital and accelerating the construction of an international communication center

An international communication center means that a city has many international organizations, and organizes various kinds of international activities and conferences that have a significant influence globally, thus enabling the city to play an important role in international communication. Today, when the traffic becomes more convenient, the means of transportation such as airplanes and high-speed trains become more popular, and the development of telecommunications, computer and Internet technologies accelerates, the communication between cities, especially across borders becomes increasingly frequent, the international division of labor is further refined, the urban economic development has a significant influence on global communication, developing countries are playing a more important role in the international arena, and all of them lay a solid foundation for the formation of international communication centers.

In order to build an international communication center, we must take the implementation of the capital's functional positioning as an opportunity, strengthen the decentralization of non-capital functions while doing well in the planning and construction of an international communication center, expand the space of development for enhancing the functions and status of Beijing as an international communication center, attract more international organizations and international resources, and create conditions and space for hosting more international conferences, international events, international tourism, and foreign affairs. The existing space for international communication cannot meet the developmental needs of Beijing, and the over-concentration in the limited space has aggravated the problems of "urban diseases". Problems such as traffic congestion, population expansion, and environmental pollution affect the construction of Beijing as an international communication center, and influence its international image. From the perspective of treating the capital's "urban diseases" and implementing the capital's functional positioning, we should strengthen the strategic planning and thematic research on building an international communication center in Beijing, so as to expand the space for building an international communication center, and provide new methods for treating the capital's "urban diseases".

First of all, for treating the capital's "urban diseases", we should strengthen top-level design, organization and leadership, and decentralize the functions. In order to strengthen the top-level design and organization and leadership of Beijing to build an international communication center, it is suggested that the Beijing Municipal CPC Committee, the Beijing Municipal Government and the relevant foreign affairs departments should jointly set up a leading group for the construction of Beijing's international communication center, with the office located in the Beijing Foreign Affairs Office, to unify, coordinate, and actively promote the construction of Beijing's international communication center. From the strategic heights of treating "urban diseases" and decentralization of non-capital functions, the expansion and development of new international organizations and embassies in the already crowded central urban areas such as Chaoyang District, should be prohibited. They should be guided and encouraged to relocate and decentralize, for example, to the surrounding areas such as Tongzhou District in the new international city and Shunyi District near the airport, thus reducing the traffic congestion and mobility of the population in the central urban areas and creating conditions for improving the security of embassies in China. If there is an overly dense population and traffic in the central urban areas, it is not conducive to the security of international organizations, international events and foreign affairs, and also the space for development is limited. It is necessary to initiate the preliminary research and special planning under the basic principles of decentralization, security, and expansion, so as to enhance the influence and competitiveness of Beijing as an international communication center.

Second, at the strategic heights of the mode of transforming, adjusting structure and promoting development, we should actively host various large-scale international events, improve the level and visibility of international communication, formulate action plans for holding various professional and comprehensive international events, and improve Beijing's capacity and level of services for international communication.

Third, at the strategic heights of implementing the capital's functional positioning and decentralizing non-capital functions, we should make a master plan and a plan for the implementation of the construction of an international communication center. An area should be planned for the construction of an international communication center to vigorously attract international organizations and in which to concentrate international institutions. The relevant policies and measures should be introduced to attract international organizations and headquarters of multinational companies, such as tax relief, expansion of export powers, and relaxation of market entry conditions. Also, an international business center area that is appropriate to the status of the capital should be planned and built. Although currently Chang'an Street and nearby areas are the political center of Beijing and the central area of international political activities, these areas are excessively crowded with national institutions, international institutions, and various kinds of organizations, but without much space for development. Hence, it is inconvenient to plan areas of an international activity center in Chang'an Street and nearby areas. It is suggested that the international business center areas, international activity center areas, as well as embassies in China, various kinds of international organizations, and headquarters of multinational companies be planned for Tongzhou New City or Shunyi New City, so as to expand broader and more comfortable, livable, and ecological new space for these organizations and their activities, decentralize the population and industries out of the central urban areas, and be substantially helpful for the treatment of "urban diseases" by the capital.

Fourth, at the strategic heights of implementing the capital's strategic positioning, decentralizing non-capital functions, and treating "urban diseases", we should vigorously build key infrastructure in the planned new area of international communication, improve the comprehensive capacity for reception, and build a number of iconic international communication facilities and bases such as large international exhibition centers, headquarters of multinational companies, and international science and technology expositions. This can make up the shortcomings of Beijing's international communication facilities, enhance the service capacity of Beijing for large-scale international communication activities, and create a favorable environment of international communication. The construction of the new area for an international communication center can not only decentralize non-capital functions and treat "urban diseases", but it can also realize the coordinated development of the new area and its surrounding areas.

9.1.2 Aiming at the goal of building a harmonious and livable city, and strengthening the construction of a new type of people-oriented urbanization

The treatment of Beijing's "urban diseases" should be guided by the basic goal of building a world-class harmonious and livable city. A harmonious and livable city is characterized by two key words: harmony and livability. From the perspective of harmony, we should emphasize the treatment of Beijing's "urban diseases", advance social harmony, safety and healthy development, and highlight a series of urban social problems such as narrowing regional disparities, urban–rural disparities, disparities between the rich and the poor. The over-concentration of education, medical, cultural, administrative, and other high-end resources in the central urban areas results in high housing prices and the existence of "school district housing", and the over-concentration of industries in the central urban areas can lead to high housing prices and rents and to the social phenomena of "snail houses" and "ants". Therefore, the construction of a harmonious capital should focus on the treatment and decentralization in these aspects. A livable city is characterized by ecological governance, environmental protection and spatial comfort, but currently the frequent smoggy weather, serious environmental pollution and overcrowded traffic and population in Beijing does not reflect the characteristics of a livable city. In order to treat these "urban diseases", we must adhere to the important goal of building a world-class harmonious and livable city, take the road towards civilized development with developed production, affluent life and good ecology, curb the pattern of "pie-spreading" for development, strictly control the urban boundaries, delineate the urban ecological red line, and boost the construction of a new type of people-oriented urbanization.

9.1.2.1 Building a harmonious and livable city, adhering to a new type of people-oriented urbanization

The treatment of "urban diseases" must first adhere to the scientific outlook of development. The scientific outlook of urban development is based on the implementation of the strategic positioning of the capital city, and must clarify the basic goal of who the city should be built for and who it should serve. The treatment of "urban diseases" serves the all-round development of people, and it should not deviate from this goal. It should be clear that urban development and the treatment of "urban diseases" should aim at the all-round development of people, and make it livable and suitable for the work of citizens, instead of the other way around, so we must stick to the people-oriented basic concept. Urbanization is an inevitable trend for the social development of human beings and an irresistible historical trend. Although there is temporarily counter-urbanization in developed cities in the West, it is basically impossible to hinder the process of urbanization or to eliminate it.

In China, the process of urbanization does not come to an end yet, and the counter-urbanization will not appear in the short term. Even so, we must follow the trend of urbanization and its laws of progress, insist on the all-round development of people as the core in urbanization, and avoid the traditional path of urbanization that does not recognize the essential connotation of serving human beings, blindly pursues the big and the fast while ignoring urban boundaries, blindly emphasizes economic construction while ignoring social and ecological development, and blindly pursuing the GDP while ignoring the efficiency and quality of development. Thus, many "urban diseases" occur. It can be said that the emergence of "urban diseases" is closely linked to the neglect of social values and all-round development of people. The new type of urbanization necessarily returns to the eternal essence of the all-round development of people.

We should adhere to the guiding idea of people-oriented development and the basic concepts and principles of innovative development, coordinated development, green development, open development, and sharing development, healthily and steadily advance the new urbanization of the capital, and realize the goal of building an international first-class harmonious and livable city in Beijing. The people-oriented innovative development aims to bring into play the wisdom and creativity of the people and serve the people with the fruits of development; the people-oriented coordinated development aims at strengthening the coordination of interests among various entities, factors, departments, and regions of the city and facilitating the coordinated development guided by people's needs; people-oriented green development aims at continuously improving the urban environment, accelerating the treatment of environmental diseases such as urban smog and water pollution, and providing citizens with a fresh airy, green, low-carbon, harmonious, and livable living space and production space; people-oriented open development requires accelerating the change in the traditional developmental path of urban self-enclosure, integrating internal and external resources, developing domestic and international markets, coordinating the role of government and market mechanisms, attracting social capital and social forces to jointly participate in urban construction and urban development, speeding up the treatment of "urban diseases", infusing more positive energy, high-quality resources and fresh blood for the development of new urbanization, providing positive energy for urban development, and improving the quality and efficiency of urban development; and people-oriented sharing development proposes that the fruits of urban development should be shared by the people in order to achieve justice and equality and truly reflect the human care and people-oriented concept because only by sharing can harmony be achieved, only by sharing can stability be achieved, only by sharing can development be achieved, and only by sharing can a win–win situation be achieved. The treatment of "urban diseases" in the capital should adhere to the people-oriented approach, in other words, to further adhere to and implement the five concepts proposed by the State, namely innovative development, coordinated development, green development, open development, and sharing development.

In order to advance the new urbanization of the capital, we should establish the basic concept of being people-oriented, change the traditional concept of object-oriented or partly people-oriented development, and gradually solve the various contradictions and developmental problems in the process of urbanization. We should highlight the guiding and leading role of new urbanization in the treatment of "urban diseases", regard the promotion of the all-round development of people as the fundamental objective, prevent and treat "urban diseases" fundamentally and fully enhance the quality and developmental efficiency of urbanization.[3] For the sake of preventing and treating "urban diseases" of the capital, we should adhere to the concept of people-oriented development and realize the five-in-one construction and coordinated development of the economy, society, politics, culture, and ecological environment.

First, we should guide citizens to actively participate in urban management and social decision-making under the principle of being people-oriented.[4] We should adhere to the people-oriented principle, insist on the orderly political participation of citizens, change the traditional mode of decision-making by the government to the decision making by active participation of the public in urban management and development, pool the wisdom and efforts of the masses to jointly treat "urban diseases" and realize the sharing in this regard, and effectively enhance the openness, transparency, and scientific nature of decision-making in urban management. To become people-oriented, the introduction of urban policies should serve and meet the public needs and expectations of citizens, instead of the needs of some classes or groups of people, enable the urban policies to be more democratic, scientific, and reasonable through citizens' participation, and improve the execution of policies, thus meeting citizens' expectations and needs, improving the efficiency of public products and the quality of public services, enhancing the satisfaction, sense of gain and happiness of urban public services, and facilitating the effective prevention and prompt treatment of "urban diseases".

Second, a people-oriented concept can be realized only with an appropriate size of the city. The inevitable connections between the urban population, traffic, and the expansion of the industrial scale must be considered in a holistic manner. The expansion of the industrial scale is inevitably connected to the expansion of the size of the city, so for treating "urban diseases", the size of the city must be appropriate. The control of the size of the city, especially the control of the urban population, should be closely integrated with the control of the industrial scale and the improvement of industrial quality. The control of the size of the city and population growth should also adhere to the people-oriented principle, without simply and mandatorily decentralizing and expelling the population out of the city. For adhering to a people-oriented approach, it is necessary to deepen the study on the close relationship between population, industry, and public services, avoid the phenomena of sleeping cities and ghost cities that there are either industries without cities, or cities without industries, enhance the absorption of the population and industries into new cities, and achieve the connection between the overall planning of new cities and land use planning and the relevant supports of public services, infrastructure and industries. The land for construction use should be arranged and the land reserved for planning should be strictly controlled pursuant to the planning, thus realizing the effective use of land resources, and further controlling the size of the city in an effective and orderly manner, so that we can adhere to the people-oriented principle and improve the comprehensive efficiency and quality of the city.

Third, we should closely integrate the insistence on the people-oriented concept and the perfection and improvement of urban functions, and improve the level of modernization of the system and capacity of urban governance. All urban construction and management, including those of new cities, must have the perfect residential, industrial, and public service functions. The functional positioning of the city should be people-oriented, use modern technology for urban planning, fulfill the basic functions of urban residents, such as living, leisure, work, and traffic, realize the balance and coordination of the overall urban functions, provide residents with diversified and integrated urban services, meet the diversified needs, and improve the quality of the city.

9.1.2.2 Building a harmonious and livable city, emphasizing the improvement of people's livelihood and the construction of a harmonious society

The ultimate goal of the treatment of "urban diseases", urban construction and development is to serve the people, and the core goal of the design of urban functions is to maximize the interests of the people. Therefore, to build a harmonious and livable city, we should pay more attention to the construction of a harmonious society and a civilized city, constantly manifest the cultural heritage and personality of the city, highlight the quality of urban construction and development, focus on transforming the mode of development, enhancing the quality of development and improving the people's livelihood, and continuously improve the quality of life of residents and the comprehensive competitive power of the city. With the scientific, rational and people-oriented urban concept and working attitude, we should emphasize the exploration and enhancement of the city's cultural heritage, preserve the city's historical and cultural monuments and cultural heritage, handle the relationship between inheritance and development, protection and construction, based on the city's traditional cultural characteristics and resource endowments, adhere to people-oriented and diversified development, inherit the city's culture, value the combination of tradition and modernity, emphasize the combination of history, culture, and modern functions, combine economic construction with cultural cultivation and social construction, foster the awareness of the modern market economy, a concept of sustainable development and an urban humanistic spirit, and build a modern livable, harmonious and civilized city that makes life better.

It is necessary to avoid overly dense industries and buildings crowding into the ecological space, prevent the central urban areas from paying too much attention to economic construction but neglecting social construction and improvement of people's livelihood, and avoid disparities and inequalities between the central urban areas and the surrounding areas in various aspects such as social construction, improvement of people's livelihood, and public services. The traditional process of urbanization attaches excessive importance to the urbanization of land, expansion of the size of the city and economic development, but it does not fully reflect the people-oriented principle. For example, not much attention is paid to the balance and coordination of the interests of farmers who lose their land and people whose houses are demolished in the process of land demolition and resettlement, nor to the social construction and improvement of people's livelihood. These problems have not been solved well for a long time, thus accumulating quite a lot of social contradictions and conflicts. In particular, the dissatisfaction of local people with the CPC and the government has not been properly solved, and hence affects social harmony and stable development of the city.

9.1.2.3 Building a harmonious and livable city, attaching importance to the improvement of the urban environment and to the construction of an ecological civilization

A city with a deteriorating ecology and serious environmental pollution can never be a harmonious and livable city. In order to build a world-class harmonious and livable city, we should regard international green and ecological cities as benchmarks, pay attention to the improvement of our urban environment and to the control of pollution, and strengthen the construction of an urban ecological civilization. We should emphasize urban ecological governance, restoration and environmental protection, and build a low-carbon city that is ecologically livable. Environmental pollution is an important manifestation and problem of modern "urban diseases", and environmental governance is the core work and key content for the prevention of "urban diseases". The treatment of "urban diseases" and urban construction and development must be compatible with the carrying capacity of urban resources, energy and the environment, adhere to the low-carbon, ecological and green concept, emphasize the construction of an ecological civilization, plan scientifically for the construction of an ecological civilization, focus on energy conservation and emission reduction, improve the efficiency of the use of resources and energy, value the development and use of new renewable energy resources, transform and replace traditional energy sources, and build low-carbon and ecological urban spaces.

Only by unifying social construction, construction of an ecological environment and economic construction, and attaching importance to the new type of people-oriented urbanization, can we fundamentally solve the long-term problems of "urban diseases". The new type of people-oriented urbanization aims at changing the traditional mode of extensive urban development with economic construction as the only goal, transforming it into a diversified path of urban development that highlights people's livelihood, social construction, and the improvement of the ecological environment, and adhering to the scientific outlook of all-round, coordinated, and sustainable development. The government should not consider GDP and the goal of economic construction only, but should play the role of macro-regulation, market supervision, social management, public services, and responsibilities in other aspects to effectively overcome the market failure, instead of acting as a market player itself. The government should give full play to the decisive role of the market mechanism in the allocation of resources, strengthen policy guidance and public services, adhere to the concept of people-oriented, harmonious and livable development, appropriately control the size of large cities, delineate the ecological red lines and urban boundaries, guide and encourage the equalization and balanced development of public resources and services such as education, medical care, culture, and sports to underdeveloped areas and small and medium-sized towns, and avoid the huge gap between the central urban areas and the surrounding areas in terms of public services. Through the new type of people-oriented urbanization, we actively promote the equalization of basic public services, effectively guide and divert non-capital functions, attract population and industries to distant suburban districts and counties and surrounding areas for coordinated development, improve the comprehensive quality and level of the modern development of cities or areas, realize the five-in-one development of the city, namely economy, society, culture, environment, and politics, and promote the construction of Beijing as an international first-class harmonious and livable city and a national capital.

9.1.3 Accelerating the transformation of urban planning and talent team building, facilitating the coordinated development of the Beijing-Tianjin-Hebei region

Urban planning is the guide for the treatment of "urban diseases" and the leader for the construction of a harmonious and livable city, because it is related to the long-term development of Beijing. A scientific urban plan can effectively save the cost of urban construction and reduce the probability of "urban diseases", while an erroneous urban plan will lead to huge economic losses and affect the social harmony and healthy and sustainable development of the city. To treat the "urban diseases" of the capital, we must emphasize the scientific planning and adopt a more strategic, forward-looking and scientific vision, principles, and methods for the urban plan of the capital, so that Beijing, the capital city, can take fewer detours and suffer "urban diseases" less often. This in itself is the basic requirement for urban planning.

Given the current situation of economic and social development, particularly the deteriorating urban ecological environment and the rigid constraints of global warming on urban development, the urban plan must highlight and avoid the negative impact of these constraints. Especially in recent years, the urban construction of China has ushered in a period of rapid development. These are problems that urban planning must face, namely how to build an ecological, environmentally friendly, low-carbon modern city, solve urban problems such as the environment and traffic, improve the quality of the life of residents and promote the sustainable and healthy development of an urban economy under the situation of global climate warming.[5] Extreme climate events triggered by global climate change have great destructive impacts on human beings, the constraints of resource and environmental bottlenecks are becoming more and more urgent for cities, the carrying capacity of the environment has reached or is close to its upper limit, and the uncontrolled size of the city has not only exceeded the traditional boundaries of urban planning, but has also become an important shackle for urban planning. Traditional urban planning is confronted with the problems of a monotonous target, a lack of foresight, and the failure of environmental protection. First, from the perspective of goal orientation, it preliminarily designs a series of ideal urban developmental goals mainly based on the existing theories and models, but the goal orientation is impractical, too ideal and monotonous. Second, there is a lack of foresight regarding the problems of "urban diseases". The main consideration in urban planning is economic growth, which means how to develop industries and how to increase GDP, but without enough consideration for issues of the environment, ecology and low-carbon development. The pursuit of the growth of the GDP and the neglect of urban livability, the separation of industry and city, the separation of work and residence, and the phenomenon of "sleeping cities" are all important failures of the traditional urban plan. It is difficult to effectively solve the bottleneck constraints of urban resources, energy, and the environment with a monotonous goal of economic growth and way of thinking. Third, the traditional urban plan is still to some extent fragmented, and cities are not developed by a sustainable model, without scientific planning that considers the practical problems of global warming and high carbon emissions. Urban development and climate change are correlated to a certain extent, and a lot of problems tend to be complicated, systematic, and sustainable. The system of urban planning lays great emphasis on technical rationality, but does not pay enough attention to the relationship between planning and management. There is a lack of the deep consideration to the environment of the urban system and urban carbon emissions. Faced with the increasingly serious "urban diseases" and related planning issues, and in response to the good expectations of urban residents for ecological space and a livable life, it is necessary to accelerate the construction of a low-carbon economy, an innovation-driven model of urban planning, and a developmental approach.

Given global climate changes, current urban development needs to coordinate the harmonious coexistence of cities and the global environment, reduce urban carbon emissions, and select and develop a low-carbon economic model. Modern urban planning should change the traditional monotonous goal orientation, actively respond to global warming, choose the low-carbon economic model, and accelerate low-carbon development. These become important requirements for urban planning. Developed cities in the Western countries make the planning for low-carbon cities, implement the "zero-emission city and regional planning" and effectively build urban spaces with clean air, a low-carbon economy, and a friendly environment. The low-carbon economy puts forward new requirements for the transformation of modern urban planning, as shown in Table 9.1.[6] In terms of the content of plans, the traditional urban plan focuses on the growth of urban material space, and pays too much attention to urban industrial and economic growth, but pays no attention to carbon emissions. Cities belong to development and construction under a high carbon mode, the planning method focuses on spatial development and composition, the concept of planning is an aesthetic perspective at the spatial level, the scope of planning is spatial optimization and the combination of urban elements, but there is a lack of the consideration for, the

Table 9.1 Comparison of traditional and modern urban planning from the perspective of low carbon

Key areas	Traditional urban planning	Modern urban planning
Content of planning	The design of a form of single material space places too much emphasis on economic growth and accumulation of material wealth, but neglects the urban environment and the control of carbon emissions.	It focuses on the coordinated development, planning and design of economic, social, cultural, environmental, and political aspects, with special emphasis on the green and low-carbon development of urban spaces.
Planning methods	The composition of spatial development highlights population, traffic, industry, and other elements, but lacks methodological guidance for the urban environment and ecological space.	Emphasis is placed on the relationship between urban climatic environment and urban planning elements, and on the use of planning methods such as response to climate change, atmospheric governance, and environmental protection.
Concepts of planning	It pays attention to the visual aesthetics of space, and the expansion of the urban scale and the high concentration of urban elements can promote economic development and solve employment problems.	It establishes the concept of low-carbon innovation, realizes low-carbon cities, promotes the construction of an ecological civilization, and focuses on the low-carbon, livable, and harmonious nature of the city.
Scope of planning	The functional organization of urban elements and the development of regional economic environment put emphasis on how to highlight industrial development and economic growth and achieve urban prosperity and development. It focuses on the relationship between population, urbanization, and economic development.	The plan considers the control of the size of the city and the delineation of an ecological red line, expands urban ecological space, enhances the comprehensive urban carrying capacity with low-carbon technological innovation, and considers the coordinated relationship between urban economic space and ecological space under the climatic system.

planning of and the design for these factors such as urban ecological space, atmospheric environment. Modern urban planning requires an emphasis on low-carbon development, and spatial planning should be transformed towards low-carbon planning with the needs of social development and ecological environment as the important orientation. Compared with traditional urban planning, modern urban planning has substantially improved in terms of technical methods, basic concepts, and scope of planning. Faced with global warming and strategic requirements of promoting ecological civilization and low-carbon development, modern urban planning must transform and develop towards low carbon, and require low-carbon planning from the source, process, and even the end of urban construction. The planning method is to realize harmony and symbiosis between the urban climatic environment and urban planning elements, and to build a system of correlation among the form of urban space, the traffic pattern, industrial distribution, and carbon emissions.

Under the new economic normal, China's economy must maintain a medium–high growth rate, overcome the bottleneck constraints of resources, energy and the environment, facilitate the construction of an ecological civilization, and realize low-carbon development and innovative drive. To achieve these goals, we must strengthen transformation at the level of urban planning and enhance planning and design at the low-carbon level. For the sake of integrating the concept of low-carbon development, solving the contradiction between urban economy and the environment, and coping with the problems of global climate change, and traditional urban planning, we need to enhance the transformation of modern urban planning for low-carbon development in Beijing. The low-carbon development puts forward the requirements of the transformation of urban planning. According to the strategic requirements of global warming and of the construction of an ecological civilization, we must strengthen the low-carbon innovative planning of the city. The development of a low-carbon economy must be supported by low-carbon scientific and technological innovation.[7] The so-called low-carbon innovation refers to the collection of various innovative means and tools of low-carbon technology, system, management, and culture in a certain area, with the basic goals of reducing carbon emissions, improving energy efficiency, and realizing regional low-carbon transformation and low-carbon economic development.[8]

First of all, for solving the problems of traditional urban planning, we should pay much attention to the important support, engine and leverage role of the innovation of low-carbon technology and of a low-carbon system, strengthen urban planning for green and low-carbon innovation, reduce the consumption of non-renewable resources as much as possible, improve the efficiency of energy utilization, rationalize industrial distribution and spatial planning, reduce carbon emissions and environmental pollution, avoid over-concentration of the population, traffic and industry, and effectively treat "urban diseases".

Second, we should promote low-carbon innovation and development in the capital city through innovation and transformation at the planning level. Urban planning of low-carbon innovation is a dynamic model of planning to achieve multiple goals of economy, society, ecology, environment, and culture, and realize the integrated development of material, society, and spatial environment. Low-carbon innovation must be integrated into urban planning and become a key technology for solving "urban diseases" and realizing low-carbon and livable urban development based on low-carbon, green and harmonious concepts and values, and planning for the value of urban development must be achieved without damage to the natural environment, but by building a livable ecological space. The urban planning of low-carbon innovation is characterized by systematization, innovation, and by being low-carbon. It should enhance the preparation, management, implementation, and feedback regarding low-carbon innovation planning through a systematic perspective and well-thought-out plan, innovative planning tools and a technical roadmap, low-carbon planning requirements, and a target selection, avoid the monotonous linear model of the traditional urban plan, emphasize a clear process of planning, prompt information feedback and timely avoidance of climate risks, build an environmental early warning mechanism, improve the ability to develop cities through low-carbon innovation, and facilitate the intensive use of resources and energy and the ecologically and environmentally friendly development of the city.

Third, the team of urban planning talents should be well established. The emergence of "urban diseases" in Beijing is to a large extent related to urban planning. The prospective, strategic and scientific nature of urban planning is often linked to the quality and level of planning talents. Hence, we should further strengthen the selection, training and introduction of planning talents and build a high-quality team of planning talents that are suitable for a world-class city. However, at present, the talents are not competent for urban planning and urban management in some areas, because they have not received formal professional training and education, they are without strong theoretical knowledge and practical ability in urban planning and urban management. They fall short of the requirements for urban planning and urban management. It is necessary to strengthen the building of a team of urban planning talents and improve professionalism.

9.2 Changing the GDP-oriented assessment system, and promoting the transformation and upgrading of the industrial structure

9.2.1 Changing the traditional GDP-oriented performance assessment system, emphasizing coordinated development

In order to treat Beijing's "urban diseases", we should establish a scientific performance assessment system of the government and incorporate social construction, the improvement of the people's livelihood, environmental protection, housing security and food safety into the performance assessment system, and change the traditional GDP-oriented performance assessment system. Due to the excessive pursuit of economic growth goals, many urban areas exceed their carrying capacity of resources, energy, and environment. For example, in the Dongcheng, Xicheng, and parts of the Chaoyang and Haidian districts, the ecological land is encroached upon for developing more high-rise office buildings that exceed the carrying capacity of resources, energy, and roads of the city itself, resulting in an over-concentration of industries, employment opportunities and working population, rigid traffic needs for commuting, and traffic congestion. Therefore, the central urban areas should not pursue GDP excessively, but should consider the comprehensive bearing capacity of central urban areas in terms of resources, energy, environmental capacity, traffic facilities, and housing conditions. The plans for and development of high-rise buildings should be moderately reduced, the city should not be too "compact" and dense, and the boundary and scale of the city should be limited by green spaces and ecological land in order to control the expansion of the urban population and the over-expansion of industries. The key to effectively controlling the over-expansion of industries is to change the city government's GDP-oriented system of performance assessment and establish a more scientific system and mechanism of performance assessment. In order to treat "urban diseases", the system of performance assessment of the government and leading cadres of Beijing at all levels should be adjusted and innovated properly. We should actively weaken economic growth indicators, and increase the setting and evaluation of indicators for social construction, improvement of people's livelihood, environmental protection, and construction of an ecological civilization, so as to weaken the GDP orientation and guide the city government to implement the people-oriented, all-round, coordinated, and sustainable scientific outlook of development.[9] By weakening the assessment of economic growth indicators, we can strengthen other aspects of construction, enhance the overall coordination of various fields, promote the coordinated development of different areas, and avoid excessive regional disparities. The balanced allocation and distribution of resources can effectively decentralize the population and industries from the core areas, and guide the balanced distribution of population and industries in each area, thus effectively treating "urban diseases".

9.2.2 Establishing a fiscal system that matches financial resources and responsibilities

According to the examination of the mechanism of formation of Beijing's "urban diseases", not only are there too many urban functions, but there is also pressure on bearing the responsibility for fiscal expenditure. Guided by the GDP growth target, it will inevitably lead to the government's impulse to strive for economic development because the government has to be responsible for too many local affairs and fiscal expenditures. For example, the core areas, despite their overly dense population, industry, traffic, and office buildings, have difficulty in controlling the impulse towards economic growth due to the existence of economic incentives and responsibilities of fiscal expenditures. The excessive pursuit of economic goals will inevitably result in the neglecting livelihood, social construction, traffic, and environmental constraints. Therefore, we must reasonably define the responsibilities for affairs and expenditures of the central and local governments. The responsibilities of expenditures between the central and local governments must be clearly defined in the fields of basic public services such as compulsory education, public health, public safety, housing supply, and social security. We must unify the powers of finance and affairs, and solve the problems that exist in the two traditional lines, namely income and expenditures, and the division of state and local taxes. In other words, the tax revenue is collected too much by the central government, while the funds for the basic construction and public services of the city are too few. As a result, it is inevitable for the local government to expand its fiscal revenue in other areas, such as relying too much on land finance and obtaining high profit returns by selling land, building houses and commercial development, so as to finance their fiscal spending.

With regard to Beijing, it not only needs to unify its financial and administrative powers, but it also needs to change its traditional GDP-first performance assessment goal according to the regional functional positioning. For example, the economic assessment indicators in the ecological conservation areas should not be set too high, even no economic growth indicators should be set. Moreover, with respect to the central urban areas, such as Dongcheng District and Xicheng District, they are strong in economic growth and can easily achieve the goals of economic development, but as the location of the CPC, the State Council and the central ministries and commissions, they assume the political responsibility of serving the central government. The excessive development of the economy will inevitably lead to the over-concentration of industries in the central urban areas and a too large proportion of construction land and commercial housing, which exceeds their own carrying capacity of the environment, resources, and energy, and existing traffic facilities, thus causing the long-standing problems of population expansion, traffic congestion, etc. Therefore, we must establish a fiscal system that unifies financial and administrative powers, build a system of "central administrative district" and "capital finance" in the Dongcheng District and Xicheng District to serve the central government, weaken or even abolish the economic growth assessment of these areas, and require all financial and tax revenues to be paid to the state treasury. The central government should guarantee the necessary financial expenditures of Dongcheng District and Xicheng District through transfer payments. The central urban areas should not rely on their own economic development and self-financing to assume their responsibilities for financial expenditures, otherwise it will be difficult to fundamentally curb their impulse to economic expansion. Considering the trend towards promoting tax reform, according to the basic principles of tax attributes and economic efficiency, the division of revenues between the central government and the government of Beijing and its districts and counties should be clarified, so as to fully arouse the enthusiasm of the central and local governments, avoid the problems of "urban diseases" on the premise of serving the political responsibility of the central government, improve the fiscal system of the capital with matched fiscal powers and affairs and dominated by transfer payments by the central government, create conditions for the government of Beijing at all levels to get rid of "land finance" and dependence on non-regulatory income, and open up a channel for solving the problems of "urban diseases" in the capital.

9.2.3 Changing the land finance system, strictly restricting industrial land, and expanding ecological land

"Land finance" is a fiscal model that relies on the transfer of land use rights and their value appreciation to obtain various types of tax revenues and support local expenditures. Land finance is called the second finance because it is an extra-budgetary revenue. The various types of tax revenues generated from land include fiscal revenues of land finance in a narrow sense, which comprise non-tax revenues such as extra-budgetary land transfer fees and fees for new construction land, and budgetary tax revenues related to land transfer, such as urban land use tax and land value-added tax. Land finance in a broad sense includes not only fiscal revenues of land finance in a narrow sense, but also government proceeds from land mortgage financing and taxes and fees charged on industries directly involved in land transfer and use.[10] By controlling land transfer, the local government trades land on the market through the transfer and development of existing state-owned land and the acquisition of non-state-owned land, at higher land prices, and hence increases their fiscal revenues. It relies on land transfer to promote GDP growth, rapid economic growth and the appreciation of land prices lead to rising housing prices, and the high cost of purchasing a house and other costs caused by high housing prices further result in risks such as rising consumer prices and increased economic pressure on homebuyers.

The system of land finance was formed after the tax sharing reform in 1994, when the central government took over the fiscal powers, and 75% of the value-added tax was transferred to the central government. After 2002, the income tax, which used to be one of the fastest growing local taxes, was changed into a shared tax. With the further devolution of affairs by the central government, local governments assume heavier responsibilities for affairs and expenditures, because they must provide more public goods and services, and bear huge amounts of fiscal expenditures such as social security expenditures, administrative expenditures, local constructive expenditures, and non-public welfare expenditures. The land transfer fees are allocated to local governments and provide plenty of room for operations by local governments to generate revenues. At the same time, the tax-sharing model transfers good tax sources to the state treasury through the state tax system, but the limited local tax revenue can hardly support the rigid expenditures of local governments in education, medical care, social construction, culture and sports, urban construction, etc. In particular, the fiscal system in regions with few local enterprises and tax resources becomes a "payroll finance", and some of them can barely support the basic expenditures, such as salaries of civil servants and teachers. Due to these contradictions and pressures, local governments must maintain their operations only through other sources of revenues, and they become enthusiastic about the active market trading of land to get huge amounts of fiscal revenues.

In the case of Beijing, owing to the influence of the land finance system, local governments have a considerable incentive for land transfer, thus leading to a series of "urban diseases". Because of functional mismatch, in addition to providing basic public goods and services, local governments must take on the political responsibility of economic development. Under the performance assessment system based on GDP and fiscal revenues, local governments are bound to promote urban economic development through land development in order to achieve political performance and economic development, and this directly leads to the sale of land at the highest possible prices and by large areas, continuous reduction of ecological land, and even modification of land planning and an increased scale of land transfer. The direct result is that developers compete to buy and raise the prices of land, which in turn raise the prices of housing and allow the land to appreciate continuously. Local governments have more incentive to develop the economy, and neglect the construction of ecological land and public land in the city, and this results in the dense distribution of office buildings and high-rise buildings and the squeezing of ecological space, land for traffic use and land for public facilities. Some local governments are highly motivated to transfer land, but less motivated to build urban infrastructures and carry out ecological construction, thus leading to many "urban diseases" such as overpopulation, traffic congestion, ecological deterioration, and high housing prices in central urban areas.

For reforming the traditional land finance system, at the strategic heights of treating "urban diseases", the State should strictly limit the scope, scale, and procedure of land acquisition, prohibit local governments from converting ecological land into construction land, set a ceiling to construction areas in central urban areas, strictly control new approvals and construction after reaching a certain scale, increase the scale and proportion of ecological land, introduce rigid constraints and guide developers and relevant departments to enhance ecological construction and improvement, increase the construction of green buildings, facilitate the expansion of the space for public land, enhance the construction of relevant traffic facilities, and avoid excessively large area and the proportion of building and ecological space and public space that is too limited in central urban areas. Currently, by taking the good opportunity of decentralizing non-capital functions, we should strengthen the decentralization of industries, institutions and organizations in central urban areas such as Dongcheng District and Xicheng District, prohibit the vacated space from being used as industrial land, which should be changed to ecological land and land for public space, and prohibit excessive commercial development. Moreover, from the perspective of solving urban social problems and promoting social harmony, the compensation for land acquisition should be increased according to the proportion of land value appreciation, and the local government should compensate land acquisition according to the market price, but should not adopt the traditional low price of land acquisition and high price of transfer for exploiting the interests of farmers who lose their land. It should strictly define land for public welfare and business construction, establish and improve the evaluation system of benchmark land prices, use the evaluation price as the reference benchmark for land market transactions and acquisition prices of the government, change the over-reliance of local governments on land finance and corporate taxation, expand the scale of ecological land in urban areas, delineate the ecological red line and urban boundaries, and promote the construction of a harmonious and livable capital, thus effectively treating the capital's "urban diseases".

9.2.4 Accelerating the transformation and upgrading of industrial structure, building a high-grade, precision and advanced economic structure

Guo Jinlong, the Secretary of Beijing Municipal Committee of the CPC, proposed to adjust and decentralize non-capital core functions with determination, always adhere to the strategic positioning of the capital and take the road toward being high-grade, precision-minded, and advanced. Deepening the implementation of the capital city's strategic positioning requires accelerating the construction of Beijing's high-grade, precision and advanced economic structure, which is mainly examined from three dimensions: global, national, and urban. From a global perspective, faced with economic globalization, accelerated scientific and technological innovation, and increasingly fierce international competition, without accelerating innovation, there is a risk of being eliminated. In order to actively participate in the global competition in science and technology and improve its technological competitive power, China must accelerate its scientific and technological innovation and take the road towards high-grade, precision, and advanced economic development. It should follow the trend of global economic development. With the advent of economic globalization, a knowledge-based economy and a network economy, acceleration of scientific and technological innovation, and more intense international competition, Beijing, as the capital of the largest developing country and the city with the second largest GDP in the world, should accelerate its strategic transformation and structural adjustment. From a national perspective, transforming the mode of development, implementing the innovation-driven strategy and building an innovative country require changing the traditional mode of extensive economic growth, and building a high-end, knowledge-intensive, technology-intensive, high-grade, precision and advanced economic structure. From the perspective of Beijing, the city is facing the serious "urban diseases" of a metropolis. In order to solve the problems of serious environmental pollution, population expansion, traffic congestion and insufficient carrying capacity of resources, energy, and the environment, Beijing must accelerate the transformation of its mode of development and economic restructuring.

For the sake of accelerating the transformation and upgrading of industrial structure, we should lay stress not only on the closure and transfer of traditional industries, transformation and upgrading and structural optimization, but also on the high-end development of modern industries, and build a high-grade, precision, and advanced economic structure. The traditional industries that are backward, energy consuming and environmentally polluting should be strictly shut down and phased out, and those to be developed must improve their industrial quality and efficiency, reduce energy consumption and improve output value and environmental benefits through upgrading and technological transformation, and further achieve high-end and efficient development and be fused with modern high-tech industries. The modern service industries, modern high-tech industries, and highly intelligent manufacturing industries must accelerate scientific and technological innovation, increase technological content and industrial competitiveness, and take the road towards high-grade, precision, and advanced development. A high-grade, precision and advanced economic structure has the following three characteristics. First, high-grade industries. Distinguishing from the traditional extensive economic model of high input, high energy consumption, high emissions, and high pollution, Beijing needs to vigorously develop high-grade industries, including new generation mobile communication technology and products, integrated circuit industry, biomedicine, new material industry, etc. Second, technological precision. A high-grade, precision and advanced economic structure must be led by precision and lean technology, driven by high-end technological innovation, and with technological progress as the core competitiveness to improve the economic competitive power of the capital. Third, being globally advanced. Secretary Guo Jinlong pointed out that the urban construction of the core areas should be on a par with international first-class standards, and must play a global leading role to construct industries and brands with global influence and competitiveness, lead the world with top technology, organizational structure, and product features, and build well-known brands with international influence.

In order to achieve the above high-grade, precision, and advanced economic structure, we must focus on the development of six industries: first, the construction of functional areas for high-grade industries; second, the active development of strategic emerging industries; third, the vigorous development of productive service industries; fourth; the healthy development of cultural and creative industries; fifth, the enhancement of the quality of the life service industries; and sixth, the vigorous development of low-carbon and energy-saving industries to improve the quality and efficiency of the capital's development.

The accelerated construction of a high-grade, precision, and advanced economic structure must properly deal with the relationship between give and take, decentralization and diversion, restrict industries with high energy consumption, high water consumption, and high pollution from the source, and decentralize overly concentrated functions, so as to lay a solid foundation for building a high-grade, precision and advanced economic structure and leave more room for the coordinated development of the Beijing-Tianjin-Hebei region. Some industries are not suitable for development in Beijing and must be diverted to the surrounding areas or shut down as soon as possible. Only through effective diversion can new market vitality be unleashed, the "urban diseases" of the capital be treated, new economic growth points be formed, and sustainable economic and social development and harmonious and healthy development be realized.

We should take the opportunity of the coordinated development of the Beijing-Tianjin-Hebei region, accelerate urban transformation and treatment of "urban diseases", speed up the transfer of low-carbon, non-core urban functions, strengthen the strategic layout, scientific planning, and top-level design, enhance the adjustment, transformation and upgrading of Beijing's industrial structure, dock with the industries in Tianjin and Hebei, and in a larger regional scope, promote the coordination of population, resources, and the environment. The industries in the capital should take the road towards connotative development and intensive development, solve the problem of excessive concentration of industrial functions, clear out industries that do not conform to the strategic positioning of the core areas as soon as possible, improve the level of development of life service industries, play the role of high-quality resources more intensively and achieve sustainable development.

We should strengthen the construction of auxiliary infrastructures, advance balanced development, focus on accelerated construction in two areas, namely the integration of traffic and the integration of the construction of an ecological civilization, realize the equalized supply of ecological civilizations, emphasize the synergy of education, medical care, and social security, and solve the issue of talents. We should accelerate industrial synergy, the docking of enterprises, the integration of resources and the coordinated development of the Beijing-Tianjin-Hebei region, and provide strong support and basic conditions for industrial transformation and upgrading and building a high-grade, precision, and advanced economic structure through construction in these areas.

9.3 Enhancing the balanced distribution of high-quality resources, and guiding the orderly diversion of the population

On July 11, 2015, the Seventh Plenary Session of the 11th Beijing Municipal Committee of the CPC voted to pass the opinions of the Beijing Municipal Committee of the CPC and Beijing Municipal People's Government on the implementation of the Planning Outline for the Coordinated Development of the Beijing-Tianjin-Hebei Region. The opinion proposed that Beijing will focus on Tongzhou, accelerate the planning and construction of the city's administrative subcenters, and strive to make significant achievements in 2017; the increase in population will be strictly under control by the two-pronged approach of "control" and "decentralization", the total population will be controlled within 23 million in 2020, and the central urban areas will decentralize 15% of their population. How to achieve and complete this goal is complex, problematic, and arduous. In this book, it is most important that the balanced distribution of high-quality resources in the core areas should be strengthened. Such high-quality resources include high-end education resources involving primary and secondary schools, colleges, and universities, Grade 3A hospitals, state-owned cultural resources, high-end employment opportunities such as central ministries and commissions, central enterprises, and state-owned enterprises, etc. The over-concentration of high-quality resources in the core areas will inevitably lead to over-expansion of the population and make decentralization difficult. In order to guide the orderly diversion of population, it must start from the principles of balance, coordination and guidance, and moderately dilute the concentration of high-quality resources in the core areas. The core areas should be slimmed down and healthy, and the non-core areas should strengthen the balanced distribution of public services and the introduction of some high-quality resources, so as to attract and guarantee the orderly diversion of the population.

The coordinated development of the Beijing-Tianjin-Hebei region is not only the integrated development of the economy, but more importantly, to ensure that all citizens in the Beijing-Tianjin-Hebei region can share the fruits of development in the regional economic, political, cultural, social, and ecological fields, and realize the universalization and equalization of basic public services in the region. We should strengthen the balanced and integrated development of infrastructures in the city circle of the capital, and equalize the supply of public services to facilitate the effective decentralization of the population, regional coordinated development and fundamental treatment of "urban diseases" of the metropolis. The "urban diseases" of the metropolis in the capital are not formed within a short period of time, and there are many reasons. However, the profit-seeking nature to avoid harm and "vote with one's feet", and the existence of regional differences such as the huge disparities of infrastructure are important reasons for the formation of "urban diseases". Only by strengthening the balanced and integrated development and construction of infrastructure in the city circle of the capital and promoting the equalization of basic public services, can the occurrence of "voting with feet" be reduced, and the population and industries in the dense central urban areas be effectively decentralized, and the balanced distribution and spatial flow of market factors be guided. Beijing's "pie-spreading" pattern of development is mainly due to the over-concentration of resources in the central urban areas, which have absolute advantages over the surrounding areas in terms of infrastructure and public services. In order to implement the strategic positioning of the capital, we should speed up the decentralization of non-capital functions, accelerate the balanced distribution of advantageous resources, and guide the orderly diversion of the population.

9.3.1 Core areas reduce increments without reducing service quality, and innovate the reasonable mechanism for mobility of talents

The core areas reduce increments, new projects, new industries, and new population. The increments of population, enterprises, industries, administrative organs and institutions, universities, hospitals, etc. should be reduced, so as to ease the pressure on the population, resources, and the environment in the core areas. However, the purpose of treating "urban diseases" is not to reduce the quality of life, but to make the citizens' life more comfortable, pleasant, and happy. Reducing increments does not mean relocating or reducing the supply of public services, but decentralizing excessive high-quality resources on the premise of meeting the basic public service needs. Only when the high-quality education, medical, cultural, and employment opportunities can be decentralized and diverted to the destinations, can talents be attracted and diverted to the destinations, can the increments and total population in the core areas be effectively decreased, thus achieving balanced development, moderate development, and livable development, jointly improving the quality of urban life and enhancing the sense of happiness and satisfaction in the city.

9.3.2 Non-core areas and core areas jointly establish branches to facilitate the effective decentralization of the population

Non-core areas and core areas should strengthen cooperation in the decentralization of high-end education, medical and cultural resources, jointly establish branches, improve the quality of public services, and increase the supply of high-end employment opportunities and other resources, and moderately increase high-quality public service resources. The increments should be transferred to the surrounding districts and counties, especially those in Hebei. The compensation for interests and market guidance should be done well in order to attract or guide the population, industries, administrative organs, institutions, and enterprises to move out. The investment and total supply of infrastructure in backward areas, and the balanced and integrated construction of infrastructure should be strengthened, such as the balanced development of traffic, education, medical care, cultural and sports facilities, etc. Famous schools and universities should establish branches in or be fully relocated to backward areas. The balanced infrastructure and equalized supply of public services can facilitate the decentralization of the population and the coordinated development of the Beijing-Tianjin-Hebei region, and ultimately contribute to the treatment of Beijing's "urban diseases".

New projects mainly consider distant suburbs and destinations for decentralization. The high-quality education, medical and cultural resources in the core areas can cooperate with the distant suburbs and destinations for decentralization by partially relocating or jointly building branches of famous schools, hospitals, and cultural venues. Through reducing increments in the core areas and decentralizing high-end quality resources, we can create an equal environment of public services for destinations for decentralization and distant suburbs, and attract the population to non-core areas. For example, Haidian District, Dongcheng District and Xicheng District have very good educational, medical, and cultural resources and employment opportunities. Schools, medical institutions, enterprises, and state ministries in these areas should be guided to establish cooperation mechanisms with neighboring areas such as distant suburbs, Hebei and Tianjin, and jointly build branches and subsidiaries as well as branch schools and sub-hospitals. For example, the High School Affiliated to Renmin University of China has established many branches in the surrounding areas. This is a good model and case that can be promoted. In addition, we can create a mechanism for the free flow and balanced allocation of famous teachers and doctors.

At present, according to the requirements of the opinions of the Beijing Municipal Committee of the CPC and the Beijing Municipal People's Government on the implementation of the Planning Outline for the Coordinated Development of the Beijing-Tianjin-Hebei Region, the functional positioning of the Tongzhou Subcenter is a centralized administrative office area of Beijing, an international first-class harmonious and livable demonstration area, a demonstration area of the new type of urbanization, and a demonstration area of the coordinated development of the Beijing-Tianjin-Hebei region. In order to construct the Tongzhou Subcenter, we should strengthen the integration of resources and functional coordination, properly balance work and residence and link the industrial upstream and downstream, strengthen the guidance of high-quality resources such as education and medical care in Dongcheng and Xicheng as soon as possible, cooperate with famous schools and Grade 3A hospitals in the core areas, establish branch schools and hospitals, enhance the quality of public services in Tongzhou, reduce the drawbacks, and thus attract the inflow of population and the decentralization of industries from the core areas. Tongzhou is currently cooperating with strong educational districts such as Haidian, Xicheng, and Dongcheng. Famous schools will establish branches in Tongzhou, such as the High School Affiliated to BIT, the High School Affiliated to Beijing International Studies University, the Beijing No. 4 High School in Xicheng District, the Beihai Kindergarten, the Huang Cheng Gen Primary School, the Beijing No. 2 High School in Dongcheng District, Jingshan School, and the Beijing No. 5 High School. Tongzhou cooperates with the central urban areas to introduce famous municipal schools, implement integrated management and improve the quality and level of education in the Tongzhou Subcenter. Moreover, we should eliminate barriers to the mobility of talents within these areas. The personnel relationships of famous teachers and doctors can remain unchanged, but they may go to underdeveloped areas for exchange and support in various forms, such as part-time, cooperation, and consultancy, to achieve common development of the surrounding areas.

The docking of high-quality resources between Tongzhou and the central urban areas needs to be further advanced and expanded to form a demonstration effect, facilitate the relatively balanced distribution of resources, change the current monocentric pattern, realize the relatively balanced distribution of the population, thus alleviating the pressure of the population, resources, and the environment in the central urban areas and solving the problems of "urban diseases".

9.3.3 Interacting between government and market, promoting balanced development and orderly diversion

The relationship between government and market is always a popular issue and a difficult point for theoretical and practical research. It is difficult to clearly reveal and properly deal with this relationship. Whether the relationship between government and market is rationalized also directly affects whether urban development is sustainable and balanced. For the treatment of Beijing's "urban diseases" and the coordinated development of the Beijing-Tianjin-Hebei region, we must attach great importance to this relationship, and treat it impartially and scientifically. The macroscopic guidance of the government mechanism and the free competition of the market mechanism become the key to realizing the coordinated development of the city. In order to guide and decentralize advantageous resources to the distant suburban districts and countries and surrounding areas, we must play the roles of "push" and "pull" of both government support and market mechanism. The government can neither simply rely on mandatory administrative intervention and on the mode of forced relocation, nor leave the situation without any action.

At the government level, through various modes such as benefiting the people, policy support and transfer payments, etc., governmental organs, social organizations, and educational and medical institutions should be guided to relocate or establish branches in the surrounding areas. The central urban areas should be restricted from development, and the surrounding areas can attract agencies, organizations, and enterprises in the central urban areas by various means such as household registration permissions, land indicators, and tax exemption. In the meantime, the government should enhance the construction of traffic facilities, particularly rail transit, and strengthen decentralization and support of famous schools and medical resources in the destinations of decentralization. Through government guidance and appropriate advancement, a favorable environment for optimal allocation of resources can be formed to guide the diversion of population and balanced distribution, give full play to the role of human capital and talent capital, attract high-quality talents to spread to the surrounding areas, and transform human capital into the wealth for economic growth and social productivity.

At the market level, we should give full play to the decisive role of the market mechanism in the balanced distribution of the city's advantageous resources and the decentralization of non-capital functions, create market conditions and a favorable market environment for the destinations of decentralization, give market players hope and space for profit in the new destinations of decentralization, foster the new space for industrial development, and form new economic growth points. The decentralization of non-capital functions and the relocation of industries and enterprises that are not suitable for development should respect the market law and adhere to the principle of compensation for market interests, and they should be guided to relocate and develop in a balanced manner by the temptation of necessary and appropriate interests. During the decentralization of advantageous resources and non-capital functions, the market mechanism should be brought into play to attract social capital and private capital for participating in the construction of new markets and investment and cooperation in various fields such as urban traffic facilities, urban education, medical culture, etc., revitalize social capital, facilitate the construction of new cities and the balanced regional development by market power, alleviate and solve various aspects of "urban diseases" in the central urban areas, and advance the construction of a harmonious and livable city.

9.4 Accelerating the construction of rail transit in the Beijing-Tianjin-Hebei city circle, and controlling the growth of motor vehicles in an orderly manner

The traffic congestion in Beijing, on the one hand, is reflected by the serious shortage of existing public transportation and related facilities, and underdeveloped rail transit; on the other hand, because of underdeveloped public transportation, the problems of crowded buses, crowded subways, and inconvenient interchanges result in the fact that more citizens drive private cars, and the ineffective control and the increase in the number of motor vehicles at a speed that is too fast aggravates the problem of "capital jam". According to the experience of international cities, the construction density and coverage of rail transit facilities may be improved to ease the pressure of traffic congestion in the capital. The experience of international cities such as New York and Tokyo reveals that the mobility of the urban population mainly relies on rail transit such as subways, and private cars are not used for commuting to and from work, but only for holiday travel. Beijing currently relies on buses, subways, taxis, and private cars for travel, especially for commuting to and from work, and private cars account for a significant proportion. This is the important reason for traffic congestion and exhaust emissions. Therefore, in order to treat Beijing's "urban diseases", the construction of rail transit must be enhanced. Rail transit such as subways and light railways has the advantages of public transportation, punctuality, short waiting time, fast interchange, large capacity, low energy consumption, and low pollution compared with the general rail transportation. Beijing should increase the density and coverage of rail transit facilities.

9.4.1 Densification of rail transit construction in the core areas

The construction of rail transit in the core areas should be densified according to the plan, commenced ahead of schedule and accelerated, so as to relieve the pressure of traffic congestion as soon as possible and meet the traffic needs of more citizens. According to the experience of international cities, such as New York, London, and Tokyo, rail transit is responsible for the traffic needs of more than 60% of the total population, but the proportion is less than half in Beijing. Hence, there is much room for rail transit development. It must speed up and increase the density of the construction of rail transit. The high density of urban living space, high-rise buildings and office space, as well as the mismatched road space and rail transit, lead to traffic congestion. The traffic needs of an overly dense urban population determines that China must give priority to the development of a high-capacity, high-speed, fast rail transit system, because it can achieve the goals and basic functions of minimizing the per capita occupancy of spatial resources of roads, energy consumption, emissions and environmental pollution, maximizing the capacity of transportation, and reducing the use of private cars. Therefore, Beijing as the national capital, for the purpose of building a world-class harmonious and livable city, needs to accelerate the construction of urban public transportation, especially the construction of urban rail transit, improve the capacity of the urban rail transit, and create the traffic conditions for the decentralization of non-capital functions. Compared with international metropolises such as Tokyo, the construction of rail transit in the core areas of Beijing should be further densified, and strive to have subway entrances every 500–200 meters, so as to facilitate the traveling of citizens in the core areas, reduce the use of private cars and the pressure of traffic, and create a convenient, harmonious, and livable traffic environment in the capital.

9.4.2 Wide coverage in distant suburban districts and counties and surrounding areas

The construction of rail transit between the core areas and the neighboring districts and counties and the border areas of Hebei and Tianjin should be accelerated to narrow the gap of traffic infrastructure in the surrounding backward areas, attract new population and industries to move to the surrounding areas, ease the pressure on the population, resources and traffic, and control the increase in the population in the core areas. At present, there is still no plan for the Beijing-Tianjin-Hebei subway, and the development seriously lags behind. To accelerate the construction of subways and other rail transit in the surrounding areas and build a "Beijing-Tianjin-Hebei region on the track" can effectively attract the input of resource factors, provide conditions and a developmental environment for various enterprises, administrative organs, and institutions that are transferred or relocated from the core areas, and enhance the attractiveness, so that they can be attracted, retained, and well developed. The construction of rail transit in the Beijing-Tianjin-Hebei city circle should reflect the principles of dense network and efficient services, and have a layered layout and well-connected Beijing-Tianjin-Hebei rail transit circle by means of special passenger lines, suburban railroads, intercity railroads, subways, and other means. According to the existing plan, relatively complete network of passenger lines will be formed before 2020, and fully cover most prefecture-level cities and counties in Beijing, Tianjin, and Hebei. However, intercity railroads, suburban railroads, and subway lines are seriously inadequate, and the density of subway lines is insufficient in the central urban areas of Beijing, resulting in the serious overload of most lines during the commuting hours and inability to meet the existing traffic needs on the subway. There are few subway lines in the distant suburban districts and counties and the surrounding areas, some of which are even not covered, so it is difficult to divert the population and industries to the distant suburban districts and counties for functional decentralization. Therefore, we must adhere to the strategy of building a "Beijing-Tianjin-Hebei region on the track", increase the density of subway lines in the central urban areas and commence the existing plan as soon as possible.

Beijing should increase the coverage of subway lines, guide the diversion of population and industries, achieve a balanced regional development, and accelerate the construction of subway lines and suburban railroads connecting distant suburban districts and counties, as well as intercity railroads. Relying on suburban railroads and intercity railroads alone can effectively meet the traffic needs from the distant suburban districts and counties to the central urban areas, but it is not conducive to the industrial development of the distant suburban and surrounding districts and counties, because in this case, the distant suburban districts and counties only serve the function of "sleeping cities" and the living function. In order to achieve balanced development between districts and counties, the subway and suburban railroad should be advanced at the same time, and the "last mile" of the existing subway lines should be linked to realize the construction of subways between some districts and counties. For example, the last station of Line 6 can build a "last mile" and be extended directly to Yanjiao Town, thus providing convenience for hundreds of thousands of people in Yanjiao. The Batong Line can also be extended further a few stops in the east, so that it can link Xianghe County in Hebei. The Fangshan Line can be extended to Zhuozhou City and other areas in Hebei to facilitate traffic in the neighboring areas, provide convenience for and create the basic conditions for the economic and social development of these areas, reduce the regional disparities and achieve the coordinated development of the Beijing-Tianjin-Hebei region.

9.4.3 Demolishing fence walls in urban areas, accelerating the construction of branch roads and cut-off roads

The formation of "urban diseases" in Beijing, especially traffic congestion, is often closely related to the lack of road accessibility, because there is too much traffic on trunk roads and too many fence walls lead to insufficient microcirculation, many intersections become single passages and form "hard obstructions", and there is a lack of capillaries and branch roads to divert traffic. This is the case in many areas of Beijing. We need to modernize the capacity and system of national governance. The existence of fence walls does not facilitate the modernization of urban governance, but hinders the accessibility of urban transportation, and artificially causes the idleness of urban spatial resources and self-enclosed obstruction.

In order to build a world-class harmonious and livable city, Beijing needs not only to keep up with international standards, but also to achieve innovative, coordinated, green, sharing, and open development. It must accelerate the demolition of most fence walls, smoothen out the capillaries of traffic, ease traffic congestion, and construct an accessible modern city.

9.4.3.1 The current situation of no fence walls and the experience of developed cities

First, in order to guarantee microcirculation and accessibility of traffic, no fence walls are built in developed countries and cities. Almost none of the universities in developed countries have fence walls. Residential buildings along streets not only do not have fence walls, but there are also very few metal security bars. In developed countries, there are basically no fence walls in cities, the roads are spaced within a few dozen meters on average, and the traffic micro-circulation is smooth. For example, Tokyo in Japan attaches great importance to the construction of branch roads and the accessibility of capillaries, and often does not allow the construction of fence walls in urban areas, so that trunk roads can be diverted and circulated with branch roads around communities, enterprises, and institutions.

Second, the sharing of urban public space is encouraged to reduce the waste of idle urban resources. Many developed countries and cities allow their citizens to use urban public space and emphasize openness to the public to improve the rate of the utilization of urban resources and the sharing of urban resources. For example, the Louvre is located in an urban core area of Paris, which neither occupies a large space, nor has fence walls to isolate it from the outside world. There are basically no fence walls in the whole city of Paris, so the roads are easily accessible, and roads between buildings can be used for traffic of external buildings. London's famous Hyde Park covers a large area, but it is not isolated from the outside with fence walls. The various arterial roads in the park are connected to the outside, so as to achieve the smoothness of urban traffic. Of course, Buckingham Palace in London is an exception, with iron fences around a small courtyard, but occupying less than 1/10 of the area of the Forbidden City in Beijing. Universities, enterprises, and institutions, and even governmental organs and residential housings in developed countries in Europe and the United States of America do not have fence walls. Even though private villas are built in forest areas, on mountains and at the waterfront, most of them do not have fence walls. For living and working there, instead of feeling insecure due to the lack of fence walls, people feel that the whole world is well connected, comfortable, open, and shared.

Third, citizens are well educated with a high level of mutual trust. A national integrity system has been established to guarantee lifelong accountability and punishment for those who fail to become honest. Citizens in developed countries and cities have a high degree of integrity. As a result, cities do not need to have various walls and security guards to prevent theft and other unsafe behavior. Developed countries and cities often establish a perfect national integrity system, where each person's behavior can be tracked, warned about, and punished at any time, and once any violation and breach is detected, they will be entered into the integrity blacklist and be held accountable for life. This system is an important humanistic environment for dismantling fence walls in urban areas because it can ensure the integrity among people.

9.4.3.2 Dismantling fence walls in urban areas, accelerating the construction of branch roads and cut-off roads

First, Beijing should strengthen the construction of microcirculation for and capillaries of urban roads and branch roads to relieve the traffic congestion on trunk roads. From the perspectives of respecting the constitution and integrating urban spatial resources, it must break the segmentation of urban space and reasonably plan the layout of an urban road network. According to Tokyo's experience, all redundant fence walls should be removed on the premise of guaranteeing security by the legal system. Except for important secret government institutions, cultural monuments, and other important areas that need fence walls for ease of management, other general enterprises and institutions, schools, hospitals, social organizations, shopping malls, parks, etc. should be open to the outside, the fence walls should be opened, and the artificially closed roads should be opened up to return land and roads that have been cut off by a few people for public use and for the sharing of urban space, and guarantee the equal rights of way for all people. Only by diverting urban traffic and valuing the equal rights of way in the city, can we truly realize urban traffic management and share the fruits of urban development. According to Tokyo's experience, Beijing should take the opportunity to remove the many excess fence walls and speed up the planning and design of branch lines for diverting traffic flows on trunk roads, especially at intersections, so that once congestion occurs at the intersection ahead, vehicles can choose other branch roads on the side of the trunk roads to avoid congested traffic, for the sake of reducing the pressure of congestion and achieving the effect of rapid accessibility. Planning, designing, and speeding up the construction of these branch roads can completely eliminate the dead ends and "hard obstruction" of roads and effectively control traffic congestion in the capital.

Second, Beijing should strengthen the planning and reuse of the space after the demolition of fence walls, and implement the project of demolishing walls and making the capital green. Considering the limited spatial resources of Beijing, especially those used for urban green space and green partitions, it should implement the strategic positioning of the capital, decentralize non-capital functions, combine decentralization and the transfer of non-capital functions, and speed up the demolition of city walls without preserving the function of historical and cultural heritage. First, the planning authority should strengthen the control over buildings, set back the lines of fence walls and forms, enhance the planning and reuse of the space after the demolition of fence walls, pay attention to the system and coordination, facilitate the coordination of the urban landscape, urban roads, urban land used for construction and other functions, and strive to create a good urban street landscape and urban interface. Second, after demolition, these spaces will no longer be used as industrial land, but changed fully to urban green spaces and land for public roads. The demolition and greening project should be implemented to increase the rate of urban greening and garden areas, and boost the construction of a green Beijing. Third, new urban areas should no longer be planned as fenced-in areas. Relevant laws and regulations should be enacted that clearly specify that fence walls can be built only for special functional needs and after approval. Under no other circumstances should enterprises, institutions, organs, and communities be allowed to build new fence walls, so that people can be closer to nature and love greenery. According to the successful international experience, the city may explore the possibility of removing fence walls around parks, and allow beautiful sceneries in parks to be visible directly from a distance and become part of the people's lives. Low plants may be planted where the former fence walls were located, or decorative metal chains can be put in to separate the landscape without blocking the field of vision. Publicity and supervision should be enhanced so that citizens can foster the habit of consciously caring for the sceneries in parks.[11]

Third, Beijing should improve the civilized attitude of its citizens, advocate civilized behavior, prevent the occupancy of public space after the demolition of fence walls in urban areas, and establish credit archives. On the one hand, the city should improve the civilized attitude of its citizens so that they have the awareness and behavior of not occupying public spaces. On the other hand, it is necessary to strengthen supervision and discipline, and establish the essential credit archives. Currently, many roads are occupied by disorderly parking and stall-keepers. In order to keep the space after the demolition of fence walls from being occupied by new disorderly parking and stall-keepers, the relevant institutional system should be constructed, and the credit archives should be established for the monitoring of disorderly parking and stall-keepers on roads, who, once found, should be recorded in the credit archives and severely punished.

Fourth, Beijing should strengthen the construction of a smart, digital, and informative city, advance the modernization of the capacity for and system of urban governance, and crack down on and punish the behavior of disorderly parking and stall-keepers on roads by technological means. All public urban spaces after the demolition of fence walls in urban areas should be planned and designed again. If it can be used as a parking lot, the space may be designated as a parking lot, and if it can be used as a green partition or green space, it should be used for other purposes. These spaces should be monitored at all times by installing cameras and be equipped with a smart management system. Any abnormality, once found, should be promptly stopped and punished accordingly, thus achieving the goal of cleaning up the public space and purifying the public environment of the city. By dismantling city walls, we will strengthen the integrity and civilized attitude of the city and build a new capital that is accessible by traffic, ecologically livable, honest, and caring, and full of vitality.

Fifth, Beijing should strengthen the linkage of cut-off roads. There are obviously quite a lot of cut-off roads, by which it is especially difficult to create links between Beijing and the surrounding areas in Hebei and Tianjin. In 2015, Beijing accelerated the commencement of the Miyun-Zhuozhou Expressway and the Beijing-Qinhuangdao Expressway. While smoothening major roads, the traffic authorities in the three regions have started the plans for the docking of ordinary trunk roads. Moreover, under the leadership of the Ministry of Transportation, the three regions are studying how to accelerate the construction of a ring expressway around the capital area. It is expected that by 2017, there will be no more cut-off roads between Beijing, Tianjin, and Hebei. When this expressway is open to traffic, Beijing will open up a new fast track to the northeast, the traffic among northern Tianjin, Tangshan, Qinhuangdao, and Beijing will be more convenient, and it will play an important role in promoting the economic development of the Beijing-Tianjin-Hebei region. According to the functional positioning, the role of the ring expressway around the capital area is to decentralize non-capital functions, guide the passage of transit traffic, and improve the freight function from northern China to the ports of Tianjin and Hebei. Beijing, Tianjin, and Hebei need to accelerate the study and jointly promote the construction of the ring expressway around the capital area.[12]

There are many cut-off roads between Beijing, Tianjin, and Hebei, but the rural roads and local roads should be constructed by local governments. This restricts the integrated development of the Beijing-Tianjin-Hebei region. The coordinated development of the Beijing-Tianjin-Hebei region must be preceded by traffic control, relying on the integration and interconnectivity of traffic, and accelerating the decentralization of non-capital functions and the diversion and balanced distribution of population and industries, so the linkage of cut-off roads must be accelerated. The establishment of the Jing Jin Ji Railway Transit Investment Co., Ltd. provides the organizational guarantee for the construction of rail transit in the Beijing-Tianjin-Hebei region. At the same time, social capital should also be attracted to participate in the integrated construction of the Beijing-Tianjin-Hebei region, and the benefit- and risk-sharing mechanisms should be established to provide convenient traffic for the coordinated development of the Beijing-Tianjin-Hebei region and facilitate the mobility and diversion of population.

9.5 Deepening the reform of the system of ecological civilization in the capital, and establishing a long-term mechanism for environmental governance

In recent years, the smoggy weather has frequently appeared in Beijing and this gives the capital the label of a polluted city. At the mention of smog, Beijing will be the first thing that comes to our mind. Given the objective reality of ecological deterioration and environmental fragility and citizens' strong desire for fresh air and a livable city, it is inevitable for us to strengthen Beijing's environmental governance and the construction of an ecological civilization. The report of the 18th CPC National Congress clearly proposes to vigorously promote the construction of an ecological civilization. The CPC and the State put forward the earnest expectation for and development goal of building an international first-class harmonious and livable city. It becomes an important project for Beijing to enhance ecological governance and environmental construction and accelerate the control of its environmental pollution. In order to speed up the construction of an ecological civilization in the capital, we must deepen the reform of the system of ecological civilization and establish a long-term mechanism for environmental governance. The reform of the system of ecological civilization involves many fields, such as the economy, society, culture, and politics, and it is difficult to boost the construction of an ecological civilization comprehensively by reforming a single field or a single region. The integration of the construction of an ecological civilization with economic, social, cultural, and political construction requires systematic institutional innovation. The reform of the system of an ecological civilization in the capital should strengthen the reform and innovation in multiple fields, such as the economy, the environment, society, and culture, and it includes key areas and paths.

9.5.1 Strengthening the innovation of the economic system, establishing an ecological industrial system

Beijing should strengthen the reform of its economic system, overcome the dilemma between economic development and environmental pollution, realize the disconnection of economic construction and environmental pollution, and achieve a win–win situation between economic development and the construction of an ecological civilization.

9.5.1.1 Establishing an ecological economic system, building a high-grade, precision-focused and advanced economic structure, accelerating industrial transformation and upgrading, and vigorously developing low-carbon, green, and ecological industries

Beijing should establish a green and ecological economic system, vigorously develop low-carbon, green, and ecological industries, reduce environmental pollution and carbon emissions, improve economic efficiency, disconnect economic growth from environmental pollution, and promote the construction of an ecological civilization in the capital with ecological industries and an ecological economy. It should also accelerate the construction of a high-grade, precision-focused, and advanced economic structure, speed up industrial transformation and upgrading, vigorously develop low-carbon industries, and establish an ecological economic system of the capital. It should seek support from the central government, lead Hebei, Tianjin, and other provinces and cities in taking measures, strengthen industrial transformation and upgrading and regional industrial cooperation, continuously reduce the proportion of heavy and chemical industries around Beijing, including those in Tianjin and Hebei, decrease pollutant emissions, and enhance the industrial transformation and development of ecological industries. These are the top priorities for promoting the construction of an ecological civilization in Beijing, Tianjin, and Hebei, and also the keys to advancing the ecological construction, reducing smog, and improving the environment of the capital.

9.5.1.2 Strengthening economic compensation in ecological areas, improving the mechanism of ecological compensation

By deepening the reform of the fiscal and taxation systems and improving the innovation of the institutional mechanism of factor allocation, the issue of economic compensation for ecological protection in ecological function areas can be solved. The areas of ecological conservation of the capital are mainly located in remote mountainous areas and other ecologically fragile areas, including Yanqing, Huairou, Miyun, Pinggu, and other districts and counties, where the economic basis and public services are relatively weak. According to international experience, the government fiscal transfer expenditure plays an important supporting role in realizing the specific policy objectives of the government, giving full play to the role of macro-control of finance, guiding the local reasonable allocation of resources, and promoting the development of local economy. The reform of the capital's system of an ecological civilization should enhance the intrinsic motivation of ecological protection, innovate the regional tax system, and explore the scale of tax sharing and tax transfer between ecological protection areas and optimized development areas and their ratios. A horizontal mechanism for ecological compensation should be established between the core areas of the capital and the distant suburban districts and counties, and between Beijing, the capital, and Tianjin, Hebei. Beijing should jointly formulate the Regulations on the Management of Ecological Compensation in the Capital with Tianjin and Hebei to clarify the jurisprudence and legal basis, so that the intra- and inter-generational ecological equity can be put on a legal track through the implementation of a mechanism for ecological compensation, and the ecological compensation funds may be raised from multiple sources.

9.5.1.3 Enhancing the reform of the energy system, vigorously developing new energy industries

The development of an ecological economy involves the field of energy economy, and the system of traditional energy supply and consumption has hindered the intensive use of resources and energy and the governance of energy emissions and environmental pollution. The reform of the energy system is an important measure for promoting economic growth, energy conservation, and emission reduction. The energy revolution mainly aims at solving the problem of excessive energy consumption. At the national level, it is recommended to coordinate the reform of state-owned enterprises and the energy industry, strengthen the market-oriented reform of the system of oil and gas and other industries, reform the system of the management of mineral resources, and bid for the transfer of undeveloped oil and gas blocks and unconventional oil and gas blocks, such as shale gas and shale oil. The system of circulation should be reformed, and entry should be allowed to the wholesale and retail activities and to the importation and exportation of oil and gas. The city should also deepen the reform of the electricity system, introduce a reform plan for the electricity system to withdraw the power grid from the role of unilateral purchaser, and realize direct transactions between power generators and electricity consumers, who can "buy more and sell more".[13] Beijing should take advantage of its energy and technological resources, enhance its innovation in new-energy technology, vigorously develop new-energy industries such as solar and wind power, increase the proportion of low-carbon renewable energy in the energy structure, and reduce carbon emissions and environmental pollution.

9.5.2 Strengthening the innovation of a system of environmental management, enhancing law enforcement of environmental protection

In order to advance the construction of an ecological civilization in the capital, it must reform and innovate the existing systems, institutions, and mechanisms that do not meet the requirements of an ecological civilization. Since the Third Plenary Session of the 11th Central Committee of the CPC, China has established a government-led system of environmental administration, and it has made certain achievements in ecological and environmental governance. However, the economic management and administration have not had the effective constraints on the extensive and externally expanding mode of economic development. As a result, many localities unilaterally pursue the growth of gross domestic product, and realize economic prosperity for a short period of time at the cost of destroying the ecological environment, with more and more consumption of natural resources, increasingly severe damage to the environment and more and more serious ecological deterioration. In the face of the serious situation, we must strengthen the institutional innovation of ecological environmental protection and pollution prevention, and strengthen the construction of a system of ecological civilization.

9.5.2.1 Strengthening the top-level design, establishing a vertical, comprehensive, and regional organization of ecological governance

Beijing should strengthen the top-level design, accelerate the innovation of the administration system of an ecological civilization, and explore the reform and innovation of the ecologically-oriented regional management system and assessment system with the transformation of government functions from the core. In terms of the system of management, innovations can be made by establishing a high-level coordination and decision-making body and introducing the reform of flat management at the grassroots level. The establishment of a high-level coordination and decision-making body for regions or fields of strategic significance is common to the design of systems of management both at home and abroad. This can, on the one hand, improve administrative efficiency, and avoid delaying the development of major strategies by following the traditional administrative procedures. On the other hand, it can also integrate resources from all aspects and focus on core issues. The development of an ecological civilization is different from conventional industrialized development, because it has an urgent need to establish a high-level coordination and decision-making body and break through the shackles of the backward administrative system. Aiming at the characteristics of ecological areas, such as a small population and a small economic aggregate, we can explore the implementation of the innovative reform of flat management at the grassroots level; establish an independent administration for ecological protection and strengthen the functions of ecological protection and management; and integrate the management resources of existing street offices and community workstations, reduce the administrative hierarchies, improve the administrative efficiency, and build a green government.

Beijing should strengthen the top-level design, play the role of the special group for the reform of the capital's system of ecological civilization, establish a vertical system of management of environmental protection, innovate the organizational structure and improve the capability of ecological and environmental governance. It should break the traditional system of setting up environmental protection agencies according to administrative regions, and keep local environmental protection agencies from being led and constrained by local governments in terms of personnel and funding. For the mechanism of management, the municipal environmental protection bureau should have sub-bureaus and dispatched agencies, whose personnel, finance, and properties are under vertical leadership and management, and delinked from the government at the district and county level. In the process of operations, we should reduce the pyramidal bureaucratic procedures, and introduce flat management, so that local environmental sub-bureaus and dispatched agencies can communicate directly with the municipal environmental protection bureau, in order to achieve vertical leadership and smooth communication, reduce the interference by local protectionism on environmental law enforcement, and enhance the authority and unity of environmental management.

The modern network platforms and technological means such as WeChat, online government, etc., should be utilized to an institutional mechanism of ecological governance that is vertical in leadership, flat in management and networking in information sharing.

Beijing should strengthen the construction of integrated environmental protection agencies, and based on the special group for the reform of the capital's ecological civilization system, integrate institutional resources, coordinate the strengths of the development and reform commission, environmental protection, landscape, agriculture, water, land, and other departments, deepen the reform of the administration system of resources and environment, and establish the interdepartmental coordination agencies of ecological civilization. The city should change the tendency towards weakening supervision, but strengthen its main responsibilities, authority, and status of the supervision of environmental protection agencies. It must avoid the phenomena of no management or multi-departmental management, incorporate all supervisions involved in environmental protection, ecology, etc. into the environmental protection agencies, clarify the responsible parties of environmental protection, and enhance punishment and hold accountable any violations according to law. The division of responsibilities between departments must be made clear to coordinate the work of environmental protection and ecological construction, and formulate environmental policies that coordinate environmental protection with economic development. The duties and powers of environmental protection should be reasonably divided between Beijing and the districts, the environmental protection agencies at the grassroots level should be enhanced, and the cross-regional environmental management should be strengthened. Beijing should enhance the building of teams of environmental protection, and increase staffing of environmental law enforcement according to the actual needs of environmental law enforcement and supervision. The environmental protection agencies should establish a joint law enforcement team together with traffic, water, and urban management authorities, so as to sink the law enforcement teams to the low levels, consolidate law enforcement teams in towns, communities, and villages, build an environmental law enforcement team that is "politically strong, diligent, good at work and strictly disciplinary", and improve the law enforcement and business competence of environmental protection agencies and the coverage of environmental law enforcement.

Beijing should strengthen the construction of the regional environmental management agencies in Beijing, Tianjin, and Hebei, and establish a joint prevention and control mechanism for environmental governance. Beijing should play a leading role as the capital, take the lead in coordinating with Tianjin, Hebei, and other neighboring areas to build a joint prevention and control mechanism for the construction of an ecological civilization in the capital's economic circle, establish the regional environmental management agencies, and realize the comprehensive pollution control, integrated planning of industrial layout, optimization of industrial structure, so as to achieve both economic development and environmental protection, and a win-win situation for environmental protection and economic development. The industrial distribution, planning of environmental protection, and control of pollution may be coordinated according to the regional social, economic, natural, and ecological situation, the previous division of management according to administrative units should be broken, and the situations of dispersive management, scattered forces, high cost but inefficiency in environmental management should be changed, in order to achieve comprehensive regional environmental governance, coordinated economic development, and harmonious and sustainable economic, environmental, and social development.

9.5.2.2 Seizing the key points of governance, strengthening the innovation of the governance system in the fields of air, water, and waste

Beijing should seize the key points in the fields of atmosphere, water, and waste. The special group for the reform of the capital's system of ecological civilization should further integrate the strengths of the special group for the reform of the system of atmospheric pollution control, the capital commission of environmental construction and the reform group of the capital's economic system, and give priority to the ecological environment. The municipal environmental protection bureau should enhance the supervision and evaluation of the construction of an ecological civilization and related environmental protection work by the planning, development, and reform commission, traffic, and industry and commerce authorities, and change the current situation by which traditional environmental protection gives way to economic construction.

First of all, Beijing should strengthen the institutional innovation of the governance of the capital's atmospheric environment. For strengthening the governance of air pollution in Beijing, President Xi Jinping put forward the basic principles and important points, such as treating both the symptoms and the root causes and giving equal importance to special treatment. In order to implement the spirit of President Xi Jinping's important speech, we must take new measures to increase the treatment of air pollution in Beijing and innovate the system of the governance of the atmospheric environment.

The first point is to give equal importance to treating both the symptoms and the root causes and applying special treatment. According to the results of atmospheric monitoring, PM2.5 has its principal sources in coal combustion, vehicle exhaust, dust, and industrial waste gas. In order to do well in the prevention and control of air pollution, we must find the crux of the problem, and identify the main polluting industries, sources, and factors. Smog is an important symptom of "urban diseases", but "urban diseases" and atmospheric diseases are mutually affected. The treatment of air pollution should first involve the treatment of "urban diseases" in order to treat both the symptoms and the root causes. For example, the control of vehicles needs the control of the population, the control of the population needs the control of the increase in the number of industries and jobs in the core areas, and the control of industries needs a reduction in or avoidance of the impulse towards GDP assessment and economic growth. The control of smog must be synergized with the decentralization of non-core functions and the control of an excessive concentration of core resources.

The second point is the coordination of regular treatment and emergency reduction of emissions. Strengthening the control of air pollution should become the new normal for Beijing's economic and social development. It should enhance environmental law enforcement, make it a normal, and strictly control pollution and emissions. The regular treatment of air pollution should be closely integrated with the development of new-energy vehicles, electric vehicles, slow-moving systems, afforestation, and other activities. To strengthen the emergency reduction of emissions, we should restart activities such as "car-free days" and traffic restrictions based on even- and odd-numbered license plates in heavy polluted weather.

The third point is that local pollution control and regional coordination should promote each other. The air pollution control in Beijing should pay attention to a further strengthening of local pollution control and enhance industrial transformation, coal reduction, and clean energy consumption. We should attach more importance to regional coordination, for example, strengthen docking and the coordinated governance of high-polluting industries, enterprises and cities in Hebei and Tianjin, cooperate to establish industrial optimization and upgrading mechanisms, jointly build the mechanisms of new service parks, tax sharing, talent, and science and technology information sharing, improve regional coordination and inner incentives for industrial transfer, and avoid transferring in a formal and hollow manner.

The fourth point is multi-strategy, multi-locality linkage, and joint action involving the whole society. Multi-strategy requires the combined use of multiple means and strategies, such as economic, legal, administrative, and information means. The Regulations on the Prevention and Control of Traffic Congestion and Pollution in the Capital should be enacted to levy the pollution emission tax and congestion tax on the exhaust emissions of motor vehicles, and raise the standards of parking fees, to guide and reduce the frequency and intensity of using motor vehicles. The multi-locality linkage requires the linkage of Beijing's core areas with functional expansion areas and ecological conservation areas, and the joint action of Beijing, Tianjin, and Hebei. The joint action of the whole society requires that Beijing should combat air pollution by allocating targets and tasks not only to districts and counties, but also to municipal enterprises and institutions, asking for instructions from the central government, and striving for the cooperation and joint action of central ministries and commissions, state units, central enterprises, and state-owned enterprises. It should strengthen the public participation and action of various social organizations and citizens, establish various associations, guilds, chambers of commerce, foundations, etc. of air pollution, and play the role of social forces and social capital to jointly combat air pollution.

The fifth point is to continuously focus on the governance of four areas, build a cross-regional coordinated system and mechanism for the governance of the atmospheric environment in Beijing, Tianjin, and Hebei, and strengthen the supervision of law enforcement. President Xi Jinping pointed out that we should continue to focus on the four key areas, coal, motor vehicles, industry, and dust, and take measures of reducing coal combustion, controlling vehicles and decreasing the need for oil, treating pollution and reducing emissions, cleaning, and dust fall. Beijing should accelerate the elimination of backward production capacity, transform and upgrade traditional industries, and actively develop a circular economy and a low-carbon economy. It must strengthen the outward relocation or transformation and upgrading of polluting industries in the capital, attach importance to the treatment of traffic exhaust, set management mechanisms for fee collection zones and low-emission zones, and vigorously combat air pollution. The city should emphasize the treatment of traffic exhaust, set up "fee collection zones" in the core urban areas of the capital, and specify that motor vehicles entering the core areas of the city must pay "congestion charges" or environmental pollution tax; the municipal environmental protection authority and traffic authority should jointly establish a monitoring and coordinated treatment center for traffic exhaust, set "low emission zones" within the fourth or third ring road, prohibit polluting vehicles from entering these zones, establish round-the-clock monitoring of motor vehicles with excessive emissions, and impose heavy fines on them; raise parking fees and increase penalties for disorderly parking to reduce the use of private cars, traffic congestion, and exhaust emissions from motor vehicles; require motor vehicles within Beijing's fifth ring road to use clean fuels, speed up the use of clean energy, and the installation of filters in buses and taxis to reduce emissions, strengthen law enforcement and inspection, and increase penalties for excessive exhaust emissions; encourage the use of electric vehicles, stipulate that license plates are to be issued for motor vehicles, improve electric-car-charging facilities, reduce the exhaust emissions of motor vehicles, and facilitate the improvement of the capital's atmospheric environment and ecological governance. The city must establish an early warning mechanism for monitoring and set the red line for the carrying capacity of the atmospheric environment. It should have strict assessment indicators, strengthen environmental law enforcement and supervision, and seriously pursue accountability. Given that the indicator of the concentration of Beijing's clean air action plan is not convenient for the operation of districts and counties and actual emission reductions, the reduction of motor vehicle emissions, industrial emissions, dust emissions, etc. should be used as the assessment criteria. Considering the difference in the air pollution base in districts and counties, the indicators for core areas, functional expansion areas, and ecological conservation areas should be designed in a hierarchical manner. Environmental protection agencies should integrate the strengths of public security, urban management, and family planning units to form comprehensive urban law enforcement teams, encourage the building of teams of environmental law enforcement wardens or volunteers, and enrich the environmental law enforcement forces at the grassroots level.

Beijing should establish a cross-regional coordinated system and mechanism for the governance of the atmospheric environment in Beijing, Tianjin, and Hebei, and strengthen strict law enforcement of pollution of the atmospheric environment. It is recommended that the special group for the reform of the capital's ecological civilization system should cooperate with Hebei and Tianjin on establishing a network of atmospheric environment information for the Beijing-Tianjin-Hebei region or the Bohai Rim and a platform for the release of information regarding pollution resources in the Beijing-Tianjin-Hebei region, should mandatorily require heavily polluting areas, industries and enterprises to set targets for pollution reduction or a schedule for phase-out, transformation, and upgrading, should make the annual tasks and targets of emission reductions clear, and should install monitoring equipment and related monitoring indicator facilities for all pollution sources in Beijing, Tianjin, and Hebei for pursuing real-time monitoring, feedback, and accountability, thus forcing the government and enterprises in heavily polluted areas to take rigid measures for continuous reduction of pollution, improvement of environmental protection and promotion of the construction of an ecological civilization in the capital and even in the Beijing-Tianjin-Hebei region. The sixth point is to promote clean energy and increase the construction of urban green areas. General Secretary Xi Jinping pointed out that for the promotion of clean energy, public transportation should be pushed forward. Based on the piloting of buses and taxis, considering how to reduce the total number of fuel vehicles in Beijing, in this book, we suggest taking measures for step-by-step realization of being clean and electric, fully promoting new-energy vehicles, striving to increase the number of new-energy vehicles to 50–60% of the total number of motor vehicles in 3–2 years, then replacing fuel vehicles year by year, and finally achieving the goal that all vehicles are new-energy vehicle and completely solve the problem of exhaust pollution.

Beijing should accelerate the formulation of implementation programs and policy measures for clean-energy vehicles in government agencies, devise a technology roadmap for clean-energy vehicles, improve related facilities, and construct charging piles in diversified ways such as government procurement, corporate sponsorship, and social participation. The city should enhance the technological research on and development of new-energy vehicles, improve battery technology, and reduce various costs regarding new-energy vehicles. Also, it must accelerate the transformation of the structure of energy consumption, encourage administrative units, institutions, schools, enterprises, social organizations, community residents to invest in the construction of distributed photovoltaic power plants on their own rooftops or vacant land. The national power grid should introduce convenient connection procedures and encouragement policies to vigorously develop new-energy sources such as photovoltaic and wind energy. Beijing must speed up the construction of urban greening and of an ecological civilization, fully implement the key projects of urban greening and beautification, lay stress on the construction of urban green infrastructures and green partitions, accelerate the construction of green ecological barriers in the capital, and improve the environmental carrying capacity and self-cleaning capacity of the atmosphere.

Second, Beijing should strengthen the innovation of the capital's system of water governance. It should enhance the reform and institutional integration of environmental protection, water affairs and other related departments for the governance of surface water and groundwater, establish and perfect a system of water governance for the whole process of river management, drainage management and protection of water sources, and integrate government departments related to water affairs or unify them into the special group for the reform of the capital's system of an ecological civilization. Beijing should actively promote the construction of ecological rivers, build an integrated treatment system of river basins, enhance systematic governance by the combination of points, lines, and faces, and establish a system of coordinated governance of water affairs in the capital. These points refer to key points and difficult points that can be resolved one by one. Reclaimed water plants should be distributed in a centralized and decentralized combination, and different kinds of sewage treatment facilities should be constructed for different types of pollution, with full consideration to local reuse after sewage treatment. Beijing should collect and treat sewage from the source, improve the network of collection pipelines of urban domestic sewage according to the layout of domestic pollution sources, complete the construction of intercepting pipelines along the line and the renovation of the combined flow of rain and sewage, strictly control and reduce the amount of sewage flowing into the river, and raise the standard of sewage treatment. Lines are divided into horizontal and vertical ones. Horizontal lines are based on the carrying capacity of water and biological resources in the river basin, and carry out the three layers of treatment from land ecology, water, and land, interlacing ecology to water ecology. Vertical lines are based on connecting rivers and creating a water landscape, constructing living rivers, restoring the biodiversity and gradually forming clean ecological corridors. Generally speaking, the comprehensive management of the river basin will drive the community ecological construction, from the ecological environment to the ecological economy and ecological humanities, build a clean community and green city, and develop a low-carbon green economy.

Third, Beijing should strengthen its institutional innovation of waste management in the capital. We should strengthen the fine management foundation of the whole process, strengthen the top-level design, take reduction as the basic approach, and explore the most strict management measures for emission source. According to different types of objects such as community, enterprise, and institution, rural area, the system of responsible person for garbage classification management shall be implemented, and the generation, discharge, and flow of all kinds of garbage in the city and various districts shall be further clarified, and the fine management basis shall be laid down. Unified waste classification and identification guidance system, unified technical specifications and setting standards of waste classification and collection facilities, unified planning of waste classification and separation, recycling and transportation system, and top-level scheme of effective connection and reasonable matching of front-end classification, recycling and transportation and incineration, biochemical and other treatment facilities, so as to promote collaborative development. With a focus on kitchen and food waste, Beijing should vigorously advance the construction of a system of waste classification, pilot the registration of kitchen waste discharge, and treat kitchen waste as local resources in places where the municipal party and governmental organs, government of districts and counties, schools, and star hotels are located. It should further improve the system of collection, transportation and treatment of waste classification, pilot the classification of waste in agencies directly affiliated to the central government, central state organs in Beijing and municipal party and governmental organs, pilot the new waste bins with the function of classification and collection in public spaces, and basically fulfill the task of renovating closed cleaning stations in urban areas.

9.5.2.3 Innovating the ecological system, establishing the systems of resource property rights, ecological compensation and public participation

First of all, a system of resource property rights should be established. The natural ecological space in the capital, such as water flow, forests, mountains, wastelands, and mudflats, are uniformly registered for confirming property rights and forming a property rights system for natural resource assets with clear ownership, clear rights and responsibilities, and effective supervision. The reform of the system of collective forest rights should be established and improved, and the system of the operation and management of state-owned forest areas should be perfected. An independent system of environmental regulation and administrative law enforcement must be built for the unified supervision of all pollutant emissions. An institutional mechanism for the protection and restoration of the ecological system and the regional linkage of pollution prevention and control should be established.

Second, ecological red lines should be scientifically delineated and protected. In the core areas, ecological conservation areas and functional expansion areas, the scope of red lines should be fully determined for forest land and forest resources, wetlands, management of stone desertification, farmland, water sources, management of water resources, protection of rivers and lakes, and of the species. The strict protection system of farmland, forest land, and water resources should be implemented, and the management of red line areas by classification should be practiced. In the first-tier control zones, all forms of development and construction activities are prohibited, and in the second-tier control zones, the development and construction activities that affect the main functions of the zones are prohibited. Within the fifth ring road, the approval of new construction land is restricted or delayed. The core areas aim at decentralizing low-end industries, diverting the population and reducing the pressure on resources, energy, and the environment, and they should expand the ecological red lines as much as possible, increase the land for landscaping and greening, and change the land destined for construction as the land for national parks in the capital.

Third, a mechanism for monitoring and early warning regarding the carrying capacity of resources and the environment should be established, and restrictive measures must be taken for areas exceeding the carrying capacity of water and soil resources and the environment. There should be adherence to the principles of paying for the use of resources and paying for the pollution of environment and damage to the ecology, speed up the reform of the prices of natural resources and their products, fully reflect the market supply and demand, the degree of resource scarcity, the cost of ecological damage and the benefits of restoration, and extend the resource tax to the occupancy of various natural ecological spaces.

Fourth, a mechanism of ecological compensation should be established. The market mechanism should play a decisive role in the allocation of resources for an ecological civilization in the capital, which must adhere to the principle of those who benefit and those who compensate, improve the mechanism of the ecological compensation for key ecological function areas, and promote the establishment of horizontal mechanisms of ecological compensation between the core areas of the capital and distant suburban districts and counties, and between Beijing and Tianjin, Hebei. Beijing should formulate the Regulations on the Management of Ecological Compensation in the Capital together with Tianjin and Hebei, and clarify the jurisprudence and legal basis, so that the intra-generational and inter-generational ecological equity will be put on a legal track through the implementation of the mechanism of ecological compensation, and raise ecological compensation funds from multiple sources. By the fiscal transfer of payments by the government, payments by ecological beneficiaries, payments by ecological users, ecological taxes, social donations, and other financing means, it can explore the establishment of a system of standards of ecological compensation, funding sources of ecological compensation, compensation channels, compensation methods, and a system of guarantees. In Yanqing, Huairou, Miyun, Pinggu, and other ecological conservation areas, the mechanism of ecological compensation has been implemented and properly extended to other areas. Beijing should actively pilot the trading of energy savings, pollution rights, and water rights, etc., and accelerate the establishment of a system of paid use and trading of chemical oxygen demand, sulfur dioxide, and other pollution rights. It should strengthen the construction of clean development projects, further the capital's system of carbon emissions trading, and expand the existing carbon trading market in Beijing to the Beijing-Tianjin-Hebei region and even to larger surrounding areas.

According to the plans for main functional areas, Beijing should establish the development and protection system of national land space and the spatial planning system of the capital, delineate the control boundaries for the development of production, living, and ecological space, implement the control of usages, and improve the system for the conservation and intensive use of energy, water, and land. It should clarify the boundaries of development, utilization, and protection of all kinds of land space, realize the classified and graded utilization of energy, water resources, and mineral resources according to their quality, and give full play to the maximum efficiency of resources.

Fifth, Beijing should establish and improve an educational system of ecological civilization, a national conservation system, a system of disclosure of environmental information, and a system of social supervision and reporting and public participation in the capital. It should use the economic and social strengths to boost the development of the environmental protection market, establish a market-oriented mechanism to attract social capital for investing in the protection of the ecological environment, and introduce the third-party governance of environmental pollution. The city should establish industry associations in key industrial fields related to the construction of an ecological civilization in Beijing, Tianjin, and Hebei. The industry associations, intermediaries and the public can play an effective role in socialized supervision, universal participation and third-party governance, strengthen the monitoring and annual ranking of emissions of enterprises in the industry, and enhance the industry supervision and emission reduction for seriously polluting enterprises. The government should punish polluting enterprises according to the assessment results of social organizations and third parties, achieve the phase-out, transformation and modification of polluting enterprises with strong social forces, and further promote the construction of an ecological civilization in the whole capital area.

9.5.2.4 Adhering to strict policies of farmland protection, improving the system of ecological land protection, establishing a land inspection system of the capital, establishing and improving the system for the transfer of development rights and plot ratio incentives

First, Beijing should push forward the integrated treatment of land, provide the "constructive" protection of farmland, freeze, and expropriate wasteland, forest land and wetlands with important ecological functions, reduce, or minimize land set aside for urban construction, and improve the ecological spaces in the capital city. It must strictly protect high-quality farmland, optimize the layout of land, raise the production capacity of farmland, stabilize the ecological environment, improve production and living conditions, bring into play the ecological functions of farmland, and create a good and livable idyllic landscape and living environment. The capital must increase the ecological spaces, relieve the environmental pressure, improve the carrying capacity of the environment, and establish a system of ecological land protection and entrusted management. The ecological land is land that serves important ecological functions, which are reflected in protecting the biodiversity, regulating the climate, nourishing the water sources, purifying the environment, preventing land degradation and reducing natural disasters, and maintaining the normal operations of regional life support systems. According to the capital's overall plans for land use, the system for controlling land use must be strictly enforced, the responsibility of land contractors for the protection of the ecological environment must be clearly defined, the protection of ecological land must be strengthened, the wasteland, forest land, and wetlands with important ecological functions must be frozen and expropriated, the amount of land used for urban construction must be reduced or decreased, the urban ecological land must be increased and protected, and the urban ecological spaces in the capital must be improved. Beijing must further improve and strictly implement the planning system of ecological land, the system for controlling the use of ecological land, the system of the ban on the expropriation of ecological land, the system of approval for the conversion of ecological land, and the system for balancing occupancy and compensation of ecological land. It must strictly protect high-quality farmland, optimize the layout of the land, raise the production capacity of farmland, stabilize the ecological environment, improve production and living conditions, give full play to the ecological functions of farmland, and create a good and livable idyllic landscape and living environment.

Beijing should abandon the greed for big-time construction. Modern civilization is not about tall buildings, dense factories, and smoking villages, but the pursuit of a livable, harmonious, and sustainable social state. By conservation and intensive use of the land, the city can take the road towards new urbanization, break the bottleneck of resource constraints, and achieve sustainable development. It must optimize the pattern of spatial development of land and increase the greening rate of the capital city. Land use should respect the laws of nature, which is the essential requirement for the construction of an ecological civilization. Based on the evaluation of the suitability of the land, the city should fully implement the overall strategy of spatial development of land; determine the direction of the development and utilization of the land at the capital level according to the geographical division of labor and productivity layout; build a "trinity" pattern of development, protection, and improvement, and promote the three-dimensional development of the whole area, so as to avoid development zones blooming everywhere, convergence and vicious competition of the industrial structure, blind expansion of new urban areas and disorderly development of backup resources. The core areas have a low carrying capacity of resources and the environment, so they should reduce the industrial layout and planning of land used for construction. The city should carry out protection by ecological red lines in the core area sand functional expansion areas, plan and distribute the construction of urban green spaces, construct more gardens and green spaces and fewer buildings, and strengthen the planning, design, and construction of three-dimensional green buildings.

Second, Beijing should establish a system of land inspection in the capital. Land inspection agencies are duty-bound to promote the construction and guarantee the realization of the strategic goals of an ecological civilization. The city must expand the number of inspections of the rationality of land usages and highlight the inspection of land use links; strengthen investigation and research, actively promote and guide the transformation of land usages and development ideas, and scientifically and reasonably use land in the inspected areas. It should highlight the implementation of planning, regular inspection, supervision, and accountability. The planning commission and environmental protection agencies should jointly enhance the investigation and punishment of illegal construction, raise the standards of punishment, maintain the legal authority of planning, and avoid illegal construction on green partitions and collective land, the continuous encroachment on ecological land, and the expansion of the urban boundary that leads to "pie-spreading".

Third, Beijing should establish and improve the system of transferring development rights and plot ratio incentives. It is suggested that the capital city should explore the policy of transferring development rights and plot ratio incentives into the ecological function areas for the overall transformation or urban renewal of areas involving historical and cultural heritage, and give additional compensation of building plot ratio to developers or development entities that can preserve the historical and cultural heritage. The plot ratio incentive refers to the authority of land development and management rewarding developers with a certain amount of building area in order to obtain their cooperation, on the premise of providing them with certain public space or for the protection of specific public welfare facilities (such as ancient cultural heritage buildings/monuments). The transfer of development rights, as a supplement and deepening of the application of plot ratio, broadens the scope of the reward by transferring the development rights in exchange for the protection of the ecological and historical environment or economic compensation on the premise that the development value of the land is affirmed by the authority of land development and management, and then the exchanged development rights are transferred to a place with more development value. The obvious advantage of the policy of plot ratio incentives and transferring development rights is that it can reconcile the contradictions between conservation, development, and construction. It is recommended that the capital should explore the policy of transferring development rights and plot ratio incentives when carrying out overall renovation or urban renewal of areas involving historical and cultural heritage in ecological functional areas: that is to say, the government-led policy of introducing social capital and giving additional compensation of building plot ratios to developers or development entities that can preserve the historical and cultural heritage.

9.5.2.5 Strengthening ecological administration, establishing a performance assessment system of an ecological civilization

Beijing should reform the existing system of the management of environmental protection and explore the establishment of a system of ecological administration. According to the requirements of the scientific outlook on development, the reform of the administrative system should play a key role, deepen the reform of the system of an ecological civilization, promote the transformation of the mode of economic development, realize the ecological mode of production and life, and advance the whole society to embark on the path of civilized development with the development of production, affluence of life, and good ecology. The government at all levels should assume important responsibilities for the protection of the ecological environment and effectively strengthen the government's public service function of ecological construction.

Beijing should establish a performance assessment system of the ecological civilization, and replace the traditional GDP-only performance assessment indicators with the indicators of an ecological civilization. It should formulate and adopt the Implementation Measures on the Assessment of the Goals for the Construction of an Ecological Civilization in the Capital, and take the superiority or inferiority of the integrated assessment indicators of the construction of an ecological civilization as an important content for comprehensively assessing the leading teams and leading cadres of districts and counties. It should implement the system of responsibility for the ecological environment, incorporate the consumption of resources, environmental damage and ecological benefits of districts and counties into the assessment system of economic and social development, and establish a target system, assessment methods and reward and punishment mechanisms that reflect the requirements of an ecological civilization in the capital. The government at all levels should be guided to value the investment in ecological construction, attach importance to the construction of urban green infrastructures and urban landscaping, and focus on the construction of green buildings, green transportation, green communities, etc.

Beijing should study and prepare the accounting system and balance sheet of natural resource assets in the capital, by combining general ledgers and journals. The general ledgers are used to reflect the total amount of natural resource assets in the capital, and the journals are used to reflect the value composition of a single natural resource asset and the stock of natural resources. Natural resources are divided into forest land, drinking water, wetlands, urban green areas, old and valuable trees, etc. The liabilities include indicators such as investment funds for the protection of drinking water resources, river management, etc. An accounting method with operability and quantitative assessment of natural resource assets should be constructed. The worse the quality of regional ecological environment, the smaller the equity in natural assets owned by management, and the further away they are from the attainment value of natural resource assets. Beijing should study and develop a system for the outgoing audits of natural resource assets in the capital, which should aim at leaders of municipal governments, various functional departments and departments of district and county governments, leaders of sub-district offices or executive deputy leaders. The content of audits includes: whether there is any damage or destruction to natural resource assets due to mistakes in individual decision-making; whether there is any illegal possession, waste, destruction or pollution of natural resources; and the investigation and handling rate of cases of illegal destruction of natural resources during the term of office, and the rate of closing the cases. According to the design of the system, the results of the outgoing audits of natural resource assets will be used as a reference for the appointment and treatment of leading cadres in the district. Those who seriously violate the state laws and regulations should be punished by the party and political disciplines; those who seriously damage natural resource assets should be dealt with by the discipline inspection and supervision organs; and those who are suspected of crimes should be handed over to judicial organs.

Beijing should improve the system of permissions for emissions of pollutants, control the total amount of pollutant emissions of enterprises and institutions, adopt a system of compensation for those who are responsible for causing ecological and environmental damage, and pursue against their criminal liabilities according to law. A system of lifelong accountability for ecological and environmental damage should be established. It must link the system of ecological environment with the systems of economic, political, cultural, and social construction to become a complete and seamless system of construction of an ecological civilization in the capital.

9.5.2.6 Establishing pilot zones for the comprehensive reform of an ecological civilization and a national park system

According to the goal of construction of an ecological civilization and the need for transformation of the mode of economic development proposed in the report of the 18th CPC National Congress, the reform of the system of ecological civilization in the capital can establish pilot zones for the comprehensive reform of an ecological civilization, and explore the path of reform for the mode of development of an ecological civilization. As a heavily polluted city, it is significant for Beijing to strengthen environmental protection and the construction of an ecological civilization. In the capital, especially in areas with relatively serious pollution and smog, such as Daxing, Tongzhou, Changping, Chaoyang, Dongcheng, and Xicheng, the national pilot zones for the comprehensive reform of an ecological civilization should be established to effectively promote that construction in the capital, have a typical demonstration effect in the country, boost the reform of the national system of ecological civilization and the construction of an ecological civilization, and play a leading and demonstrating role for the construction of a beautiful China and a beautiful city.

At present, Yanqing, Huairou, Miyun, and Pinggu are the ecological conservation areas of the capital, and Miyun and Yanqing have been selected as the national demonstration areas for the ecological civilization. The ecological construction of these districts and counties is relatively good, and the environmental pollution there is not as serious as what it is in the core areas of the capital and the functional expansion areas. Given that the core areas of Beijing suffer from the most serious urban pollution, ecological deterioration, and "urban diseases", these districts, such as Dongcheng, Xicheng, Chaoyang, Daxing, Changping, and Haidian, should be chosen as important pilot or experimental zones for the reform of the system of ecological civilization and the construction of an ecological civilization. The construction of an ecological civilization and its effect in these areas are directly related to the ecological and environmental protection of the city of Beijing. Since the core areas are seriously polluted, strengthening the construction of an ecological civilization in the capital should first enhance the construction of an ecological civilization in these seriously polluted areas. Therefore, the so-called demonstration and experimental zones for the construction of the ecological civilization should not be placed only in the conservation areas with a better ecological foundation, but also in the most seriously polluted core areas of the city. Because the policy innovation for the construction of an ecological civilization involves finance, land, administration, and other aspects, it should carry out the mission of early and pilot implementation, select heavily polluted areas as the national pilot zones for the comprehensive reform of the ecological civilization, study these core urban areas with relatively serious pollution and low carrying capacity of the environment, advance the construction of the ecological civilization in these areas through industrial adjustment, technological innovation and improvement of systems, and guide these areas to take the road towards ecological and low-carbon urban development that is good and fast.

Beijing should establish a system of national parks in the capital, strengthen the zoning, realize the unification of powers, responsibilities, and benefits, prevent departmental interests, and establish a unified system of the management of national parks in the capital. It must strengthen the integration of land planning, institutional settings, and other supporting systems of the capital's national parks from the perspective of urban development and public welfare, and complete the scientific investigation and master plans. For the main functional areas with national parks as the core function, the city must establish a system for the development and protection of the land space, build a funding mechanism mainly by financing from the high-level government, and improve the mechanism of ecological compensation for these areas in order to realize the innovation of the funding mechanism for national parks.

Beijing should integrate the strengths of multiple departments such as forestry, development and reform commission, planning, land, cultural relics, religion, and tourism to establish a unified system of the management of national parks in the capital and avoid problems such as multiple-party management and cross management. It should emphasize the comprehensive management of ecological and environmental resources in the national park area and the intensive use of the surrounding land, strengthen the planning, monitoring, and evaluation of the management of national parks, remove the limitations of departmental interests, and build an efficient system of resource management and operations.

Beijing should increase investment by the government, encourage social capital and social forces to actively participate in the construction of national parks, innovate the diversified financing mechanisms for their construction and operation, and improve the operating efficiency and social benefits of national parks. It should include the investment for the basic construction of parks and personnel expenses into the financial budget, increase the investment by the government, encourage social capital and social forces to participate in the construction of national parks on the basis of protection, encourage enterprises to assume social responsibilities, attract the participation of social capital by means of charity, sponsorship, and adoption, and establish and innovate a diversified financing mechanism for national parks. It should attract excellent talents, improve the configuration of infrastructure, and carry out normal management and care activities.

Beijing should increase the number and area of national parks within the Beijing-Tianjin-Hebei region. It should estimate based on the urban ecological capacity and the carrying capacity of the environment of the capital, and plan the unbuilt and unapproved vacant land in Beijing, especially within the sixth and fifth ring roads as the land for national parks so as to expand the capital's ecological land and ecological space, relieve the pressure on its resources, energy, and environment, improve its ecological carrying capacity, and reserve space for future development. In terms of land use, it should regard the strict control of the size of the city and its boundaries and the delineation of ecological red lines as rigid constraints, reduce the approval of construction land in the core urban areas, increase urban ecological land as much as possible, change land destined for construction to ecological land, further expand the scope of ecological land on the premise of protecting ecological red lines, mandatorily specify the construction of green buildings and rooftop greening and increase the urban ecological space and greening coverage.

9.5.3 Strengthening the innovation of the social system, actively fostering ecological and environmental organizations

The goal of construction of an ecological civilization is to achieve social justice, which requires the effective integration and cohesion of the strengths from all fields and classes of the society, promoting reforms that are consistent with the interests of the general public, being able to promptly reflect the will of the majority of the society, effectively integrating the will and interests of the majority of the society in the institutional reforms, institutional arrangements, and procedural design, establishing laws and systems that reflect social justice, centralize strengths, and consider interests, weakening conflicts of interest and social confrontation, promoting social progress, rebuilding the cultural and moral order, improving the ecological civilization in the deep structure, and maintaining social justice. Therefore, the reform of the system of ecological civilization in the capital needs to strengthen and pay attention to the ecological governance in the social fields. The innovation of the system of social governance reflects the integration of the strengths of various social fields and classes in the construction of an ecological civilization and their role as the main forces, embodies the institutional innovation of pluralistic participation, favorable interaction and grassroots democracy in the ecological civilization, thus being the institutional innovation to realize the construction of an ecological civilization from domination, management and control to treatment, good government, and good governance.

9.5.3.1 Clarifying the relationship among the government at all levels, individuals, and social intermediaries or civil organizations

The public interests, especially the interests of an ecological civilization, should be regarded as the highest pursuit of values. Beijing should incorporate and integrate the strengths, interests, and wisdom of the general public in the system of ecological civilization, and reach a consensus on the public interests of ecological civilization in the capital through pluralistic participation and in dialogue, communication, and exchange. The innovation of the system of social governance should reflect the joint participation of multiple parties, which should include, in addition to the government at all levels and their affiliated functional departments, enterprises, and institutions, various non-governmental organizations, social intermediaries, civil organizations, individual citizens, and private enterprises related to the construction of an ecological civilization.

9.5.3.2 Actively fostering social intermediaries for the construction of an ecological civilization and social service organizations of environmental protection, and actively promoting the third-party governance of environment

Beijing should establish a regular mechanism of environmental protection by the joint action of enterprises, government, and the public, enliven the social development of the construction of an ecological civilization, rely on the integration of resources of social forces and public organizations, and improve the level of social governance and social supervision of the construction of an ecological civilization. In order to activate social organizations in the construction of an ecological civilization, the city must accelerate the separation of government and the society, and clarify the rights and responsibilities, self-governance according to law, and the role of social organizations. Public services and matters that are suitable for social organizations in the field of ecological civilization should be provided and solved by social organizations. It should support and develop voluntary service organizations in the field of ecological and environmental protection, truly enable social organizations to take over the governmental functions of the construction of an ecological civilization and environmental governance, fulfill social responsibility, pool the public wisdom, and jointly strengthen the construction of an ecological civilization and environmental governance. The Third Plenary Session of the 18th Central Committee of the CPC clearly proposed "to establish a market-oriented mechanism to attract social capital for investment in the protection of an ecological environment and practice the third-party governance of environmental pollution". Third-party governance means changing the traditional government-led model of pollution control by enterprises. It emphasizes that enterprises emitting pollution should pay for pollution control services from environmental protection companies, social intermediaries for environmental protection and social service organizations, which have the obvious advantages of professional governance. The environmental protection agencies should centralize the supervision, reduce the costs of law enforcement, enhance the effects of pollution control and improve the environment. Beijing should establish a market-oriented mechanism to attract social capital for investment in the protection of the ecological environment and practice third-party governance of environmental pollution.

9.5.3.3 Strengthening the construction of ecological and low-carbon communities, improving the mode of social governance

Beijing should encourage and support the participation by community residents, and realize favorable interaction among the governance of the government, social self-regulation and residents' autonomy in the construction of an ecological civilization. It should adhere to the principles of governance from the source, community governance, treatment of both the symptoms and the root causes, and focus on treating the root causes, aim the directions of grid-based management, community-based services and ecological governance, improve the platform for the management of comprehensive services and the service network of community participation at the grassroots level, promptly reflect and coordinate the interests of the people in the construction of an ecological civilization, and enhance their awareness of ecological and environmental protection, as well as the awareness, ability, and level of participation in the construction of an ecological civilization.

9.5.4 Strengthening the innovation of the cultural system, creating a cultural atmosphere for ecological and environmental protection

Beijing should highlight the construction of an ecological civilization and ecological culture in the field of cultural development, and value the innovation of a cultural system in the field of ecological and environmental protection.

1 It must establish a cultural awareness of ecology and greenery and create a cultural atmosphere that attaches importance to the construction of an ecological civilization. It should enhance the country's cultural soft power of ecology, environmental protection, and low-carbon aspect; cultivate and practice the core values of a socialist ecological civilization in which mankind lives in harmony with nature; and raise the ecological cultural awareness of the whole society.
2 It should adopt a green and low-carbon lifestyle, enrich the connotation of an ecological culture, and take actions of conservation and emission reduction. It should make use of radio, TV, the Internet, WeChat, and other platforms for activities for the popularization of science on green and low-carbon life, guide residents in the capital to widely use energy-saving appliances and water-saving equipment, encourage green consumption, advance the green traffic, and promote green buildings.
3 It should establish a complete system of the ecological and low-carbon cultural market and attach importance to the development of ecological cultural industries. The reform of the cultural system should focus on the need to scientifically distinguish the boundaries between cultural undertakings and cultural industries, cultural market. It should not follow the traditional mode of management of cultural undertakings under the system of a planned economy, but activate the resource elements of the cultural market. For the management of cultural industries, the market mechanism should play a decisive role in the allocation of cultural resources, improve the mechanism for entry into and exit from the cultural market, encourage various market players to actively participate in the production and innovation of cultural products for ecological propaganda and ecological construction, and build a modern system of cultural communication of an ecological civilization.
4 It should build a system of public cultural services for the construction of an ecological civilization. Beijing must establish a mechanism of coordination for the construction of an ecological civilization, coordinate the construction of a network of service facilities, and promote the effective docking of ecological and cultural projects for the benefit of the public with the cultural needs of the masses. It should integrate facilities for the publicity of an ecological civilization, the popularization of ecological and environmental protection technology, and the fitness of green and environmental protection and build comprehensive ecological and cultural service centers.
5 It should protect and develop ecological and cultural resources, and build a number of areas for ecological and cultural reserves in the capital. With a long history as the national capital, Beijing has very rich resources of historical culture and ecological culture. These resources of ecological culture should not be covered and extinguished due to urbanization, and attention must be paid to maintaining the capital's diversity and individual characteristics of its ecological culture. The ecological protection of the capital's historical and cultural towns (villages) and neighborhoods

and traditional villages should be strengthened, and it should construct and form a number of publicity and education bases of ecological culture with a focus on green enterprises, low-carbon communities, and ecological villages.

9.6 Establishing a mechanism for social participation, solving social problems and achieving synergy of governance

The treatment of Beijing's "urban diseases" needs the collective participation of the general public, and it is difficult to rely on the government or enterprises alone to obtain achievements. The treatment of "urban diseases", urban construction, and management are definitely not just the responsibilities of a single governmental department, nor are they tasks that can be accomplished by the residents of the city, but a mechanism for social participation must be established to concentrate collective efforts and improve the capital's capability of the treatment of "urban diseases". Beijing has the resources of massive talents and a large population. If the advantages and potential of the existing talents or population can be unlocked, they will be turned into positive energy and productivity for Beijing's treatment of "urban diseases" and economic and social development, otherwise they are the pressure and burden for Beijing's urban development. Therefore, we must lay stress on Beijing's talents and population, and take effective measures to stimulate the vitality and creativity of the general public, which should become the consensus of every citizen of the capital. During the treatment of the capital's "urban diseases", it is necessary to establish a mechanism for the orderly participation of the public, so that they can work together to solve social problems and become active in governance.

9.6.1 Strengthening the quality education of citizens, enhancing the degree of civilization of urban citizens

The treatment of "urban diseases" cannot be achieved without the active participation of all citizens, their widespread support and practical actions. Beijing must enhance the civilized quality and the quality the education of its citizens, so that they can play a dominant role in the control of traffic congestion, environmental protection, waste recycling, energy saving, etc. The incidence of many "urban diseases", such as traffic congestion, disorderly parking, stall-keepers on roads, littering, and other problems, is related to some citizens who do not obey the order and rules. Hence, the quality of citizens determines the degree of urban civilization.

Beijing must strengthen the quality education of its citizens and the degree of civilization of urban citizens, and build a civilized city and a civilized Beijing-Tianjin-Hebei metropolitan area. It should enhance the spread of knowledge throughout the population and improve the education regarding the treatment of "urban diseases" and participation in urban construction, raise citizens' awareness of traffic rules, environmental protection, hygiene, services, etc., establish among its citizens a sense of ownership of the city, continuously improve the degree of civilization of those citizens, guide them to share the fruits of urban civilization, actively prevent and jointly participate in the process of treating "urban diseases". Through quality education and the spread of knowledge throughout the population, it can enhance ideas and the value orientation for the development of urban civilization, improve the moral standards of the citizens, and create a good atmosphere of social opinion and spiritual support for the treatment of "urban diseases".

9.6.2 Building smooth channels and mechanisms for citizens' participation in urban governance

The treatment of "urban diseases" requires the extensive and orderly social participation of the citizens. We must not only raise the awareness of participation, but also open up the channels, mechanisms and platforms for participation, so that the strengths of the public can be promptly transformed into positive energy and intrinsic motivation for the development of the capital. The orderly participation of citizens will not only resolve various conflicts, but it will also pool the wisdom and strengths of citizens, facilitate the prevention and treatment of "urban diseases", and truly reflect the tenets that people love the city for the people, people build the city of the people, and the city is built for the people. Therefore, we need to further open up the channels and mechanisms for the expression of public opinion, encourage citizens to make suggestions for the treatment of "urban diseases", encourage citizens to participate in the treatment of "urban diseases" and in the supervision of urban construction, and improve the quality and level of urban construction in the capital.

Encouraging and guiding the public to participate in the urban governance of the capital is a sacred mission and inevitable requirement to reflecting the people-oriented, socially responsible construction of a better capital. Beijing has a large population with a complex structure, because the resident population exceeds 20 million, and its structures of social classes, interests, and demands are increasingly differentiated. It is located at the hub of the flowing population, materials and funds. There are millions of members of the floating population. In such a case, it is a very huge project to promptly know the dynamics and information and guide the public opinion. The only way to meet the challenge and solve the dilemma is to build a public platform and long-term mechanism for the participation of citizens.

First, Beijing must strengthen the guidance and diversion of the floating population, raise the awareness of citizens to participate in and care about the development of the city, jointly treat the "urban diseases", give up uncivilized social behavior and create a good atmosphere of urban civilization.

Second, Beijing must enhance the services, management, and guidance of the floating population, establish an early warning mechanism for the orderly flow and decentralization of the population, improve the comprehensive mechanism of social security and social participation, and facilitate the harmonious, stable, and healthy development of the capital. Third, citizens should be guided to participate in the supervision and evaluation of urban planning and construction, so as to eliminate various "urban diseases" at the bud. For example, many green areas are occupied by illegal construction. If citizens can actively participate in the supervision and promptly report on illegal activities, and there are special institutions and personnel responsible for implementation, many "urban diseases" can be dealt with and prevented in a timely manner, so as to not only reduce losses, but also create a good environment for urban development. For overcoming the traditional difficulties such as indifferent participation of citizens, unsmooth channels for participation and obstruction of participation, we should establish a long-term mechanism for timely communication, interaction and supervision between citizens and the government.

9.6.3 Fostering various social organizations for the treatment of "urban diseases" in the capital

According to the theory of new public management, the government should change from the traditional regulatory and monopolistic type to the service-oriented and market-oriented type, strengthen the transformation of governmental functions, and outsource or entrust more public services that can be socially undertaken and completed to social organizations or enterprises, especially third-party sectors and other non-profit social organizations, which can play a role that cannot be replaced by the government in undertaking various social public affairs. During the treatment of "urban diseases", we must also rely on the active participation of social organizations. The third-party sectors can make up for failures of the government and the market, play the role of intermediary and bridge for social organizations, and actively participate in various aspects of the treatment of "urban diseases", such as governance, supervision, and evaluation. Social organizations should take the initiative in undertaking the transformation of governmental functions and play an important role in the treatment of "urban diseases", thus reflecting the principle of building and sharing the capital city. Beijing should establish a long-term mechanism of cooperation among citizens, social organizations, enterprises, and governmental departments, concentrate efforts on the treatment of "urban diseases", and play the role of participation of the public and social organizations in various fields such as decentralization of non-capital functions, diversion of the population, relocation of industries, environmental governance, and traffic diversion.

9.6.4 Strengthening the building of teams for urban management, modernizing the capacity and system of urban governance

The governmental departments at all levels should raise awareness about, attach great importance to the governmental functions of supervision, control and services in the treatment of "urban diseases", and improve the capacity and level of urban governance. The higher the concentration of the population, the more order and rules are needed, otherwise chaos is likely to occur. The incidence of "urban diseases" is related to the inability of city managers to organize urban production and life, and any city with an expanding population needs to improve the capacity and system of urban governance. Beijing is an international metropolis and the capital of a developing country. The advent of urbanization and post-industrialization puts forward many new requirements for urban governance. The city must undertake arduous tasks of serving the central government and the people of the capital. The treatment of "urban diseases" urgently needs to enhance the urban management and team-building of urban construction. On the one hand, we must enhance the quality and level of knowledge of the urban management team so that they can meet the high requirements of modernization and metropolitan management. On the other hand, the government must enhance the execution and credibility of policies, take the initiative in performing their duties well, respond to the expectations and various needs of the public in a timely manner, and strengthen the prevention and treatment of "urban diseases" and various risks that may arise. From training, selection, and appointment to assessment and evaluation of cadres, we should strengthen the building of teams and the organization of urban governance, continuously improve the basic ability of urban governance, respond to major emergencies and risks, and realize the modernization of the capacity and the system of the urban governance of the capital.

9.7 Advancing the coordinated low-carbon development of the Beijing-Tianjin-Hebei Region, and accelerating the decentralization of non-capital functions

The so-called coordinated low-carbon development refers to strengthening multiparty coordination and cooperation with the goal of low-carbon development, jointly changing the traditional model of high-carbon growth based on integration, coordination and cooperation, and developing a low-carbon economy with low energy consumption, a low degree of pollution and high efficiency. Coordinated low-carbon development lays stress on the basic principles of coordination, cooperation, and integration, strengthens the innovation of low-carbon technology and system, continuously improves the efficiency of the utilization of energy of the whole region, actively develops new energy sources and low-carbon industries, reduces carbon emissions, and forms a low-carbon and efficient economic system.[14] The coordinated development of the Beijing-Tianjin-Hebei region provides the good opportunities of policy and development for the treatment of the capital's "urban diseases" and the decentralization of non-capital functions. On April 30, 2015, the meeting of the Political Bureau of the CPC Central Committee considered and adopted the Planning Outline for the Coordinated Development of the Beijing-Tianjin-Hebei Region, which pointed out that promoting the coordinated development of the Beijing-Tianjin-Hebei region is a major national strategy, and its core is the orderly decentralization of Beijing's non-capital functions. The realization of the coordinated development of the Beijing-Tianjin-Hebei region, change in the traditional model of extensive urban growth with high energy consumption, high pollution, and high emissions, and avoidance of the traditional "pie-spreading" pattern of urban development should be guided by the direction and principle of resource intensive, environmentally friendly, green low-carbon development to boost the coordinated development of the Beijing-Tianjin-Hebei region. For the treatment of the capital's "urban diseases", we must look beyond Beijing, change the traditional thinking of "care only about one's own interests", and take the road towards coordinated low-carbon development of innovation, coordination, green, openness, and sharing.

First, innovative development can break through the inertia of the traditional path, innovation can unleash new energy and strength, and the innovation drive is an important engine in the coordinated development of the Beijing-Tianjin-Hebei region. Innovative development is the core driving force of historical progress, the key support for the development of the times, and the eternal topic of future development. Comrade Xi Jinping put forward the "Five Concepts for Development", namely innovation, coordination, green, openness, and sharing, at the Fifth Plenary Session of the 18th Central Committee of the CPC, which put innovation in the first place, point out the direction and requirements of China's development, represent the current trend of development in the world and reflect the deepening of the CPC's understanding of the law of development. Innovation is the basis for continuous development and advancement, and the core of the overall development of the country. Innovation, especially scientific and technological innovation, has become a theme, a tide and a trend in the world. A new round of scientific and technological revolution and industrial change is ready to start worldwide, and the information technology, biotechnology, new-material technology and new-energy technology are penetrating widely. The world's major countries are actively strengthening the deployment of innovation, such as the United States' re-industrialization strategy and Germany's Industry 4.0 strategy. Putting innovation at the core position of the developmental landscape reflects the firm determination and historical commitment of the CPC Central Committee with Comrade Xi Jinping as the General Secretary.[15] Scientific and technological innovation is the first productive force. The accelerated development of the Beijing-Tianjin-Hebei region must adhere to the double-wheel drive and role of the engine of scientific and technological innovation and cultural innovation, and achieve the transformation and leap-frog development of the Beijing-Tianjin-Hebei region driven by innovation.

Second, coordinated development is an essential part of the coordinated development of the Beijing-Tianjin-Hebei region, which aims at facilitating the communication and coordination among different areas, promote the coordination of interests and policies, and finally achieve the joint development and a win–win situation. The coordinated development of the Beijing-Tianjin-Hebei region should be strategically considered on a larger regional scale. That is to say, to achieve the coordinated development of different administrative areas, the capital, as a concept on a larger regional scale, should not be limited to the administrative division of Beijing, but cover a large city circle of Beijing, Tianjin, and Hebei. Through the coordinated and joint development of the three regions, we can accelerate the decentralization of non-capital functions, moderately disperse the over-concentrated resources in the capital, and achieve balanced allocation and optimized configuration of resources. Only this way can we truly solve the problems of Beijing's "urban diseases", and change the siphoning effect of Beijing as the economic, political, educational, and medical heights on Hebei and Tianjin's talents and capital.

Third, green development is the inevitable choice for resolving the problems of serious smoggy weather and deterioration of ecological environment in the Beijing-Tianjin-Hebei region. Green low-carbon development is the road to sustainable development, but the traditional model of extensive development with high carbon and high emissions is not sustainable. We must strengthen the transformation and upgrading of industries with high energy consumption and high emissions in the Beijing-Tianjin-Hebei region, especially in Hebei and Tianjin, and attain new heights by green and low-carbon development. In order to change the traditional model of extensive development with high energy consumption, high pollution and high emissions, we must take the road towards low-carbon, green and ecological development so as to build an international first-class harmonious and livable city.

Fourth, open development is a necessary condition for the coordinated development of the Beijing-Tianjin-Hebei region. Connections and communications among the three regions are important aspects of opening-up, and the three regions also strengthen opening-up and communications with domestic and foreign resources. Only through opening-up and reform can we achieve new coordinated development.

Fifth, sharing development is the ultimate goal of the coordinated development of the Beijing-Tianjin-Hebei region. On the one hand, the purpose of the coordinated development of the Beijing-Tianjin-Hebei region is to serve the people, not the people of one region, but the people of the three regions, all of whom should share the fruits of the development. On the other hand, the development of the three regions cannot be achieved without the participation and wisdom of the people, and the people of the three regions need to pool their wisdom and collective efforts, strengthen the coordinated development of the Beijing-Tianjin-Hebei region, and serve the leapfrog, sustainable and low-carbon development of the three regions.

Guided by the above five concepts, this book proposes that the coordinated development of the Beijing-Tianjin-Hebei region should adhere to the concept of low-carbon development, in which coordination embodies the connotations of innovation, coordination, openness, and sharing, while the low-carbon aspect reflects that the coordinated development must follow the basic principle of green and low carbon, adhere to green and low-carbon innovative development, coordinated development, open development, and shared development. To be specific, the following paths of development should be adopted:

9.7.1 Strengthening the macroscopic layout of the coordinated low-carbon development of the Beijing-Tianjin-Hebei region

In order to promote the coordinated low-carbon development of the Beijing-Tianjin-Hebei region according to the theory of a low-carbon city and the strategic needs for the construction of an ecological civilization, a leading group for the coordinated development of the Beijing-Tianjin-Hebei region must be established at the national level, with the group for the construction of an ecological civilization responsible for the construction of an ecological civilization and low-carbon development of Beijing, Tianjin and Hebei. The framework for cooperation on organization, legal system and information technology should be constructed for the coordinated low-carbon development of the Beijing-Tianjin-Hebei region. At the strategic heights of the construction of an ecological civilization, functional distribution and balanced development, Beijing's non-core functions should be diverted to Tianjin and Hebei to promote the coordinated and balanced development of Beijing, Tianjin, and Hebei. Considering the pressure of Beijing's urban population, resources and traffic, except high-tech R&D, high-end services, and high-grade manufacturing industries, Beijing should relocate general manufacturing, industries not belonging to core functions, most central enterprises, some institutions or non-core administrative agencies to Hebei and Tianjin, and channel capital, human resources, and some administrative resources for the coordinated development of Tianjin and Hebei, so that the three regions can complement each other in terms of industrial layout and economic form, avoid duplication and similarity as much as possible, and form relative advantages in high-end manufacturing. Hebei plays an important role in taking over industries transferred from Beijing and Tianjin and adjusting the general layout of functions. The three regions must transition from multi-win to win-win with staggered development, and gain the relative competitive advantages and synergies. For the development of a low-carbon economy, the active cooperation and joint participation of the governments of Beijing, Tianjin, and Hebei are required to prevent the monopoly of industries, promote market competition, and prevent the regional monopoly of a low-carbon economy.

9.7.2 Strengthening the innovation of low-carbon technology and industrial division of labor, establishing a public service platform for low-carbon science and technology

The government at all levels in the Beijing-Tianjin-Hebei region should pay special attention to measures in low-carbon technology and encourage technological innovation. Beijing should actively make use of its advantages in R&D and talents to develop low-carbon technology and strengthen information exchange in the field of low-carbon technology in the Beijing-Tianjin-Hebei region. It should actively explore the mechanism for cooperation and innovation in low-carbon technology, facilitate the horizontal cooperation of universities, research institutes, and enterprises in the three regions, and advance the research, development, promotion, and application of low-carbon technology. The construction of an ecological civilization and coordinated low-carbon development should strengthen the collaborative division of labor in industries, avoid homogeneous and vicious competition, carry out a reasonable division of labor in different parts of industrial chains and achieve the complementarity of functions. In the case of Baoding's manufacturing of solar and wind energy equipment, the energy-saving services and the applications of new energy industries should be encouraged in various districts and counties in Hebei, Tianjin, and Beijing. It is recommended to set up R&D centers for low-carbon technology and other terminals for consumption and application of low-carbon products in Beijing, and promote solar-powered street lights, photovoltaic buildings, solar water heaters, etc. on a large scale. The solar and wind energy equipment and products made in Baoding can be widely used in various districts and counties in Beijing, and the manufacturing can be retained in Baoding, where there are convenient traffic and abundant resources and manpower. The development of low-carbon industries in Beijing, Tianjin, and Hebei should emphasize the integration and complementary advantages of these resources, accelerate the establishment of a public service platform for low-carbon science and technology, break through the barriers of the administrative system, provide high-quality services for low-carbon development in the Beijing-Tianjin-Hebei region, such as the information sharing of low-carbon science and technology, the integration of resources, the diffusion and transformation of low-carbon technology, and industrial incubation, promote the division of labor, gradient transfer and the concentration of low-carbon industries among different areas in Beijing, Tianjin, and Hebei, and build an integrated mechanism of low-carbon innovation with complementary functions, a macroscopic layout and market interconnection.[16]

9.7.3 Strengthening the talent development of low-carbon technology, providing a guarantee for the cooperation of Beijing, Tianjin, and Hebei

The talent development and the building of teams in low-carbon technology should be accelerated to provide talent support and basic guarantees for the low-carbon cooperation and development of Beijing, Tianjin, and Hebei. The related majors and courses of low-carbon technology may be offered to foster, attract, and retain talents of low-carbon technology. In the case of the Beijing-Tianjin-Hebei region, the education related to the low-carbon economy and low-carbon technology may be given at different levels of higher education, such as vocational, undergraduate, and postgraduate education, and universities and enterprises are encouraged to cooperate on the development of talents. With Beijing at the center, a regional cooperation platform should be built for cultivating human resources in low-carbon technology and giving full play to the advantages of cooperation in the education industry. The Beijing-Tianjin-Hebei region should improve the policies to facilitate the mobility of talents, break the restrictions on hukou (household register), strengthen the equalized supply of public services in the three regions, change the current recruitments limited to Beijing hukou only and extend it to cover those with hukou of Beijing, Tianjin, and Hebei, gradually unleashing the shackles of identity and hukou, narrowing and equalizing the gap of interests between Beijing hukou and those of Tianjin and Hebei, removing the institutional barriers that restrict the free mobility of factors, especially talents, and boldly reforming the systems of personnel management and hukou management, so that the labor force can move freely and voluntarily according to market rules.

9.7.4 Introducing carbon trading in the Beijing-Tianjin-Hebei region, building a mechanism for ecological compensation

General Secretary Xi Jinping clearly proposed to expand the environmental capacity and ecological space and strengthen cooperation in the protection of the ecological environment. The coordinated low-carbon development of the Beijing-Tianjin-Hebei region initiates the coordinating mechanism for the prevention and control of air pollution, improves the long-term mechanism of cooperation in the fields of the construction of protective forests, the protection of water resources, urban greening, environmental governance and the use of low-carbon energy, pilot the system of assessment for the intensity of carbon emissions, explore the institutional mechanisms for the control of greenhouse gas emissions, and introduce carbon emissions trading in specific areas or industries.[17] First, the three regions should actively introduce carbon trading, strengthen cross-provincial and cross-basin coordinated governance, positively advance the joint prevention and control of atmospheric pollution, improve the regional ecological environment, expand the environmental capacity, extend the ecological space, and achieve coordinated economic, social, and environmental development. Second, they should explore the system of joint ecological protection in the Beijing-Tianjin-Hebei region, and set up a special fund for regional ecological compensation, which can be used for compensating the loss of rights to the use of water resources and ecological forest land. The compensation of Beijing and Tianjin for Hebei in reforestation, the transfer of water resources and the transformation of rice fields to dry land should be increased, and a long-term mechanism of ecological compensation must be established. Third, through the mechanism of ecological compensation, they should establish an industrial system oriented towards low-carbon development and help underdeveloped areas to establish a mechanism for coordinated development and cooperation in low-carbon fields.

9.7.5 Creating self-owned brands of low carbon, enhancing the development of low-carbon industrial clusters

The coordinated low-carbon development of the Beijing-Tianjin-Hebei region should seize the opportunities of low carbon and coordinated development, strengthen the construction of self-owned low-carbon brands, accelerate the transformation, phase-out or upgrading of industries with high energy consumption, and open some new low-carbon industrial parks. Hebei Province should purposefully cultivate and develop the clusters of emerging industries, high-end industries, and low-carbon industries. The three regions should create self-owned low-carbon brands, emphasize the planning of industrial clusters and the publicity of low carbon, strengthen the construction of related facilities from proposing concepts to brand packaging, registration and online operation, and offer preferential policies in tax relief, technological innovation, infrastructure, land use, and administrative approval. The Beijing-Tianjin-Hebei region should strengthen the leading role of the government in the industrial clusters of low-carbon activities, create a favorable environment for enterprises, and build up the clusters of low-carbon enterprises with different characteristics according to the different advantages of localities.

9.7.6 Decentralizing non-capital functions, building six service circles for the coordinated low-carbon development of the Beijing-Tianjin-Hebei region

The key to decentralizing non-capital functions and ensuring that these industries, population and other factors can flow out lies in the integrated and equalized development of infrastructure and public services such as traffic, education, healthcare, culture, and sports. The existence of objective and subjective disparities in infrastructure and public facilities makes it difficult to attract the transfer of Beijing's non-core functions. Therefore, it is necessary to strengthen the coordinated and integrated development of infrastructure in Beijing, Tianjin, and Hebei. On the one hand, we should continue to increase the total supply of infrastructure. For example, Beijing's subway construction still has a lot of "historical debts", insufficient density and coverage, and inadequate radiation over the surrounding areas; thus it lags behind international cities like Tokyo, London, and New York. We must increase the total supply, reduce the historical debts, and continuously alleviate Beijing's traffic congestion. On the other hand, we should pay attention to the construction of several "coordination circles" in the Beijing-Tianjin-Hebei region.

First of all, the construction of subway circles in the Beijing-Tianjin-Hebei region. Unlike the existing national railway system, the subway system, including the urban light railway, has the advantages of one card, convenient interchanging, short waiting time, and low fares. Accelerating the docking of the subway in Beijing with those in the surrounding cities of Tianjin and Hebei can effectively ease the traffic pressure and promote the coordinated development of the surrounding areas. For example, in order to solve the current problems of "tidal waves" in commuting hours and difficulty of taking buses in Yanjiao, Line 6 or the Baitong Line should be extended to Yanjiao and Xianghe as soon as possible.

Second, the construction of an ecological protection circle. A circle of coordinated development of green infrastructure should be established with joint plans and construction.

Third, the construction of an education service circle. The three regions should unify the policies and treatment of college entrance examinations. Colleges and universities from Beijing may have campuses in Hebei and Tianjin, or relocate some colleges and universities affiliated to the Ministry of Education, or the undergraduate or postgraduate education to Hebei, so as to advance the decentralization of the population to Hebei.

Fourth, the construction of a medical service circle. Prestigious hospitals or specialty hospitals may establish branches in Hebei, such as the Union Medical College Hospital and the 301 Hospital. An industrial park of medical services for the Beijing-Tianjin-Hebei region could be planned and constructed, and in this park, there would be branches of major hospitals in Beijing, for the sake of diverting and decentralizing the working population and those accompanying patients in Beijing.

Fifth, the construction of a tourism service circle. The advantageous tourism resources of Beijing, Tianjin, and Hebei can be integrated for coordinated development. There are rich tourism resources and great historical and cultural heritage locations in the three regions, which are not interconnected. Tourism enterprises, relevant governmental departments, social organizations of tourism in the three regions do not have in-depth cooperation and collaborative innovation, so it is difficult to profit from group advantages and the clustering effect. In the case of Beijing, tourism resources are not well integrated and developed, there are serious homogenization and fierce competition, tourism facilities are not perfect, the six areas have not been improved and integrated, namely food, accommodation, traffic, entertainment, shopping and visiting, and the whole Beijing-Tianjin-Hebei region does not have a good service chain.

The purpose of strengthening the construction of a tourism service circle in the Beijing-Tianjin-Hebei region is to fully integrate tourism resources of districts and counties of Beijing, sufficiently integrate the high-quality tourism resources of the surrounding areas, including Hebei and Tianjin, select the best tourism lines according to different characteristics, jointly launch a travel pass covering a number of tourist attractions in Beijing, Tianjin, and Hebei, carry out large-scale network marketing and online sales, enhance the advertising of tourism, improve the quality of services, prevent improper behavior such as rip-offs and deception, and improve the brand quality and image of tourism in the three regions. Given the facts that tourist attractions in Beijing are overwhelmed by tourists during holidays and there are problems of poor services, over-concentration of population and traffic congestion, a tourism service circle in the Beijing-Tianjin-Hebei region should be established for reasonable diversion of tourists, so as to meet their consumption needs from multiple aspects and at multiple levels and improve the level of the services of the tourism industry. The problems of "urban diseases" are being solved, and meanwhile a tourism service company of the Beijing-Tianjin-Hebei region may be founded to increase the tourism service industry into a big and strong industry, highlight its integrity, improve the innovation capacity of tourism services, constantly enhance the quality and efficiency of the tourism industry and facilitate the coordinated development of the Beijing-Tianjin-Hebei region.

The construction of a tourism service circle in the Beijing-Tianjin-Hebei region should accelerate the establishment of a working mechanism for the coordinated development of tourism, and expedite the integration of tourism organizations; further mutually expand the tourism market, and speed up the integration of tourism markets; deepen cooperation in tourism supervision, accelerate the integration of tourism management; strengthen the overall arrangements of important issues such as the development of the tourism industry, planning, and project construction, and accelerate the integration of the coordination of tourism.

Sixth, the construction of a cultural and sports circle. The cultural and sports facilities in the Beijing-Tianjin-Hebei region can be put under unified plans and construction, sharing of resources, and joint organization of large-scale international or national events. Beijing is the international communication center and the national sports and cultural center, and Tianjin and Hebei also have abundant sports resources and historical and cultural resources. Such resources should be integrated to establish a cultural and sports circle in the Beijing-Tianjin-Hebei region, including "one core and three rings". The core areas comprise Beijing, Tianjin, and Langfang, which aim to develop sports clubs, are suitable for the development of projects of indoor fitness and short-distance tourism, widely carry out marketing activities, and promote the sports tourism business and characteristics of the other three rings. This is the core of the entire cultural and sports circle. The first ring area consists of Baoding, Tangshan, Zhangjiakou, and Chengde, which are also the focal point of development. The second ring area includes Shijiazhuang, Qinhuangdao, and Cangzhou, where appropriate sports tourism projects according to the local characteristics should be designed. The third ring area is composed of Xingtai, Handan, as well as Inner Mongolia, Northeast China, Shanxi, Shandong, etc. Currently, with the further improvement of traffic conditions, a one-hour circle of high-speed rail or an intercity railway circle is gradually taking shape, and the fast and convenient high-speed railway, one-stop access to tourist attractions, and a smooth high-speed road network constitute a half-hour or one-hour tourism circle in the Beijing-Tianjin-Hebei region, thus promoting the integration of tourism and the construction and development of a tourism service circle.

The above six circles for the coordinated development of the Beijing-Tianjin-Hebei region should establish a new service network of coordinated development, facilitate the equalized supply, integrated construction and balanced distribution of basic public services through integrated, coordinated, and networked development, share the fruits of urban development of the capital, jointly realize the convenience, comfort, livability, and happiness of urban life and work, and work together to treat the capital's "urban diseases". Through the key construction of the above six service circles, we can advance the equalized supply of infrastructure and public services in the Beijing-Tianjin-Hebei region, improve related service facilities and industrial development, effectively attract talents, capital and industries to Hebei and Tianjin, boost balanced, low-carbon and coordinated development, and provide the support and basis for developing a world-class city cluster.

9.8 Innovating the model of urban management, advancing urban intelligence and building a smart capital

The treatment of "urban diseases" is a systematic project that needs to innovate the mode of urban management and strengthen the delicacy management of the city. The delicacy management highlights the perfect pursuit of urban managers for the treatment of "urban diseases", the rigorous attitude to urban governance and the mind of pursuing excellence, the introduction of advanced technology for systematic thinking and process optimization, improvement and upgrading of urban governance, and the use of standardized, procedural, data-based, and scientific means to allow urban governance to become more precise, efficient, collaborative and sustainable. The treatment of "urban diseases" needs to innovate the methods of urban management, focus on the standardized process, regulated operation, optimized resources, quantified responsibility, supervision and control according to the law of the operation of metropolises, realize the service concept of urban governance, pay attention to details and institutionalized management, and improve the level of urban governance, service efficiency, and the quality of management.

Beijing must innovate its modes of urban management, enhance the level of grid management, and pull down the center of urban management. The so-called grid management is an innovation of the management model based on digital technology, with the management of grids as a basic feature, and the systematic re-engineering of ideas, means, organizational structure and workflow of urban management as the important content. Compared with the traditional model of urban management, the grid management has unique features, which are mainly reflected in the characteristics and concepts of digital, closed-loop, delicacy and dynamic management. The key technologies are: first, 3S technology, namely Geographic Information System (GIS), Global Positioning System (GPS), and Remote Sensing (RS). Second, distributed database and distributed computing technology. A distributed database is a system composed of interrelated databases, and the design of distributed database requires the use of distributed computing technology. Third, grid and grid computing technology. Grid computing is the connection of computers and information resources. Fourth, components and component library technology. Components refer to software components that can be used to construct reusable software and other software, and they may be encapsulated object classes, class trees, functional modules, software architectures, analytics, design patterns, etc. The basic characteristics of the grid management model of a city are shown in Table 9.2.[18]

Beijing, as an important practice base of the grid management model, should further strengthen the experience of networked management, enhance sub-districts and communities, give full play to the political advantages of Beijing's citizens, who are to have good quality, high political awareness, and strong executive power, and focus on autonomy of urban communities and urban self-management. By the grid, participatory and coordinated governance, we can effectively prevent and control "urban diseases" such as traffic congestion, reduce simple and mechanical administrative interventions, emphasize the regulation of urban traffic management by laws, policies and self-governance of communities, use economic means, ideological education and other means, guide citizens of the capital to choose green and low-carbon traffic, and facilitate the construction and development of low-carbon traffic in the capital. By grid, participatory and coordinated governance, we can resolve the problems of "urban diseases", play an important role in solving many urban social problems such as group housing rental, unemployment, juvenile delinquency and beggars, and promote the construction of a harmonious and livable city and the construction of the capital. By grid, participatory and coordinated governance, we can improve the pattern of urban social management and the system of prevention and control of public security, and perfect the mechanisms for the mediation and resolution of social conflicts, urban monitoring and early warning, emergency response, coordination, joint action, etc.

Beijing must facilitate urban intelligence, build a smart capital, and effectively prevent and control "urban diseases". The construction of a smart city is an inevitable trend for the development of international metropolises, and an important means to achieve the treatment of "urban diseases". A new round of scientific and technological revolution is emerging with information technology at the core, where modern network technology, computer technology, and communications technology become important driving forces for scientific and technological innovation and technological progress, and mobile Internet, IoT, cloud computing, big data, and intelligent hardware become the quality standards for the new generation of information technology and promote the development of smart cities. A smart city is a deep expansion and integrated application and one of the important directions for the breakthrough of the new generation of information technology, thus becoming the strategic height in the information field.[19] For the treatment of the capital's

Table 9.2 Basic characteristics of the grid management model of a city

Characteristics	Main manifestations
Digital management	The grid management model of a city uses the modern 3S technology, massive data storage technology, mobile communication technology, middleware technology, etc., to achieve a high degree of integration of modern scientific and technological means with management. For example, the "ChengGuanTong" app for terminal management is the fruit of modern digital technology, because it can achieve a high degree of unification of instrumental and social rationalities and serve the practice of management.
Closed-loop management	The grid management model of a city realizes all-round and closed-loop management from the source to the terminal, and builds a two-layered system of urban management with separate supervision. The supervisory center is responsible for both signal input and evaluation results, and the public participates in supervision and evaluation, directly gives feedback to managers and urges the improvement of management performance. Hence, the management system achieves a closed-loop type of control.
Delicacy management	Delicacy management highlights the details and depth of management, focuses on the optimization of details, clarifies key control points and builds efficient business processes. All urban components, as small as manhole covers, street lights, mailboxes, fruit boxes, street trees, and as large as parking lots, construction sites, overpasses, telephone booths, public toilets, etc., are coded, and each supervisor controls the codes within his or her own area. This can highlight the features and qualities of details and lean management, and improve the performance of management.
Dynamic management	Grid management avoids the traditional model of management by abrupt inspections and campaigns, but emphasizes the concept of daily, regular, and dynamic management. With the grid-based information platform of urban management as the technical support, it realizes the real-time updating and dynamic monitoring of information. Once a problem occurs in a city component within the grid, it will be detected, solved, fed back and inspected within the shortest possible time, thus achieving accurate, timely, and efficient dynamic management and active management.

"urban diseases" and the coordinated development of the Beijing-Tianjin-Hebei region, we must accelerate the construction of smart cities characterized by perception, interconnection, and intelligent applications, expedite the integration of urbanization, modernization, and agricultural modernization, and enhance the capacity and quality of the sustainable development of Beijing as the capital.

The construction of a smart capital must utilize modern network technology and information technology to strengthen the control of urban traffic congestion, disorderly parking and difficulty in parking. All trunk roads and arteries, including communities, units, institutions and all other places that may be used as parking spaces, should be marked with unified coding and input into the system for accelerating the construction of parking guidance systems. In 1971, Aachen, a German city, built what is recognized as the world's first parking guidance system, and set up parking guidance signs with photoelectric display for 12 parking lots in the city. In the mid-1990s, Leicester in England designed and implemented a parking guidance system consisting of 21 variable message boards to serve eight multi-story parking garages with a total capacity of 5,200 parking spaces. The parking guidance system was first used in the United States of America in February 1996 in the commercial district of St. Paul. The $1.2 million system managed seven parking garages and three parking lots. In April 1993, Tokyo constructed the first parking guidance system located in Shinjuku in the center of the city, with perfect guidance functions and successful application. Compared with advanced countries, China's construction of parking guidance systems is still in the early stages, and the vast majority of parking lots are still in the era in which car owners themselves find parking spaces in the parking lots. Strengthening the construction of parking guidance systems can further alleviate the parking problem, achieve the rational use of social resources and create more value.[20] According to international experience, Beijing should make full use of modern network technology, digital technology, intelligent technology, and other means to build a smart capital and accelerate the construction of intelligent, information-based parking guidance systems, thus further improving the efficiency of traffic and road use, and resolving a series of "urban diseases" such as traffic congestion and difficulty in parking.

Moreover, the construction of a smart capital, in addition to the use of modern technological means to accelerate the construction of intelligent traffic, must also enhance the quality education of traffic safety and civilized traffic, and maintain good orderly traffic in the capital. The means of integrated governance must be adopted to integrate the capital's parking resources, be clear about the quantity, do well in planning, strengthen management, consider local conditions, continuously innovate and improve the efficiency of the use of parking resources. We must further optimize and improve the regional differentiated parking fees, especially to raise parking fees, use economic leverage to reduce vehicle parking, reduce the use of vehicles in the central urban areas, and guide citizens to take buses or subways. A network has been established for all parking spaces in the city, to obtain and update parking information in a timely manner, enhance the real-time monitoring of parking spaces, and increase penalties for disorderly parking.

Promoting urban intelligence and building a smart capital can provide important information support and a technical guarantee for the new form of information development in the capital and the popularization of information in Beijing, and for the effective treatment of "urban diseases", enhancement of the core functions of the capital and decentralization of non-capital functions. In order to promote urban intelligence and build a smart capital, we must give full play to the active role of "Internet+", integrate various resources, strengthen cross-border integration and development, and lead the flow of capital and talents with the flow of information to better serve the development of the city and build a smart capital. The city must change a single-center model of urban development to the integrated development of Beijing's districts and counties and the coordinated development of the Beijing-Tianjin-Hebei region, formulate the strategy of development for a smart city cluster and achieve resource sharing and interconnection.

9.9 Summary

This chapter mainly studied the treatment of Beijing's "urban diseases" and the countermeasures for the low-carbon development of the Beijing-Tianjin-Hebei region. The treatment of Beijing's "urban diseases" should not only consider the general experience and laws of international treatment of "urban diseases", but also choose the scientific countermeasures of development according to Beijing's own characteristics. Beijing should accelerate its treatment of "urban diseases" and the coordinated low-carbon development of the Beijing-Tianjin-Hebei region under the guiding principle of the implementation of the strategic positioning of the capital, aiming at the basic goal of building an international first-class harmonious and livable city. To be specific, the following countermeasures should be taken:

First, to realize the functional positioning of the capital, and enhance top-level design and unified coordination. Beijing should implement the functional positioning of the capital, clarify the direction of urban development, aim at the goal of building a harmonious and livable city, strengthen the construction of a new type of people-oriented urbanization, accelerate the transformation of urban planning, and facilitate the low-carbon development of the capital. Second, to change the GDP-oriented assessment system, and promote the transformation and upgrading of the industrial structure. Beijing should change traditional the GDP-only system of performance assessment, emphasize coordinated development, establish a fiscal system that matches financial resources and responsibilities, change the land finance system, strictly limit industrial land, expand ecological land, accelerate the transformation and upgrading of the industrial structure, and build a high-grade, precision, and advanced economic structure. Third, to enhance the balanced distribution of high-quality resources, and guide the orderly diversion of the population. Fourth, to accelerate the construction of rail transit, and control the growth of the number of motor vehicles in an orderly manner. Fifth, to deepen the reform of a system of ecological civilization in the capital, and establish a long-term mechanism for environmental governance. Sixth, to establish a mechanism for social participation, solve social problems, and achieve synergy of governance. Seventh, advance the coordinated low-carbon development of the Beijing-Tianjin-Hebei region, and accelerate the decentralization of non-capital functions. Eighth, to innovate the model of urban management, advance urban intelligence, and build a smart capital.

Notes

1 Wang Gefang, "Urban Diseases" in the Rapid Urbanization of China and Their Treatment, *Journal of the Party School of the Central Committee of the C.P.C.*, 2012(5).
2 A Central Administrative District generally refers to an area where the central government or local government is located and where there is a high density of related government departments in the surrounding area. It is the political heart of a country or a locality. The central administrative district is where the offices of the central administration and its departments are located.
3 Yang Chuankai and Li Chen, Treatment of Urban Diseases against the Background of New Urbanization, *Reform of Economic System*, 2014(3).
4 Ding Denglin, Thinking about Paths to Prevent and Treat Urban Diseases, *Truth Seeking*, 2012(S2).
5 Lu Wei and Zhang Dan, Research on Low Carbon Urban Planning against the Background of Global Warming, *Real Estate Information of China*, 2013(5).
6 Zhang Hongbo, Tao Chunhui, Pang Chunyu, Liu Shengjun, and Jiang Yun, Low Carbon Urban Planning Innovation System under the Impact of Global Climate Change, *Sichuan Building Science*, 2012(5).
7 Yue Xueyin, Tan Xinmin, and Huang Wenyi, The Role of Innovation of Low Carbon Technology in the Development of a Low-Carbon Economy and Countermeasures, *Science &Technology Association Forum*, 2011(4).
8 Lu Xiocheng, Research on the Cultural Restriction and the Construction of a Service System of Regional Low-Carbon Innovation, *Journal of North China Electric Power University (Social Sciences)*, 2012(2).
9 Lin Jiabin, An Institutional Analysis of China's "Urban Diseases", *Urban Planning Forum*, 2012(3).
10 Xu Antuo and Xiu Junqiang, Breaking the Perverse Developmental Model of Local Dependence on Land Finance, *People's Tribune*, 2012(8).
11 Zhao Jie, Removing Fence Walls of Parks to Open up City Sceneries, *Tonight News Paper*, January 26, 2015.
12 Beijing Municipal Commission of Transportation: The Elimination of "Cut-off Roads" in Beijing, Tianjin and Hebei by 2017, *Beijing Daily*, June 29, 2015.
13 Fan Bi, Without Removing the Smog of the Energy System, the Atmospheric Smog Cannot Be Eliminated, http://finance.sina.com.cn, March 2, 2015.
14 Lu Xiaocheng, Promoting the Coordinated Low-Carbon Development of the Beijing-Tianjin-Hebei Region, *Qianxian*, 2015(2).
15 Ren Lixuan, Sticking to Innovative Development–Interpretation of the "Five Concepts for Development", *People's Daily*, December 21, 2015.
16 Lu Xiaocheng, *Research on the Theory and Practice of Regional Low-Carbon Innovation System–Thinking Based on Global Climate Change*, Chinese Literature and History Press, 2011, pp. 190–295.

17 Lu Xiaocheng, *A Cluster Model for Productive Service Industries Based on a Regional Low-Carbon Innovation System*, Intellectual Property Publishing House, 2010, p. 3.
18 Jiang Ailin and Ren Zhiru, Gridding: A New Model of Modern Urban Management – A Preliminary Study on Some Issues of the Grid-based Urban Management Model, *Shanghai Urban Planning Review*, 2007(1).
19 Ya Wenhui, Construction of Smart City Faces a New Situation, the Development Must Adapt to Local Conditions, *China High-Tech Industry Herald*, May 2, 2015.
20 Domestic v.s. Foreign Parking Guidance Information Systems, www.qianjia.com/html/2015-03/13_245785.html.

10 Summary and outlook

"Urban diseases" are a worldwide concern that is attracting great attention in the international community. The general experience of the formation and control of "urban diseases" in Western developed countries is valuable for other countries to draw lessons from; in particular, the experience in the control of "urban diseases" accumulated for a long time in international cities such as London, New York, and Tokyo is of special significance. In the longterm and rapid development of Beijing, "urban diseases" such as population expansion, traffic congestion, frequent smog and environmental pollution have been accumulated and formed, and attract the great attention of the CPC Central Committee and the State Council. Based on the integration of theory and practice, this book analyzed the law of evolution and phased characteristics of "urban diseases", compared the basic experiences of typical international cities in treating "urban diseases", such as New York, London, and Tokyo, made an analysis of Beijing's "urban diseases" and their causes, and proposed some policy recommendations for the treatment of Beijing's "urban diseases" and the coordinated low-carbon development of the Beijing-Tianjin-Hebei region.

10.1 Review and interpretation of relevant theories on the treatment of "urban diseases", to provide a theoretical basis for the study of this book

There are commonalities in the studies of "urban diseases", but differences also exist for different countries at different phases of development. Moreover, the academic community has achieved relevant research results and theoretical systems on "urban diseases" and their treatment. The theories of classical sociology, human ecology, community school, garden city, and low-carbon city are reviewed, and the important theoretical underpinnings are proposed to guide the treatment of Beijing's "urban diseases" and the low-carbon development of the Beijing-Tianjin-Hebei region. The theory of classical sociology focuses on early "urban diseases" and their treatment, and provides the fundamental theoretical support for the study and treatment of "urban diseases". The theory of human ecology is an important theoretical basis for the treatment of "urban diseases". The community theory is a generic term for the theories, doctrines, and perspectives developed in the studies on various aspects of the community-wide issues. This school of thought pays attention mainly to the microscopic perspectives of cities. In contrast to the traditional de-ruralization model of cities, the theory of a garden city depicts a beautiful picture of the integration of urban production and life with nature. The theory of a low-carbon city offers new theoretical tools for the treatment of urban diseases and sustainable urban economic and social development.

10.2 Study and investigation of the general rules and phased characteristics of the evolution of "urban diseases"

The so-called "urban diseases" refer to the problems of population expansion, traffic congestion, serious pollution, ecological deterioration, and social conflicts caused by the over-concentration of urban resources, industries, and functions during long-term urban development. The various manifestations of urban diseases include the expansion and aging of the population, traffic congestion, environmental pollution, resource shortage, social conflicts, etc. Generally speaking, the evolution of cities is subject to the typical phases of the rapid growth of urban centers, suburbanization, and metropolitanization, each of which has different characteristics and faces different "urban diseases". The evolution of "urban diseases" is closely related to the industrial development of cities, because they are formed and developed with the rise, development, prosperity, and decline of the industry in cities. The formation of many "urban diseases" is related to the continuous concentration of industries inside cities, the expansion of the size of the city, and population expansion, all of which further lead to the shortage of resources and energy and the stagnation of industrial development. The industrial expansion in cities is constrained by the bottlenecks in resources and energy, and the upgrading of economic structure has set new requirements for the mode of city operations, thus leading to the evolution of "urban diseases".

10.3 Study of New York's experience in treating "urban diseases" from the perspective of cross-regional coordination

New York experienced the evolution from urbanization and suburbanization. Because of the problems of "urban diseases" brought about by accelerated industrialization and urbanization, the government at all levels of New York chose new development strategies, strengthened urban planning, and shifted to the direction of suburbanization based on the original urbanization. The evolution of New York from urbanization to suburbanization effectively alleviated the problems of "urban diseases" and roughly went through the phases from the suburbanization of the residential function, the suburbanization of the commercial and industrial functions, the suburbanization of the integrated functions through satellite towns, to the cross-regional coordination of the functions of the city. Based on the transition from urbanization to suburbanization, New York further realized cross-regional coordinated development, established the coordinated pattern of the Greater New York Metropolitan Area, effectively alleviated the problems of New York's "urban diseases" and promoted the coordinated development of different regions.

10.4 Examination of London's experience in treating "urban diseases" from the perspective of smog control

By combating the smog, London transformed from a foggy city to a green city. London's smog problem originated from the smog incident in 1952, which resulted in the British people's reflections on the bitter consequences of air pollution. The main experience of London for treating smog was the use of various means together. After more than half a century of iron-fisted pollution control, London finally got rid of the shadow of smog and became an ecological and livable green capital of the world with clean air. London's experience of smog control and its inspirations for Beijing are mainly embodied as follows: to formulate regulations governing clean air and strengthen the institutional construction of smog control; to set up points of pollution detection and strictly control exhaust emissions; to enhance the technological research of smog control and promote control by innovation in technologies; to develop green public transportation, use clean and low-carbon energy and reduce carbon emissions; and to attach importance to the public participation in the control of smog in the capital city.

10.5 Exploration of Tokyo's experience in treating "urban diseases" from the perspective of subcenter construction

Tokyo took effective measures to deal with "urban diseases" and treat them from multiple aspects, including planning and guidance, decentralization of functions, construction of subcenters, industrial adjustment, decentralization of the population, and allocation of resources. These experiences are worthy of reference for Beijing. Tokyo's "urban diseases" mainly included: the growth of population that was too rapid, over-concentration of industrial enterprises in the center of the city, rapid development of steel, shipbuilding, machinery, chemical and electronic industries, concentration of large amounts of manufacturing enterprises in Tokyo, and the attraction of a large population from other places, thus resulting in housing difficulties, high pressure of traffic, as well as an increase in emissions and serious environmental pollution in the city caused by the overcrowding of enterprises.

10.6 Examination of Ruhr's experience in treating "urban diseases" from the perspective of cultural transformation and industrial upgrading

The Ruhr area relied on the coal resources to develop traditional industries, and de-industrialization led to the dilemma of urban transformation. The Ruhr area transformed and upgraded the traditional industrial areas with a cultural connotation, and concluded the experiential model of regional control, museums, public recreation spaces, comprehensive development, and low-carbon development. According to the Ruhr experience, cities in China should place emphasis on the cultural transformation, formulate the plans for regional rehabilitation, never copycat other cities, focus on the construction of cultural infrastructures, strengthen ecological restoration and environmental governance of the city, enhance industrial optimization and upgrading, and promote low-carbon development.

10.7 Empirical study and exploration of problems in terms of interaction and correlation effects of population, resources and environment, to analyze the main manifestations and internal causes of the problems of Beijing's "urban diseases", and identify the key elements for treating "urban diseases" and their influencing relationships

Beijing's "urban diseases" are mainly manifested as follows: first, the population growth is slowing down, but the total population continues to rise, and the sustainable development of Beijing is plagued by the "urban diseases" of a metropolis; second, the total traffic capacity continues to grow, and the problem of "capital jam" persists; third, the industrial structure is not reasonable, with difficulty in decentralizing low-end industries; and fourth, the total energy consumption is on the rise, smog had become serious and the carrying capacity of the environment is on the decline. There are many influencing factors to the formation of Beijing's "urban diseases" that have complex relationships. In essence, "urban diseases" result from the accumulation of conflicts between the carrying capacity of urban resources and the environment and the speed of urbanization-oriented development.

10.8 In-depth study and specific measures for the treatment of Beijing's "urban diseases" and the low-carbon development of the Beijing-Tianjin-Hebei region

The treatment of Beijing's "urban diseases" should consider both the general international experience and practice and choose the scientific countermeasures for development based on its own characteristics, adhere to the guiding concept of implementing the strategic positioning of the capital city, and regard the construction of a world-class harmonious and livable city as the basic goal, so as to accelerate the treatment of Beijing's "urban diseases" and the coordinated low-carbon development of the Beijing-Tianjin-Hebei region. To be specific, the countermeasures should be: first, to implement the strategic positioning of the capital city, and enhance top-level design and overall coordination; second, to change the system of GDP-based performance assessment, and promote the transformation and upgrading of industrial structure; third, to strengthen the balanced distribution of advantageous resources and guide the orderly diversion of the population; fourth, to accelerate the construction of rail transit in the city circle of Beijing, Tianjin, and Hebei, and control the growth of motor vehicles in an orderly manner; fifth, to deepen the reform on the system of ecological civilization in the capital and establish a long-lasting mechanism for environmental governance; six, to build a mechanism of social participation, solve social problems and concentrate joint efforts of governance; seventh, to promote the coordinated low-carbon development of the Beijing-Tianjin-Hebei region, and speed up the decentralization of non-capital functions; and eighth, to innovate the mode of urban management, advance the intelligent city and build a smart city.

References

Cai Meng and Wang Yuming, A Study on the Transition of Tourism Cities Based on a Low-Carbon Perspective, *Human Geography*, 2010(5).
Chang Jiang and Feng Shanshan, The New Dynamism of the Ruhr Area, *Dongfang Daily*, November 1, 2012.
Chang Xinxin, Chinese Characteristics and Institutional Confidence in Modern State Governance, *Scientific Socialism*, 2014(1).
Chen Guisheng, Public Governance System and Its Path in Low-Carbon Cities, *Social Sciences in Yunnan*, 2011(5).
Chen Keshi, Wang Long, and Deng Tingting, The Cultural Path of Building Beijing as a World-Class City from the Perspective of the Coordinated Development of Beijing-Tianjin-Hebei – Inspiration of the Paris Experience, *Commercial Times*, 2014(28).
Chen Liuqin, Construction and Development Trend of Healthy Cities, *China Market*, 2010(33).
Chen Liuqin, The Practices of the Low Carbon Cities' Development at Home and Abroad, *China Value*, 2010(9).
Chen Rongzhuo and Tang Ming, Township Governance Transition and Optimization under the Guidance of Scientific Development Concept, *Marxism & Reality*, 2014(1).
Chen Shuhua, The Development of Industrial Tourism in Northeast Resource-Based Cities – Analysis from the Perspective of the Ruhr Area in Germany, *Academic Exchange*, 2010(3).
Chen Wenjian and Huang Dong, Dynamics and Obstacles of Low Carbon Technology Innovation in China, *Science and Technology Management Research*, 2011(20).
Chen Xiaochun and Jiang Daoguo, Connotation and Realization Path of Low-Carbon Development of New Urbanization, *Academic Forum*, 2013(4).
Chu Chunli, Ju Meiting, Wang Yannan, and Wang Yuansheng, Study on the Planning Principles and Framework of Low Carbon Development of Cities in China, *Ecological Economy*, 2011(3).
Chu Mingyu, The Development Status of Low-Carbon Cities, *Modern Science*, 2010(23).
Cui Yuqing, On IPR and Low Carbon Technology Transfer, *China Opening Herald*, 2011(1).
Dang Xiuyun, The New Strategy of Public Governance: Partnerships between Governments and NGOs, *Chinese Public Administration*, 2007(10).
Ding Denglin, Thinking about Paths to Prevent and Treat Urban Diseases, *Truth Seeking*, 2012(S2).

Ding Jinhong, On Urban Explosion and Population Regulation, *Qianjin Luntan*, 2011(2).
Ding Xin, An Analysis of the Problem of Professional Beggars in China's Cities, *Heihe Journal*, 2008(8).
Du Yu and He Yuxin, 300 of 657 Cities Nationwide Is "Short of Water", *Beijing Daily*, May 18, 2014.
Fan Bi, Without Removing the Smog of the Energy System, the Atmospheric Smog Cannot Be Eliminated, http://finance.sina.com.cn, March 2, 2015.
Fu Lili, 17 Cities of China Are Facing Serious Water Pollution, *Science and Technology Daily*, November 19, 2014.
Gao Bingxiong and Zhang Jiangtao, Public Governance: Theoretical Origin and Model Change, *Socialism Studies*, 2010(6).
Ge Xiaofang and Fu Zhenghua, Path Selection of Technological Innovation under Low-Carbon Economy, *Value Engineering*, 2011(13).
Guo Pibin, Zhou Xijun, Li Dan, and Wang Ting, Predicament and Its Solution in the Transformation of Coal Resource Based Economy: A Perspective of Energy Technology Innovation, *China Soft Science*, 2013(7).
He Jiankun, The Strategic Choice of Chinese Energy Revolution and Low Carbon Development, *Wuhan University Journal (Philosophy & Social Sciences)*, 2015(1).
He Taozhou and Shi Danfen, Low-Carbon Cities and Establishment of Navigator Model, *Shanghai Urban Management*, 2010(1).
Hou Baizhen, City Transformation: Cycle, Strategy and Mode, *Urban Planning Forum*, 2005(5).
Hu Angang, *How China Responds to the Challenge of Global Warming, On Low Carbon Economy*, Beijing: China Environmental Science Press, 2008.
Huang Dong, Technology Innovation and Policy Support of Low Carbon, *Forum on Science and Technology in China*, 2010(2).
Huang Haifeng and Li Bo, Analysis of the Decoupling Transition in Beijing's Economic Development, *Environmental Protection*, 2009(2).
Huang Jiangsong and Lu Chunjiang, What Kind of Livable City Does Beijing Want to Build?, http://theory.people.com.cn/GB/41038/526534.html, January 10, 2007.
Huang Rongbing, Liu Guoyu, and Ding Yan, Revelation of Houston, Ruhr and Lorraine's Economic Transformation for China, *Journal of Liaoning Technical University*, 2004(6).
Huang Rongqing, Urbanization in Developing Countries, *China Population Science*, 1988(1).
Huangpu Yue, Zhang Jingxing, and Deng Huayuan, Metropolitanization: The New Characteristics of Urbanization in Metropolis Areas – A Case Study of Nanjing, *Modern Urban Research*, 2008(1).
Hu Xin and Jiang Xiaoqun, *Urban Economics*, Shanghai: Lixin Accounting Press, 2005.
Industrial Transformation Research Group in Liaoning, Learning from the Experience of French Lorraine to Accelerate Liaoning's Industrial Transformation, *China Soft Science*, 1998(10).
Jiang Aihua and Zhang Chi, "Urban Diseases" in the Process of Urbanization and Analysis of the Path for Treatment, *Academic Journal of Zhongzhou*, 2012(6).
Jiang Ailin and Ren Zhiru, Gridding: A New Model of Modern Urban Management – A Preliminary Study on Some Issues of the Grid-based Urban Management Model, *Shanghai Urban Planning Review*, 2007(1).

References

Jiang Changliu and Han Chunhong, Endogenous Constraints of Low Carbon Urbanization Transition: Mechanism Analysis and Governance Framework, *Urban Studies*, 2015(9).

Jiang Su, Difficulties and Countermeasures of Renewable Energy Development in China, *Macroeconomic Management*, 2009(8).

Jiao Binlong, How the Cultural Industry Promotes the Adjustment of Industrial Structure, *Ideological Work*, 2008(1).

Jiao Xiaoyun, The Plights, Emphasis and Countermeasures in Local Urbanization of the New Process of Urbanization: Another Idea for Controlling the "Urban Problems", *Urban Studies*, 2015(1).

Jin Jianguo and Li Yuhui, Governance Innovation in the Transition of the Resource-Depended Cities, *Comparative Economic and Social Systems*, 2005(5).

Jin Leqin and Liu Rui, Low Carbon Economy and Transformation of China's Economic Development Model, *Inquiry into Economic Issues*, 2009(1).

Jin Qiwen, Building a Technical Support System for Developing Low-Carbon Economy, *Guangming Daily*, March 15, 2010.

Jin Xiaoling, Zhao Xiaoying, and Hu Xijun et al., Summary of Roof Garden Construction, *Ecological Economy (Academic Edition)*, 2007(2).

JinYong, Wang Zhuo, Hu Shanying, and Zhu Bing, Low Carbon Economy: Idea, Application and Innovation, *Engineering Sciences*, 2008(9).

Kong Lingcheng and Xie Jiaping, *Research on the Circular Economy Promotion Strategy*, Beijing: China Times Economic Publishing House, 2008.

Lang Lang and Ning Yuyu, Numerous Symptoms of "Urban Disease", *World Vision*, 2010(13).

Lan Qingxin, Peng Yiran, and Feng Ke, Research on the Evaluation Index System and Evaluation Methods of the Construction of an Urban Ecological Civilization – An Empirical Analysis Based on the Four Cities of Beijing, Shanghai, Guangzhou and Shenzhen, *Research on Financial and Economic Issues*, 2013(9).Leng Yanju, The Cultural Thinking on the Transition of the Resource Exhausted Cities, *Urban Studies*, 2011(5).

Li Chen, Classical Theories and the Main Problems of "Urban Diseases" Abroad, *Northwest Population Journal*, 2013(3).

Li Chenghui, Study of the Industrial Structural Adjustment of Mining Cities – Taking the Ruhr as the Example, *China Population Resources and Environment*, 2003(4).

Li Chunyan, Value Orientation and Construction of Low-Carbon Technology Innovation, *Industrial & Science Tribune*, 2011(5).

Li Gangyuan, An Analysis of the Urban Diseases in the UK and Their Treatment – An Inquiry into the Pattern of British Urbanization, *Journal of Hangzhou Teachers College (Social Sciences Edition)*, 2003(6).

Li Jiajie, What Is the Crux of Beijing's Traffic Congestion?, *Guangming Daily*, October 24, 2003.

Li Leilei, De-industrialization and Development of Industrial Heritage Tourism: The Actual Process and Development Model of the Ruhr Area in Germany, *World Regional Studies*, 2002(3).

Li Xiangyang, Huang Fang, and Li Ruiqing, The Present Situation and Development Trend of Low-Carbon City Theory and Practice, *The Journal of Gansu Administration Institute*, 2010(3).

Li Xuemin and Wu Zhenguo, An Analysis of the Urban Diseases of Big Cities in Inner Mongolia and Study of Countermeasures, *Journal of Inner Mongolia University of Finance and Economics*, 2015(3).

Li Xuemin and Zhao Hui, The Experience of Industrial Transformation in the Ruhr Industrial Area of Germany, *China Economic Times*, November 24, 2005.

Li Yanjun, Industrial Wavelength, Urban Life Cycle and the Transition of Cities, *Development Research*, 2009(11).

Li Yingbo and Zhu Huiyong, Study on the Coordination between Urban Growth and Industrial Innovation under New Urbanism Perspective, *Urban Development Studies*, 2013(7).

Li Youhua, Lv Jing, and Xu Shanshan, Low-Carbon Economy Evaluation Index System, *Journal of Harbin University of Commerce*, 2010(6).

Li Yunyan, Evaluation Methods and Implementation Ways of Low-Carbon Cities, *Macroeconomic Management*, 2011(3).

Li Yunzhao and Yue Wu, A Study on Urban Diseases in China from the Perspective of the Scientific Outlook on Development, *The Border Economy and Culture*, 2015(12).

Liang Li, Technological Path for Treating "Urban Diseases" in the Era of Big Data, *E-Government*, 2016(1).

Lin Jiabin, An Institutional Analysis of China's "Urban Diseases", *Urban Planning Forum*, 2012(3).

Lin Xi, Valuable Experience: How Japan Controlled Smog, *Life Times*, March 11, 2014.

Liu Chang, Thoughts on the Transformation of Resource-Exhausted Cities – A Case Study of the Urban Transformation of Zaozhuang, *Theoretical Research on Urban Construction*, 2012(4).

Liu Chunbin, Dual Society Structure and Urbanization – Urban Diseases and Urban Size, *Society*, 1990(4).

Liu Fengchao, Pan Xiongfeng, and Shi Dingguo, Research on the Evaluation of Regional Independent Innovation Ability Based on Set Pair Analysis, *China Soft Science*, 2005(11).

Liu Guojian, Low-Carbon Development in the Context of Chinese Dream, *Journal of Guangdong University of Technology (Social Sciences Edition)*, 2014(1).

Liu Jianping and Yang Lei, The Risk of China's Urbanization and Governance Transformation, *Chinese Public Administration*, 2014(4).

Liu Jianping, Chen Songling, and Yi Longsheng, Choice and Cultivation of the Leading Industries of Resource-Based Cities' Transformation, *Journal of China University of Mining & Technology (Social Science)*, 2007(1).

Liu Jiping and Liu Chenxiao, An Analysis of the Embodiments, Causes and Countermeasures of Urban Diseases in China, *Journal of Jiaozuo Teachers College*, 2014(2).

Liu Junqing and Miao Zhengqing, Priority of Hebei Chemical Industry, *China Computer Users*, 2013(19).

Liu Lili, How Can Mexico City "Remove Smoke", *Xinhua Daily Telegraph*, September 29, 2014.

Liu Qi, Research on the Expansion and Application of Urban Grid Management Mode – Taking Changing District as an Example, *Shanghai Jiaotong University*, 2008(5).

Liu Rong, Xu Zheng, and Li Yue, Indicator System and Empirical Research on Low-Carbon Economy Evaluation – Taking a County in Hebei Province as an Example, *Economic Forum*, 2010(5).

Liu Sha and WangPeihong, The Development of Low Carbon Economy Appeals to Scientific and Technological Innovation, *Energy Research & Utilization*, 2010(2).

Liu Shujun, Environmental Kuznets Curve and Energy Conservation and Emission Reduction, *Environmental Protection*, 2007(12).

Liu Wei, Research on the Construction of Beijing-Tianjin-Hebei Regional Ecological Civilization Circle, *Coastal Enterprises and Science & Technology*, 2013(6).

Liu Wei, Study on Beijing's Developing Low-Carbon Economy, *Commercial Research*, 2010(9).

Liu Wenting and Wang Jianming, Summary of Research on Evaluation of Regional Innovation Capability at Home and Abroad, *Science & Technology and Economy*, 2008(6).

Liu Xuemin, Issues on the Transformation of Resource-Based Cities, *Macroeconomics*, 2009(10).

Liu Yan, Low-Carbon Eco-City – Strategies for Future Urban Sustainable Development under the Influence of Global Climate Change, *Urban Development Research*, 2010(5).

Liu Yan, Low-Carbon Eco-City – Strategies for Future Urban Sustainable Development under the Influence of Global Climate Change, *Urban Studies*, 2010(5).

Lu Dadao, Functional Orientation and Coordinated Development of the Urban Agglomeration of Beijing-Tianjin-Hebei, *Progress in Geography*, 2015(3).

Lu Jun, Existing Problems in the Construction of Ecological Civilization of China and Thoughts on Countermeasures, *Journal of Socialist Theory Guide*, 2010(9).

LuWei and Zhang Dan, Research on Low Carbon Urban Planning against the Background of Global Warming, *Real Estate Information of China*, 2013(5).

Lu Xiaocheng, *A Cluster Model for Productive Service Industries Based on a Regional Low-Carbon Innovation System*, Intellectual Property Publishing House, 2010, p. 3.

Lu Xiaocheng, Exploring the Model for Low-Carbon Innovation System of Green Transformation in China's Cities, *Journal of Guangdong Institute of Public Administration*, 2013(2).

Lu Xiaocheng, Promoting the Coordinated Low-Carbon Development of the Beijing-Tianjin-Hebei Region, *Qianxian*, 2015(2).

Lu Xiaocheng, Research on the Construction of Public Service Platform of Low Carbon Technology: Problems and Countermeasures, *Journal of Southwest Petroleum University*, 2012(1).

Lu Xiaocheng, Research on the Low Carbon Transition in Chinese Cities from the Perspective of Ecological Civilization, *Journal of Hebei University of Science and Technology*, 2013(2).

Lu Xiaocheng, *Research on the Theory and Practice of Regional Low-Carbon Innovation System – Thinking Based on Global Climate Change*, Chinese Literature and History Press, 2011, pp. 190–295.

Lu Xiaocheng, The Construction of Regional Low-Carbon Innovation System: From the Perspective of Technology Foresight, *Science Technology and Dialectics*, 2008(6).

Lu Xiaocheng, *Urban Transformation and Green Development*, Economic Press, China, 2013, pp. 94–95.

Lu Xiocheng, Research on the Cultural Restriction and the Construction of a Service System of Regional Low-Carbon Innovation, *Journal of North China Electric Power University (Social Sciences)*, 2012(2).

Lv Bin and Qi Lei, Compact City: A Sustainable Way of Urbanization, *Urban Planning Forum*, 2008(4).

Meng Chibing, Requirement of Unified Understanding for Low-Carbon Economy Development, *China Venture Capital*, 2010(11).
Ministry of Ecology and Environment of the People's Republic of China, *2014 Annual Report on Prevention and Control of Solid Waste in China's Large and Medium-Sized Cities*.
Pei Dan, Review of Green Infrastructure Planning Methods, *City Planning Review*, 2012(5).
Peng Hongbi and Yang Feng, Scientific Connotation of New Urbanization, *Theoretical Exploration*, 2010(4).
Peng Jian and Wang Xuesong, A Comparative Study of Visions, Objectives and Strategies of the Latest Comprehensive Transportation Plans for Metropolitan Areas of International Cities, *Urban Planning Forum*, 2011(5).
Qi Benchao and Zhou Da, Environmental Management of Tokyo and Enlightenment to Beijing, *Social Sciences in Ningxia*, 2010(5).
Qi Jishun, Meng Xiaomei and Du Fayi, Conflicts between Shenyang's Fence Wall Culture and Urban Modernization and Countermeasures, *Theory Circle*, 2005(2).
Qi Yunlei and Sun Shan, Sector Differences in Jobs-Housing Mismatch and Their Causes: A Case Study of Beijing Metropolitan Area, *Modern Urban Research*, 2015(1).
Qian Zhenming, Global Analysis on the Transformation of Public Governance, *The Journal of Jiangsu Administration Institute*, 2009(1).
Qu Yang, The Legal Path of Air Pollution Control in Japan, *Legal Daily*, January 22, 2013.
Ren Lixuan, Sticking to Innovative Development – Interpretation of the "Five Concepts for Development", *People's Daily*, December 21, 2015.
Shan Zhuoran and Huang Yaping, An Analysis of the Concept, Goals, Contents, Planning Strategies and Misunderstandings of New Urbanization, *Urban Planning Forum*, 2013(2).
Shen Chen and Qie Haixia, The Synergetic Development between the University and the City – A Study of Interactive Mode of the University of London and the City of London, *China Higher Education Research*, 2015(8).
Shen Peijun, Fence Wall Culture and Urban Traffic Congestion, *Comprehensive Transportation*, 2011(10).
Shen Yufang, Liu Shuhua, Zhang Jing, et al., The Correspondence among Industrial Cluster, City Group and Port Group on the Yangtze Delta Area, *Economic Geography*, 2010(5).
Sheng Guangyao, Reflection and Transformation of China's Urbanization Model, *Economic Review*, 2009(9).
Shi Minjun and Liu Yanyan, Urban Green Development: An International Comparison and Perspective of Problems, *Urban Development Studies*, 2013(5).
Song Yingchang, Explorations on the Treatment of "Urban Diseases of Big Cities", *City*, 2015(2).
Tang Jianxin and Yang Jun, *Infrastructure and Economic Development: Theory and Policy*, Wuhan University Press, 2003.
Tang Juan, *Theory of Government Governance*, Beijing: China Social Sciences Press, 2006.
Tang You'an, Inspirations from London's Change of "City of Fog", *Legal Daily*, January 30, 2013.

Tao Xidong, Inclusive Urbanization: The New Strategy of Urbanization in China, *City Planning Review*, 2013(7).

Tian Chengchuan and Chai Qimin, Japan's Experience of Building a Low-Carbon Society and Significance, *Macroeconomic Management*, 2016(1).

Tian Zhiyu and Yang Hongwei, Problems and Challenges of Green Low-Carbon City Development in China – Taking the Beijing-Tianjin-Hebei Region as an Example, *Energy of China*, 2014(11).

Wan Guanghua and Zhu Cuiping, Problems and Thoughts Faced by China's Urbanization: Literature Review, *World Economic Papers*, 2016(6).

Wang Bin and ChenYao, Measurement of the Development Gap of Beijing, Tianjin and Hebei City Group and Study on Their Coordination Development, *Shanghai Economic Review*, 2015(8).

Wang Dawei, Wen Hui, and Lin Jiabin, International Experience and Enlightenment in Dealing with Urban Diseases, *China Development Observation*, 2012(7).

Wang Dong, Urban Poverty and Social Problems in the Contemporary World, *Zhejiang Daily*, May 5, 2008.

Wang Fengyun, Resources and Environment Cost in the Suburbanization of US Cities and Its Alarming Effects, *Shanghai Urban Management*, 2013(5).

Wang Gefang, "Urban Diseases" in the Rapid Urbanization of China and Their Treatment, *Journal of the Party School of the Central Committee of the C.P.C.*, 2012(5).

Wang Guixin, Solution to City Diseases, *People's Tribune*, 2010(32).

Wang Huaping and Sheng Xiaoming, Three Ideal Sources of Social Constructivism, *Studies in Science of Science*, 2005(5).

Wang Jiacheng, Clean Utilization and Structural Adjustment of Coal – An Inevitable Choice for the Sustainable Development of Coal in China, *Coal Economic Research*, 2003(4).

Wang Jiaqiong, Sheng Lihui, and Chen Pengfei, Analysis of Functions and Characteristics of Regional Innovation System, *China Soft Science*, 1999(2).

Wang Jiating, Research on China's Urban Development Model from the Perspective of Low-Carbon Economy, *Jiangxi Social Sciences*, 2010(3).

Wang Jici et al., *Industrial Clusters and Regional Development*, Beijing: Peking University Press, 2001.

Wang Jun and Qiu Shaonan, Mode Shift and Structure Adjustment: Thinking about the Transformation of the Old Industrial Area of Qingdao with the Experiences of Ruhr in Germany as Reference, *China Development*, 2012(3).

Wang Junli, A Brief History, Present Situations of Green Roof and Ways to Develop It, *Chinese Agricultural Science Bulletin*, 2005(12).

Wang Kaiyong, Yan Bingqiu, Wang Fang, and Gao Xiaolu, Countermeasures of Urban Planning to Manage "Urban Diseases": The Experiences from Foreign Countries, *World Regional Studies*, 2014(1).

Wang Ning, Defects in Spatial Structure and the Treatment of the "Urban Diseases" of Extra-large Cities, *Regional Economic Review*, 2015(1).

Wang Qian, Huang Rui, and Shuang Xing, "Carbon Trap": Theoretical Discrimination and Policy Orientation, *Economist*, 2011(10).

Wang Ranghui, *Regional Response to Global Change*, Beijing: China Meteorological Press, 2008.

Wang Ru and Wang Hongmei, Research on the Key Factors of Local Government's Low-Carbon Economy Development Evaluation, *Review of Economic Research*, 2010(29).

Wang Weidong, A Study on the Mechanism of Coordinated Innovative Development of City Clusters in the Yangtze River Delta, *Enterprise Economy*, 2011(12).

Wang Wenjun, Experience & Enlightenment of Foreign Countries and China's Development of Low-Carbon Economy, *Journal of Northwest A&F University*, 2009(6).

Wang Xiangyang and Hu Chunyang, Governance: A New Issue of Theory of Modern Public Management, *Fudan University Journal*, 2000(4).

Wang Xiaolu, Urbanization Path and City Scale in China: An Economic Analysis, *Economic Research Journal*, 2010(10).

Wang Xiaoming, Strategic Research on Transformation and Development of Resource-Based Cities in China, *Research on Financial and Economic Issues*, 2011(1).

Wang Yahong, British Experts Say London's Experience of Smog Control Is Applicable to Beijing, www.chinadaily.com.cn, March 1, 2013.

Wang Yali and Wang Yan, The New Normal of China's Low-Carbon Economic Development Mechanism and Its Path Construction, *Seeker*, 2015(4).

Wang Yanhong, Never a City of Fog – History of London in Controlling Air Pollution, *Xinhua News Agency*, August 26, 2001.

Wang Yunjia, The Suggestions on Boosting the Transformation of Resource-Exhausted Cities, *China Development*, 2012(6).

Wei Houkai, Strategy of Urban Transformation in China, *Research on Urban and Regional Planning*, 2011(4).

Wei Jiang, Tao Yan and Hu Shengrong, Research on Multi-level Architecture of Innovation Systems, *Journal of Dialectics of Nature*, 2007(4).

Weng Zhiyong, Construction of an Ecological Civilization: Study on Problems and Countermeasures, *Studies on Mao Zedong and Deng Xiaoping Theories*, 2011(11).

Wu Changhua, Roadmap of Technology Development for Low Carbon Innovation, *Bulletin of Chinese Academy of Sciences*, 2010(2).

Wu Haiyan, Mexico City in Mexico: Poverty and Pollution Caused by Over-urbanization, *Reference News*, http://news.xinhuanet.com, March 1, 2013.

Wu Hongyan, Mode and Enlightenment of the Ruhr District Industrial Heritage Tour in Germany, *Journal of Taiyuan University*, 2010(3).

Wu Jinjing and Zhu Huanghe, Ecological Civilization Construction from the Perspective of the "Five-sphere Integrated Plan", *Marxism & Reality*, 2013(1).

Wu Nan, Wang Xuelan, Yang Jun, and Liu Zheng, Carbon Reduction and Sequestration Strategy in Urban Planning, *Planners*, 2012(S1).

Wu Qiaowen, UK Takes the Lead in the Low-Carbon Economy, www.ccchina.gov.cn/Detail.aspx?newsID=27742&TId=58.

Wu Wei and Fu Xi'e, The Concept of Green Infrastructure and Review of Its Research Development, *Urban Planning International*, 2009(5).

Wu Yanping, Research on the Legal Path of Low-Carbon Economy, *Journal of Hebei University of Science and Technology*, 2010(3).

Xia Jianzhong, The Main Theories and Methods of Modern Western Urban Community Studies, *Journal of Yanshan University*, 2000(2).

Xiang Chunling, "Urban Disease" and Its Treatment in China's Urbanization, *Journal of Xinjiang Normal University (Edition of Philosophy and Social Sciences)*, 2014(2).

Xiao Hong, Urban Ecological Construction and Urban Ecological Civilization, *Ecological Economy*, 2004(7).

Xiao Jincheng and Ma Yankun, Coordination of Beijing, Tianjin and Hebei and Treatment of the Urban Diseases in Big Cities, *China Finance*, 2016(2).

Xiao Yang and Liu Sisi, China's "Carbon Diplomacy" in the Post-Copenhagen Era, *Contemporary International Relation*, 2010(9).

Xiao Yang, International Shipping Emission Reduction Game and Carbon Trap Faced by China, *Contemporary International Relation*, 2013(6).

Xie Jingbo, Research on Promoting the Innovation Mechanism of Industry-University-Research Cooperation, *People's Tribune*, 2009(17).

Xing Tianhe, Thoughts on the Coordinated Development of Beijing-Tianjin-Hebei, Economy and Management, 2014(5).

Xu Antuo and Xiu Junqiang, Breaking the Perverse Developmental Model of Local Dependence on Land Finance, *People's Tribune*, 2012(8).

Xu Fengjun, Zhao Tao and Yuan Lanjing, Study on the Synthetic Evaluation System of Circular Economy, *Journal of Inner Mongolia University*, 2008(6).

Xu Kangning, *Comparative Study on Urban Economic Development Environment between China and Foreign Countries*, Nanjing: Southeast University Press, 2003.

Xu Lin, On the Suburbanization of Chinese Feature and Countermeasures, *Journal of Fuqing Branch of Fujian Normal University*, 2009(4).

Xu Zheng and Quan Heng, Transitional Economy and Political Economy Significance in China – Experience and Theoretical Analysis of China's Transformation, *Academic Monthly*, 2003(3).

Xu Zhenghua, *UK's Experience of Building a Low-Carbon Economy and Significance*, People's Tribune, 2011(11).

Xue Lan and Zhang Qiang, Transformation Needs of China's Public Governance, *Policy Making Consultation*, 2003(6).

Xue Yongmin and Wang Jichuang, On the ecological value significance of low carbon development, *Journal of Shanxi University (Philosophy and Social Sciences Edition)*, 2012(2).

Xue Yongmin and Wang Jichuang, On the Ecological Value Significance of Low Carbon Development, *Journal of Shanxi University (Philosophy and Social Sciences Edition)*, 2012(2).

Ya Wenhui, Construction of Smart City Faces a New Situation, the Development Must Adapt to Local Conditions, *China High-Tech Industry Herald*, May 2, 2015.

Ya Wenhui, Smart City Construction Is Facing a New Situation, the Development Needs to Adapt to Local Conditions, *China High-tech Industry Herald*, May 25, 2015.

Yan Wentao, Research on Urban Ecosystem Health Attribute Synthetic Assessment Model and Application, *Systems Engineering – Theory & Practice*, 2007(8).

Yan Yanming, Research on the Evolution Mechanism and Prevention of Urban Diseases in the Process of Industrial Transformation, *Modern Economic Research*, 2012(11).

Yang Chuankai and Li Chen, Treatment of Urban Diseases against the Background of New Urbanization, *Reform of Economic System*, 2014(3).

Yang Hongjuan and Guo Binbin, Discussion on the Performance Evaluation of Low-Carbon Supply Chain Based on DEA Method, *Inquiry into Economic Issues*, 2010(9).

Yang Huafeng and Jiang Weijun, Research on Comprehensive Evaluation Index System of Energy Saving and Emission Reduction Effect of Enterprises, Industrial Technology & Economy, 2008(10).
Yang Ka, Analysis of the Nature and Root Causes of "Urban Diseases" and Their Paths of Treatment Based on the Theory of a Self-organizing System, *Jinan Journal (Philosophy and Social Sciences)*, 2013(10).
Yang Yaowu, Basic Concept of Technology Foresight, *World Science*, 2003(4).
Yang Zhangqiao, Urbanization and Urban Social Problems in China, *Zhejiang Journal*, 1988(5).
Yi Liqi, Current Situation of the Management of Urban Land Resources in China and Countermeasures, *Management Observer*, 2009(3).
Yi Zhenli, Low Carbon Urbanization: The Only Way for China's Sustainable Development, *Guangming Daily*, April 2, 2010.
You Jianxin, To Develop a Low-Carbon Economy, Action Is the Key and Innovation Is the Success, *Shanghai Enterprise*, 2008(8).
Yu Junhua and Yuan Wenyi, Public Governance: Concept and Properties, *Chinese Public Administration*, 2013(12).
Yu Keping, Scientific Outlook on Development and Ecological Civilization, *Marxism & Reality*, 2005(4).
Yu Keping, Good Governance and Happiness, *Marxism & Reality*, 2011(2).
Yu Wenlie, Circular Economy and Technological Innovation in Green Cities, *Southern Forum*, 2006(2).
Yuan Dongzhen, How to Deal with City Disease in Foreign Countries, *Decision Making Magazine*, 2005(8).
Yuan He and Yang Ben, Research Progress and Analyze of Practice of Low Carbon Urban Planning in China, *Planners*, 2011(5).
Yuan Yi and Wang Shuangjin, Literature Review of the Theory of Low-Carbon Urban Development, *Northern Economy*, 2010(20).
Yue Xueyin, Tan Xinmin and Huang Wenyi, Role and Countermeasures of Low-Carbon Technology Innovation in the Development of Low-Carbon Economy, *Science & Technology Association Forum*, 2011(4).
Yue Xueyin, Tan Xinmin, and Huang Wenyi, The Role of Innovation of Low Carbon Technology in the Development of a Low-Carbon Economy and Countermeasures, *Science & Technology Association Forum*, 2011(4).
Zang Shuying, Li Dan, and Han Dongbing, The Research of the Transformation of Resource-Based City and the Development of Circular Economy – Take Yichun City of Heilongjiang Province as an Example, *Economic Geography*, 2006(1).
Zeng Changqiu and Zhao Jianfang, "Urban Sickness" in Modernization Advancement and Its Solutions in China, *Journal of Hunan City University*, 2007(5).
Zeng Guangyu and Wang Shengquan, On China's Urbanization and "Urban Diseases", *Economic Affairs*, 2005(1).
Zeng Hong, An Exploration of Building a Livable City, *Journal of Shenyang Official*, 2014(1).
Zeng Lijun, Sui Yinghui, and Shen Yusan, Study on the Sustainable Coordinated Development of Science & Technology Industry and Resource-Based City Based on System Dynamics, *China Population Resources and Environment*, 2014(10).
Zeng Wantao, Changsha-Zhuzhou-Xiangtan Urban Agglomeration Construction, *City*, 2009(1).

Zeng Xiangang and Pang Hanshuang, The Status, Trend and Countermeasures of Carbon Dioxide Emission in Provincial Level of China, *China Soft Science*, 2009(S1).

Zhang Chen and Liu Chunbin, The Cost Analysis and Timing Choice of Green Transformation of Resource-Based Cities, *Ecological Economy*, 2009(6).

Zhang Chenguang, Li Jian, and Yan Yanming, New York's Urban Industrial Transformation and Its Enlightenment to Beijing's Construction of a World City, *Invest Beijing*, 2011(9).

Zhang Dunfu, *Principles of Urban Economics*, Beijing: China Light Industry Press, 2005.

Zhang Fang, Water Shortage of Beijing Still Reaches 100 Million Cubic Meters, *Beijing Times*, September 8, 2015.

Zhang Hongbo, Tao Chunhui, Pang Chunyu, Liu Shengjun, and Jiang Yun, Low Carbon Urban Planning Innovation System under the Impact of Global Climate Change, *Sichuan Building Science*, 2012(5).

Zhang Hongjun, The Policy Choices and the System Innovation of Developing Low-Carbon Economy in China, *Science & Technology and Economy*, 2011(3).

Zhang Jian, Development Level and Spatial Distribution of China's Mega-Cities' Infrastructure, *Urban Problems*, 2012(6).

Zhang Jinggan, Resource Shortage in the Urbanization Process of China, *Urban Problems*, 2008(1).

Zhang Jingwei, Developing Low-Carbon Economy Is an Inevitable Choice for the Transformation and Development of Resource-Based Cities, *Journal of Shanxi Institute of Economic Management*, 2011(3).

Zhang Jingwu, Awareness, Concepts and Strategies: Discussion on "Urban Diseases" and Their Treatment, *City*, 2014(1).

Zhang Kunmin, Pan Jiahua, and Cui Dapeng, *On Low Carbon Economy*, Beijing: China Environmental Press, 2008.

Zhang Lianguo, Trap of Low-Carbon: The Low-Carbon Economy under the Background of Democratic Socialism, *Henan Social Sciences*, 2011(4).

Zhang Mingdou, Potential Crisis Faced by New Urbanization and Its Direction of Governance – With Rural Diseases, Town Diseases and Urban Diseases as the Chain of Study, *Journal of Zhengzhou University (Philosophy and Social Sciences Edition)*, 2015(2).

Zhang Quan, Ye Xingping, and Chen Guowei, Low-Carbon Urban Planning: A New Vision, *City Planning Review*, 2010(2).

Zhang Xuan, Delicacy and Traffic Demand Management: Tokyo's Control of Traffic Congestion, *Journal of Jiangxi Radio & TV University*, 2014(4).

Zhang Yixiao, Ranking of World's Congested Cities: Chongqing and Tianjin Surpassed Beijing, *The Beijing News*, April 7, 2015.

Zhang Zhanbin, Strategic Significance and Reform Problems of New Urbanization, *Journal of China National School of Administration*, 2013(1).

Zhao Hong, A Good Remedy to Beijing's "Urban Diseases", http://finance.sina/com.cn, May 4, 2014.

Zhao Jian, An Appeal to Break Institutional Barriers of a Developing Metropolitan Area with a Bottom-line, *Journal of Beijing Jiaotong University*, 2015(1).

Zhao Jie, Removing Fence Walls of Parks to Open up City Sceneries, *Tonight News Paper*, January 26, 2015.

Zhao Xiaohan, Study on Land Use in the Course of Suburbanization, *Journal of Huazhong Agricultural University (Social Science Edition)*, 2004(2).

Zhao Xiaohui and Fan Xi, Moderately in Short of Water in China, the Key Solving the Water Crisis Is Water Conservation, www.mwr.gov.cn/slzx/slyw/200404/t20040423_143805.html, April 23, 2004.

Zheng Yaping and Nie Rui, The Expansion of City Scale Should Be "Moderate", *Macroeconomics*, 2010(12).

Zhong Maochu and Pan Liqing, Study on Eco-economic Cooperation Mechanism to Beijing, Tianjin and Hebei and Povertybelt Issues around Beijing and Tianjin, *Forestry Economy*, 2007(10).

Zhou Jialai, Definition, Laws and Prevention of "Urban Diseases", *China Urban Economy*, 2004(2).

Zhou Jun and Ma Xiaoli, The Planning and Path of Low-Carbon Urban Development from the Perspective of the Coordinated Development of Beijing-Tianjin-Hebei, *People's Tribune*, 2015(32).

Zhou Weili, Four Questions on Trial Levying of Congestion Charges in Beijing in 2016, *Guangzhou Daily*, December 14, 2015.

Zhou Wuqi and Nie Ming, Practice and Enlightenment of Public Policies of Promoting Low-Carbon Technological Innovation, *Forum on Science and Technology in China*, 2011(7).

Zhou Xiaomeng, How Japan Integrates Low Carbon into the Whole Society, *China Energy News*, May 3, 2010.

Zhu Dajian and Chen Fei, The Connotation, Objectives and Strategies of Shanghai's Low-Carbon Growth, *Urban Insight*, 2010(2).

Zhu Tianxin, The Construction of Green Open Spaces in London Started Early, *China Flower & Gardening News*, April 2, 2015.

Zhuang Guiyang, An Analysis of Low Carbon Path Potentials in China's Economic Growth, *Pacific Journal*, 2005(11).

Zhuang Guiyang, Energy Saving and Emission Reductions: Their Significance to China's Transition to a Low-Carbon Economy, *Advances in Climate Change Research*, 2008(5).

Index

Note: Page numbers in **bold** indicate tables; those in *italics* indicate figures.

3S technology 296
301 Hospital 294

Aachen, Germany 299
accounting system, Beijing's natural resources 277–278
aging population 77
agricultural wholesale markets, Beijing 184, 185–187
air pollution *see* atmospheric pollution
air quality: green low-carbon development 24, 25; population growth 76; *see also* atmospheric monitoring; atmospheric pollution
air travel 193, 231
alienation, urban 68
Anhui Province 26
art 22
Asakusa-Ueno 136
Asian Development Bank (ADB) 83–84
atmospheric monitoring: Beijing 128, 132, 269, 270; China 176; London 125, 127
atmospheric pollution 80–81, 83–84; Beijing 128, 190–191, 193, 211, 267–271; Beijing-Tianjin-Hebei region 207, 292; China 221; New York 108, 116; Tokyo 134, 144; *see also* smog
audits, Beijing's natural resources 278

Baiyin 24
Baliqiao wholesale market 185
Baltimore 112, 113
Baoding 291, 295
beggars 88; poverty 86; unemployment 87
Beihai Kindergarten 253

Beijing 224, 306; choice of countermeasures for treating "urban diseases" 16, 17; connotations and causes of "urban diseases" 7, 8, 194–224; control of "urban diseases" 64, 226–301, 303, 306–307; coordinated urban development 28, 131, 227, 244; deficiencies and review of research studies 31, 32; ecological civilization and environmental governance 262–284; evolution of "urban diseases" 67; Forbidden City 258; Foreign Affairs Office 232; functional positioning 226–243; garden city, theory of 54; green low-carbon development 24, 25, 158, 206–207, 230, 235, 238, 239, 242, 249, 262–263, 269, 283; industrial transformation 101, 149–151, 158, 159, 224, 248–250, 262–263, 268, 269; Korean Town 50; livable city, theory of 58; London's lessons 119, 127–131, 132, 305; mechanism for social participation, solving social problems and synergy of governance 284–287; Municipal CPC Committee 232, 250, 253; Municipal People's Government 232, 250, 253; New York's lessons 107; performance assessment system and industrial transformation 243–250; phases of urban evolution 90, 93; phenomena of the problems of "urban diseases" 178–193; political center 227–228; pollution 83, 84, 150, 154, 156, 158, 178, 188, 190–192, 193, 197, 198, 200, 206, 207, 210, 218–219, 221–222, 223, 226, 227, 231, 233, 235,

238, 248, 249, 256, 262–263, 264, 271, 272, 273, 278, 279, 282; population growth 76, 142, 159, 178, 179–183, **180**, *181*, **182**, 183, 188, 190, 194, 196, 197, 206, 208, 211, 212, 216, 224, 226, 229, 231, 236, 244, 245, 248; research ideas and contents 35, 36; research key points and difficulties 37, 38; research methods 38, 39; research significance and purpose 34; resource scarcity 84; Ruhr area's lessons 161; separation of work and residence 105n10, 156–157; smart capital 296–300; Tokyo's lessons 133, 138, 140, 141, 146–159; traffic congestion 77–78, 79, 140, 142, 147, 150, 151, 152, 154, 154, 156, 157–158, 159, 178, 179, 180, 182, 183–184, 187, 188, 193, 194, 197, 198, 201, 202, 206, 210, 211, 212, 214, 217, 222, 223, 224, 226, 227, 231, 244, 245, 247, 248, 255, 256, 257, 258, 269, 284, 293–294, 295, 297, 299
Beijing No. 2 High School 253
Beijing No. 4 High School 253
Beijing No. 5 High School 253
Beijing-Qinhuangdao Expressway 261
Beijing-Tianjin-Hebei region 178; accelerated decentralization of non-capital functions 287–296; atmospheric pollution 207, 292; causes of "urban diseases" 14; choice of countermeasures for treating "urban diseases" 16, 17; civilization 284; coal combustion 217; control of "urban diseases" 64, 303; coordinated development 28–29, 151, 185, 196, 200–201, 211, 212, 213, 239–243, 250–251, 253, 254, 261, 287–296, 298, 300; deficiencies and review of research studies 32; fence walls 257–261; GDP-based performance assessment 207–208; green low-carbon development 23, 27, 146, 226, 240–243, 250, 287, 289–296, 300, 307; high-quality resources and orderly diversion of population 250–255; industrial structure 185, 186; national parks 280; pollution 207–208, 220, 266–270, 288, 289, 292; population control 209; population growth 76, 250–251; rail system 215, 254, 255–257, 293, 295; research background 4; research ideas and contents 35, 36–37; research key points and difficulties 38; research significance and purpose 34; road system 259–261; smart cities 298; smog 207, 216, 289; Tokyo's lessons 146, 147, 151, 159
Beijing Xizhihe Stone Market 188
Beijing Zoo 188, 196
bicycles: Beijing 130, 153; London 124, 126; Ruhr area 166, 168, 169
big data 17, 297
Birmingham, England 22
Bloomberg, Michael 115, 117
Boston 112, 113
brain drain, Ruhr area 163
branding of Beijing 229
Brazil **78**
Bristol, England 60
Burgess, Ernest 48
buses: Beijing 129, 130, 139, 152, 153, 154, 183, 212–213, 255, 269, 270, 299; Beijing-Tianjin-Hebei region 294; congestion charges **155**; London 124; New York 114, 115, 116; Tokyo 139, 153

C40 Cities Climate Leadership Group 81
cadres 202–203, 278, 287
Cai Meng 25
Cairo 84
Cangzhou 295
Cao Zhongxiong 5, 12
Capital Airport 193
carbon emissions: Beijing 129–130, 132, 150, 158, 190, 193, 207, 212–213, 238, 249, 255, 263, 264, 268, 269, 278; Beijing-Tianjin-Hebei region 217, 220, 240, 242, 287, 288, 289; China 174, 175, 176; coordinated urban development 29; deficiencies and review of research studies 32; green low-carbon development 19, 20, 21, 22; industrial transformation 101, 103; London 119, 123, 125; low-carbon city, theory of 59, 60, 61–62, 63, 64; New York 107, 108, 115; pollution 80; Tokyo 133, 144–145, 159; traffic congestion 79
carbon trading 273, 292
Central Administrative Districts 228
Central Plains City Cluster 76
central urban areas, growth of 88, 89
Chang'an Street 232–233

Changchun 81
Changping: ecological civilization 279; pollution 193; smog 278
Changsha-Zhuzhou-Xiangtan City Cluster 76
Chaoyang 157; ecological civilization 279; GDP-oriented performance assessment system 243; international communication center 232; pollution 193; smog 278
Chen Jiliang 24
Chen Jing 23, 25
Chen Keshi 28
Chen Ning 23, 25
Chen Songling 26
Chen Yao 29
Cheng Jianwen 24
Chengde: culture and sports 295; pollution 81
Chi Zihua 13
China: causes of "urban diseases" 12–14; choice of countermeasures for treating "urban diseases" 15–17; connotations and causes of "urban diseases" 5, **6**; coordinated urban development 27–29; current situation of "urban diseases" 9–10; evolution of "urban diseases" 67; green low-carbon development 17–18, 20–26, 171, 174–175, 176, 177, 242; industrial transformation 103; international comparative studies on "urban diseases" 10, 11; manifestations of "urban diseases" 69, 104; phases of urban evolution 90, 92, 93; pollution 80, 81–84; population growth 76–77; research background 2–4; resource scarcity 84–85; separation of work and residence 105n10; traffic congestion 77–79, 204, 205, 206; urbanization 212, 226, 234; *see also* Beijing; Beijing-Tianjin-Hebei region; Hebei; Pearl River Delta; Tianjin
Chongqing: pollution 83, 84; traffic congestion **78**, 78
circular economy: Beijing 269; China 171, 176; deficiencies and review of research studies 31, 32; green low-carbon development 20
City of London 28
city size classification 179, **179**
civilization, Beijing 284–285
civilized attitude 260, 261

classical sociology 46–47, 64, 303–304
climate change: Beijing 242; Beijing-Tianjin-Hebei region 239, 240, 242; China 171; green low-carbon development 18; low-carbon city, theory of 59, 60, 61, 62; pollution 81; research background 2; resource scarcity 84
coal: Beijing 128, 192, 216, 222, 267, 268, 269; Beijing-Tianjin-Hebei region 217; China 24; London 119, 120, 122, 125; pollution 81; Ruhr area 161, 162–165, **164**, **165**, 169, 173, 175, 177; Tokyo 134
colleges *see* universities and colleges
commercialization 10
communication: phases of urban evolution 91; urban community, theory of 50, 51; urban functions 98
communication center, international 231–233
Communist Party of China (CPC) 178: 11th Central Committee 264; 18th Central Committee 4, 31, 171, 202, 282, 288; 18th National Congress 3–4, 17–18, 31, 128, 171, 198, 202, 262, 278; Beijing 238, 245; Beijing Municipal Committee 232, 250; cadre selection 202–203; natural resource audits 278; Political Bureau of the Central Committee 287–288; political center 227, 228
community, theory of 49–52, 65, 304
community liberated, theory of 50–51
community lost, theory of 49–50
community saved, theory of 50
compensation, ecological 263, 273–274, 292
compensation mechanisms, lacking in Beijing 199–200
components and component library technology 297
concentrated outbreak, period of 95, **95**, 96, 97
conferences 231
congestion *see* traffic congestion
congestion charges: Beijing 128, 155, 156, 184, 214, 269; Lisbon **155**; London **121**, 123, 132, **155**, 214, 223; Singapore 214; Tokyo 154, **155**
construction 52, 54, 192; Beijing 146–147, 148, 151, 153, 157, 180, 183, 187, 188, 193, 197, 201, 202, 212,

Index 323

213, 216, 218, 229, 232, 234, 235, 236, 237, 238, 246, 247, 248, 267, 273, 275, 276, 277, 280, 285, 286; Beijing-Tianjin-Hebei region 250, 253, 256, 294; China 176, 203, 204, 205; connotations and causes of "urban diseases" **5–6**, 7–8; countermeasures for treating "urban diseases" 15, 16, 17; green low-carbon development 20; industrial transformation 102; livable city, theory of 54, 55; low-carbon city, theory of 63; New York 113, 114; noise pollution 82; phases of urban evolution 96; research background 1; resource scarcity 85; Tokyo 134, 135, 136, 138, 141, 146; *see also* demolition and reconstruction

consumption: Beijing 150, 216, 249; China 174–175; energy *see* energy consumption; green low-carbon development 19, 20, 21, 23, 24, 26; industrial transformation 103; low-carbon city, theory of 62, 64; New York 109; resource *see* resource consumption; Ruhr area **164**; Tokyo 136; water 85, 150, 249

continuous development, period of 95, 95, 96

control of "urban diseases" 46, 64–65, 303–304; classical sociology, theory of 46–47; garden city, theory of 52–54; human ecology, theory of 47–48; livable city, theory of 54–58; low-carbon city, theory of 59–64; urban community, theory of 49–52

controlling urban functions 98, 99

coordinated development: Beijing 28, 131, 227, 244; Beijing-Tianjin-Hebei region 28–29, 151, 185, 196, 200–201, 211, 212, 213, 239–243, 250–251, 253, 254, 261, 287–296, 298, 300; deficiencies and review of research studies 32; literature review 26–29; livable city, theory of 55

coordinating body, lacking in Beijing 198–199

counter-urbanization 234

Crawford, Jenny 22

credit archives 260

crime: beggars 88; New York 108; phases of urban evolution 96; population growth 76, 77; poverty 86; unemployment 87

cross-regional coordination: Beijing 147; New York **110**, 111–113, 118

culture: Beijing 149, 152, 157, 194, 195, 197, 210, 226, 228–229, 233, 237, 239, 246, 249, 260, 276, 282–284; Beijing-Tianjin-Hebei region 251, 252, 253, 255, 293, 294, 295; China 171, 173, 174, 175, 176, 177, 203, 204; coordinated urban development 28; green low-carbon development 22; industrial transformation 100, 101, 102; livable city, theory of 54, 55, 56, **57**, 58; New York 108, 111, 114; phases of urban evolution 93; Ruhr area 161, 162, 165, 168–169, 170, 173, 174, 176; Tokyo 139, 142, 144; urban community, theory of 50, 51

Dahl, R. A. 52
Dahongmen: Decentralization Office 199; market 196
Daning reservoir 189
Daxing: ecological civilization 279; pollution 193; smog 278
Dayang Road wholesale market 185
decentralization: Beijing 184–188, 196, 198, 199–201, 209, 210, 222, 231, 232, 233, 244, 247, 249, 256, 260, 286, 293–296, 300; Beijing-Tianjin-Hebei region 211–212, 215, 251, 252–255; China 206
de-industrialization, Ruhr area 162–165, **165**
demolition and reconstruction 192; Beijing 193; China 205
Deng Tingting 28
depression 87
development rights, transfer of 276
Dhaka 84
distributed database and distributed computing technology 296–297
Dong Guoliang **5–6**
Dongcheng 142, 157; decentralization 247; ecological civilization 279; education 253; fiscal system 245; GDP-oriented performance assessment system 243; health care 195; orderly diversion of the population 253; political center 228; population density 181; smog 278
Dongzhimen 153
drinking water pollution 81–82
drug addiction 77

drug trafficking 77
Du Yong 23, 25
Durkheim, Émile 47

ecological administration, Beijing 277–278
ecological civilization 173; Beijing 218, 221, 238–239, 242, 244, 262–266, 270–271, 273–283; Beijing-Tianjin-Hebei region 206–207, 242, 250, 290, 291; China 171, 176; deficiencies and review of research studies 31–33; literature review 17–26; research background 3–4; Ruhr area 161, 171
ecological compensation 263, 273–274, 292
ecological crisis 2
ecological deterioration: Beijing 247, 262, 279; defining the connotation of "urban diseases" 68; industrial transformation 103; low-carbon city, theory of 60; New York 108; phases of urban evolution 96; research background 1, 2; research significance and purpose 34; Ruhr area 161, 162, 175
ecological economy 32
ecological governance: Beijing 130, 131, 215–222, 238, 262, 264–272, 277–278, 281–282; Beijing-Tianjin-Hebei region 292; China 177; London **122**, 125–126, 132; Tokyo 146
ecological health **57**, 58
ecological land: protection 275–276; research background 1
ecological organizations, actively fostering 280–282
ecological protection 19
ecological red lines 272–273, 275, 280
ecological security 18
economic crises *see* financial crises
economic growth: Beijing 131, 180, 182, 188, 192, 197, 206, 215, 227, 229, 237, 240, 243–244, 245, 246, 247, 250, 263, 264, 266, 267, 268; Beijing-Tianjin-Hebei region 208, 254, 255; China 174, 203, 206, 242, 248; coordinated urban development 29; deficiencies and review of research studies 30, 31; green low-carbon development 18, 19, 20, 23; industrial transformation 101; livable city, theory of 55; low-carbon city, theory of 59; manifestations of "urban diseases" 69; New York 111–112; research background 2, 4; Ruhr area 162, 163; Tokyo 134, 136, 141
economic system, Beijing 262–264, 267
edge cities 90–91
Edinburgh 125
education: Beijing 147, 149, 152, 156, 157, 178, 180, 182, 186, 195, 200, 202, 209, 210, 223, 233, 239, 245, 246, 274, 284–285; Beijing-Tianjin-Hebei region 250, 251, 252, 253, 254, 255, 291–292, 293, 294; connotations and causes of "urban diseases" 8; countermeasures for treating "urban diseases" 15, 17; ecological civilization 274; industrial transformation 101; livable city, theory of 58; London 123; manifestations of "urban diseases" 69; New York 111, 112, 114; phases of urban evolution 96; poverty 86; research background 1; Tokyo 142, 143–144, 148–149; unemployment 87; urban functions 98, 99; *see also* universities and colleges
El Niño 3
elderly people: Beijing 202; population growth 77
electric vehicles: Beijing 130, 155, 156, 158, 183, 269, 270; London 123; Tokyo 145, 156
electromagnetic wave pollution 83
elite, theory of the 52
embassies 232, 233
emigration *see* migration
employment 69, 87, 178; Beijing 150–151, 157, 178, 182, 183, 188, 208–209, 210, 211, 229, 236, 244; Beijing-Tianjin-Hebei region 251, 252, 253; causes of "urban diseases" 14; connotations and causes of "urban diseases" 8; countermeasures for treating "urban diseases" 15; defining the connotation of "urban diseases" 68; green low-carbon development 22; livable city, theory of 56; New York 109, 111; phases of urban evolution 90; population growth 76, 77; research background 1, 2; Ruhr area 168; separation of work and residence *see* spatial dislocation/separation of residence and job; Tokyo 133, 135, 136; urban functions 99; *see also* underemployment; unemployment

energy conservation: coordinated urban development 29; green low-carbon development 19; low-carbon city, theory of 62, 63, 64; New York 115, 116, 118
energy constraints: green low-carbon development 23; industrial transformation 101
energy consumption: Beijing 129–130, 132, 150, 156, 158, 187, **190**, 190, 197, 210, 216, 224, 238, 243, 249, 255, 264; Beijing-Tianjin-Hebei region 288, 289, 293; China 174, 176; green low-carbon development 19, 21, 22, 24, 26; industrial transformation 101; London 125; low-carbon city, theory of 59, 61; Ruhr area 161, 165–166, 170–171, 175; Tokyo 136
energy depletion: deficiencies and review of research studies 33; research background 1, 2
energy policy 63
energy reforms, Beijing 264
energy resources: Beijing 190, 192; green low-carbon development 22
energy scarcity: Beijing 188; China 171; coordinated urban development 29; low-carbon city, theory of 60; unemployment 87; research background 2
energy supply 26
entertainment: Ruhr area 166, **167**, 170; Tokyo 136
entropy theory 25
environmental awareness 23
environmental deterioration: Beijing 194, 210; China 204, 206; garden city, theory of 54; low-carbon city, theory of 59; pollution 81; population growth 76, 77; research background 1, 2; Tokyo 141; unemployment 87
environmental governance *see* ecological governance
environmental organizations, actively fostering 280–282
environmental pollution *see* pollution
environmental protection: Beijing 190–191, **191**, 216, 217, 221–222, 243, 244, 264–280, 276, 277, 278, 279, 281–284; China 176, 203, 220–221; countermeasures for treating "urban diseases" 16; deficiencies and review of research studies 30, 31; green low-carbon development 19, 20; London 125
environmental taxes 63
evaluation index systems 25–26
evolution of "urban diseases" 67, 103–104, 304; defining the connotation of "urban diseases" 67–69; industrial transformation 99–103; manifestations of "urban diseases" 69–88, **70–75**; phased characteristics 88–99, 95
exhaust emissions *see* traffic pollution
exhibition centers 233
export powers 232

Fang Yaming 13
Fangshan District 208–209
farmland protection 274–275
fence walls 215, 257–261
Feng Ke 25
Fengtai District 199
financial center, building a national 228
financial crises: green low-carbon development 18, 22; phases of urban evolution 97
financial resources and responsibilities, matching 244–246
fiscal system: Beijing 244–246, 263, 273; Beijing-Tianjin-Hebei region 207; China 202, 204–205, 206, 207
Fischer, Claude S. 51
Fong, W. K. 22
food safety 243
French, Will 22
Fu Guanghui 3
Fu Guanyun 24
Fukuda Yasuo 62
fundamental urban functions 98, 99

gangs: poverty 86; unemployment 87
Gaobeidian wholesale market 187
garden city, theory of 52–54, 65, 304
Geng Tianzhao 25
Geographic Information System (GIS) 296
Germany: Aachen's parking guidance system 299; Industry 4.0 strategy 288; *see also* Ruhr area
ghost cities 236
Ginza 136
Glasgow 22
Global Positioning System (GPS) 296
global warming *see* climate change

globalization 173; Beijing 230, 248; Ruhr area 165; Tokyo 135; urban functions 97
governance: Beijing 128, 129, 130, 131, 147, 153, 157, 158, 179, 184, 187, 188, 198–201, 215–222, 223, 224, 236, 238, 244–245, 246, 260, 262, 264–274, 277–282, 284–287, 296–297, 299; Beijing-Tianjin-Hebei region 250, 254–255, 261, 287–288, 290–293; as cause of "urban diseases" 12–13; China 171, 173, 175, 176, 177, 202–203, 204–206, 207–208, 258; coordinated urban development 27; countermeasures for treating "urban diseases" 15, 16, 17; deficiencies and review of research studies 31–32; ecological *see* ecological governance; green low-carbon development 20, 21; industrial transformation 102; London 119, 120, **121**, **122**, 124, 125–127, 132; low-carbon city, theory of 60–63; market and government, relationship between 254–255; New York 112, 113, 118; phases of urban evolution 94, 97; research background 4; research significance and purpose 34; Ruhr area 162, 166, 171, 173, 175; social *see* social governance; Tokyo 134, 136, 144–146, 154, 156
Great Britain *see* United Kingdom
green belts: Beijing 130, 197; London 126
green chains 126
green economy 32
green governance *see* ecological governance
green low-carbon development: Beijing 24, 25, 158, 206–207, 230, 235, 238, 239, 242, 249, 262–263, 269, 283; Beijing-Tianjin-Hebei region 23, 27, 146, 226, 240–243, 250, 287, 289–296, 300, 307; China 17–18, 20–26, 171, 174–175, 176, 177, 242; deficiencies and review of research studies 31, 32, 33; literature review 17–29; London 125–126; New York 115, 116–117, 118; research background 2, 3, 4; research significance and purpose 34; Ruhr area 161, 165–166, **167**, 168, 170–177; Tokyo 146
greenhouse gas emissions *see* carbon emissions

grid computing 297
grid management 296–297, **298**
gross domestic product (GDP): Beijing 182, 188, 192, 197, 200, 202–208, 224, 238, 240, 243–244, 245, 246, 247, 248, 264, 268; China 234; deficiencies and review of research studies 31; green low-carbon development 23, 26; low-carbon city, theory of 60; performance assessment 13, 202–208, 224, 243–244, 245, 277
ground subsidence 179
Gu Shengzu 15
Gu'an 213
Guangyuan market 196
Guangzhou: green low-carbon development 25; industrial transformation 101; separation of work and residence 105n10
Guanyuan wholesale market 188
Guo Jinlong 248, 249

Haidian 142, 157; ecological civilization 279; education 253; GDP-oriented performance assessment system 243; orderly diversion of the population 253; wholesale markets 188
Hammond, John and Barbara 119, 131
Handan: culture and sports 295; pollution 192
happiness index 17
harmonious and livable city 233–239
He Jiankun 21
health care: Beijing 147, 149, 157, 178, 180, 182, 186, 195, 200, 202, 209, 210, 233, 239, 246; Beijing-Tianjin-Hebei region 250, 251, 252–253, 254, 255, 293, 294; connotations and causes of "urban diseases" 8; industrial transformation 101; livable city, theory of 58; New York 111, 112, 114; phases of urban evolution 93; poverty 86; research background 1; Tokyo 142, 144; urban functions 98, 99
health problems: Beijing 191; defining the connotation of "urban diseases" 67; London 119–120; mental illnesses 87; New York 108, 117; phases of urban evolution 89; pollution 81, 82, 83; research background 1; Tokyo 134, 146
Hebei: agricultural products 186, 187; atmospheric pollution 268, 269,

270; compensation mechanism, lack of 199; coordinated urban development 29; coordinating body, lack of 199; decentralization 200; ecological civilization 274; ecological compensation 263, 273; education 209; environmental management 266; GDP-based performance assessment 206; green low-carbon development 207, 293; industrial transformation 150, 207, 263; migration flows 210; orderly diversion of the population 252, 253; phases of urban evolution 90, 92; pollution 192, 222; public transport 130; rail system 152, 256, 257; road system 261; scientific and technological innovation 231; *see also* Beijing-Tianjin-Hebei region
Hegang 24
Heilongjiang 186
High School Affiliated to Beijing International Studies University 253
High School Affiliated to BIT 253
High School Affiliated to Renmin University of China 253
Hollingshead, August 49
Hou Jingxin 24
Hou Weili 23
housing: Beijing 142, 178, 179, 180–181, 182, 183, 187, 188, 193, 194, 210, 211, 217, 233, 243, 244, 245, 246, 247; countermeasures for treating "urban diseases" 16; defining the connotation of "urban diseases" 68; industrial transformation 100; international comparative studies on "urban diseases" 11; livable city, theory of 58; London 119; manifestations of "urban diseases" 69; New York 107, 108, 109, 111, 112, 117, 118; phases of urban evolution 91, 93, 96; population growth 76, 77; research background 1; Ruhr area 168; Tokyo 133, 135, 141, 143, 144, 149, 159; UK 119; urban functions 98, 99; *see also* slums
housing rental market: Beijing 183, 211, 233; New York 113
Houston 22, 84
Howard, Ebenezer 52–54
Hu Angang 21
Hu Xin 9
Huairou: ecological civilization 279; ecological compensation 273;

ecological conservation 263; reservoir 189; subways 213
Huang Cheng Gen Primary School 253
Huang Rongqing 14
Huilongguan: trading markets 188; wholesale market 185
hukou 292
human ecology, theory of 47–48, 64–65, 304
Hunter, Floyd 52
hybrid vehicles: Beijing 130; Tokyo 145
hygiene issues 69

Ikebukuro 135, 141
immigration *see* migration
inclusion 55
India *see* Mumbai
industrial boom phase, Ruhr area 162, **163**
industrial clusters, low-carbon 293
industrial decline phase, Ruhr area **163**, 162–165
industrial development: connotations and causes of "urban diseases" 6, 9; research background 2
industrial parks, New York 111
industrial policies 27
industrial pollution, Beijing 128, 158
industrial structure, Beijing 184–188, 224
industrial transformation: Beijing 101, 149–151, 158, 159, 224, 248–250, 262–263, 268, 269; Beijing-Tianjin-Hebei region 207; evolution of "urban diseases" 99–103, 104; green low-carbon development 19; London 125; low-carbon city, theory of 59, 61, 62; Ruhr area 162, **163**, 165–166, 170, 175, 176; Tokyo 133, 136–137, 146, 150, 159
industrial upgrading 161, 177, 306; implications 171–176; models 166–171; reasons for 161–166
industrialization 178; Beijing 195, 216, 226; connotations and causes of "urban diseases" 5; control of "urban diseases" 46; deficiencies and review of research studies 30; defining the connotation of "urban diseases" 67; evolution of "urban diseases" 67; garden city, theory of 52; green low-carbon development 20, 24, 25; industrial transformation 100, 101, 102, 103; international comparative

studies on "urban diseases" 10, 11; London 119; low-carbon city, theory of 59; New York 107–108, 111, 117, 118; phases of urban evolution 89, 90, 91; pollution 81, 82; population growth 76; poverty 86; research background 1, 2, 3, 4; Tokyo 135; UK 119
information: Beijing 180; New York 111; urban functions 98, 99
information and communication technologies: Beijing 155, 157–158, 297; Beijing-Tianjin-Hebei region 290; China 176; countermeasures for treating "urban diseases" 17; Tokyo 142–143
informatization: Beijing 157; industrial transformation 100, 102; research background 1
infrastructure: Beijing 183, 188, 196, 202, 209, 210, 233, 247, 271, 277; Beijing-Tianjin-Hebei region 250, 251, 252, 256, 293, 294, 296; China 175, 176, 177, 203, 204, 212; connotations and causes of "urban diseases" 8, 13, 14, 68; countermeasures for treating "urban diseases" 15, 16, 17; industrial transformation 102; New York 114, 116–117; phases of urban evolution 90, 91, 92, 95, 96; population growth 76; research background 1; Ruhr area 166, 171, 175; Tokyo 146; urban functions 98, 99
initial formation, period of 95, 95–96
Inner Mongolia: agricultural products 186; countermeasures for treating "urban diseases" 16; culture and sports 295; current situation of "urban diseases" 10
institutional causes of "urban diseases" 13, 14
institutional countermeasures for treating "urban diseases" 15, 16, 17
integrity 259, 261
intellectual property rights 230
international communication center 231–233
international events 232
International Water Association 81
Iran 84
Isomura, Eiichi 5
Istanbul **78**, 78
Italy 83

Jakarta 84
Japan: low-carbon society 61–64; phases of urban evolution 93; *see also* Tokyo
Jiang Aihua 10, 13, 15
Jiang Xiaoqun 9
Jiangsu 92, 93
Jiao Xiaoyun 10, 17
Jilin 186
Jinan 83, 84
Jing Jin Ji Railway Transit Investment Co., Ltd. 261
Jingshan School 253
Jingshen wholesale market 185–186
Jinxiudadi wholesale market 185, 186
juvenile delinquency 87–88

kidnapping 77
kindergartens 202
Knott, John 21
knowledge-based economy 23
Kotkin, Joel 5, 67
Kunshan 92, 93
Kyoto Protocol 62

Lagos 84
Lan Qingxin 25
land finance system, Beijing 246–248
land inspection system 276
land ownership system 17
land prices/value: Beijing 151; industrial transformation 100; New York 109; phases of urban evolution 90; Tokyo 133, 141
land protection 275–276
land shortages 85–86
land supply 100
land system, China 202, 205, 206
land use 92
Lang Lang 15
Langfang 295
Lanzhou 83, 84
Latin America 76
law *see* legislation
law enforcement, Beijing 152, 219, 220–221, 266, 268, 269–270, 282
law of urban evolution *see* evolution of "urban diseases"
Leeds, England 60
legislation: Beijing 128, 132, 158, 198, 217, 220, 222, 223, 266, 268, 278, 297; Beijing-Tianjin-Hebei region 290; China 205; London 120, **121**, 122–123,

132; New York 111, 115, 116; Tokyo 137, 144–146, **145**, 147–148, 150
Lei Lei 24
Leicester, England 299
Leighton, B. 51
leisure: Beijing 236; livable city, theory of 54; New York 111; Ruhr area 166, **167**, 169–170, 171; Tokyo 136
Letchworth, England 52
Lewis, Oscar 50
Li Gangyuan 10
Li Xuemin 10, 16
Li Yanjun 4, 20
Li Yingbo 27
Li Yunzhao 14, 16
Liang Li 17
Liaoning 186
Lin Jiabin 11, 13
Lisbon **155**
Liu Chang 24
Liu Chenxiao 10, 14, 16
Liu Chunbin 13–14, 21
Liu Jianping 26
Liu Jiping 10, 14, 16
Liu Shuhua 27
Liu Yanyan 24
Liu Yongliang 8, 15
Liu Youzhao 3
livable city, theory of 54–58, **57**, 65
livelihood, improving people's 237–238
London 223, 226; Buckingham Palace 258; congestion charges **121**, 123, 132, **155**, 214, 223; coordinated urban development 28; fence walls, lack of 258; Hyde Park 258; industrial transformation 101, 102; international comparative studies on "urban diseases" 11; livable city, theory of 58; manifestations of "urban diseases" **70–71**; motor vehicle control 184; phases of urban evolution 89; rail system 124, 213, 256; research ideas and contents 35; research key points and difficulties 37; research methods 39; smog control 119–132, 305; subways 124, 293
Long Island 111
Los Angeles: manifestations of "urban diseases" **75**; research ideas and contents 35; resource scarcity 84
low-carbon city, theory of 59–64, 65, 304
low-carbon development *see* green low-carbon development

low-carbon economy 32
Lu Dadao 28
Lu Jun 18, 23
Lu Lixin 8
Lu Xiaocheng 24

Ma Xiaoli 29
Ma Yankun 17
Maine 112
Malaysia 22
Manchester, England 60
market entry conditions 232
market failure, as cause of "urban diseases" 12, 13
media: Beijing 283; London 127, 130, 132
medical care *see* health care
medical problems *see* health problems
mental illnesses 87; *see also* psychological issues
metropolitanization: evolution of "urban diseases" 88, 92–94, 96; industrial transformation 101; New York 111–113, 118; urban functions 99
Mexico 11; *see also* Mexico City
Mexico City: manifestations of "urban diseases" **74–75**; pollution 83; resource scarcity 84; traffic congestion **78**; urban community, theory of 50
migration: Beijing 188, 210; causes of "urban diseases" 12; countermeasures for treating "urban diseases" 15; New York 108; research background 1; Tokyo 133, 159
migratory urban functions 98–99
military command, Beijing 210
mining 26
Miyun: ecological civilization 279; ecological compensation 273; ecological conservation 263; subways 213
Miyun-Zhuozhou Expressway 261
modernization: Beijing 154, 215, 236, 260, 287; Beijing-Tianjin-Hebei region 298; China 171; connotations and causes of "urban diseases" 8, 13; population growth 77; research background 2, 4
Moscow **78**
multinational companies' headquarters 232, 233

Mumbai: international comparative studies on "urban diseases" 11; poverty 86
museums, Ruhr area 166, **167**, 168–169, 177

Nanhua wholesale market 185
Nanyuan Airport 193
national park system 279–280
natural gas: Beijing 192, 222; London 125
Nature Conservancy 81
neighborhoods and social networks of urban community 49–51
new public management, theory of 286
New Urbanism 27
New York 107, 117–118, 304–305; critical problem 107–108; cross-regional coordination and equal allocation 112–117; evolution from urbanization to suburbanization 108–113; green low-carbon development 24; industrial transformation 101, 102; international comparative studies on "urban diseases" 11; livable city, theory of 58; manifestations of "urban diseases" 71; motor vehicle control 184; phases of urban evolution 89; rail system 114, 213, 255, 256; research ideas and contents 35; research key points and difficulties 37; research methods 39; subways 114–115, 293
Ni Pengfei 13
Ning Yuyu 15
Ningxia 186
noise pollution 82; Beijing 153; industrial transformation 101; New York 111
Northeast China 295

overpasses: Beijing 139, 154, 183; Tokyo 139
overpopulation: Beijing 150, 179, 180, 181, 193, 195, 197, 201, 216, 228, 233, 247; connotations and causes of "urban diseases" **5**, 7, 12; countermeasures for treating "urban diseases" 15; deficiencies and review of research studies 33; defining the connotation of "urban diseases" 68; garden city, theory of 53; research background 1; resource scarcity 85; Tokyo 135; *see also* population growth

Pan Baocai 12
Paris: coordinated urban development 28; fence walls, lack of 258; industrial transformation 102; livable city, theory of 58; Louvre 258
Park, Robert E. 48
parking 78, 79; Aachen, Germany 299; Beijing 140, 156, 184, 198, 202, 212, 214–215, 260, 261, 268, 269, 284, 299; London 124; New York 115; Tokyo 140, 154, **155**
Parsons, Talcott 51
Pearl River Delta 76
Peng Yiran 25
people-oriented urbanization 234–237, 238–239
performance assessment, Beijing 202–208, 224
Perman, Roger 22
Philadelphia 112, 113
photovoltaic energy 270
Pinggu: ecological civilization 279; ecological compensation 273; ecological conservation 263; subways 213
Pittsburgh 22
planning 192; Beijing 146–147, 148, 153, 193, 196–197, 201, 223, 231, 236, 238, 261, 286; Beijing-Tianjin-Hebei region 239–243, 260, 294; China 173, 202, 205–208; connotations and causes of "urban diseases" 7, 8, 12, 13, 14; coordinated urban development 29; countermeasures for treating "urban diseases" 15, 16, 17; garden city, theory of 52, 54; green low-carbon development 22, 240–243, **241**; international comparative studies on "urban diseases" 11; livable city, theory of 54; London 123, 126; low-carbon city, theory of 63; New York 109–110, 112, 113, 118; phases of urban evolution 90; population growth 77; research background 1; Ruhr area **172**, 173; talent team building 243; Tokyo 135, 136, 141, 146, 147–148
plot ratio incentives 276
policy measures, London **121**, 123–124, 132

political center, building a national 227–228
political harmony and stability 56, **57**
political participation *see* public participation
political pluralism, theory of 52
pollution 69, 79–84, 178; Beijing 83, 84, 150, 154, 156, 158, 178, 188, 190–192, 193, 197, 198, 200, 206, 207, 210, 218–219, 221–222, 223, 226, 227, 231, 233, 235, 238, 248, 249, 256, 262–263, 264, 271, 272, 273, 278, 279, 282; Beijing-Tianjin-Hebei region 207–208, 220, 266–270, 288, 289, 292; as cause of "urban diseases" 12, 14; China 171, 174, 176; countermeasures for treating "urban diseases" 16; deficiencies and review of research studies 33; defining the connotation of "urban diseases" 67, 68; green low-carbon development 19, 20, 23; industrial transformation 101, 102; international comparative studies on "urban diseases" 11; low-carbon city, theory of 59, 60; New York 107, 108, 111, 115, 116, 117; phases of urban evolution 89, 90, 96; population growth 76; research background 2, 3, 4; research significance and purpose 34; Ruhr area 161, 163, 165, 166, 168, 170, 171, 175; Tokyo 133, 134, 143, 144–146; traffic congestion 77; UK 119; urban functions 99; *see also* smog
population control measures, lacking in Beijing 208–212, 224
population growth 69–77; Beijing 76, 142, 159, 178, 179–183, **180**, *181*, **182**, 183, 188, 190, 194, 196, 197, 206, 208, 211, 212, 216, 224, 226, 229, 231, 236, 244, 245, 248; Beijing-Tianjin-Hebei region 76, 250–251; China 204, 206, 212; connotations and causes of "urban diseases" 7–8, 14; deficiencies and review of research studies 30; green low-carbon development 23; industrial transformation 99, 101, 102, 103; international comparative studies on "urban diseases" 10; London 119; New York 107–108, 117; phases of urban evolution 93, 96; pollution 81; research background 1, 4; research significance and purpose 34; Tokyo

133, 144, 159; urban community, theory of 50; *see also* overpopulation
ports, New York 114
post-industrialization: Beijing 226, 287; industrial transformation 101; New York 112
poverty 86; connotations and causes of "urban diseases" 8; countermeasures for treating "urban diseases" 15; green low-carbon development 23; New York 108; urban community, theory of 50
power of urban community 51–52
preservation of old buildings 192; Beijing 193
prosperity: Beijing 264; green low-carbon development 20; industrial transformation 99; livable city, theory of 55, **57**; New York 107; research background 4; Ruhr area 162; Tokyo 136, 137
prostitution: population growth 77; poverty 86
psychological issues: population growth 77; traffic congestion 77; urban community, theory of 50, 51; *see also* mental illnesses
public health: Beijing 245; population growth 76
public housing, New York 113–114, 118
public participation: Beijing 130–131, 132, 158, 222–224, 235–236, 268, 274, 282, 284–286; China 205; London 126–127, 132; Tokyo 146, 147
public services: Beijing 142, 147, 148–149, 157, 159, 186, 195, 200, 210, 229, 236, 237, 238–239, 245, 286; Beijing-Tianjin-Hebei region 251, 252, 253, 291, 293, 296; causes of "urban diseases" 13, 14; China 203, 204, 205; countermeasures for treating "urban diseases" 15; defining the connotation of "urban diseases" 68; industrial transformation 101, 102; New York 113–114, 118; phases of urban evolution 89, 91; Tokyo 142, 143–144, 146, 148, 159
public transport: Beijing 129–130, 132, 142, 183, 212–213, 255, 256, 270; Beijing-Tianjin-Hebei region 215; garden city, theory of 54; livable city, theory of 58; London 120, **122**, 123, 124, 126, 132; New York 111,

114–115, 116, 118; phases of urban evolution 90, 93; Tokyo 137–143, 159; traffic congestion 78–79

Qie Haixia 28
Qin Hailin 12
Qingdao 81
Qinhuangdao: culture and sports 295; road system 261

rail system: Beijing 130, 147, 148, 151–155, 157, 159, 183, 212–213, 224; Beijing-Tianjin-Hebei region 215, 254, 255–257, 293, 295; countermeasures for treating "urban diseases" 16; international communication center 231; London 124, 213, 256; New York 114, 213, 255, 256; phases of urban evolution 92; Ruhr area 162; Tokyo 137–143, 145, 151, 159, 213, 255, 256
recessions: green low-carbon development 20; research background 4; Ruhr area 163; unemployment 87
recreation *see* entertainment; leisure; sports facilities
recycling *see* waste recycling
regional rehabilitation model of industrial heritage: China 177; Ruhr area 166–168, **167**, 177
Remote Sensing (RS) 296
renewable energy 63, 64
Renmin University of China 253
research: background and the problems 1–4; ideas and contents 34–37; key points and difficulties 37–38; literature review 4–33; methods 38–39; significance and purpose 33–34
residence and work, separation of *see* spatial dislocation/separation of residence and job
resource allocation 67–68
resource-based cities 27–28
resource conservation 21
resource constraints: green low-carbon development 23; industrial transformation 100–102
resource consumption: Beijing 187, 210, 216, 238, 243; deficiencies and review of research studies 30; green low-carbon development 19, 20, 21; Ruhr area 161, 170; Tokyo 136
resource depletion/scarcity 69, 84–86, 178; Beijing 188–189, 194, 197, 216; China 171; coordinated urban development 29; deficiencies and review of research studies 33; defining the connotation of "urban diseases" 68; green low-carbon development 18, 21; low-carbon city, theory of 59, 60; population growth 76; research background 1, 2; Ruhr area 161, 163, 165; unemployment 87
resource endowments: China 174; Ruhr area 162, **164**, 174
resource property rights, Beijing 272
resource scarcity *see* resource depletion/scarcity
resource security 2
retail: Beijing 184, 188; livable city, theory of 58; New York 109, 110, 111; phases of urban evolution 90; Ruhr area **167**, 170; Tokyo 136
Rio de Janeiro **78**
road system: Beijing 141, 153, 154–155, 157–158, 183, 187, 214, 299; Beijing-Tianjin-Hebei region 259–261; connotations and causes of "urban diseases" 7; industrial transformation 100; New York 108, 109, 114; phases of urban evolution 92; Tokyo 137, 141, 142–143, 258, 259; *see also* traffic congestion
robbery: population growth 77; unemployment 87
Rome 83
Ruhr area 161, 177, 306; geographical advantages and influences of industrial development **164**; history of development 161–166, **163**; industrial transformation 101; manifestations of "urban diseases" **72–73**; models of industrial upgrading 166–171; policy suggestions 171–176; research ideas and contents 36; research key points and difficulties 37
rule of law 4
rural to urban migration: connotations and causes of "urban diseases" 8; research background 1
rural–urban imbalance *see* urban–rural imbalance
Russia **78**

safety *see* security; traffic safety
St. Paul, USA 299
St. Petersburg **78**

Salvador 78
Sanhe City 93
São Paulo: poverty 86; resource scarcity 84
satellite cities/towns: Beijing 151, 157; New York 111, 112, 118; phases of urban evolution 90
schooling *see* education
science: Beijing 195, 226, 230–231, 233, 248, 296, 297; expositions 233; global trends 288; New York 114
scientific development 32
security: Beijing 178, 181, 213, 214, 232, 243, 245; defining the connotation of "urban diseases" 68; livable city, theory of 55, 56; phases of urban evolution 96; population growth 76, 77; poverty 86; urban functions 98
self-organizing systems 15
service sectors: Beijing 150, 184, 192, 207, 209, 249; China 176; phases of urban evolution 93; Tokyo 136, 137
sewage: Beijing 128, 188–189, 190, 217, 218–219, 220, 271; New York 117; Ruhr area 169, 175; water pollution 81
Shaanxi 92, 93
Shandong 295
Shanghai: green low-carbon development 24, 25; industrial transformation 101; phases of urban evolution 93; resource scarcity 84; separation of work and residence 105n10
Shanxi: agricultural products 186; culture and sports 295
Sharif, Hamid L. 84
Sheffield 125
Shen Chen 28
Shen Yufang 27
Shen Yusan 27
Shenghongda market 188
Shenzhen: green low-carbon development 25; pollution 81; separation of work and residence 105n10
Shi Minjun 24
Shi Yishao 13
Shibuya 135, 141
Shijiazhuang: culture and sports 295; pollution 83, 84
Shilihe market 187–188, 196
Shimen market 185
Shinjuku 135–136, 141

shops *see* retail
Shuitun wholesale market 185
Shunyi: international communication center 232; New City 233; pollution 193; population control 208
Si Yanming 15
Simmel, Georg 49
Singapore: congestion charges 214; green low-carbon development 24; resource scarcity 84
sleeping cities 236; Beijing 147, 148, 151, 183; Beijing-Tianjin-Hebei region 240, 257; phases of urban evolution 90; traffic congestion 79
slow fading, period of 95, 95, 96–97
slums 86; Beijing 210; London 119; population growth 76
smart cities: Beijing 296–300; countermeasures for treating "urban diseases" 17
smart grids 61
smog: Beijing 127–131, 154, 155, 156, 178, 188, 190–193, 207, 212, 215–217, 220, 222, 224, 233, 235, 262, 263, 267–268, 278; Beijing-Tianjin-Hebei region 207, 216, 289; industrial transformation 102; London 89, 119–132, 305; New York 116; phases of urban evolution 89, 96; research background 3, 4; research significance and purpose 34; Tokyo 134, 144, **145**
social conflict/problems 178; Beijing 181, 215; research background 1
social elite, theory of the 52
social governance: Beijing 282; London **122**, 126–127
social organizations, Beijing 286
social participation *see* public participation
social security: Beijing 245, 246, 286; Beijing-Tianjin-Hebei region 250; international comparative studies on "urban diseases" 11; livable city, theory of 56, **57**; poverty 86; unemployment 87
social services: industrial transformation 101; livable city, theory of 56, **57**, 58
social system, strengthening its innovation 280–282
sociology, classical 46–47, 64, 303–304
solar power: Beijing 264; Beijing-Tianjin-Hebei region 291; China 174;

low-carbon city, theory of 63; New York 116; Ruhr area 170, 171
solid waste pollution 82–83
Song Yajie 24
spatial dislocation/separation of residence and job 79, 105n10; Beijing 105n10, 156–157; Beijing-Tianjin-Hebei region 240; Tokyo 141–142
sports facilities: Beijing 239, 246; Beijing-Tianjin-Hebei region 252, 293, 295; Ruhr area 170, 171; Tokyo 144
State Council 227, 228, 245
status symbols 79
steel industry, Ruhr area 162, 163, **164**, 165, 169
Stern, Nicholas 60
subcenter cities: Beijing 146–148, 156–157, 159; Tokyo 134–136, 146–148, 159
subsidence 179
subsidies, London 123
suburbanization: Beijing 256–257; Beijing-Tianjin-Hebei region 252–253, 254; evolution of "urban diseases" 88, 89–92, 96; industrial transformation 101, 102; New York 108–111, **110**, 112, 114, 118
subways: Beijing 129, 139, 151, 152, 153, 154, 183, 212–213, 293–294, 299; Beijing-Tianjin-Hebei region 255, 256, 257; London 124, 293; New York 114–115, 293; phases of urban evolution 92, 93; Tokyo 137, 138–139, 142, 153, 293; traffic congestion 79
Sui Yinghui 27
Sun Jiuwen 15
Sun Yajing 24
sustainable development: Beijing 179, 186, 187, 202, 215, 216, 224, 227, 230, 237, 239, 244, 250, 275, 298; Beijing-Tianjin-Hebei region 254, 267, 289; China 202, 203, 212; coordinated urban development 26, 28, 29; deficiencies and review of research studies 30; green low-carbon development 18, 19, 20–21, 23; industrial transformation 99, 103; livable city, theory of 55; low-carbon city, theory of 59, 64; New York 112, 113, 117; phases of urban evolution 92, 95; pollution 79–80; population growth 77; research background 1, 2, 3; resource scarcity 84, 85; Ruhr area 161; social problems 86; Tokyo 135, 137; urban functions 98

Taiyuan 83, 84
Tangshan: culture and sports 295; pollution 192; road system 261
Taoranting ornamental flower market 188
taxation: Beijing 155, 200, 206, 220, 232, 245, 246, 248, 263, 268, 269, 273; Beijing-Tianjin-Hebei region 207, 254, 293; China 202, 204–205, 206; London 123; New York 113; Ruhr area 166, 175; Tokyo 140
taxis: Beijing 130, 255, 269, 270; New York 116
Taylor, Graham 111
teachers, Tokyo 143–144, 148–149
technology: beggars 88; Beijing 129, 132, 150, 180, 195, 206–207, 227, 230–231, 233, 236, 248, 249, 296–300; Beijing-Tianjin-Hebei region 291, 293; China 174, 176; countermeasures for treating "urban diseases" 17; expositions 233; global trends 288; green low-carbon development 19, 20, 21; London **121–122**, 124–125, 132; low-carbon city, theory of 59; New York 114; phases of urban evolution 91; Ruhr area 175; Tokyo 137; urban functions 99; see also information and communication technologies
Tehran 84
theft: population growth 77; unemployment 87
Tian Zhiyu 23, 24, 26
Tiananmen Square 213
Tianjin: agricultural products 186, 187; atmospheric pollution 268, 269, 270; compensation mechanism, lack of 199; coordinated urban development 29; coordinating body, lack of 199; culture and sports 295; decentralization 200; ecological civilization 274; ecological compensation 263, 273; environmental management 266; GDP-based performance assessment 206; industrial transformation 150, 263; orderly diversion of the population 253; pollution 81, 268, 269, 270; public transport 130; rail system 152, 256, 257; road system 261; scientific

Index   335

and technological innovation 231; traffic congestion 78; *see also* Beijing-Tianjin-Hebei region
Tiantongyuan 151, 183; phases of urban evolution 90
Tianyi Di'anmen Store 188
Tokyo 133, 159, 223, 305; control of "urban diseases", key experience of 134–146; control of "urban diseases", lessons learned and policy implications 146–158; industrial transformation 101; international comparative studies on "urban diseases" 11; livable city, theory of 58; manifestations of "urban diseases" **72**, 133–134; parking guidance system 299; phases of urban evolution 89; rail system 137–143, 145, 151, 159, 213, 255, 256; research ideas and contents 36; research key points and difficulties 37; research methods 39; road system 137, 141, 142–143, 258, 259
tolls: Beijing 155, 157; Tokyo 143
Tongzhou 147, 151, 156, 183, 228; focus on 250; international communication center 232, 233; orderly diversion of the population 253–254; phases of urban evolution 90; pollution 193; smog 278
Tönnies, Ferdinand 46–47
tourism: Beijing 213, 231; Beijing-Tianjin-Hebei region 294–295; China 174, 176; green low-carbon development 22, 25; Ruhr area 161, 165, 166, 168–169, 170, 174, 176; Tokyo 136, 138
traffic accidents *see* traffic safety
traffic congestion 69, 77–79, **78**, 178; Beijing 77–78, 79, 140, 142, 147, 150, 151, 152, 154, 156, 157–158, 159, 178, 179, 180, 182, 183–184, 187, 188, 193, 194, 197, 198, 201, 202, 206, 210, 211, 212, 214, 217, 222, 223, 224, 226, 227, 231, 244, 245, 247, 248, 255, 256, 257, 258, 269, 284, 293–294, 295, 297, 299; as cause of "urban diseases" 12, 14; charges *see* congestion charges; China 77–79, 204, 205, 206; connotations and causes of "urban diseases" 7, 8; countermeasures for treating "urban diseases" 16; defining the connotation of "urban diseases" 67, 68; industrial transformation 101, 102, 103; London 119, **121**, 123, 124; New York 108, 109, 111, 114–115, 117, 118; phases of urban evolution 90, 91, 96; population growth 77; research background 1, 2, 4; Tokyo 133, 134, 135, 137, 139, 141, 142, 143, 144, 153, 154, 159; urban functions 99; *see also* road system
traffic noise 82
traffic pollution: Beijing 128–129, 130, 132, 152, 154, 158, 191, 193, 198, 211, 212–213, 216, 217, 219, 222, 233, 255, 268, 269, 270; London 120, **121**, 122, 123, 124, 125; Tokyo 140, 144, 145, 146, 154
traffic safety: Beijing 152, 153, 154, 156, 157, 299; and congestion 77, 79; Tokyo 139, 141, 143
traffic system: Beijing 147, 188, 212–215, 219, 224, 247, 297; Beijing-Tianjin-Hebei region 254, 255, 293, 295; China 203; coordinated urban development 28, 29; industrial transformation 100, 102; international comparative studies on "urban diseases" 11; livable city, theory of 58; New York 111, 112, 114; phases of urban evolution 91, 93; population growth 76; poverty 86; research significance and purpose 34; urban functions 98, 99
tragedy of the commons 12, 222
trams: London 124; Tokyo 137, 138–139, 145
transportation system: Beijing 153, 157–158, 231; London 126; low-carbon city, theory of 63; phases of urban evolution 92; Ruhr area **164**; Tokyo 142–143, 153; *see also* buses; rail system; road system; subways; taxis; traffic system; trams
Turkey **78**, 78

unemployment 87; connotations and causes of "urban diseases" 9; green low-carbon development 22; phases of urban evolution 96; population growth 76; poverty 86; Ruhr area 161, 163, 165
Union Medical College Hospital 294
United Kingdom: connotations and causes of "urban diseases" 5; defining the connotation of "urban diseases" 67; garden cities 52–53;

green low-carbon development 22; industrialization 119; international comparative studies on "urban diseases" 10–11; Leicester's parking guidance system 299; low-carbon cities/economy 60–61, 64; population growth 76; satellite cities 111; *see also* London
United Nations Conference on Human Settlements 54
United States: Chinatown 50; fence walls, lack of 258; green low-carbon development 22, 24; international comparative studies on "urban diseases" 11; Little Italy 50; phases of urban evolution 91, 92, 93; preservation of old buildings 192; re-industrialization strategy 288; St. Paul's parking guidance system 299; separation of work and residence 105n10; *see also* Los Angeles; New York
universities and colleges: Beijing 149, 182, 209, 210, 213; Beijing-Tianjin-Hebei region 251, 253, 291, 292, 294; fence walls, lack of 258
University of London 28
upstream industries, Ruhr area **164**
urban alienation 68
urban community, theory of 49–52, 65, 304
urban coordination systems 25
urban development: Beijing 181, 196–197, 227, 234, 235, 237, 240, 250, 284, 300; Beijing-Tianjin-Hebei region 240, 288; causes of "urban diseases" 12, 13; China 173, 174, 176, 202, 205; coordinated *see* coordinated development; countermeasures for treating "urban diseases" 16, 17; green low-carbon development 19, 20, 23, 25; human ecology, theory of 48; international comparative studies on "urban diseases" 11; phases of urban evolution 88, 91; poverty 86; resource scarcity 85; Ruhr area 161, 175; scientific outlook of 234; Tokyo 135; urban functions 97, 98, *100*
"urban diseases": connotations and causes 4–9, **5–6**; control of *see* control of "urban diseases"; countermeasures for treating 15–17; current situation 9–10; evolution *see* evolution of "urban diseases"; international comparative studies 10–11; literature review 4–33; research background 1–4; research ideas and contents 34–38; research key points and difficulties 37–38; research methods 38–39; research significance and purpose 33–34; studies of causes 11–14; *see also specific "urban diseases"*
urban functions: Beijing 147–148, 159, 181, 187, 195, 196, 210–211, 236, 237, 244; Beijing-Tianjin-Hebei region 185; evolution of "urban diseases" 97–99, *100*; New York 111–112, 118; Tokyo 134–136, 142
urban management, Beijing 201–202
urban parks, London 125–126
urban planning *see* planning
urban registration system 15
urban–rural imbalance: causes of "urban diseases" 14; connotations and causes of "urban diseases" **6**, 8–9; countermeasures for treating "urban diseases" 15; defining the connotation of "urban diseases" 68
urban support systems 25
Urban Water Blueprint report 81
urbanization 178; Beijing 192, 194, 195, 199, 201, 215, 216, 224, 226, 234–237, 238–239, 275, 283, 287; Beijing-Tianjin-Hebei region 253, 298; causes of "urban diseases" 12, 13, 14; China 212, 226, 234; connotations and causes of "urban diseases" 5, **6**, 8; control of "urban diseases" 46; coordinated urban development 29; countermeasures for treating "urban diseases" 16, 17; current situation of "urban diseases" 10; deficiencies and review of research studies 30; defining the connotation of "urban diseases" 68; garden city, theory of 52; green low-carbon development 18, 20, 23, 24, 25, 26; industrial transformation 100, 102, 103; international comparative studies on "urban diseases" 10, 11; London 119; low-carbon city, theory of 59; manifestations of "urban diseases" 69, 104; New York 107–108, 109, **110**, 111, 117, 118; people-oriented 234–237, 238–239; phases of urban evolution 89–97; pollution 81, 82;

population growth 76, 77; poverty 86; research background 1, 2, 3, 4; resource scarcity 84, 85; Ruhr area 161; Tokyo 133, 135; UK 119; urban functions 99
Urumqi 83, 84

vagrancy 88
viaducts 137
Virginia 112

Wang Anshun 8
Wang Bin 29
Wang Dawei 11
Wang Guixin 12
Wang Huan 25
Wang Kaiyong 11
Wang Long 28
Wang Mengxin 8, 15
Wang Ning 14, 16
Wang Shengquan 13
Wang Weidong 27
Wang Yuming 25
Wang Yunjia 26
Wangsiying market 185
Wanjiadenghuo market 188
Wantong market 188
Warsaw 84
Washington 112
waste management: Beijing 271–272; industrial transformation 101
waste recycling: low-carbon city, theory of 64; New York 115, 118
water consumption, Beijing 150, 249
water pollution 81–82; Beijing 217, 235; New York 117; phases of urban evolution 96
water quality 25
water resources: Beijing 179, 188–190, **189**, 271; Beijing-Tianjin-Hebei region 292; New York 116, 117
water shortages 84–85, 101; industrial transformation 100
weather: research background 3; *see also* climate change; smog
Weber, Max 47, 51
Wei Houkai **6**
Wellman, B. 51
Welwyn, England 52
Wen Hui 11
Weng Zhiyong 22
wholesale markets, Beijing 184, 185–188, 196

wind power: Beijing 264, 270; Beijing-Tianjin-Hebei region 291; China 174; New York 116
Wirth, John 47, 50
Wu Guancen 3
Wu Liangcheng 5, 12
Wu Zhenguo 10, 16
Wuhan City Circle 76

Xi Jinping: Beijing 179, 186, 194, 195, 199, 208, 215, 216, 217, 226, 267, 269; Beijing-Tianjin-Hebei region 178; clean energy 270; deficiencies and review of research studies 31; environmental protection 292; "Five Concepts for Development" 288; research background 4
Xi'an: phases of urban evolution 93; pollution 81
Xiang Chunling 16
Xianghe: buses 213; rail system 257; subway system 294
Xianyang 92, 93
Xiao Hong 20
Xiao Jincheng 17
Xicheng 142, 157; decentralization 247; ecological civilization 279; education 253; fiscal system 245; GDP-oriented performance assessment system 243; health care 195; orderly diversion of the population 253; political center 228; population density 181; smog 278
Xinanjiao wholesale market 185
Xinfadi wholesale market 185, 186–187
Xing Tianhe 28
Xingtai: culture and sports 295; pollution 192
Xu Chuanchen 12
Xu Zhiqiang 11

Yan Bingqiu 11
Yan Yanming **6**
Yang Bo 24
Yang Hongwei 23, 26
Yang Ka 15
Yang Shisong 15
Yangqing 263
Yangtze River Delta region: coordinated urban development 27, 29; population growth 76
Yanjiao 151; buses 213; phases of urban evolution 90, 92–93; rail system 257; subway system 294

Yanqing: ecological civilization 279; ecological compensation 273
Yaoshun building material market 188
Yi Longsheng 26
Yu Keping 18
Yuan Dongzhen 11
Yuan Zhibin 24
Yue Tian 24
Yue Wu 14, 16
Yuegezhuang wholesale market 185

Zaozhuang 24
Zeng Changqiu 9
Zeng Guangyu 13
Zeng Hong 55
Zeng Lijun 27
Zhang Chen 21
Zhang Chi 10, 13, 15
Zhang Dunfu 5
Zhang Hanfei 5
Zhang Jing 27
Zhang Mingdou 14, 17
Zhang Shuhua 11
Zhangjiakou 295
Zhao Hong 14, 16
Zhao Liming 24
Zhaoyuan 24
Zhongguancun National Independent Innovation Demonstration Zone 230–231
Zhongyang wholesale market 185
Zhou Jialai 5, **5**, 12
Zhou Jun 29
Zhu Dajian 23, 25
Zhu Huiyong 27
Zhu Yinghui 9
Zhu Yu 25
Zhuang Guiyang 21
Zhuozhou: buses 213; rail network 257